Collective Rights and the Cultural Identity of the Roma

Studies in International Minority and Group Rights

Series Editors

Gudmundur Alfredsson
Kristin Henrard

VOLUME 3

The titles published in this series are listed at brill.com/imgr

Collective Rights and the Cultural Identity of the Roma

A Case Study of Italy

By

Claudia Tavani

MARTINUS NIJHOFF PUBLISHERS

LEIDEN · BOSTON
2012

Library of Congress Cataloging-in-Publication Data

Tavani, Claudia.
Collective rights and the cultural identity of the Roma : a case study of Italy / by Claudia Tavani.
p. cm. -- (Studies in international minority and group rights, ISSN 2210-2132 ; v. 3)
Includes bibliographical references and index.
ISBN 978-90-04-20261-0 (hardback : acid-free paper) -- ISBN 978-90-04-23383-6 (e-book)
1. Romanies--Italy. 2. Romanies--Ethnic identity. 3. Italy--Ethnic relations. 4. Romanies--Civil rights--Italy. I. Title.

DX233.T38 2012
305.891'497045--dc23

2012027143

This publication has been typeset in the multilingual "Brill" typeface. With over 5,100 characters covering Latin, IPA, Greek, and Cyrillic, this typeface is especially suitable for use in the humanities. For more information, please see www.brill.com/brill-typeface.

ISSN 2210-2132
ISBN 9789004202610 (hardback)
ISBN 9789004233836 (e-book)

This book is printed on acid-free paper.

MIX
Paper from responsible sources
FSC www.fsc.org FSC® C109576

Printed by Printforce, the Netherlands

CONTENTS

ACKNOWLEDGEMENTS

My special thanks go to those who offered valuable insights and professional and moral support throughout this project. I wish to thank my PhD supervisors, professors Geoff Gilbert and Jane Wright for their indispensable advice, for their constant professional and emotional support and for believing in me even when I did not believe in myself. I am thankful to professor Antonio Bultrini, for letting me share my thoughts and doubts and for always helping me to find hidden documents. I must thank my parents, Franco and Marcella, and my sister Elisabetta for giving me a shoulder to cry on and for always supporting me and being there for me. Finally, I should thank Micra for keeping me company during the long, sleepless nights of work, for helping me relax with her soft purrs and for loving me just the way I am.

ABSTRACT

In this book, the author argues that the best way to protect disadvantaged minorities such as the Roma is through the protection of their cultural identity by means of adopting a system that applies the principles of equality and non-discrimination and encompasses the recognition of a collective right to cultural identity. After a brief introduction, in chapter I, the author clarifies the concepts of culture and cultural identity, important for the identification of groups and ethnicity, and argues that the Roma are an ethnic group. In chapter II, the author explains that an internationally accepted definition of minority is missing but that this has not been an obstacle to the application of existing instruments or to the protection of the cultural identity of minorities. The author also clarifies that recognition of groups such as the Roma, whose status is not always clear, might not be a simple task but that according to the recommendations of international monitoring bodies, they are to be considered a minority. Recognition of minorities is important because, as the author explains in chapter III, when groups are not recognised as such, they cannot claim special rights for their protection and their members can only resort to individual human rights, non-discrimination and equality to have their rights guaranteed. However, these individual rights are not sufficient in protecting the cultural identities of minorities. In chapter IV, the author explains that the best way to protect minorities such as the Roma is through the recognition of collective rights, particularly the collective right to cultural identity. In chapter V, the author uses Italy as a case study to prove the importance of adopting an internationally accepted definition of the term minority so that states cannot discriminate between groups when granting recognition and thus special rights. Italy illustrates the limits of non-discrimination provisions when dealing with minority issues and the need to recognise the collective right to cultural identity to advance the protection of minorities.

LIST OF ABBREVIATIONS

ACFC	Advisory Committee under the Framework Convention for the Protection of National Minorities
CAHMIN	Ad Hoc Committee for the Protection of National Minorities (Council of Europe)
CEDAW	Convention on the Elimination of all Forms of Discrimination Against Women
CERD	Committee on the Elimination of Racial Discrimination
CESCR	Committee on Economic Social and Cultural Rights
CoE	Council of Europe
COHRE	Centre On Housing Rights and Evictions
CPRSI	Contact Point for Roma and Sinti Issues
CSCE	Conference on Security and Cooperation in Europe
ECHR	European Convention on Human Rights and Fundamental Freedoms
EChRML	European Charter for Regional or Minority Languages
ECJ	European Court of Justice
ECommHR	European Commission on Human Rights
ECRI	European Commission Against Racism and Intolerance
ECtHR	European Court on Human Rights
ERRC	European Roma Rights Centre
EU	European Union
FCNM	Framework Convention for the Protection of National Minorities
HCNM	High Commissioner on National Minorities
HRC	United Nations Human Rights Committee
ICCPR	International Covenant on Civil and Political Rights
ICERD	International Convention on the Elimination of all Forms of Racial Discrimination
ICESCR	International Covenant on Economic, Social and Cultural Rights
ICJ	International Court of Justice
IGO	Inter-governmental Organisation
ILO	International Labour Organisation
NGO	Non-governmental Organization
ODIHR	Office for Democratic Institutions and Human Rights

OSCE	Organisation for Security and Cooperation in Europe
PCIJ	Permanent Court of International Justice
UDHR	Universal Declaration on Human Rights
UN	United Nations
UNAR	Ufficio Nazionale Antidiscriminazioni Razziali
UNESCO	United Nations Educational, Scientific and Cultural Organisation
UNGA	United Nations General Assembly
WWII	World War II

INTRODUCTION

The Roma[1] minority is the most marginalised in Europe and in Italy. The living conditions of Roma in Italy are below acceptable standards. With little consideration for how the Roma view themselves, they are labelled as nomads in Italy. This label allows the cultural legitimation of their exclusion to the point that, regardless of whether they want to live nomadically or settle into a location and be sedentary, they are forced to live in camps outside cities in unsanitary conditions and with little or no access to education, employment or health care.

Roma are the target of racial profiling by public authorities and police forces. The media contribute to the perpetuation of negative stereotypes. News of Roma who have been caught kidnapping children is given great emphasis. Research shows, however, that in every case in which a Roma has been accused of kidnapping a child, it has been easily proven that this did not actually happen. Nevertheless, even when the police point out that the alleged crime was not committed, the media give little space to this news, especially when compared to the space given to the news that reported the alleged crime. People remain thus convinced that Roma kidnap children, even when the facts prove the contrary, and this perception is often used to foment hatred and violence. For example, following the news that a young Roma had attempted to kidnap a child in Ponticelli (Naples), on May 13, 2008 people living in the area set the nearby Roma encampment on fire and Roma families were forced to escape.

Roma are also marginalised through law. Indeed, despite the fact that Italy has ratified most international human rights instruments, the Italian Parliament has so far denied the Roma the status of national minority as well as that of linguistic minority – a move which would make the application of national laws on the protection of the cultures and identities of minorities and the implementation of international instruments more straightforward. The fact that an internationally accepted definition of

[1] During the course of this book, I use the word "Roma" to refer generally to all Roma groups – whether Roma, Sinti, Travelers and so on – that commonly fall under the umbrella of Romany people. The words "gypsy" or "nomad" (mistakenly but commonly used in Italy to refer to the Roma and often also appearing in documents and reports of international and regional organisations) will only be used if they are also used in the articles, books and documents to which I am referring or which I am quoting.

minority is missing has thus given Italy the chance to marginalise the Roma. Furthermore, a number of emergency decrees have been adopted in the past year that single out the Roma as the cause of social alarm. Conversely, little interest has been shown in the integration of the Roma minority and in the promotion and protection of its culture and its cultural identity.

These legal and sociological issues prompted me to ask myself what would be the best ways of protecting highly marginalised groups such as the Roma. This book will show that the best way to protect minorities such as the Roma is through the protection of their cultural identity, and most of all, through the recognition of a collective right to cultural identity and not through a mere application of the principle of non-discrimination.

The starting point for this argument is that no internationally accepted definition of culture exists, although an understanding of what culture is and of what it implies exists.[2] It is thus understood that culture has strong links with ethnicity, and in this way, culture helps determine whether a group can be considered an ethnic group. Provided that the concepts of culture and cultural identity are understood, questions regarding the status of the Roma as a group still exist and, if it is recognised that they are a group, regarding what kind of group – could the Roma be considered an ethnic group? Moreover, no internationally accepted definition of minority exists, which means that recognising the groups which ought to be the subject of special rights, such as the protection of their cultural identity, is not always a straightforward task and that states have the opportunity of unilaterally establishing which groups living on their territory constitute a minority. States are thus able to discriminate between groups and frustrate their international obligations. In this framework, it should be pointed out that, provided the Roma are indeed recognised as an ethnic group, they might not necessarily fit the descriptions of minority used by international law instruments because they set criteria that Roma do not necessarily meet.

When minorities are not officially recognised by the state, this implies that they are not granted special rights and they cannot demand to be the subject of measures to preserve their cultural identity (which, I believe, is the real essence of minority protection). The only way members of minorities thus have to receive satisfaction of their rights and to protect their

[2] *See* for example the recent United Nations, Committee on Economic, Social and Cultural Rights, *General Comment 21, Right of Everyone to Take Part in Cultural Life*, E/C.12/GC/21, 21 December 2009, as well as United Nations Human Rights Committee, *General Comment 23(50), Article 27*, UN Doc. CCPR/C/21/Rev.1/Add.5, 1994.

cultural identity is through individual human rights and through equality and non-discrimination clauses, which do not necessarily suffice because hardly any instrument explicitly recognises a right to cultural identity.

Additionally, international law instruments that forbid discrimination and promote equality are not necessarily enforced at the domestic level. States have a choice regarding whether to ratify international human rights law instruments and when they do so, they can even avoid the implementation of some of the principles and rights contained therein by adopting reservations on a number of articles. The fact that instruments have been signed and ratified (even without reservations) does not necessarily mean they are properly implemented.[3]

Having established that members of non-recognised minorities can only make recourse to individual human rights instruments to claim protection of their rights, it might be argued that if individual human rights and the prohibition of discrimination were properly implemented, there would be no real reason to grant minorities special rights. However, even if individual human rights were indeed properly implemented, it is still questionable that these would be the best way to protect the cultural identities of minorities such as the Roma. Furthermore, individual human rights take little account of the importance of the group and of group identity for minorities.

Hence, the need to adopt special measures for the protection of minorities should also include the recognition and the protection of collective rights, particularly the collective right to cultural identity, considered the best way to protect the Roma as a group and their collective identity. Furthermore, the implementation of collective rights would also ensure the proper application of individual human rights.

The importance of adopting an internationally accepted definition of minority, the limits of non-discrimination provisions when dealing with minority issues and the importance of recognising collective rights and in particular the collective right to cultural identity as the best way to advance

[3] In this sense, the most valuable instrument for the protection of human rights is the ECHR and the decisions of the ECtHR because all members must allow the procedure of individual complaints to the ECtHR and because the views expressed by the ECtHR in its judgements are binding on members. Conversely, states are not obligated to allow the individual complaints procedure under the ICCPR, and even when this procedure is allowed through the ratification of Optional Protocol 1, the views expressed by the HRC in its judgements and in its concluding observations on states reports, despite having a high degree of authority, are not binding on states. Similarly, no individual complaints procedure exists under the FCNM, whose application is monitored through a state reporting system, and the views expressed by the ACFC in its opinions are not legally binding on members.

the protection of minorities is exemplified through the case study of Italy, in which some groups received the label of minority whereas others, such as the Roma, have not been recognised and have thus been excluded from the benefits that would derive from recognition. This has happened despite the fact that the Roma are considered a minority by a number of international bodies even if they do not fulfil the international criteria for minority recognition that international law uses in a straightforward way.

Book Outline

Chapter I will first define culture and cultural identity, to then provide an overview of the history of the Roma and focus on the main characteristics and identification of the Roma today. It will consider whether the Roma are a group and, if so, whether they should be considered an ethnic group.

Chapter II will review the working definitions of minority provided by the most important international and regional instruments, with a view to determine whether the Roma are to be considered a minority according to them.

Chapter III will consider the ineffectiveness of individual rights in protecting the cultural identity of minorities. An overview will be given of the main instruments on individual human rights (and the case law developed from these) that are relevant for the protection of minorities' cultural identities. The principles of equality and non-discrimination and the idea of special measures for the protection of minorities will also be analysed.

The recognition of collective rights as a possible way to advance the rights of minorities will be discussed in chapter IV. After reviewing the protection of collective rights granted by international instruments, chapter IV will focus on the debate between opponents and supporters of collective rights. It will also analyse the concept of cultural rights and finally concentrate on the collective right to cultural identity.

Chapter V will focus on the current situation and normative framework in Italy by studying the constitutional norms on non-discrimination and minority protection and examining the law which, in 1999, allowed for the recognition of several minority groups but not of the Roma. The juridical status of the Roma in Italy will be reviewed, the latest developments reported and analysed together with measures supposed to be in favour of the Roma. Strategies will be suggested to end the discrimination experienced by Roma in Italy, to ensure their integration in the majority society and to ensure the full implementation and application of international human rights laws and standards.

CHAPTER ONE

AN OVERVIEW OF THE ROMA AND THEIR CULTURE

1.1 Introduction: The Importance of Recognising the Roma As an Ethnic Group

The importance of recognising the Roma as an ethnic group should not be underestimated because their possibility to be granted minority rights and the chance to avail themselves of legal provisions prohibiting racism and discrimination depends on it. It is my belief that recognition of a collective identity is necessary for the protection of the Roma as a minority. Similarly, recognition of a collective identity is necessary for the protection of the Roma as a *national* minority.[1] However, it must be acknowledged that the diversity of the Roma communities poses significant problems: *"any notion of group-based rights necessitates the drawing of ethnic boundaries in a manner which cannot precisely mirror the reality of the groups concerned."*[2]

To deny the Roma ethnicity is to relegate them to the status of parasitic and troublesome outsiders – even the denial of compensation for their suffering during the Nazi holocaust was based on the argument that the Roma were not a legitimate ethnic group.[3] The importance of the recognition of the Roma as an ethnic group, therefore, rests on their need to be brought within the legal provisions outlawing racism and discrimination, and even more so, within those that protect minorities: to recognition as an ethnic group are linked issues of civil rights from which ethnicity cannot be separated.[4]

---

[1] H. O'Nions, *Minority Rights Protection in International Law. The Roma of Europe* (United Kingdom: Ashgate, 2007), at 20. [hereinafter O'Nions] It should be underlined that the concept of "national minority" has not been defined in any specific manner in international documents.

[2] Id.

[3] D. Mayall, *Gypsy Identities 1500–2000* (London: Routledge, 2004), at 243 [hereinafter Mayall].

[4] Id., at 243. Controversies and debates about Roma identity and on whether or not they constitute an ethnic group are highly politicised. This has been the case in Italy, where political pressure has caused the exclusion of the Roma from the groups who have been granted the status of minority by law 482 of 1999 on the protection of minorities.

Roma groups exist in very different political systems,

> *but in every system, since the way the group is defined in academic and policy literature is related to policy justifications, these groups [...] are usually attached to a conceptual category with general implications for the discourse of ethnic/national/anti-racist politics.*[5]

In other words, different political systems define Roma groups differently and thereby can change the policies that regard them most closely. Labeling the Roma in a particular way serves the purpose of affording or denying them particular rights. For example, in the case of groups who deny their Romany identity states can point out that because they are not a national or ethnic (or linguistic or cultural) group, they cannot have special rights, hence campaigns about the rights of Roma in other countries cannot apply to them because they are not real Roma.[6]

Similarly,

> *In England, councilors who have never knowingly spoken with a Gypsy believe that somehow Gypsies do not deserve the protection of the Race Relations Acts. In Eastern Europe, despite Indian diplomatic intervention in the last decade as a putative country of origin, Romany people are still not seen to conform to the standard pattern of a "national" or "historic" minority* [...].[7]

This has led politically minded Romany individuals to assert ethnic solidarity expressing the feeling that they belong to the same and to distinct people, who share common and enduring cultural traits, similar patterns of interaction with multicultural environments and common problems resulting from widespread prejudice, ethnic hostility, racial hatred, and violence.[8]

The diverse multicultural mosaic of people formed by the Roma contradicts the need felt amongst the Roma elite to define themselves as a unified, particular ethnic group.[9] The need to find ethnic unity exists to combat a common threat: racism.[10]

> *It is still difficult to imagine how multiculturality and multi-territoriality could become the basis for the cultural affirmation and development of people, or at*

---

[5] T. Acton and N. Gheorghe, 'Dealing with Multiculturality: Minority, Ethnic, National and Human Rights,' in *Office for Democratic Institutions and Human Rights Bulletin Spring* (1995) Vol. 3, 2, at 32 [hereinafter Acton and Gheorghe].

[6] Id., at 33.

[7] Id., at 34.

[8] Id., at 34–35.

[9] Id., at 30.

[10] Id.

> *least of communities, which strive to identify themselves in respect of other groups in terms of unity and specificity.*[11]

The historic diversity within the Roma creates a serious constraint on the formalisation and codification of Romany culture and such issues will need to be adequately addressed and resolved to have effective minority rights protection.[12]

Minority protection is often justified by referring to the protection of culture, and culture, being a fundamental feature of ethnicity, has an intrinsic relation to the right to identity of minorities such as the Roma. It is thus necessary to define culture and cultural identity, and to determine whether the Roma are indeed a group; if so, whether they are a national or ethnic group and thus can be afforded protection under minority rights law and under the provisions prohibiting racism and discrimination, including the protection afforded by group rights. In the course of this chapter, the concepts of culture and cultural identity will be reviewed, together with the history and culture of the Roma, to then analyse the main characteristics and identification of Roma today. It will finally be agreed that Roma should be considered as an ethnic group.

1.2. Culture and Cultural Identity

Although no definition of culture exists in international law,[13] an understanding of what culture is and of what it implies exists. It is understood that culture is inseparable from the quality of being human, from the sense of self-respect of a person or a community. It is about human relations and as such "cross-influencing, cross-fertilization, conflict and change are part of culture."[14] In November 1966, the UNESCO Declaration of the Principles of International Cultural Co-operation (which was adopted by a Resolution of the UNESCO General Conference and is not legally binding), recalled in its preamble the Constitution of UNESCO, which states that

[11] Acton and Gheorghe, *supra* note 5, at 30.

[12] Id.

[13] P. Thornberry, *International Law and the Rights of Minorities* (Oxford: Oxford University Press, 1991), at 187 [hereinafter Thornberry].

[14] E. Stamatopoulou, *Cultural Rights in International Law. Article 27 of the Universal Declaration of Human Rights and Beyond* (Leiden: Martinus Nijhoff Publishers, 2007), at 107–108 [hereinafter Stamatopoulou].

> *since wars begin in the minds of men, it is in the minds of men that the defence of peace must be constructed'* and that *'the wide diffusion of culture and education of humanity* [...] *are indispensable to the dignity of men* [...].[15]

Article 1 of the Declaration states that

> *(1) Each culture has a dignity and value which must be respected and preserved. (2) Every people has the right and the duty to develop in culture. (3) In their rich variety and diversity, and in the reciprocal influences they exert on one another, all cultures form part of the common heritage belonging to all mankind.*

The Declaration gives no definition of culture. However, although vague and not legally binding, it is important because it acknowledges the importance of culture, of all cultures and of the value of cultural diversity.

The first international conference on cultural rights was organised by UNESCO in July 1968, two years after the International Covenant on Economic Social and Cultural Rights (ICESCR) was adopted. One of the main issues during the conference was the clarification of "cultural rights" through a definition of the term "culture."[16] Culture was considered to be

> [...] *the totality of ways by which men create designs for living* [...] *Culture is everything which enables man to be operative and active in his world, and to use all forms of expression more and more freely to establish communication among men.*[17]

In the final statement of the conference it was underlined that cultural rights are important because culture enables persons to maintain and perpetuate life.

The concept of culture is a very broad one with diversified meanings and includes inter alia language, religion and education. Language and education are of great importance for minorities. In particular, the regulation of education plays a central role in maintaining a separate and distinct identity, in passing certain values, culture and ways of life to new generations.[18]

---

[15] 1966 UNESCO Declaration of the Principles of International Cultural Co-operation, UNESCO Doc 14C/8.I., 4 Nov. 1966. The Constitution established a close link between culture, peace and human dignity.

[16] Y.M. Donders, *Towards a Right to Cultural Identity?* (Antwerp: Intersentia, 2002), at 69 [hereinafter Donders].

[17] *Cultural Rights as Human Rights* (Paris: UNESCO, 1970), at 10–12 and 105–106.

[18] K. Henrard, *Devising an Adequate System of Minority Protection* (The Netherlands, Kluwer Law International, 2000), at 66–67 [hereinafter Henrard].

> *Among the principal problems facing ethnic minorities and indigenous peoples in the world is the question of educational and cultural policies by governments [...] The first issue of course is language. Linguistic minorities [...] demand respect and status for their languages, which are an essential element in the maintenance of ethnic and cultural identity.*[19]

Even access to and adequate coverage in the media is a guarantee for the reproduction of a certain culture (which is once more related to the right to identity of minorities).

> *Without access to media, which overreaches space and distance, and recombines, re-unites disparate speakers, it is doubtful if relatively weak and embattled minority communities can survive intact.*[20]

Culture is usually described in terms of its sources or aspects. Thus, "[...] *a culture is distinguished by such characteristics as language, religion, and race, and more broadly by shared attitudes, customs and traditions.*"[21] Culture can be seen as the particular way of life of a group of people and not only includes the traditional way of life of minorities, but also systems of customary law of indigenous peoples.[22] A definition of culture normally consists of a series of cultural attributes, such as religion, law, art, customs, language, literature and philosophy among others.

---

19 R. Stavenhagen, *The Ethnic Question: Conflicts Development and Human Rights* (Tokyo: UN University Press, 1990), at 142. This statement further highlights the importance of language for culture and the intrinsic relation between culture and the right to identity of minorities – for whom the right to education is thus vital. In 1992, the CoE adopted the Charter for Regional or Minority Languages, whose purpose is expressed in the Explanatory Report. This states that *"as is made clear in the preamble, the Charter's overriding purpose is cultural. It is designed to protect and promote regional or minority languages as a threatened aspect of Europe's cultural heritage. [...] [...] emphasis is placed on the cultural dimension and the use of a regional or minority language in all aspects of the life of its speakers." See European Charter for Regional or Minority Languages, Explanatory Report,* Council of Europe, DELA (92)2, at paras. 10–11. Following this line of reasoning, Meyer-Bisch considers cultural rights as a category that includes linguistic rights. *See* P. Meyer-Bisch, 'Le Droits Culturels Forment-ils une Catégorie Spécifique de Droits de l'Homme? Quelques difficultés logiques,' in P. Meyer-Bisch (ed.), *Le Droits Cultures, une catégorie sous-développée de droits de l'homme, Actes du VIIIe Colloque interdisciplinaire sur le droits de l'homme* (Switzerland: Editions Universitaires Fribourg Suisse, 1993), pp. 17–43, at 18–20 and 23–24.

20 C.H. Williams, 'The Cultural Rights of Minorities: Recognition and Implementation,' in J. Plichtova (ed.), *Minorities in Politics: Cultural and Language Rights* (Bratislava: Czechoslovak Committee of the European Cultural Foundation, 1992), pp. 107–120, at 113–114. The right of minority peoples to respect for their identity, language and cultural tradition is by some considered a cultural right. *See* H.L.V. Prott, 'Cultural Rights as Peoples Rights,' in J. Crawford (ed.), *The Rights of Peoples,* (Oxford: Clarendon, 1988), pp. 93–106, at 97 [hereinafter Prott].

21 V. Van Dyke, 'The Cultural Rights of Peoples,' *Universal Human Rights,* Vol. 2 No. 2, April-June 1980, pp. 1–21, at 2.

22 Henrard, *supra* note 17, at 65.

> *Culture* [...] *comprehends all that is inherited or transmitted through society* [...] *its individual elements are* [...] *diverse. They include not only beliefs, knowledge, sentiments and literature* [...] *but the language or other system of symbols which are their vehicles. Other elements are the rules of kinship, methods of education, forms of government and all the fashions followed in social relations.*[23]

Culture is also described as

> [*a*] *historically created system of meaning and significance* [...] *a system of beliefs and practices in terms of which a group of human beings understand, regulate and structure their individual and collective lives.*[24]

Culture is articulated at several levels. At the most basic level, it is reflected in language; thus, societies sharing a common language share at least some cultural features.[25] The culture of a society is also embodied in aspects such as proverbs, rituals, body language, jokes, customs and manners of greeting. On a different level, culture is embodied in its arts, music, literature and moral life. Culture is also articulated in the rules and norms that govern such basic activities as social relations.

Several definitions of the concept of culture have been distinguished by the U.N. bodies and analysed by a number of scholars: culture in the material sense, as a product, as the accumulated material heritage of mankind, as a whole or as a part of human groups (including but not only limited to monuments or artifacts); culture in the sense of the process of artistic or scientific creation, as the highest intellectual achievements of people: for example, music, art, literature, philosophy, rituals, and so on; culture in the more anthropological understanding of it,[26] as *"the totality of the*

---

[23] M. Leiris, *Race and Culture* (UNESCO, 1958), at 20–21, as quoted in Thornberry, *supra* note 13, at 188.

[24] B. Parekh, *Rethinking Multiculturalism – Cultural Diversity and Political Theory*, (Basingstoke: Macmillan Press, 2000), at 143 [hereinafter Parekh].

[25] Id. Parekh notes that "[...] *when a group of individuals acquires a wholly new language as many colonial subjects did, they also learn new ways of understanding the world.*".

[26] Stamatopoulou, *supra* note 14, at 109. In a study about culture and poverty, the World Bank cuts down the meaning of culture to two main ideas, the first being the more anthropological aspect and the second intended as the process of artistic creation. The first is *"particular shared values, beliefs, knowledge, skills and practices that underpin behavior by members of a social group at a particular point in time (with potentially good and bad effects on processes of poverty reduction). The second definition describes creative expression, skills, traditional knowledge and cultural resources that form part of the lives of people and societies, and can be a basis for social engagement and enterprise development. These include, for example, craft and design, oral and written history and literature, music, drama, dance, visual arts, celebrations, indigenous knowledge of botanical properties and medicinal applications,*

knowledge and practices, both intellectual and material, of each of the particular groups of a society and at a certain level, of a society itself as a whole...." Culture is thus important in the wider sense, because *"the understanding of cultural development, may well require the care of everyday objects and practices which do not constitute peaks of cultural achievements."*[27]

Others, conversely, distinguish between three concepts of culture: one is that of culture as *"the accumulated material heritage of humankind as a whole or of particular human groups;"* another is that of culture as *"the process of artistic and scientific creation;"* and the last is that of culture as *"the sum total of the material and spiritual activities and products of a given social group which distinguishes it from other similar groups."* This last concept also covers culture as *"a coherent self-contained system of values and symbols."*[28] Such a broad concept of culture is also supported by Capotorti in his study on Article 27 of the International Covenant on Civil and Political Rights (ICCPR), in which he mentions a long series of elements of culture which include language, literature, libraries, museums, educational institutions, historical monuments, arts, religion, places of worship, traditions and legal traditions.[29] Similarly, the Human Rights Committee (HRC) observed that *"culture manifests itself in many forms, including a particular way of life associated with the use of land resources, specially in the case of indigenous peoples."*[30]

Kymlicka identifies two main definitions of culture. One is "localized" and refers to distinct customs, perspectives or ethos of a group or association. The other is wider, and if we used that meaning we could say that all Western democracies have a common culture – they all share a modern,

---

architectural forms, historic sites, and traditional technologies." See http://web.worldbank.org/WBSITE/EXTERNAL/EXTABOUTUS/EXTWEBARCHIVES/0,,MDK:22201421~menuPK:64654237~pagePK:64660187~piPK:64660385~theSitePK:2564958,00.html, last visited Mar. 19, 2012.

[27] Prott, *supra* note 19, at 93–94.

[28] R. Stavenhagen, 'Cultural Rights and Universal Human Rights' in A. Eide (ed.), *Economic, Social and Cultural Rights: A Textbook* (Dordrecht: Martinus Nijhoff, 1995), pp. 63–77, at 65–67 [hereinafter Stavenhagen (1995)].

[29] F. Capotorti, *Study on the Rights of Persons belonging to Ethnic, Religious and Linguistic Minorities,* UN Doc. E/CN.4/Sub.2/384/Rev. 1, 1979, paras. 218–224 and 327–385 [hereinafter Capotorti].

[30] United Nations Human Rights Committee, 'General Comment 23(50), Article 27': UN Doc. CCPR/C/21/Rev.1/Add.5, 1994, para. 7. [hereinafter General Comment 23(50)] *See also* the cases of *Ivan Kitok v. Sweden,* Communication No. 197/1985, CCPR/C/33/D/197/1985 (1988) [hereinafter *Kitok v. Sweden*] and of *Ilmari Länsman* et al. *v. Finland,* Communication No. 511/1992, A/50/40 (1995) [hereinafter *Ilmari Länsman v. Finland*].

urban, secular, industrialised civilisation. If culture is defined as its first meaning, then we might find that even the most ethnically homogeneous state would be "multicultural," because it contains a number of associations. If, conversely, it refers to the "civilization" of a people, then virtually all modern societies would share the same culture. The term culture is thus a synonym of the terms "nation" or "people."[31]

A strong connection exists between the concepts of culture and ethnicity. Indeed *"the quality of ethnic distinctiveness partakes of religious and cultural values as well as of linguistic separatism, but can also have geographical and even historical dimensions."*[32] It follows that an ethnic group is *"a form of social organisation in which the participants themselves make use of certain cultural traits from their past, a past which may or may not be verifiable."*[33] The relationship between culture and ethnicity can also be deduced from the formulation of Article 27 of the ICCPR, in the sense that the right to enjoy one's culture is textually linked to ethnic minorities.

Although some aspects of each culture are certainly more prone to change and adaptation, cultures usually have certain permanent features at their core which are only marginally open to change; hence, the constant search for a proper balance between the need to hold onto the basic features of a culture (and of a minority identity) and being sufficiently open to changes in society. Not all members of different cultural groups are ready to give up their distinctive culture to embrace a common culture. Surely, interactions between groups in a multicultural society will lead to changes in each group and some groups might even disappear, but in general, significantly different groups will still exist.[34] Thus, a culture and a distinctive way of life do not need to be rigid or tied to the past to be recognised as a separate, distinctive minority culture.[35]

---

[31] *"A State is then multicultural if its members either belong to different nations (a multinational State), or have emigrated from different nations (a polyethnic State) and if this fact is an important aspect of personal identity and political life." See* W. Kymlicka, *Multicultural Citizenship: a Liberal Theory of Minority Rights* (Oxford: Oxford University Press, 1995), at 18 [hereinafter Kymlicka (1995)].

[32] G. Alderman, 'Conclusions,' in G. Alderman (ed.) *Governments, Ethnic Groups and Political Representation. Comparative Studies on Governments and non-dominant Ethnic Groups in Europe 1850–1940* (Dartmouth: New York University Press, 1993), at 279–280.

[33] E. Roossens, *Creating Ethnicity: The Process of Ethnogenesis* (Newbury: Sage, 1989), at 12.

[34] C. Liew Ten, 'Liberalism and Multiculturalism' in G.L. Clark et al (eds.), *Multiculturalism, Difference and Postmodernism* (Melbourne: Cheshire, 1993), pp. 54–67, at 60.

[35] Henrard, *supra* note 18, at 254.

Furthermore, the fact that cultures are normally exposed to modification or erosion does not mean that states have no positive obligation to protect and promote minority cultures. Indeed, the preservation of a culture requires the granting of political rights and a certain degree of "internal self-determination" that allows a group to preserve and develop a separate minority identity. It can thus be said that the right to identity of minorities has a political dimension, because ethnic rights which are:

> *the rights that have to do with the survival of the ethnic group as such, the preservation of ethnic cultures, the reproduction of the group as distinct entity, the cultural identity attached to group life and social organisation,*

not only relate to the use of language, educational and cultural matters, but also to self-government and political autonomy.[36]

Cultures change all the time and the degree of development and change of a culture which is desirable can be a subject of debate between members of the group. In this sense, the right to development might go against the right to preserve or develop a culture.[37]

The HRC has accepted that culture is not static and may develop without losing its protected character. For example, economic activities that are a part of the identity or culture of a minority do not have to remain old-fashioned or strictly traditional to be protected.[38] In fact,

> *cultures live and grow, change and sometimes wither away; they amalgamate with other cultures or adapt themselves to geographical or democratic necessity. (...) To preserve or protect [a culture], or some favoured version of it, artificially, in the face of that change, is precisely to cripple the mechanisms of adaptation and compromise. (...) It is to preserve part of the culture, but not what many would regard as its most fascinating feature: its ability to generate a history.*[39]

The Committee on Economic Social and Cultural Rights (CESCR) has underlined that:

> *culture is a broad, inclusive concept encompassing all manifestations of human existence. The expression "cultural life" is an explicit reference to culture as a living process, historical, dynamic and evolving, with a past, a present and*

---

36 Stavenhagen (1995), *supra* note 28, at 65.

37 Prott, *supra* note 20, at 95 and 102–103.

38 In any case, it has been established that traditional activities may not be protected against the interests of the majority society in furthering the economic well-being of the State.

39 J. Waldron, 'Minority Cultures and the Cosmopolitan Alternative,' *University of Michigan Journal of Law Reform*, Vol. 25 n. 3/4, 1991, pp. 751–794, at 787–788.

> *a future. The concept of culture must be seen not as a series of isolated manifestations or hermetic compartments, but as an interactive process whereby individuals and communities, while preserving their specificities and purposes, give expression to the culture of humanity.* [...] *The Committee considers that culture* [...] *encompasses, inter alia, ways of life, language, oral and written literature, music and song, non-verbal communication, religion or belief systems, rites and ceremonies, sport and games, methods of production or technology, natural and man-made environments, food, clothing and shelter and the arts, customs and traditions through which individuals, groups of individuals and communities express their humanity and the meaning they give to their existence, and build their world view representing their encounter with the external forces affecting their lives. Culture shapes and mirrors the values of well-being and the economic, social and political life of individuals, groups of individuals and communities.*[40]

I view culture as encompassing a broad range of aspects, which include, among others, language, religion, customs (along with the way of life), traditions and beliefs, as well as literature, art, music, methods of education and forms of government. For the purposes of this research, I shall think of culture in such terms. The idea of a strong link between ethnicity and culture, and the idea that certain customs and cultures are typical of certain ethnicities is also supported. Furthermore, I believe that cultures should not be seen as static or never changing, but as modifying according to the times and the other cultures they encounter, without being unworthy of protection for this reason. While supporting the value of cultural diversity, I also think that although culture ought to be protected and that a right to cultural identity exists, it does not imply that all cultures should always be protected at all costs. It is indeed doubtful that groups which express and promote extremely racist and discriminatory views and violent ideas and actions (and which often shield themselves behind the appellative of cultural associations) ought to be protected.[41]

Cultural identity is viewed as the personification of culture.[42] It is not static and homogenous, but dynamic and heterogeneous. Various aspects of cultural identity exist, and these include language, religion, art as well as customs and traditions. Cultural identity gives members of a

[40] United Nations Committee on Economic, Social and Cultural Rights, *General Comment 21, Right of Everyone to Take Part in Cultural Life*, E/C.12/GC/21, 21 December 2009, paras. 11–13 [hereinafter *General Comment 21*].

[41] The issues presented by intolerable cultural practices are analysed further in the course of this book.

[42] Donders, *supra* note 16, at 30.

community a sense of belonging and, as such, concerns their human dignity. The concept of belonging is important because it gives individuals a sense of personal integrity and a feeling that they can represent themselves and be recognised.[43] Cultural identity means that:

> [...] *everyone, alone or in community with others, may freely choose his or her cultural identity in its various aspects such as language, religion, heritage and traditions; that everyone may have one or several cultural identities and may freely decide whether or not to identify with one or more cultural communities.*[44]

In this sense, cultural identity is seen as a process, according to which individuals identify themselves through many different aspects. Conversely, it could be said that cultural identity is usually determined by birth rather than by deliberate choice.[45] I maintain that although some aspects of culture – such as religion and way of life – can be chosen by individuals (one might, for example, decide to adopt a religion or way of life other than the one in which he was raised), other aspects of cultural identity – such as language – are not as freely chosen. For example, if one wants to communicate, he has to speak the language spoken by the community in which he lives; however, a language might die because its people stop speaking it for various reasons, including a lack of state support. Whether a culture endures depends therefore on whether there are individuals who are part of the culture in an active way.

1.3. Historical Background

Throughout the centuries, and despite their movements across the European continent and beyond, the Roma have remained easily distinguishable from the people around them, in part as a result of their fight to preserve their culture and identity and in part as a result of the states' segregationist policies. Fearful of persecution in most countries, they fled from place to place, to the point that their diaspora has often been compared with that of the Jews, although:

---

[43] Donders, *supra* note 16, at 31.

[44] J. Symonides, 'Cultural Rights,' in J. Symonides (ed.), *Human Rights: Concept and Standards* (Paris: UNESCO, 2000), pp. 267–278, at 189. By extension, it could be said that being a member of a minority is seen as a matter of individual choice.

[45] C. Kukathas, 'Are There Any Cultural Rights?,' in W. Kymlicka (ed.), *The Rights of Minorities Cultures* (Oxford: Oxford University Press, 1995), pp. 228–256, at 231–249.

> *theirs was the diaspora of a people with no priestly caste, no recognised standard for their language, no texts enshrining a corpus of beliefs and code of morality, no appointed custodians of ethnic traditions.*[46]

All Roma originate from Northern India, from which they started moving between 800 and 950 AD.[47] Linguists helped delineate their origins by demonstrating that the Roma language is strictly related to the main dialects spoken in North-Western India. Further ethnological and ethnographic studies demonstrate the existence of analogies between Roma customs and those of Indian tribal groups such as the Banjara of Hindustan.[48] Even the name Rom or Roma recalls the name of a group of tribes (Dom) well-known in ancient India.

Although the reasons for their migration are not yet clear, it is known that it took them several centuries to reach Europe, making their first appearance around 1100 AD, settling in a region corresponding to today's Armenia. From there they reached Greece, from which they moved to the rest of the Balkans and then to the rest of Europe. When they first arrived in Greece, Roma were called "Atsinganos" ("untouched, untouchable"), due to their practice of magic.[49] From this word derives a variety of others used to identify Roma in different countries ("Zingari" in Italy, "Tsiganes" in France, "Zigeneur" in Germany). The word Gypsies alludes to a presumed Egyptian descent. Indeed, many Eastern regions at that time were called Little Egypt and this would explain why, when the travellers moved from the Balkans to other countries, they were identified as Egyptians (of which the word Gypsies in English and Gitanos in Spanish is a variant).[50]

Upon arrival in Europe, some Roma kept moving from one region to another until the beginning of the XVII century, others became semi-permanent and joined the local economic life starting their own trade or doing seasonal agricultural jobs. In a few cases only were the Roma

---

[46] A. Fraser, *The Gypsies* (United Kingdom: Blackwell, 1995), at 44 [hereinafter Fraser].

[47] C. Silverman, 'Persecution and Politicization: Roma (Gypsies) of Eastern Europe,' Vol. 19 No. 2 (Summer 1995) *Nationalism in Eastern Europe.*

[48] A. Arlati, 'La lunga marcia del popolo senza patria' 606 *Gli Zingari* 7 (1997), at 7. Conversely, some scholars, such as Fraser, believe that the argument that Romanes is a language of Indian origin is unproven. *See* Fraser, *supra* note 46.

[49] J.P. Liégeois and N. Gheorghe, *Roma/Gypsies: a European Minority*, Minority Rights Group International Report, 95/4, 1995, at 7 [hereinafter Liégeois and Gheorghe].

[50] Liégeois and Gheorghe, *supra* note 49. Although the Roma are commonly referred to as "Gypsies" (even in documents of the CoE and of the UN) it has been underlined that this term has a derogatory, pejorative and offensive meaning. *See*, for example, Mayall, *supra* note 3.

well-integrated in the life of the country in which they lived. One example is the Kingdom of Hungary, where the creation of a Roma quarter in Buda during the XVI century could be seen as proof of the absence of policies of persecution or ghettoization. Here, the Roma were particularly appreciated as musicians, but also as metal workers who could be of great help in the course of the many wars against the Ottoman Empire. Roma's art, music and dances were initially appreciated in Britain too (where they made their first appearance in 1505).[51]

In Moldavia and Wallachia (part of the Ottoman Empire until the XIX century) Roma were enslaved. Their skills as artisans, metal workers and traders were considered quite useful and enslavement was seen as a way to prevent them from moving. All the Roma who did not have a master were to be considered property of the state.[52] Enslavement implied the deprivation not only of liberty, but also of the most basic rights and produced inhuman and degrading treatment. In addition to enslavement, in the XV and XVI centuries, Roma who lived in countries with a colonial empire – such as France, Spain and Portugal – were forced to leave, and if they failed to do so, they would be sent to the galleys and colonies.[53]

Several decrees established the prohibition of further arrivals of Roma and their expulsion from Venice (1483), the Duchy of Milan (1493), the Holy Roman Empire (Germany and Switzerland) (1498, 1500, 1510), the Low Countries (part of the Habsburg Empire), Denmark (1536 and 1554) and Britain (1530 England and 1541 Scotland).[54] Those Roma who failed to leave – and the locals who failed to turn in the Roma or those who protected them – would undergo severe penalties, including death. Several other decrees established the impunity of anyone who killed a Roma.[55]

In addition to the aforementioned decrees, attempts were made to change the way of life of the Roma. These consisted of several practices, such as: the denial of admittance to anyone who conducted a similar way of life (Low Countries); forceful settlement – in 1758, in the Austro-Hungarian Empire, Maria Theresa of Habsburg issued a decree which forced the Roma to settle, pay taxes and do mandatory service to churches

---

[51] Fraser, *supra* note 46, at 23.

[52] Z. Barany, *The East European Gypsies*, (USA: Cambridge University Press, 2002), at 85.

[53] A.S. Spinelli, *Baro Romano Drom* (Rome: Meltemi editore, 2003), at 39 [hereinafter Spinelli].

[54] Fraser, *supra* note 46, at 89, 95–96, 98–100.

[55] *See*, for example, A. Arlati, 'Le persecuzioni contro gli zingari: una pagina tragica e poco conosciuta,' 606 *Gli Zingari* 27 (1997) at 27.

and landowners (the decree also prohibited them to move freely; similar policies were adopted by Bismarck's Germany in 1886); the conscription of the Roma to the army (decree of 1761, Austro-Hungarian Empire); the prohibition of marriages between the Roma and the order to send all children away to foster homes (decree of 1773, Austro-Hungarian Empire); the prohibition of pursuing their traditional occupations.[56]

It can be generally seen that wherever they settled, the Roma were met with hostility from the local community. It was a common belief in all European states that the Roma were spies and thieves. They were considered a threat to public health and security. In many countries, Roma children were taken away from their families because their way of life was considered unsanitary and a nuisance and several attempts were made to force them to change it. *"In Hungary, Germany, Spain and elsewhere, children as young as two or four could be forcibly removed from their mothers and given to non-Romanies to rear."*[57] In Austria *"through a series of legal orders, nomadism, Roma/Gypsy costume, language and trades were forbidden or regulated, and children were taken from their parents to be brought up by local families."*[58] As a containment policy, the removal of Roma children by force from their families had been recommended in many states, and in fact occasionally put into practice.[59]

The participation of the Romany communities in the economic life of the country in which they live has always been considered marginal: their traditional occupations (such as craftsmanship) are mostly auxiliary, which could explain the need of a nomadic lifestyle with continuous resettlements to support themselves. Unfortunately, their encounters with other cultures resulted in clashes as soon as craftsmanship lost its value in the face of the necessities of modern industrial society, which

---

[56] For example, in Spain decrees were passed by Charles III that gave the Roma ninety days to find a stable home and a "legal occupation" and abandon their traditional activities. *See* Spinelli, *supra* note 53, at 44.

[57] Brearley adds that *"the fact that Gypsy children often sought to escape and their parents attempted to rescue them may have led to the myth that Gypsies steal non-Gypsy children. In fact, non-Gypsies stole Gypsy children for forced assimilation." See* M. Brearley, *The Roma/Gypsies of Europe: A Persecuted People*, Institute for Jewish Policy Research Policy Paper, No. 3 December 1996 [hereinafter Brearley].

[58] Liégeois and Gheorghe, *supra* note 49, at 9.

[59] An important and quite recent example of this concerns Switzerland and the work of the charitable organization Pro Juventute which in its "Children of the Road" division, from 1926 to 1973, removed Roma children from their families and placed them in institutions until they could be fostered or adopted; this had no legal consequence and was in fact approved by the authorities. *See* Liégeois and Gheorghe, *supra* note 49, at 9.

demanded large-scale production and maximum profit. In a capitalist society, Roma often ended up abandoning their traditional activities and became outcasts.

1.3.1. *The Gypsy Holocaust*

The origins of the policies that ultimately led to the mass extermination of the Roma (*Samudaripen,* or 'the Gypsy Holocaust') during the Nazi period started in the XIX century. In 1889, a special "Gypsy Affairs Section" was created in Bavaria, later on accompanied by a clearinghouse which had the aim of registering all Roma. Policies curtailing the freedom of the Roma were implemented in the Weimar Republic and received the approval of public opinion, according to which Gypsies were dirty and lazy wanderers who made their living from begging, stealing and prostitution.[60]

The bases of the Nazi racial policies against the Roma were set on April 1929, when the Bavarian Gypsy Affairs Section became national under the name "Central Office for Combating the Gypsy Nuisance." The reasons for the policies against the Roma were fundamentally different from those against the Jews. Indeed, it was clear that the persecution and execution of the Jews had racial origins and motives, but in the case of the Roma, Nazi scientists were faced by one of the oldest "Aryan" groups in Europe, as their language was related to Sanskrit and belonged to the Indo-Aryan group. Thus, the Roma could not be discriminated against on the simple basis of race. However, they were discriminated against due to their anti-social behaviour which, according to research of the time, was genetically induced, making the Roma "parasites."[61] On July 14, 1933 the German government issued a statement according to which Roma were unworthy of life.[62] By the end of the year, the Ministry of Interior announced a plan, according to which all persons without a fixed residence (mainly Roma) could be arrested and placed in detention camps where they would be

[60] Fraser, *supra* note 46, at 249–250.

[61] Already in 1876, Cesare Lombroso, in "L'uomo Delinquente" characterised Roma as atavistic and criminal. *See* M. Brearley, 'The Persecution of Gypsies in Europe,' *American Behavioral Scientist*, Vol. 45, No. 4 (2001), 588–599, at 589. *See also* Fraser, *supra* note 46.

[62] I. Hancock, 'Genocide of the Roma in the Holocaust,' in *Patrin Web Journal*, available at http://www.reocities.com/~patrin/genocide.htm, last visited Mar. 19, 2012. *See also* I. Hancock, 'A Brief Romani Holocaust Chronology,' available at http://www.osi.hu/rpp/holocaust.html, last visited Mar. 19, 2012.

rendered "criminally harmless" and "biologically futureless" through mass sterilization.[63]

Under the "Combating the Gypsy Plague Decree," all documents issued had to specify the percentage of Gypsy blood in a person. At the end of 1938, the first racial law against Roma, "Fight against the Gypsy Menace," was enacted and in March 1939 identity documents were issued. These were grey for non-Roma, brown for pure Roma, brown with blue stripes for part-Roma (those with two or more Roma great-great-grandparents — a stricter classification than for part-Jews). The aim of the 1938 law was the racial separation of Roma from Germans, the prevention of miscegenation and tight control of all pure and part-Roma.[64]

Deportation to concentration camps began for the Roma in 1937. There, they would have to attach a black triangle to their clothing implying "asocial status". They soon became victims of torture and live medical experiments. They were often killed on "humanitarian grounds" because their situation was considered hopeless. Roma were also sent to concentration camps from the countries under Nazi control. Between 500,000 and 1,500,000 Roma died in the *Samudaripen*, but the exact number is difficult to establish.[65] The registers of the concentration camps do not have records of those who fled, or of those who were released or transferred to other camps. In any case, the number of those who died is higher than that reported in the registers. Very few of the Roma who asked for compensation after the end of the war received any.[66]

1.3.2. *Post-WWII*

Under the communist regimes of post-WWII, the Roma attracted suspicion because of their peripatetic life-style and disregard of national boundaries. The cultural and economic assistance given to Roma as "victims of capitalism" soon changed and in post-war communist countries, Roma were compelled to abandon nomadism. Use of the Romany language was discouraged and forced assimilation caused sedentarization as well as loss of identity and traditional cultural values. The viable lifestyles developed over centuries and based on self-sufficiency, previously prized, were now being destroyed, and the projects funded in some countries to

---

63 H. Tanner, 'The Roma Persecution,' in *Patrin Web Journal*, available at http://www.reocities.com/~patrin/porraimos.htm, last visited Mar. 19, 2012.

64 Brearley, *supra* note 57.

65 Hancock, *supra* note 62.

66 Id.

improve education, provide better housing and ensure employment were proving unsuccessful.[67] Lacking education and land, the situation of the Roma further worsened with the fall of the communist regimes: paradoxically, the lifting of restrictions on freedom of expression encouraged non-Roma to express their resentments against the Roma.

In post-WWII Western Europe, most Roma were still nomadic as opposed to Central and Eastern Europe, where nomadism, although permitted by law, became progressively more difficult because of the increased control by central governments over marginal groups. Several countries enacted legislation to settle the nomadic Roma on authorised sites (one example is the Caravan Sites Act adopted in the United Kingdom in 1968). Roma wishing to remain nomadic faced harassment and violent eviction from unauthorised sites.[68] In addition, WWII affected the traditional livelihood of the Roma who, due to rapid industrialization, agricultural mechanisation and increasing difficulty in staying nomadic, lost their traditional and seasonal occupations and ended up in the larger cities in search of unskilled or semi-skilled labour. The economic recession of the 1980s forced many of them to look for unemployment or social benefits – available only for the sedentary Roma – which in turn attracted widespread criticism and negative stereotypes by the majority population.[69] As a result, traditional Romany culture risks disappearing and Roma groups need protection. The situation of Roma in Italy is particularly oppressive, as the following discussion, as well as chapter 5, will demonstrate.

1.3.3. *A Brief History of the Roma in Italy*

The first Roma arrived in Italy from Hungary in 1422 in an attempt to escape the Ottoman invasion of the Balkans. Since then, several other groups of Roma have settled in different parts of the country. They generally identified themselves as pilgrims and showed letters of safe conduct, which allowed them to circulate freely. They were mostly horse dealers, musicians, magicians and craftsmen. In the XVI century, some of the nomadic groups (those which are now known as "Sinti") began to settle down in the different states into which Italy was divided at the time.[70]

Other groups of Roma arrived in Italy in the second half of the XV century, mostly coming from the Balkans, once more fleeing the Turkish

[67] Brearley, *supra* note 57, at 11.
[68] Id.
[69] Id., at 12.
[70] A. Arlati, *Gli Zingari in Italia,* 606 Gli Zingari 36 (1997), at 36.

invasions. Some of these groups – which today compose the large family of southern Roma – arrived in Venice, coming from the Croat coast and the Greek Islands. This movement intensified between 1467 (when the Ottomans invaded Albania) and 1499 (with the fall of Lepanto, where a large community of Roma used to live). From the Adriatic and Ionic coast, the Roma spread into central and Southern Italy and moved only seasonally (mostly during fairs). The next large arrival of Roma in Italy occurred at the end of the XIX century, after the unification of the territories.

Although for a time after their arrival, relationships between Roma and the local population were friendly, soon the various Italian states began a policy of expulsion. Venice was among the first to issue decrees against their presence: in 1483 Romany communities were to be expelled following accusations of theft and of being Turkish spies. These measures were quickly adopted by the Duchy of Milan: in 1493 Ludovico il Moro issued two edicts that ordered all Roma to leave at once on the grounds that they had become too numerous and thievish.[71] Many decrees against the Roma emanated also in the Papal state, where they were accused of attacking social cohesion and the homogeneity of the local population.[72] In 1522, Governor Gerolamo di Rossi issued an edict that spoke of scandal, disorder and theft caused by Roma.[73]

The French acquisition of Milan brought stricter penalties. In 1506, two decrees declared Roma a public menace and possible carriers of the plague. In 1517, Francis I ordered all Roma to leave the Duchy within three days or undergo severe penalties. In 1523, his son, the last of the Sforza dynasty, added to the penalty a fine of 25 golden ducats for anyone who would help any Roma to escape. In 1534, Francesco Sforza expelled all Roma: those remaining would be hanged. Similar laws were passed throughout the peninsula. The decrees published under the Spanish dominion sanctioned impunity to anyone who killed a Roma.[74]

The Italian legislation was based on the French model, as were the laws on mendicancy which had the largest impact on the lives of the Roma. The Sardinian penal code of 1859, extended to the rest of the Kingdom of Italy in 1865, prescribed the arrest and detention of those who begged on a regular basis, as did the Zanardelli penal code.[75] Although such laws were

---

[71] Fraser, *supra* note 46, at 107.
[72] Spinelli, *supra* note 53, at 40.
[73] Fraser, *supra* note 46, at 107.
[74] Spinelli, *supra* note 53, at 41.
[75] A. Simoni, 'La mendicità, gli Zingari e la cultura giuridica italiana: uno schizzo di tappe e problemi,' Anno XIV 3 *Polis* 371 (2000), at 373 [hereinafter Simoni].

rarely enforced (even the Italian Fascist government did not apply pressure on this),[76] it is clear that they were largely intended to target the Roma population.

The Italian Fascist government manifested little tolerance for the Roma, who were considered a threat to the security and public health of the country. For these reasons, it tried to curb their life style, and in particular to put an end to their movements. Although Roma were not mentioned in the anti-Jewish laws of 1938, the issues they presented were also treated as racial and were "solved" by deporting as many Roma as possible to the South and to the islands. When Italy entered the war, it adopted more repressive racial measures, along Nazi lines, especially against the foreign Roma who were sent to concentration camps. The situation became even more dramatic following September 8, 1943, after Italy surrendered and the remaining Fascists began a manhunt for the remaining Jews, Roma and partisans.[77]

After the genocide of WWII, Roma found a favourable harbour in Italy and word spread so fast that soon the welcoming climate turned into one of hostility. A few authorised camps were created, either by local or central government. The creation of camps was soon discontinued as policy turned toward the integration of the Roma, which would begin with education. However, the creation of special classes for Roma children made it soon clear that the intention was not so much that of integrating the Roma, but of segregating them or, at best, assimilating them.[78]

1.4. The Roma Today: Main Characteristics and Identification

Today, Roma live virtually everywhere in Europe, and in most countries they suffer discrimination on many grounds. Following the collapse of the Eastern European regimes, most Eastern European states experienced political and social transformation. Ironically, many people have been using the possibility to freely express their opinion as an opportunity to manifest their hatred against the Roma, making them *'the scapegoat for wider social ills.'*[79] The situation is not much better in Western Europe, where the repercussions of the changes in neighbouring countries have sometimes caused severe economic stagnation.

---

[76] Simoni, *supra* note 75, at 372–377.
[77] A. Arlati, 'Gli Zingari e il Fascismo,' 606 *Gli Zingari* 34 (1997), at 34.
[78] This aspect will be further reviewed in chapter 5.
[79] Liégeois and Gheorghe, *supra* note 49, at 5.

Most of today's Roma are neither stationed on a specific territory nor have they ever made any territorial claim: Roma never had a promised land as the focus of their dreams and this, in any case, would be in contrast with their (presumed) way of life. They are sometimes citizens of the country in which they live; but they are often stateless (having given up their documents while fleeing from one country to another in the hope of being granted refugee status), reflecting the refusal of governments to grant them citizenship.[80] Even their language is not a single one. Different groups speak varying dialects that are the result of linguistic contamination, and the absence of a written language has led to some divergences among the varieties of Romanes. The International Romani Union[81] proposed the unification of all dialects in one official language, the "Romanes," which is the most widely spoken amongst Roma. Most Roma groups have the same geographic origin in common, the same degrading life conditions and suffer the same rejection in most countries, which at times, leads states to classify them as "foreigners."

1.4.1. *Roma "Identity"*

Roma generally consider themselves to be a nation. Although great differences sometimes exist among themselves,[82] they share a feeling of closeness strengthened by the experience of separation from the *Gadje* (non-Roma).

> [...] *insofar as these groups share a common experience of discrimination based on dominant ethnic groups regarding them as non-white, and insofar as culture is experientially determined, that common identity will become an increasing reality.*[83]

[80] *See*, for example, Council of Europe, Commissioner for Human Rights, July 2009, 'Many Roma in Europe are stateless and live outside social protection,' July 6, 2009, available at http://www.unhcr.org/refworld/docid/4a7023c72.html, last visited Mar. 19, 2012.

[81] The International Romani Union (IRU) is a non-governmental organisation that represents the Romani community across the world. IRU co-ordinates a large number of regional and national organizations of thirty different countries and promotes the reunification of Roma people under their culture and language. IRU was fully recognised by the United Nations Economic and Social Council (ECOSOC) in March 1979, and in March 1993 it obtained consultative status with ECOSOC.

[82] Fraser notes that European Roma today are a heterogeneous community with many different cultural values as well as religious and linguistic diversity. *See* Fraser, n. 44 above. *See also* I. Pogány, 'Minority Rights and the Roma of Central and Eastern Europe,' (2006) *Human Rights Law Review* 6:1, at 17–18.

[83] Acton and Gheorghe, *supra* note 5, at 30.

Roma have a common ancestry which can be used to supply evidence of a core of values and traditions, some of which have been changed by contact with the majority society and the need to adapt to the conditions of the host country.[84]

The High Commissioner on National Minorities of the Conference for Security and Cooperation in Europe stated that:

> [...] *there are significant commonalties perceived as binding the Roma together: commonalties in origin, language, culture, historical experience, and present-day problems in the region. In addition to a Romani cultural heritage, including a strongly itinerant tradition that is both cause and effect of their history, the Roma also share the use (or the remembrance) of a common, though highly variant language, also known as Romani or Romanes. Modern-day Roma group identity is being further strengthened by the recognition and development of these cultural and linguistic commonalties, as well as by an understanding of their similar historical experiences, particularly of discrimination, within the region.*[85]

The Romany holocaust that took place during WWII helped to develop a feeling of nationhood.[86] The multiculturalism and trans-nationality[87] of Roma populations are then peculiarities that underline a way of life and are a full expression of their (common) identity.[88]

A number of definitions have been put forward that attempt to capture the essence of Romany identity. In trying to define the Roma and clarifying their status, various "alternative faces of the Gypsy"[89] can be distinguished. The first is "racial:" this refers to the race of the Gypsies – in other words, to the "real" or "true blood" Gypsies, it is related to their separateness, to their "foreign," Indian origin and ancestry. This provides the basis for a

---

84 O'Nions, *supra* note 1, at 4.

85 Conference for Security and Cooperation in Europe, High Commissioner on National Minorities, *High Commissioner on National Minorities' Report on the Roma in the CSCE Region*, 1993, at 3.

86 N. Gheorghe and A. Mirga, 'The Roma in the Twenty-First Century: A Policy Paper,' available at http://www.eurozine.com/article/2001-03-12-mirga-gheorgh-en.html, last visited Mar. 19, 2012, at 10 [hereinafter Gheorghe and Mirga].

87 Romany intellectuals have introduced innovative concepts such as "stateless nation" and "nonterritorial," "transnational" or "truly European" people (in the Brussels Declaration) to describe their position. All of these terms indicate that, in demanding recognition, Romany leaders are not claiming an ethnic territory or nation-state, but rather are searching for a broader political framework in which to address their cause. *See* Gheorghe and Mirga, *supra* note 86, at 10.

88 And it is for the preservation of their culture, their way of life and their identity that the Roma fight.

89 Mayall, *supra* note 3, at 5.

picture of the group which emphasises its peculiar attitudes and behaviours; the continued cultural practices and the *obvious* physical differences such as skin, hair and eye colour.[90] Also of importance is the retention of a distinctive language with Indian roots – Romani or Romanes.[91] In addition, nomadism is seen as an important part of Roma culture and as a way of life (although not all Roma lead a nomadic lifestyle and nomadism has often been abandoned to live a sedentary life). Finally, *"the idea of a single race allows the group a worldwide identity which unites Gypsies across national borders."*[92]

A second definition is based on the combination of a way of life with low socio-economic and social status: in this case, the main criterion for defining the group is not its origins, but the nomadic way of life which distinguishes travelling families pursuing itinerant occupations from the settled population. Nomadism is equated with gypsyism and being a nomad with being a "Gypsy."[93]

To these can be added two further and competing ethnic versions of the "Gypsy." The ethnic-racial classification – possessing the same characteristics as the racial one but with some important differences: this emphasises the Indian origin, cultural distinctiveness and linguistic continuity. This definition however rejects fixed and permanent differences, in particular in relation to psychological, mental and cultural attributes, while stressing the ethnic minority status of the Roma and a transnational identity based on common origins, lifestyle, culture and experience, allowing for diversity and variants within the group.[94] Another classification gives priority to the historical and contemporary oppression of the group, stressing the

---

[90] Mayall, *supra* note 3, at 5–6.

[91] Id., at 6.

[92] Id., at 6.

[93] Id. Mayall pointed out that nomadism is a major component present in every definition of Gypsy identity, to the point that it is almost universally agreed that nomadism and Gypsy go hand-in-hand: nomadism used to be seen as an inherited instinct, and not something that could be controlled or denied. To try to prevent the Roma from travelling was thought to be the denial of their nature and essence, to the point that Roma were thought to become ill if they were to live in houses and would recover only when returned to their tents. Nomadism would explain the inability of the Roma to settle; but it was also considered a state of mind – in which case a Roma could remain a mental or spiritual nomad and retain the essence of gypsyness, while having a settled lifestyle. Inevitably these ideas caused increasing criticism as scholars had to explain why some Roma had given up their nomadic lifestyle for settled employment and a permanent home, if not for their whole life, at least for parts of it. Various explanations were given, including those according to which only the non-pure Roma born through intermarriage would be able to settle and abandon nomadism. *See* Mayall, *supra* note 3, at 11–12 and 130.

[94] Id., at 7.

persecution and victimisation of the Roma and thus finding a parallel with Jewish history and identity.[95]

The final face of the Gypsy can be termed "ethnic/cultural." In practice, this means that an ethnic specificity of the Gypsy exists, except this is not located in foreign origins but rather in its nomadic ancestry. In other words, this definition borrows from both the ethnic/racial elements and the socio/economic elements already outlined.[96] *"No criterion interpreted from the outside provides a satisfactory method of identifying Gypsies, whether it be a country of origin, race, language, occupation or general culture."*[97] Conversely, the criteria for the definition should come from the inside; from the Roma. Nomadic descent can thus be identified as the necessary condition for Roma identity, in which aspects such as self-employment, language, an ideology for travelling, dress, cleanliness rituals, shared values and ideological separation between Roma and non-Roma are secondary. Furthermore, the place of origin does not seem significant for the Roma.[98]

There is a separate "racial" identity of the Roma which is constructed around notions of foreign origins and distinct language, cultural and behavioural differences, their way of earning a living and even a belief in physiological distinctiveness. Not all the racial components have to be present for the racial picture to be affirmed.[99] Central to the racial definition of the Roma is the conviction that they all originate from a single lineage. *"By identifying one origin for the Gypsies it then became possible to establish a coherent identity for all those people said to be able to claim ancestry back to this one source."*[100] Race is thought to refer to physical traits (including skin colour and facial features) and discernible characteristics, but these are not the only things that allow us to distinguish the Roma.

As previously stated, all Roma speak different varieties of one language, Romanes, further supporting the view according to which the Roma are an ethnic group.

---

[95] Mayall, *supra* note 3, at 7.

[96] Id.

[97] J. Okely, 'Gypsy Identity,' in B. Adams, J. Okely, D. Morgan and D. Smith (eds.), *Gypsies and Government Policy in England: A Study of the Travellers' Way of Life in Relation to the Policies and Practices of Central and Local Government* (London, 1975), pp. 27–54, at 28 [hereinafter Okely (1975)].

[98] J. Okely, 'Ethnic identity and place of origin: the Traveller Gypsy in England,' in H. Vermeulen and J. Boissevain (eds.), *Ethnic Challenge: The Politics of Ethnicity in Europe* (Göttingen, 1984), at 5 [hereinafter Okely (1984)].

[99] Mayall, *supra* note 3, at 118–119.

[100] Id., at 119.

> *In relation to the emergence and development of the racial definition of Gypsies, the study of the Romany language became a key element of the attempt to prove their existence as a separate racial group.*[101]

Studies dating back to the XVIII century have shown that Romanes is closely connected to Sanskrit, the various arguments in favour of this being based on comparisons of words, similarities in spelling, pronunciation and meaning, as well as grammatical structures and conventions of the languages. The extent of the purity or corruption of the language was considered an indication of how long the Roma had dwelled in a particular area or country, as well as the degree of contact and assimilation with the indigenous populations and, on some occasions, also of the persecution suffered by the Roma on their travels and of the purity or decay of their "race" as a result of intermixing, intermarriage and assimilation.[102] Indeed, when persecuted, the Roma would use their secret language to survive and so the language remained pure, while the opposite happened when they were treated humanely.[103]

To further build on the idea of Roma as a separate "ethnicity," importance is given to their physical appearance, customs, manners, behaviour and manners of thought, which – as far as language is concerned – have been traced back to their Indian roots.[104] The main features of the Roma are *"olive or tawny-coloured flesh, black hair, dark eyes* [...]*"* which all have Indian roots. Emphasis is also given to their *"keenness or brilliance of eye, long eyelashes, sallow cheeks, thin curled lips, brilliant white teeth, wiry figures and their lithe and graceful form."*[105] Added to this unscientific description was the distinctive style of dress: women were believed to

---

[101] Mayall, *supra* note 3, at 124.

[102] Id., at 122–123. Marriage within the group (endogamy) served to preserve the identity of the group, and intermarriage and intermixing were seen, conversely, as great threats to the group's survival. It is however known that intermarriage and intermixing have long occurred between Roma and non-Roma. To respond to the evidence of intermarriage (exogamy) as not having threatened the Roma identity, three explanations were given. According to the first, in any crossbreeding, it would be the Roma blood that would prevail and thus non-Roma would take on the Roma way of life rather than the opposite: this was seen as proof of the "Gypsies racial assertiveness." The second explanation was that crossbreeding allowed the renewal of the racial stock and it gave it extra vigour. Finally, it was recognised that by the XIX century intermixing had occurred to the extent that dilution of the race was taking place and the true Roma was being threatened. Arguments for racial purity thus depended on the view that assimilation had not occurred since the first arrival of the Roma and that it was not to be desired if the Roma wanted to retain their separate identity. *See* Mayall, *supra* note 3, at 134–135.

[103] Id., at 123.

[104] Id., at 124.

[105] Id., at 125.

have a love of gay colours and personal adornments (taken as indications of a persistent Oriental tradition); whereas men were less colourful but wore slouching hats, corduroy trousers and velveteen coats.[106]

Okely and Acton agreed that the Roma constitute an ethnic group, although they disagreed over the basis of that ethnicity and the relative significance of Indian origins and nomadic ancestry. Even in Liégeois' work, the concept of ethnic Gypsy remains vague and he seems to deny the importance of original foreign ancestry from India when he acknowledges that in Europe from the XVI century there was exchange, mixing and absorption amongst the travellers coming from India and the indigenous ones.[107]

Roma are also thought to be significantly different from non-Roma because of their separate customs and culture, which have remained virtually unchanged over centuries and which are made up of not only Romany language, but also music, diet and dress as well as various rituals, taboos and ceremonies relating to marriage, divorce, courtship, pollution and death.[108] Other differences between Roma and non-Roma which further separate them from the people among whom they live are in their nature, manner of thought, ambitions and attitudes toward life.[109] Furthermore, many of the racial representations of the Roma also incorporate statements on their political and social organisation, claiming that Roma remain outside the dominant social and political institutions and favour their internal systems of organisation and rule.[110]

Based on the various premises identified, I will consider the Roma as an ethnic group and not exclusively a racial one,[111] united not only by common genealogy or ancestry and thus visible physical traits, but also by language, culture, behaviour, religion and lifestyle. I will also allow for

106 Mayall, *supra* note 3, at 126.

107 J.P. Liégeois, *Roma in Europe* (Strasbourg: Council of Europe Publishing, 2007), at 17–22.

108 Mayall, *supra* note 3, at 126.

109 R.A.S. Macfie, 'Gypsy Lore,' *University Review* Vol. 7, No. 38, November 1908, at 104, as reported in Mayall, *supra* note 3, at 129.

110 Mayall, *supra* note 3, at 128.

111 Although the term "race" has been generally used to identify a person by biological characteristics, the term "ethnicity" reflects the social, cultural, and geographical environment from which an individual or his ancestors have come. This determination includes factors such as language and culture that are passed down through learning. The idea that the Roma are an ethnic group is further explored in the course of this chapter. It should be pointed out that no definition of ethnicity exists in international law and that although Article 1 of the ICERD gives a list of aspects that fall within the concept of race, it does not provide a definition.

diversity and differences among the various Roma groups and will not demand them to be homogeneous to consider them an ethnic minority.[112] Nomadism will be considered an important but not fundamental trait that distinguishes the Roma: considering the change in circumstances that has led to the sedentarization of many Roma, it will not be deemed as the most important factor in defining the Roma ethnicity.

1.4.2. *The Roma as an Ethnic Group?*

Most definitions of ethnicity include notions of common origin in time and place, descent, customs, culture and the commitment to a distinctive way of life which is handed down to new generations. One of the most complete definitions was given in 1983 by the House of Lords in the United Kingdom in the case of *Mandla v. Dowell Lee*,[113] in which it was stated that for a group to constitute an "ethnic group" it should regard itself, and be regarded by others, as a distinct community with certain characteristics, two of which are fundamental. These are: a long-shared history; a cultural tradition; and, in addition, either a common geographical origin; language; literature; religion different from that of the group surrounding it; or the characteristic of being a minority or an oppressed or dominant group within a larger community.

The concept of ethnicity, searching for common characteristics and emphasising a number of features as the primary definers and essence of a people, inevitably has a homogenising effect on group identity. Priority is given to those features shared by the majority – if not all – of the members of the group.[114] Of course, the identification of shared characteristics as the basis of group identity is valid; however, differences within the group must be acknowledged and accommodated. As has been previously pointed out in this chapter, major differences between Roma exist in different countries, as well as in various Roma groups within the same country. The common approach taken to ensure that the Roma are recognised as an ethnic group is thus to simply ignore the differences between the various groups dispersed in the world and to reassert the image of the Roma as one group sharing the same features, ancestry, physical appearance, way of life, values and so on. Another approach is that of allowing and even highlighting the differences among the various groups.

---

[112] *See below* the discussion of the case *CRE v Dutton* [1989] 1 All ER 306 [hereinafter *CRE v Dutton*].

[113] *Mandla v. Dowell Lee*, [1983] 2AC 548.

[114] Mayall, *supra* note 3, at 239.

> *It is a mistake to think* [...] *that Gypsies constitute a homogeneous population. As the migrating population spread out into Europe, the different groups became associated with different countries, over time acquired local characteristics, and intermarried with local populations.*[115]

The acquisition of local characteristics and the partial or total assimilation of the Roma in the culture of the various countries in which they have lived and still live, has led to the admission that they do not form a "unified ethnic whole"[116] and that no such thing as a single Roma culture exists. The idea of "multiculturality" has appeared in the ethnic discourse. The Roma often have features in common with those of the majority population of the country in which they live. Somehow, they are part of that community, with a sense of loyalty to the state (shown by their willingness to fight for the country in times of war). Conversely, they are separate from the majority community because of their trans-national identity, which extends beyond national borders and unites all Roma. This characteristic can be called "the dual identity and dual nationalism" of the Roma.[117]

The recognition of these differences has allowed the construction of the image of a heterogeneous group which does not share a common nationality, language or dialect, social or economic organisation, occupations, customs or culture – yet, it is still recognised as an ethnic group. Indeed, a sense of shared common identity is derived from the sense of collective awareness of the Roma.[118] *"Gypsies are a part of our world and yet are distinct from the rest of us. They live in the world we know, yet they seem to offer an alternative way to be in our world."*[119] The Roma identity is also reaffirmed by their separation and distinctiveness from the host population: tribal differences are seen as perfectly compatible with the "one people" definition.[120]

In recent years, it has been admitted that identities are not fixed but fluid and mobile rather than self-perpetuating. In view of this, it can be noted that Roma culture is in constant evolution, borrowing from and

---

115 I. Hancock, 'American Roma: the hidden Gypsy world,' *Interface 28,* November 1997, pp. 19–22, at 21 [hereinafter Hancock].

116 Mayall, *supra* note 3, at 239.

117 Id., at 240.

118 J.P. Liégeois, *Gypsies. An Illustrated History,* translated by Tony Berre (Al Saqui Books, London, 1986), at 83–84. [hereinafter Liégeois (1986)] Liégeois notes that *'despite the diversity, the feeling of belonging to the same category of individuals is stronger than the sense of difference that divides them.'*

119 M. Stewart, *The time of the Gypsies* (USA, Westview Press, 1997), at 12 [hereinafter Stewart (1997a)].

120 Mayall, *supra* note 3, at 241.

interacting with the majority culture, and that this is part of a process of creating and recreating the Roma's culture.[121]

> *Gypsies and Travellers as a whole must not be considered a static society, rigidly set since time immemorial and reproducing itself in an identical mould.* [...] *Gypsy culture, like all cultures, is in constant evolution, and more so than others because change is one of its traditions and adaptation a constant necessity.*[122]

In short, Roma culture is not static but dynamic, able to borrow from and interact with non-Roma societies: the concept of adaptation is identified as a distinguishing feature of the Roma, linked to processes of survival in a hostile environment.[123]

Today, the Roma are generally considered an ethnic group – one that shares not only certain physical characteristics, but also common descent, customs and culture. The recognition of the Roma as an ethnic group, however, did not occur without difficulties. For example, in the United Kingdom, following the judgment of *Mandla v. Dowell Lee*, which granted Sikhs the status of ethnic group, in the case of *CRE* (Commission for Racial Equality) *v. Dutton*,[124] some Roma challenged the notion according to which, in the United Kingdom, the words "gypsy" and "traveller" are synonyms and that neither one could be defined as a racial or ethnic group. When the case appealed, it was confirmed that the meaning of "traveller" is not synonymous with "gypsy" and the judgment according to which Gypsies do not constitute an ethnic group was overturned because it was stated that they do indeed satisfy the key criteria for ethnicity, incorporating the two essential features identified in the case of *Mandla v. Dowell Lee* as well as some of the non-essential characteristics. The ruling was that Gypsies possessed: a long-shared history; a historically determined social identity; common geographical origins in North India and a pattern of migration through Persia; certain – although limited – customs, including some related to cooking and the manner of washing; distinctive cultural features, such as a traditional style of dressing, which meant they had not been absorbed into the majority society; their own language (in this case a

---

[121] Okely, J., 'Cultural ingenuity and travelling autonomy: not copying, just choosing,' in Acton, T. and Mundy, G. (eds.), *Romani culture and Gypsy identity* (Great Britain: University of Hertfordshire Press, 1997), pp. 188–203.

[122] J.P. Liégeois, *Gypsies and Travellers: Socio-cultural Data, Socio-political Data*, (Strasbourg, 1987), at 46 and 80 [hereinafter Liégeois (1987)].

[123] Stewart (1997a), *supra* note 119, at 5.

[124] *CRE v Dutton*, *supra* note 112.

combination of Romanes and English) as well as their dialect; and a repertoire of folktales and music passed from one generation to the next (although no common literature or religion).

Origins are the essence and heart of Roma identity. It is argued that *"to assert common Indian origins is to provide the Gypsies with a shared homeland."*[125] Conversely, it is maintained that the theory of Indian origins should be abandoned – for this being accused of depriving the Roma of the roots of their identity and ethnicity. However, the notion of the Roma as a legitimate ethnic group is generally supported, although the vision of ethnicity has moved away from the Indian roots and suggests that the (English) Roma[126] are indeed groups of people who at some point in the XV and XVI centuries, at the time of the collapse of feudalism and socio-economic change, rejected wage labour and adopted itinerant trades and services.[127]

> *Often this search for origins has been rather haphazard – any Indian, or, more particularly, northern Indian, custom that reminds people of Gypsy behaviour is seen as ancestral. Sadly this kind of explanation is widely seen as acceptable.*[128]

It is often arbitrary as well as irrelevant *"to separate groups of Indian from those of indigenous origins (and sometimes even impossible to do so)."*[129]

Cultural features such as language and customs have their roots in the original homeland. The subsequent migrations and relations to a number of 'host' societies also contribute to a shared past and history.[130] Persecution is thus just one of the various components that allow the ethnic classification of the Roma. Most scholars and Roma activists point out how the Roma history and present position are dominated by various forms of persecution and harassment. Great emphasis has been placed on the Nazi persecution of the Roma, which is seen as a continuum of the persecutions that the Roma experienced throughout history, although most would agree that the Nazi holocaust and the various forms of persecution used by early modern states – such as enslavement, forced labour, banishment and imprisonment – are not comparable.[131] It is important

---

125 Mayall, *supra* note 3, at 220–221.
126 However, the argument could be extended to the Roma of all Europe.
127 Okely (1984), *supra* note 98, at 52.
128 Stewart (1997a), *supra* note 119, at 236.
129 Liégeois (1987), *supra* note 122, at 45.
130 Mayall, *supra* note 3, at 221.
131 Id., at 235.

now to point out that the persecution and the Nazi holocaust lend support to the recognition of the Roma as an ethnic group. Persecution (whether experienced directly or learnt as part of the group history) helps to establish the Roma ethnicity by consolidating a sense of group identity and establishing ethnic credentials in the eyes of the non-Roma. Furthermore, discriminatory treatment by outsiders strengthens the group identity by creating a defensive response to such hostility.[132] In addition, the knowledge and experience of hostile treatment in the past and the present, becomes part of the oral tradition and culture of the group. Persecution thus increases the sense of difference, strengthens in-group feelings and creates an "us and them" mentality.[133]

Knowledge of the persecutions faced by Roma in the past and the present brought demands for equal rights and for their recognition as a legitimate ethnic group – even more so because other ethnic groups such as the Jews have a similar history.[134] Diaspora, dispersal and persecutions could have broken up a sense of collective identity by spreading the Roma around the world. Roma were dispersed not only across the world, but also within states in which they united in relatively small groups, family units and encampments; a factor that delayed or prevented the creation of the normal ideological and institutional mechanisms for asserting common identity.[135] Indeed, the history and experience of persecution can cause members of the group to deny their identity and to adopt strategies to minimise the differences with the host societies to avoid further persecution. Such strategies might involve the use of the same language and clothing style, the adoption of indigenous names and of a way of life that does not mark the group for any special treatment – in other words, the identity is concealed or lost through the process of integration and assimilation.[136] However, in the case of the Roma, the diaspora contributed to providing a sense of common history and past in which constant movement and persecution have served to strengthen a sense of otherness.[137]

The emphasis on common descent and ancestry of the Roma provides them with a past and identity shaped around kinship and family networks. Thus, a "Gypsy identity" as well as ethnicity is *"something an individual is*

---

132 Mayall, *supra* note 3, at 235.
133 Id.
134 Id., at 236.
135 Id., at 221–222.
136 Id., at 236.
137 Id., at 222.

born with rather than something that can be acquired, or even abandoned, later."[138] However, descent and ancestry are not believed to be sufficient to establish Roma identity – which is reinforced by the way of life, culture and value of the Roma community. A shared culture is a key aspect in defining any group as being ethnic. Already in 1979, Caportorti, in trying to define the term "minority" for the purpose of the interpretation of Article 27 of the ICCPR, noted the clear link between ethnicity and culture, to the point of stating that:

> *on the basis of a logical and literal interpretation of Article 27 the rights relating to culture have been regarded as referring to members of ethnic minorities* [...] *It is evident that when a minority is both ethnic and linguistic, its members should enjoy both categories of rights. It should also be borne in mind that the dividing line between culture and language* [...] *is not as clear as it may appear.*[139]

The Roma culture is presented in two main ways. According to the first, this is strictly linked to the Roma's alleged Indian origins.[140] A second modified version accepts that traditions, cultures and beliefs are distinctive and although possibly rooted in an Indian past, have evolved and been transformed through the incorporation of features from the non-Roma society.[141] The main components of the Roma culture are thought to be self-employment, knowledge of the Romani language, an ideology of travelling, distinctive habitat, dress, rituals and codes of behaviour, forms of economic, social and political organisation and a general ideological separation from non-Roma. Laws and customs relating to pregnancy, childbirth, baptism, puberty, virginity, clothes, food, cooking, hygiene, marriage, death and funerals comprise the core system of Roma beliefs and practices.[142] These codes, belief and practices (mostly invisible to non-Roma) which influence the daily life of the Roma, define and maintain the boundaries between Roma and non-Roma.[143]

---

138 Mayall, *supra* note 3, at 229. Okely points out that the main criterion used by Roma to identify themselves as such is that at least one of their parents is also a Roma. *See* Okely (1975), *supra* note 97, at 28.

139 Capotorti, *supra* note 29, para. 590.

140 I. Fonseca, *Bury Me Standing. The Gypsies and their Journey* (New York: Vintage Departures, 1996), at 106 [hereinafter Fonseca].

141 I. Hancock, 'The Gypsies/Roma,' *Shmate. A Journal of Progressive Jewish Thought*, Issue 17, Winter 1987, at 6–7; as quoted in Mayall, *supra* note 3, at 230.

142 Mayall, *supra* note 3, at 229–230.

143 Id., at 231.

Even nomadism, as the expression of a culture and way of life, as demonstrated herein, plays an important role in defining the Roma ethnicity. As previously explained, a nomadic way of life is seen as traditional, and to settle down is seen as a break from the traditional practices – a break that is however occurring more often. Settlement could imply that the Roma groups are being assimilated into the ways of life of settled societies, losing their distinctive traits and adopting the ways of the dominant hosts.[144] The settlement of the Roma has long been an ambition of the governments of the countries in which they lived because it would undermine the negative aspects of travelling and allow assimilation into the host society. However, it is argued that settlement does not necessarily mean the loss of those distinctive traits – as was established earlier, nomadism is a state of mind more than an actual situation or way of living.[145]

> *If you are a Gypsy or Traveller, it is something you know, feel and live. It is a lifestyle based on ways of being that are undefinable and intangible, and on ways of doing which may be variable or ephemeral.*[146]

Thus, sedentary Roma remain Roma as much as the nomadic ones by retaining the values and spirit of nomadism.

The social organisation of the Roma group, and the codes and rituals which reinforce this consolidate the ethnic image. Many scholars refer to the extended family and kinship networks as the core structure of Roma societies. In this picture, intermarriage serves the purpose of excluding outsiders from the Roma groups and maintaining stability in the community. Even the political organisation of the Roma is distinctive from that of their host societies. The idea that they have kings and queens as a system of formal leadership is no longer accepted; but various ideas exist according to which the Roma have courts and councils,[147] which exist in the form of a more informal arrangement based around kinship ties – a loose, unstructured form of political, social and judicial organisation that overcomes the diversity of the population by the existence of a shared and autonomous system of justice.[148]

In the past, some scholars believed that speaking Romanes would be a test of Roma identity, the argument being that while other cultural traits

144 Mayall, *supra* note 3.
145 Id., at 231.
146 Liégeois (1987), *supra* note 122, at 75.
147 Mayall, *supra* note 3, at 233.
148 Liégeois (1986), *supra* note 118, at 64.

are variable and changing, language remains somewhat consistent.[149] However, as it has already been pointed out, Romanes is not a single language understood by all Roma: there is growing acceptance that, although Romanes might have a single origin, it consists of more than 100 dialects or even separate languages, often mutually unintelligible despite the existence of some core words.[150]

A number of scholars who believe that the Roma are an ethnic group argue that their separateness and ethnicity can also be defined by a distinctive "Gypsy spirit," character, state of mind or even Romany worldview.[151] The Romany language is a linguistic expression of a much broader Roma personality. The language is seen as *"hyperbolic, gregarious, typically expressive of extreme emotions:"*[152] the spirit of the language and the character of the people are the same – they are both emotional as well as passionate. Some of the common traits of the groups are the love of noise, the lack of the need for privacy and the use of misrepresentation and secrecy as a means of survival.[153] To these characteristics, one could add the disdain of Roma for non-Roma ways, referring to their sense of egalitarianism and individualism, their way of doing things, the ethos of sharing and the idiom of brotherhood.[154] The Roma love of freedom, their need to live in accordance with the rhythm of nature and their desire to be their own masters should also be pointed out.[155]

It cannot be denied that there have been changes (even if minimal) in the Roma's culture, social structure, normative systems and values and taboos. Traditional features are however the core of the Roma culture, whereas modern features, acquired through contact with the host societies, are superficial, deliberate façades.[156] The Roma have resisted outside pressures and their essence has remained strong; a trait that can be explained by their status as outsiders and by the tradition of persecution which left them isolated from other groups.[157]

---

149 Mayall, *supra* note 3, at 232.

150 Id.

151 Id.

152 Fonseca, *supra* note 140, at 58.

153 Id., at 24–25.

154 M. Stewart, 'The puzzle of Roma persistence: group identity without a nation,' in T. Acton and G. Mundy (eds.), *Romani culture and Gypsy Identity*, (Great Britain: University of Hertfordshire Press, 1997), pp. 82–96, at 86–87.

155 J.P. Clebert, *The Gypsies* (Harmondsworth, 1967), at 20.

156 Mayall, *supra* note 3, at 238.

157 It has also been argued that traditional Roma culture only allows as much involvement with non-Roma as is strictly necessary for the social and economic survival of the

1.5. Conclusions: The Roma as an Ethnic and Transnational Minority

Many commentators are still not convinced that the Roma constitute an ethnic group because of their changing identities and lack of homogeneity. Some believe that individuals and groups are constantly in the process of negotiating and renegotiating identity.[158] In his discussion on Jewish identity, Webber observed that:

> *the idea that Jews are a single people possessing a single, or at least united history assuredly has great power at the level of theology or political ideology; but, in practice, the overwhelming majority of European Jews today also function as citizens of the respective countries in which they live.* [...] *they are only partially Jewish in the sense that their cultural identities as Frenchmen, Italians, and so on operate alongside, if not in competition with, their identities as Jews* [...].[159]

The word "Jew" in this passage could be easily substituted with the word "Gypsy."[160]

This chapter has shown that despite the lack of homogeneity among the various Roma groups, the Roma should indeed be considered an ethnic group: their common ancestry proves this with evidence of a core of values and traditions, only some of which have been modified through contact with the host countries. The problems faced by Roma are similar across Europe, and this has helped in their identification as a united group.

Regarding the recognition of the Roma as a "national minority," the terms "national minority" presuppose the existence of a national identity and perhaps even a homeland, forcing the construction of a separate nationality.[161] This has led some Romani intellectuals and activists to call for a new status as a legally recognised transnational minority, which could be afforded irrespective of citizenship and residence.

According to the Committee on Legal Affairs and Human Rights of the Council of Europe,

> *The Roma are recognized legally a. as a national or ethnic minority group in Austria, Croatia, the Czech Republic, Hungary, "the former Yugoslav Republic of Macedonia", Norway, Poland, Romania, Slovakia, Sweden, Ukraine and the*

---

group – whereas intermixing might lead to defilement and spiritual disharmony. *See* Hancock, *supra* note 115, at 19.

158 Mayall, *supra* note 3, at 244.

159 J. Webber, 'Jews and Judaism in contemporary Europe: religious or ethnic group,' *Ethnic and Racial Studies*, Vol. 20, No. 2, April 1997, pp. 257–279, at 259.

160 Mayall, *supra* note 3, at 244.

161 Acton and Gheorghe, *supra* note 5.

Federal Republic of Yugoslavia; b. as a traditional national minority in Finland; c. as a racial group protected under the Race Relation Act 1976 in the United Kingdom. The Roma have no special legal status in Belgium, Denmark, Germany, Greece, Italy, the Netherlands, Slovenia and Switzerland. There are no Roma living in Andorra, Iceland and Malta. The rapporteur of the Parliamentary Assembly of the Council of Europe has not received any official information about the legal status of the Roma from the following member states: Albania, Bulgaria, Cyprus, Estonia, France, Georgia, Ireland, Latvia, Liechtenstein, Lithuania, Moldavia, Portugal, the Russian Federation, San Marino, Spain, and Turkey.[162]

As Thelen suggested, "*the Roma are an ethnic or national minority in each country and a transnational minority in Europe, and/or a nation.*"[163] "*Gypsies form a specific ethnic community that has no parallel among other European nations.*"[164]

Drawing attention to the need to draw on transnational perspectives, Kawczynski noted that:

As a de facto non-territorial minority in Europe, the Roma occupy a unique position, both historically and politically, and their situation is comparable with that of the European Jews. Unlike the Jews, however, the Roma do not have an independent national homeland state providing a framework of political sovereignty. Efforts to improve the situation of the Roma in Europe must acknowledge this special position.[165]

Discrimination and hostility are experiences common to almost all Roma in Europe,[166] and this is one of the factors that allows for the identification of Roma as a transnational minority.[167] European Union citizenship might provide an opportunity for transnational minorities to assert their rights,

---

162 Council of Europe, Committee on Legal Affairs and Human Rights, *Legal Situation of the Roma in Europe,* Report, 19 April 2002.

163 P. Thelen, 'Roma Policy: The Long Walk Towards Political Participation,' in *Roma in Europe. From Social Exclusion to Active Participation,* P. Thelen (ed.) (Skopie: Friedrich Ebert Stiftung, 2005), pp. 7–74, at 41.

164 E. Marushiakova and V. Popov, 'Historical and Ethnographic Background: Gypsies, Roma and Sinti,' in W. Guy (ed.), *Between past and future, the Roma of Central and Eastern Europe,* (Hatfield: University of Hertfordshire Press, 2001), pp. 33–53, at 33.

165 R. Kawczynski, 'Nationality: Roma Citizenship: Europe,' in *Roma Rights*, available at http://www.errc.org/cikk.php?cikk=1760, last visited Mar. 20, 2012. Kawczynski is the Program Director of the Regional Roma Participation Program of the Open Society Institute in Budapest, Hungary.

166 A. Bancroft, *Roma and Gypsy Travellers in Europe: modernity, race, space and exclusion* (Aldershot: Ashgate, 2005), at 47 [hereinafter Bancroft].

167 Aside, of course, from self-identification: being a member of a minority is, first of all, a subjective factor.

considering that European recognition will not depend solely on national identity.[168]

Although I would not reject the idea of considering the Roma as a transnational minority, I argue that the fact that some Roma activists call for their recognition as a transnational minority need not imply that they are not an ethnic minority as well. The fact that a minority might be (trans) national does not mean that it cannot also be ethnic, historic, linguistic and so on. Hence, as has already been stated, in the course of this book, the Roma will be considered an ethnic minority which should be guaranteed all the rights normally afforded to minorities and which can be the subject of collective rights.

168 Bancroft, *supra* note 166, at 171.

CHAPTER TWO

THE DEFINITION OF MINORITY AND THE PROTECTION OF ROMA IN INTERNATIONAL LAW INSTRUMENTS

2.1. Introduction

As of today, no international, legally accepted definition of minority exists. Furthermore, the types of minority protected by international instruments vary because this lack of a definition has made it necessary for them to confine their scope of applicability to certain types of minorities. In this sense, Article 27 of the 1966 International Covenant on Civil and Political Rights (ICCPR) includes "ethnic, linguistic and religious" minorities but not "national minorities." The *travaux preparatoires* indicate that the non-inclusion of "national minority" in the formulation was a conscious choice, as the proposal of the Russian delegation to include it (and to exclude "ethnic, religious or linguistic minority") was not accepted because "national minority" would imply a higher threshold and thus exclude from protection those minorities which would not develop into national minorities.[1]

The Council of Europe and the Organisation for Security and Cooperation in Europe (OSCE, formerly Conference for Security and Cooperation in Europe, CSCE), conversely, use the term "national" minorities, although, regardless of the widespread use of the expression "national minority" to date, no commonly accepted definition for it exists either.[2]

---

[1] K. Henrard, *Devising an Adequate System of Minority Protection* (The Netherlands, Kluwer Law International, 2000), at 53. [hereinafter Henrard] This reasoning implies that "national minorities" have an extra dimension in addition to the characteristics of ethnic, religious or linguistic minorities. The U.N. Declaration on the Rights of Persons Belonging to National or Ethnic, Religious, and Linguistic Minorities adds "national minorities" among the beneficiaries of Article 27. *See* H. Heintze, 'Article 1,' in M. Weller (ed.), *The Rights of Minorities in Europe* (Oxford: Oxford University Press, 2005), pp. 77–96, at 83. [hereinafter Heintze] Indeed, as the Commentary to the Declaration states, *"there is hardly any national minority, however defined, that is not also an ethnic or linguistic minority." See* A. Eide, *Final Text of the Commentary to the Declaration on the Rights of Persons Belonging to National or Ethnic, Religious, and Linguistic Minorities*, UNGA Res. A/47/135. 1992, para. 6.

[2] M. Tabory, 'Minority Rights in the CSCE Context' in Y. Dinstein and M. Tabory (eds.) *The Protection of Minorities and Human Rights* (Dordrecht: Kluwer, 1993), pp. 187–211, at 196. *"The concept of "national minorities" seems [...] something that only Europeans can explain.*

The lack of definition is usually blamed on the complexity of the subject and also on the traditional fear that talk of minority rights invokes in national governments: minority rights are seen as one step on the road to secession.[3] The problem of defining a minority for the purposes of international law has troubled international lawyers and academics; however, *"definitional difficulties should not be considered fatal to affording special minority protection."*[4] In most cases, indeed, recognising a group as a minority is not a major problem (*"most of the time it is rather self-evident which groups constitute minorities"*[5]) and international law will not treat as conclusive the status ascribed to groups by the particular state in which they live.[6] Nevertheless, some codification in the area is needed. Indeed, currently states can easily elude their obligations to protect unpopular minorities and if necessary can invoke the lack of international clarification to support their domestic policies[7] and arbitrarily decide which groups on their territory should be considered minorities and be granted the special protection and rights deriving from this status. Minorities are left at the mercy of the state in which they live, and it is thus even more important that states recognise minorities living on their territory because the lack of an international legal regime means that minorities in need of protection should at least be able to refer to domestic legislation.[8]

It is a concept very much founded in the last century of European history, and it does not include nations, as you call them, with a certain historical and territorial content. It is not necessarily applicable to all ethnic or cultural or all religious groups." See H. Hannum, 'Contemporary Developments in the International Protection of the Rights of Minorities' *Notre Dame Law Review,* Vol. 66 (1991), 1431–1448, at 1454. *"While there is no universally agreed-upon definition of the term, it has a long history in European diplomacy, where it has referred to historically-settled minorities, living on or near what they view as their national homeland." See* W. Kymlicka, *Minority Rights and the New International Politics of Diversity*, a paper presented at the Colloquium in Legal & Social Philosophy, The Global Diffusion of Minority and Indigenous Rights, 28 Feb. 2007, University College London [hereinafter Kymlicka].

[3] J. Packer, 'On the Definition of Minorities' in J. Packer and K. Myntti (eds.), *The Protection of Ethnic and Linguistic minorities in Europe* (Ebo/Turku: Ebo Akademi University, 1993), 23–65, at 26–27 [hereinafter Packer].

[4] H. O'Nions, *Minority Rights Protection in International Law. The Roma of Europe* (United Kingdom: Ashgate, 2007), at 61 [hereinafter O'Nions].

[5] G. Alfredsson, "Minority Packer Rights and Democracy," discussion paper on Human Rights, fundamental freedoms and the Rights of Minorities, submitted to the Third Strasbourg Conference on Parliamentary Democracy, Strasbourg, 1991 [SXB.CONF (III) 8], reproduced in Compendium of Documents from this Conference, Parliamentary Assembly of the Council of Europe, Strasbourg, 1992, pp. 85–101, at 93.

[6] F. Capotorti, *Study on the Rights of Persons Belonging to Ethnic, Religious or Linguistic Minorities*, UN doc. E/CN.4/Sub.2/384/Rev.1, 1979, para. 570 [hereinafter Capotorti].

[7] O'Nions, *supra* note 4, at 61.

[8] The case of the Roma of Italy, as reviewed in chapter 5, is emblematic in this sense: they have not been recognised as a minority and as such are not the subject of special

In this chapter, I will analyse the existing international law instruments that have an impact on the protection of minorities, review their working definition of minority and determine whether, according to these, they are of any use for the advancement of the status of the Roma and concomitantly protect their cultural identity.

2.2. Article 27 of the Covenant on Civil and Political Rights

Article 27 of the ICCPR calls for the protection of minorities by stating that:

> *In those states in which ethnic, religious or linguistic minorities exist, persons belonging to such minorities shall not be denied the right, in community or with the other members of their group, to enjoy their own culture, to profess and practice their religion, or to use their own language.*

Due to difficulties in the interpretation of Article 27, which does not contain a definition of minority, in 1979 the Sub-commission on the Prevention of Discrimination and Protection of Minorities (later renamed Sub-Commission on the Promotion and Protection of Human Rights) appointed a Special Rapporteur, Professor Capotorti, to undertake a special study on its application and to define the term "minorities" in relation to Article 27. Capotorti first noted that:

> *although the expression "rights of minorities" is used in common parlance, it is persons belonging to minorities, in community with the other members of their group, who are regarded in Article 27 as having the right to enjoy their own culture, to practice their own religion and to use their own language.*[9]

Although never adopted, Capotorti's definition is generally considered the most widely accepted. He defined a minority as:

> *A group numerically inferior to the rest of the population of a state, in a non-dominant position, whose members – being national of the state – possess ethnic, religious or linguistic characteristics differing from those of the rest of the population and show, if only implicitly, a sense of solidarity, directed towards preserving their culture, traditions, religion or language.*[10]

protection, which makes the consequences of the lack of a definition of minority even more serious.

[9] Capotorti, *supra* note 6, at 35.

[10] Id., para. 568.

In this definition Capotorti makes a distinction between the "objective" and the "subjective" elements.[11] The objective elements are: numerically smaller in size;[12] non-dominance (strictly linked to the size); nationality (intended as citizenship); possession of ethnic, religious or linguistic characteristics. The subjective element is the sense of solidarity to preserve traits. Capotorti emphasises its importance and asserts that it should be up to the group concerned to assess if it wants to be preserved as such or not.[13] Indeed, *"a group cannot have an identity throughout history if its members have no wish to help preserving it."*[14]

The subjective element of Capotorti's definition is rather dangerous.[15] Indeed, it must be underlined that although some groups might have the chance to voice their needs and their concerns, others might be silent; however, this silence should not necessarily be interpreted as willingness

---

[11] Capotorti, *supra* note 6, paras. 565–567.

[12] *"In principle, even quite a small group has the right to claim the protection provided for in Article 27, to the extent to which it seems reasonable to expect the state to introduce special measures of protection." See* Capotorti, *supra* note 6, at 12. It is very difficult to give an absolute number or percentage that can be used as a numerical threshold and thus not advisable to include such a threshold in a definition. *See* M. Nowak, *UN Convention on Civil and Political Rights: CCPR Commentary* (Strasbourg: N. P. Engel, Kehl, 1993), at 488. [hereinafter Nowak] Conversely, the size of the group concerned has a legitimate role to play in the determination of the demands that can be made. *See* J. Deschênes, 'Qu'est-ce qu'un minorité? Conclusion générale sur les droits des minorités' Les Cahiers de Droit, Vol. 27, No. 1 (1986), pp. 255–291, at 269. "[...] *while a minority must be numerically smaller than the majority population, it must also constitute a sufficient number for the state to recognise it as a distinct part of the society and to justify the State making effort to protect and promote it. There must be a group, not simply a few individuals." See* G. Gilbert, G. 'The Legal Protection Accorded to Minority Groups in Europe' Netherlands Yearbook of International Law Vol. 23 (1992) 67, at 72–73. [hereinafter Gilbert (1992)] Several authors conclude that the proportionality principle should be used to determine the scope of positive State obligations by taking into account the scale of the respective minority group. *See*, for example, Packer (1993), *supra* note 3, at 48–49. Packer however points out that the practice of States demonstrates that a great deal can be done even for tiny groups (in real and relative numbers). *See* J. Packer, 'Problems in Defining Minorities' in D. Fottrell and B. Bowring (eds.), *Minority and Groups Rights in the New Millennium* (Netherlands: Kluwer Law International, 1999), pp. 223–274, at 262.

[13] Capotorti, *supra* note 6, paras. 565–567.

[14] Id., at 12. This distinction applied by Capotorti's definition is particularly restrictive because it refers to "minorities by will" (voluntary minorities) and not to "minorities by force" (involuntary minorities). The first wish to maintain their distinctive cultures, languages or religion; the latter only require a guarantee of non-discrimination so that their integration into the wider society can move forward. *See* P. Thornberry, *International Law and the Rights of Minorities* (Oxford: Oxford University Press, 1991), at 9–10 [hereinafter Thornberry].

[15] M.N. Shaw, 'The Definition of Minority in International Law' *Israel Yearbook on Human Rights* Vol. 20 (1990), pp. 13–43, at 27–28.

to maintain the status quo.[16] In some cases, social and political factors such as oppressive conditions or policies of assimilation applied by the authorities might result in the lack of expression of dissident voices by minority groups. Even Capotorti admits that *"it would be too easy for a state to so pressure a minority that its members felt unable to make a positive declaration regarding the collective will to survive as a group."*[17] He thus explains that the will to preserve a distinctive identity *"generally emerges from the fact that a given group has kept its distinctive characteristics over a period of time"*[18] and indeed, in the wording of his definition, the sense of solidarity can also be expressed implicitly.

The objective and subjective elements in Capotorti's definition are interlinked:

> *when the members of a group strive in their everyday life to preserve their identity, their language, their culture, displaying a sense of unity within the collectivity, then the subjective criterion is fulfilled. There is no need for statements by a group representative, even though the fact that the group is organised and has developed a structure might be used as proof for assessing the unity and the collective will of the group.*[19]

Keeping this in mind, along with Capotorti's explanation that the sense of solidarity of a minority can also be expressed implicitly, it appears that the Roma satisfy the criteria for the subjective element of the definition. Indeed, it should be underlined that the Roma have recently started raising their voices and expressing their views and needs.[20] Furthermore, they have kept their distinctive characteristics and culture over the centuries, despite being subjected to persecution and discrimination.

Through its jurisprudence and general comments, the Human Rights Committee (HRC or Committee) helped to identify the sphere of action of Article 27 and noted that this "*confers rights on persons belonging to minorities which 'exist' in a state party;"*[21] thus, making it clear that the Article is

---

16 P.V. Ramaga, 'Relativity of the Minority Concept,' (1992) *Human Rights Quarterly* 104, at 115.

17 Capotorti, *supra* note 6, at 96.

18 Id.

19 A. Spiliopoulou Åkermark, *Justification of Minority Protection in International Law* (The Hague: Kluwer Law International, 1997), at 90 [hereinafter Spiliopoulou Åkermark]

20 *See*, for example, the creation of the "Federazione Roma e Sinti Insieme," joining together Roma and Sinti organisations in Italy to express Roma views. *See* http://comitatoromsinti.blogspot.com/, last visited Mar. 20, 2012. This aspect will be further explored in chapter 5.

21 U.N. Human Rights Committee, 'General Comment 23(50), Article 27,' UN Doc. CCPR/C/21/Rev.1/Add.5, 1994, para. 5.2 [hereinafter General Comment 23(50)].

designed to protect individuals who belong to minority groups rather than groups themselves. These individuals should share a common culture,[22] a religion and/or a language.[23] The Committee further added that the existence of a minority within a state does not depend on a decision by that state, but must be established by objective criteria (although these have not been identified by the Committee).[24]

Capotorti's definition of a minority, having among its criteria that of nationality, excludes foreigners residing in a country (such as migrant workers, refugees and stateless persons) whose case he found different from that of persons who possessed the nationality of the country in which they lived. Indeed, Capotorti observes that aliens traditionally enjoy special protection under international law which is not available to citizens of the state and thus have a different status.[25] Following Capotorti's definition, only minorities whose members are nationals of a state may qualify as such.[26] This automatically excludes the Roma, who would have to be nationals of a state to fulfil the requirements of belonging to a minority but who are often stateless or simply move from one country to another.

However, the HRC has expressed the view that the concept of "minority" is not limited to persons having the nationality of the state concerned and that the length of residence in that state is irrelevant; thus, immigrants and even visitors could qualify as minorities for the purpose of

---

[22] One of the many manifestations of culture is the way of life. *See* General Comment 23(50), *supra* note 21, para. 7. The HRC has been keen in recognising the right of individuals who are members of minorities to enjoy their culture. *See*, for example, the cases of *Lovelace v. Canada,* Communication No. 24/1977 (31 July 1980), CCPR/C/OP/1 at 37 (1984) [hereinafter *Lovelace v. Canada*], *Kitok v. Sweden,* Communication No. 197/1985 (10 August 1988): CCPR/C/33/D/197/185 [hereinafter *Kitok v. Sweden*], and *Ominayak, Chief of the Lubicon Lake Band v. Canada,* Communication No. 167/1984 (10 May 1990): CCPR/C/38/D/167/1984 [hereinafter *Lubicon Lake Band*].

[23] General Comment 23(50), *supra* note 21, para. 5.1.

[24] Id., para. 5.2. In doing so, the Committee followed the argument held by the Permanent Court of International Justice (PCIJ) in the case *Rights of minorities in Upper Silesia (Minority Schools)* in which the question was whether it should be up to the individual to declare whether he or she belonged to a minority (as recognized by the German party to the case after the authorities of the Polish Upper Silesia had annulled the enrolment of many children in the German minority school because they did not speak the language of the minority) or whether this decision should be based on objective criteria (as the Polish segment stated, arguing that minority status was a question of fact and not intention). The Court supported the Polish argument and indeed pointed out that the test of minority status had to be an objective one. *See Rights of Minorities in Upper Silesia (Minority Schools)* (PCIJ, Series A/12, 1928).

[25] Capotorti, *supra* note 6, at 12.

[26] On this aspect, *see* G. Gilbert, 'The Council of Europe and minority rights' 18 (1996) *Human Rights Quarterly* 160, at 166 [hereinafter Gilbert (1996)].

Article 27.[27] This implies that even the Roma who are not nationals of the state in which they reside (even just temporarily) would qualify as a "minority" under Article 27.

Another problem with the Roma is also that they are generally geographically dispersed and not a well-defined group living in a specific territory. Capotorti has found that Roma are rarely recognised by states as being a legal minority targeted with special measures:

> *It is important to remember that in most cases the groups recognised as "minorities" or as communities which are to benefit from special treatment are well-defined groups. Certain groups, including those which are scattered throughout the territory of a country, seldom appear among those forming the subject of recognition by the state with legal effect. Such is the situation, for instance, of the groups described as "Gypsies" in a large number of European countries.*[28]

The HRC, specifically referring to the Roma in its Concluding Observations on Italy, pointed out that *"the absence of connection with a specific territory does not bar a community for qualifying as a minority under Article 27 of the Covenant."*[29] It would thus follow that the Roma are to be fully protected under Article 27, despite that they might not be a well-defined group and that they would have to be recognised as a minority even by those states (such as Italy) which have so far refused to grant them official minority status under national law due to the fact that they are spread throughout the territory of the country.[30]

---

[27] General Comment 23(50), *supra* note 21, para 5.2. Tomuschat and Nowak, slightly detaching themselves from the Committee's views in terms of duration of presence of a group on the territory of a state, observed that the concept of minority presupposes an element of stability and thus long-established immigrant groups may fulfil the criteria of "minority." *See* Nowak, *supra* note 12, at 490. Nowak also argued that, at least in contemporary Europe, the reality of migration goes against any distinction of minority groups based on time. Indeed, *"any type of a more unified Europe will necessarily lead to more mobility and a higher degree of inter-ethnic mixture among Europeans. In such multi-ethnic and multicultural society with high immigration rates it will be difficult to justify why only long-established "old minorities" should enjoy special protection. Members of "new minorities" also rightly claim their right not to be assimilated into a melting pot type of newly created "European citizens" but to enjoy their traditional culture, practice their own religion and speak their mother tongue irrespective of where they actually live* [*or for how long there*]*." See* M. Nowak, 'The Evolution of Minority Rights in International Law, Comments' in C. Brölmann, R. Lefeber and M. Zieck (eds), *Peoples and Minorities in International Law* (Dordrecht: Nijhoff, 1993), pp. 104–117, at 118.

[28] Capotorti, *supra* note 6, para. 77.

[29] U.N. Human Rights Committee, *Concluding Observations of the Human Rights Committee: Italy,* CCPR/C/ITA/CO/5, 24 April 2006, para. 22.

[30] On the Italian exclusion of the Roma and Sinti amongst the recognised minorities, *see* chapter 5.

2.3. International Labour Organisation Convention 169 on Indigenous and Tribal Peoples

Rights normally afforded to indigenous peoples are generally more specific and far reaching than rights granted to minorities, to the point that various groups are now debating whether to adopt the label of indigenous peoples, including the Roma. Whether this is a real possibility, however, depends on the definition of what constitutes "indigenous peoples."

The 1989 C 169 Indigenous and Tribal Peoples Convention[31] (hereinafter International Labour Organisation ILO Convention 169) contains several provisions on the protection of cultural identity that are relevant for the protection of the Roma. Indeed, Article 2(b) states that actions to protect the rights of indigenous peoples and guarantee respect for their integrity shall include measures for:

> *promoting the full realisation of the social, economic and cultural rights of these peoples with respect for their social and cultural identity, their customs and traditions and their institutions.*

Article 5(a) goes on to state that in applying the provisions of Convention 169 *"the social, cultural, religious and spiritual values and practices of these peoples shall be recognised and protected* [..]." However, Convention 169 is only applicable to "indigenous peoples."

Although no generally accepted definition of "indigenous peoples" exists, the one specified in Convention 169 is the one commonly used. Article 1(b) states that Convention 169 applies to:

> *Peoples in independent countries who are regarded as indigenous on account of their descent from the populations which inhabited the country, or a geographical region to which the country belongs, at the time of conquest or colonisation or the establishment of present state boundaries and who, irrespective of their legal status, retain some or all of their own social, economic, cultural and political institutions.*

Self-identification is also endorsed as a fundamental criterion for determining the communities to which Convention 169 applies.

It is questionable that ILO Convention 169 is applicable to the Roma. Few indigenous people have been recognised in Europe (amongst which, the Sami in Northern Europe) and so far only four countries have ratified

[31] For the full text *see* http://www.ilo.org/ilolex/cgi-lex/convde.pl?C169, last visited Mar. 20, 2012.

Convention 169.[32] Furthermore, the Roma would have difficulty claiming their indigenous status because they arrived in Europe before the majority population.[33] However, it should be pointed out that the Inter-American Court has also recognised as "indigenous" groups which did not arrive first.[34] That ILO Convention 169 would be relevant for the Roma is proven, *a contrario*, by the refusal of countries such as Switzerland to ratify it, as stated in the Swiss report to the ACFC under the FCNM, because it would prove a useful instrument for furthering Roma claims.[35]

2.4. The United Nations Declaration on The Rights of Indigenous Peoples

The United Nations Declaration on the Rights of Indigenous Peoples[36] contains a wide range of cultural rights and a strong collective focus. In Article 8(1), it states that *"indigenous peoples and individuals have the right not to be subjected to forced assimilation or destruction of their culture."* States should thus refrain from applying assimilationist policies and take effective measures to protect indigenous cultures, including language, religion and education. The Declaration does not contain a right to cultural identity as such, although Article 8(2) forbids threats to the integrity and cultural values of indigenous peoples (thus making it relevant to the protection of cultural identity). Several provisions on cultural heritage also exist, the protection of which is essential to the economic and cultural survival of indigenous peoples.

---

[32] Only Denmark, Spain, the Netherlands and Norway have ratified ILO Convention 169. As of 2 March 2010, Italy has not yet ratified it.

[33] C. Cahn, 'Lawmaking in Traditional Romani Communities and International Human Rights Law and Norms: Case Study of the Real and Potential Role of the Romani Kris,' forthcoming in the *European Yearbook of Minority Issues*, 2010, at 19.

[34] *See*, for example, the *Case of Moiwana Village v. Suriname*, in which the Court relied on testimonies to prove the existence of communal institutions and demonstrated community autonomy and cohesion of the N'djuka People, rather than seeking evidence of their occupation of land previous to European arrival. *Case of Moiwana Village v. Suriname*, Inter-American Court of Human Rights, Judgment of June 15, 2005, para. 86.

[35] Council of Europe, Advisory Committee on the Framework Convention for the Protection of National Minorities, *Second Report Submitted by Switzerland Pursuant to Article 25, Paragraph 1 of the Framework Convention for the Protection of "National Minorities*, 31 January 2007, ACFC/SR/II(2007)002, para. 35.

[36] U.N. Declaration on the Rights of Indigenous Peoples, adopted by the General Assembly with Resolution A/RES/61/295, 13 September 2007. For the full text *see* http://www.un.org/esa/socdev/unpfii/documents/DRIPS_en.pdf, last visited Mar. 20, 2012.

Several aspects of the Declaration remained unclear, in particular who constitutes indigenous peoples: a definition is not provided. This implies, therefore, that it is not completely clear to whom the Declaration applies. Several reasons for which the Declaration does not contain a definition of indigenous peoples exist. Not only were states hesitant to include a definition, but indigenous peoples also opposed the inclusion for fear that any definition might exclude certain groups wrongly and thus deny them the rights of the Declaration.[37] Furthermore, some indigenous peoples thought that a definition would violate the right to self-determination and self-identification, according to which indigenous peoples are entitled to define themselves.[38] It could thus be said that because the Declaration does not contain a definition of indigenous peoples and it is therefore not clear to whom it should be applied (purposely done so that its scope can be as wide as possible), it might also be applicable to the Roma.

2.5. The Organisation for Security and Cooperation in Europe

The importance of the protection of minorities is underlined by OSCE in its Helsinki Final Act 1975,[39] in which it makes several references to the protection and rights of "national" minorities by stating that they are fundamental for the political stability of Europe. However, even the OSCE never defined the term "minority" because of the strong opposition posed by its members. The expression "national minorities" is used to refer to minorities, although in 1991 the Experts on National Minorities of the CSCE concluded that *"not all ethnic, cultural, linguistic or religious differences necessarily lead to the creation of "national minorities."*[40] The OSCE High Commissioner for National Minorities (HCNM), appointed for the first time in 1992, has observed that a minority is a group with linguistic, ethnic or cultural characteristics which usually seeks not only to maintain, but also to give "stronger expression" to its identity.[41] Max van der Stoel, former HCNM, believes that *"the existence of a minority is a question of fact*

---

[37] Y.M. Donders, *Towards a Right to Cultural Identity?* (Antwerp: Intersentia, 2002), at 217 [hereinafter Donders].

[38] Id.

[39] Conference on Security and Co-Operation in Europe Final Act, Helsinki, 1975, at 6 and 51.

[40] Report of the CSCE Meeting of Experts on National Minorities, 30 ILM 1692 (1991).

[41] R. Zaagman, *The Role of the High Commissioner on National Minorities in OSCE Conflict Prevention*, A report prepared by the Office of the HCNM, the Hague, 1995, at 22. As reported in Spiliopoulou Åkermark, *supra* note 19, at 93.

and not of definition." He also stated: *"Even though I may not have a definition of what constitutes a minority, I would dare to say that I know a minority when I see one."*[42]

The 1990 Copenhagen Document (adopted during the Copenhagen Conference on Human Dimension and establishing a set of commitments for OSCE members) links the right of persons belonging to national minorities to fully exercise their human rights without discrimination to the obligation of states to adopt, when necessary, special measures for the purpose of ensuring members of national minorities full equality with other citizens in the enjoyment and exercise of human rights and fundamental freedom (paragraph 31). In other words, states have the possibility of adopting special, positive measures to restore effective equality without these measures being considered discriminatory against the majority.[43] The Copenhagen Document states that persons belonging to national minorities have the right to freely express, preserve and develop their *"ethnic, cultural, linguistic or religious identity"* and to develop their culture in all its aspects.[44] Other rights that can be exercised either individually or in community with other members of the group are granted (paragraph 32). Paragraph 35 can be seen as a step toward the recognition of collective rights and toward forms of self-determination for minorities.[45] With the intention of undermining any attempt by a State to include or exclude a person from membership to a national minority based on governmental criteria, paragraph 32 of the Copenhagen Document stipulates that *"to belong to a national minority is a matter of a person's individual choice and no disadvantage may arise from the exercise of such choice."* Paragraph 40 deals with issues such as intolerance, xenophobia, discrimination, racial and ethnic hatred and contains a special mention of the Roma.

It is interesting to notice that the Copenhagen Document has sets of commitments in relation to various groups. Commitments on national

---

[42] OSCE Office for Democratic Institutions and Human Rights, *Human Dimension Seminar, Case Studies on National Minorities Issues: Positive Results,* Warsaw 24–28 May 1993, Key-Note Address of Mr. M. van der Stoel, CSCE High Commissioner on National Minorities, at 5.

[43] F. Benoit-Rohmer, *The Minority Question in Europe: Towards a Coherent System of Protection for National Minorities* (Strasbourg: Council of Europe, 1996), at 25 [hereinafter Benoit-Rohmer].

[44] Conference for Security and Co-operation in Europe, *second Conference on the Human Dimension of the CSCE, Copenhagen 5 June – 29 July 1990, Document of the Copenhagen meeting of the Conference on the Human Dimension of the CSCE.*

[45] *"The provision adopts the view that individual rights can only be properly protected where the groups have political control over their own affairs." See* Gilbert (1992), *supra* note 12, at 95.

minorities and on Roma and Sinti are separate, possibly intending that, in addition to the rights to be granted to national minorities, due to their peculiar situation and needs, Roma and Sinti would also be the subject of special rights providing them additional support. In this sense, it can be seen that in 1992, the HCNM already dealt with issues pertaining to the Roma and Sinti as minority issues. In 1994, the OSCE established, within the Office for Democratic Institutions and Human Rights (ODIHR), a Contact Point for Roma and Sinti Issues (CPRSI), whose aim is to promote *"full integration of Roma and Sinti Communities into the societies they live in, while preserving their identity."*[46] That the Roma fall under the remit of the HCNM is also confirmed by the many reports dedicated to the Roma and Sinti in the OSCE Area. In addition, the OSCE has been reviewing the proposal for a "Charter of Romani Rights," which would be based on the idea that the Roma are a "transnational minority" rather than a "national minority."[47]

2.6. The Council of Europe and the Framework Convention for the Protection of National Minorities

The Council of Europe has adopted the expression "national minority" to refer to a minority. In 1973, a Committee of Experts of the Council of Europe was asked to draft an additional protocol to the European Convention for Human Rights and Fundamental Freedoms (ECHR). The Committee pointed out that:

> [...] *In most cases a "national minority" would also constitute an ethnic, linguistic or religious minority. On the other hand, there are clearly certain ethnic, linguistic or religious minorities which do not constitute "national minorities."* [...] *These different factors illustrate further the difficulty of finding any generally accepted definition of the term "national minority." For this reason, the experts found it difficult to provide any satisfactory definition of "national minorities."*[48]

[46] OSCE 1998 Oslo Ministerial Decision, 'Decision on the enhancement of the OSCE's operational capabilities regarding Roma and Sinti Issues': MC(7).DEC/5.

[47] W. Kymlicka, *Minority Rights and the New International Politics of Diversity*, a paper presented at the Colloquium in Legal & Social Philosophy, The Global Diffusion of Minority and Indigenous Rights, 28 Feb. 2007, University College London, at 16. *See also* the text of the European Roma And Travellers Forum (ERTF) Statement on Roma and Sinti at the Working Sessions 6 and 7 of the Annual Human Dimension Implementation Meeting of the OSCE - ODIHR, Warshaw, September 2007, HDIM.IO/205/07, Sept. 27, 2007.

[48] Report of the Committee of Experts on Human Rights to the Committee of Ministers, Council of Europe, DH/EXO (73), 47, 9 Nov. 1973.

It thus concluded that it was not legally necessary for the protection of minorities to be the subject of a special provision laid down in an additional protocol.[49]

The Parliamentary Assembly of the Council of Europe gave a first indication of its understanding of the meaning of "national minority" in 1990, with Recommendation 1134. According to this, national minorities are:

> *separate or distinct groups, well defined and established on the territory of a State, the members of which are nationals of the state and have a certain religious, linguistic or other characteristics which distinguish them from the majority of the population.*[50]

In 1991, the European Commission for Democracy through Law (the Venice Commission) proposed the creation of a European Convention for the Protection of Minorities which should include an Article (draft Article 2) defining the concept of minority. This stated that:

> *for the purposes of this text, "minority" shall mean a group which is smaller in number than the rest of the population of a state, whose members, although nationals of that State have ethnical, religious or linguistic features different from those of the rest of the population, and are guided by the will to safeguard their culture, traditions, religion or language.*[51]

In the same draft article, the Venice Commission proposed that any group coming within the terms of the proposed definition should be treated as an "ethnic," "religious" or "linguistic" minority and that to belong to a "national" minority should be a matter of individual choice.[52]

In recommendation 1201 (1993), the Parliamentary Assembly asked the Committee of Ministers to adopt an additional protocol to the ECHR. The draft Protocol[53] gave a further explanation of the expression "national minority" in Article 1, by stating that this refers to a group of persons in a state who:

---

[49] Benoit-Rohmer, *supra* note 43, at 36.

[50] Parliamentary Assembly, Council of Europe, Recommendation 1134 (1990) *On the Rights of Minorities.*

[51] European Commission for Democracy through Law, *Proposal for a European Convention for the Protection of Minorities*, Council of Europe, CDL(91)7, 1991.

[52] As already seen, even the OSCE in its Copenhagen Document affirms that to belong to a minority is a question of individual choice. No comment on the difference of the terms used is made in the Explanatory Report, CDL(91)8, 1991.

[53] The draft protocol was rejected by the Council of Ministers on 26 January 1999 because it contained certain elements which did not find the support of all member States [Document 8306 (Communication) 'Recommendations of the Assembly – Replies by the Committee of Ministers']. Conversely, Recommendation 1201 displays a certain force through its incorporations in bilateral agreements.

> *a. reside on the territory of that state and are citizens thereof; b. maintain long standing, firm and lasting ties with that state; c. display distinctive ethnic, cultural, religious or linguistic characteristics; d. are sufficiently representative, although smaller in number than the rest of the population of that state or region of that state; e. are motivated by a concern to preserve together that which constitutes their common identity, including their culture, their traditions, their religion and their language.*

This definition requires not only firm ties to a state, but also citizenship, and it defines the subjective element as the concern to preserve the minority identity. It should also be noticed that although no requirement of non-dominance exists, clear conditions are necessary, such as a certain degree of permanence and a numerical threshold. Furthermore, this definition acknowledges the fact that a minority can also be determined at a regional level and not necessarily at the state level (something that is not reiterated, however, by any international or European documents).[54]

The Roma hardly fit the criteria of this definition because it should, in theory, exclude foreigners, immigrants and refugees from protection and include nomadic populations and Roma, based on the assumption that they must be citizens of the country in which they reside. In practice, however, most Roma are stateless, refugees or claiming refugee status, and thus would not receive the protection of the proposed additional Protocol, which, contrary to its intentions, is not applicable to groups of Roma still practising nomadism, who, although they are not citizens, may still have a strong tie with a State simply because they have lived in it for a long time.

The 1994 Framework Convention for the Protection of National Minorities (FCNM) is a fundamental addition to the system for the protection of minorities. It follows the traditional terminology of the CoE in speaking of "national" minorities and was inspired in its content by the OSCE Copenhagen Document. Although the protection of minorities is its main aim, the FCNM does not in itself contain a definition of national minority, for fear that, to avoid too many reservations, a definition reflecting the lowest common denominator would be adopted. Drafters of the

---

[54] Henrard, *supra* note 1, at 26. The idea that minorities can also be determined at the regional level was considered by the HRC in the case of *Ballantyne, Davidson, McIntyre v. Canada*, for which the Committee adopted a restrictive stance and argued that the English-speaking persons in the French-speaking province of Quebec could not be considered a minority because they constitute the majority nationwide. Accordingly, Article 27 of the ICCPR only applies to minorities at the national level. *See Ballantyne, Davidson, McIntyre v. Canada*, Communication nos. 359/1989 and 385/1989, UN Doc. CCPR/C/47/D/359/1989 and 385/1989/Rev.1 (1993).

FCNM explained that it would be impossible to arrive at a definition capable of meeting general support of all the members of the Council of Europe. They considered that the circumstances of groups considered minorities differ greatly from one state to another and it would thus be impossible to create a definition encompassing all categories of minorities. They eventually called for a pragmatic approach in its application.[55]

The explanatory report comment on Article 5 of the FCNM, which obliges members to promote the conditions necessary for national minorities to maintain and develop their culture and to preserve the essential elements of their identity, clarifies that the provision *"does not imply that all ethnic, cultural, linguistic differences necessarily lead to the creation of national minorities."*[56] Indeed, it cannot be contended that the term national minority as used in the FCNM refers only to those with state citizenship. Furthermore, it cannot be argued that the FCNM applies only to minorities with a kin state because no scope for such a limitation in its text exists.[57] In fact, the preamble of the FCNM makes reference to all the minority rights commitments of its parties, including Article 27 of the ICCPR, which, as assessed by the HRC, does not include citizenship of the State in question among the criteria for its application.

The omission of the criterion of citizenship among those necessary for the recognition of minority status implies the protection of all persons living on the territory of a state party, whether or not they are nationals or immigrants.[58] If the criterion of citizenship was adopted in this case, this would be particularly problematic for the Roma, who are generally regarded as a minority but may be excluded from nationality legislation. Whether the Roma constitute a "national minority" in this sense could

---

[55] Council of Europe, 'Framework Convention for the Protection of National Minorities and Explanatory Report:' H(1995)010, para. 12 [hereinafter FCNM and Explanatory Report].

[56] Id., para. 43.

[57] P. Thornberry and M.A. Martín Estébanez, *Minority Rights in Europe*, (Germany: Council of Europe Publishing, 2004), at 94.

[58] France, consistent with the 1997 European Convention on Nationality (which, in its Article 1 defines "nationality" as *"the legal bond between a person and a State and does not indicate the person's ethnic origin"*) associates the concept of nationality to that of citizenship, in which all citizens belong to the French nation. Conversely, Germany thinks of national minorities as linguistic and cultural communities and does not necessarily associate the idea of nationality to that of citizenship; therefore, a national minority must be connected to a larger nation already represented by a State, forming a so-called kin State. *See* Heintze, *supra* note 1, at 82–84. France and Turkey, in the name of national unity, have denied the existence of minorities. Both countries have ratified the FCNM and made reservations to Article 27 of the ICCPR to the point that this article is not applicable.

prove to be debatable.[59] It should be observed, however, that various States have made declarations which recognise the application of the FCNM to the Roma.[60] Macedonia and Slovenia accept that the FCNM applies to members of the Roma community living in their territory. Conversely, Germany has declared that the FCNM applies to Roma and Sinti who are of German citizenship. Similar declarations have been made by Switzerland and Estonia.[61] Italy has declared that the FCNM applies to the Roma, although they are not a recognised minority[62] and no specification exists regarding whether this applies only to Italian Roma.[63] In any case, the Advisory Committee for the Framework Convention (ACFC) tends to ignore the difference between citizens and non-citizens, following the principle that minorities are a matter of fact, not of law, to the point that exclusionary moves by members are normally ignored.[64]

---

[59] G. Gilbert (1996), *supra* note 26, at 176–177. Similarly, it has been argued that if a restrictive definition of national minority was applied, many of the groups excluded would be those desperately in need of international protection and with no other means of legal protection than the FCNM, such as the Roma. *See* Kymlicka, *supra* note 2.

[60] Thirty-nine State parties to the FCNM exist and of these, most include the Roma as a group to be covered by the FCNM, including Italy. Countries recognising Romani as a minority language do not necessarily include the Roma in the protection afforded by the FCNM – one example of this is the Netherlands. The only countries that recognise Roma as a national minority (either explicitly or implicitly) in their national legislation are Croatia, Norway, Poland, Ukraine, Hungary (July 7, 1993), Romania (Article 6 of the 1991 Constitution), Slovenia (Article 65 of the 1992 Constitution), Slovak Republic (Articles 33 and 34 of the 1992 Constitution), the Czech Republic, Sweden, Macedonia, Serbia and Montenegro. In 1993, Austria recognised the rights of Roma and Sinti to create their own "Councils of Ethnic Groups." Finland modified its Constitution in 1995 to include the Roma among the protected minorities. *See also* I. Castangia, *L'Europa delle persone e le minoranze zingare*, year XLVI, *Jus, Rivista di Scienze Giuridiche* 191(January–April 1999), at 206 [hereinafter Castangia].

[61] *See* Committee of experts on issues relating to the protection of national minorities (DH-MIN), *Results of the exchange of information on the question to which groups the Framework Convention will be applied*, Strasbourg, 15 January 1999, DH-MIN (98) 4, Addendum I.

[62] *See* Law 482/1999 of December 15, 1999, *Norms concerning the protection of linguistic and historical minorities*, Gazzetta Ufficiale n. 297 of December 20, 1999.

[63] Council of Europe, Advisory Committee on the Framework Convention for the Protection of National Minorities, *Second Opinion on Italy*, 24 February 2005, ACFC/INF/OP/II(2005)003, para. 11.

[64] For example, the ACFC, in its first opinion on Germany, stressed that *"the implementation of the Framework Convention should not be a source of arbitrary or unjustified distinctions." See* Council of Europe, Advisory Committee on the Framework Convention for the Protection of National Minorities, *Opinion on Germany,* ACFC/INF/OP/I(2002)008, 1 Mar. 2002, para. 14. More generally, the ACFC has encouraged all countries to apply an "inclusive" understanding of national minorities, not requiring minorities to have a historic presence or traditional territory in the country, or even to be citizens of the country: the FCNM is to be applied also to persons belonging to "new" minorities. *See* R. Hoffman,

The application of the FCNM to the Roma is thus less problematic than that of other existing instruments. Conversely, the impact of the FCNM is partly limited by the fact that it only provides for a monitoring system through the submission of states parties' reports, while not allowing a more immediate justiciability through an individual complaint procedure. Therefore, the effectiveness of the FCNM depends on the real commitment of states toward the protection of Roma. Indeed, once more, the recognition of the peculiarity of the Roma minorities has not been translated into specific norms intended to protect their rights. However, the FCNM asks for the full respect of the cultural identity of the individuals who are part of national minorities, and this may prompt some states to apply measures of protection in favour of Roma minorities.

2.7. The European Charter for Regional or Minority Languages

Although the European Charter for Regional or Minority Languages (EChRML)[65] does not directly protect minorities as such, it is an important instrument for the protection of the Roma because their language is an expression of their identity. Excluding from its remit the languages and dialects of migrants, it defines as a regional or minority language one that is traditionally spoken in a given territory by citizens of the territory who are numerically inferior to the rest of the population and that is different from the official language of the state (Article 1(a)). Moreover, it specifies that a regional language is one spoken in a limited part of the territory and by the majority of the people residing in that same territory; whereas a minority language is one not necessarily limited to a specific territory but spoken by the minority of people living in that territory (Article 1 (b)).[66] Thus, the EChRML has identified certain elements of a minority group,

---

'The Framework Convention for the Protection of National Minorities: An Introduction,' in M. Weller (ed.), *The Rights of Minorities in Europe* (Oxford: Oxford University Press, 2005), pp. 1–24, at 16–17. *See also* Kymlicka, *supra* note 2.

[65] Entered into force on 1 March 1998 but only ratified by Italy in March 2012.

[66] The Explanatory Report of the European Charter contains a clarification of the term "regional." It denotes languages spoken in a limited part of the territory of the State (even if they are spoken by the majority of citizens of the State concerned). Conversely, "minority language" refers to languages spoken either by a scattered group or by a group which only lives in a specific area but which is smaller than the population of the region who speak the majority language of the State. *See* Council of Europe, 'European Charter for Regional or Minority Languages – Explanatory Report,' DELA(92)2, para. 18.

and endeavours to secure specific rights relating to a single issue (linguistic expression), but it is clear that these are not intended to be a comprehensive definition of a minority.

The connection between territory and language excludes minority languages such as Romanes from the actual protection provided by the EChRML, unless the state grants it the status of minority language without a territory, on the basis of Article 7(5) which says that states

> *Undertake to apply, [...], the principles listed in paragraphs 1 to 4 to non territorial languages [...]. However, as far as these languages are concerned, the nature and the scope of the measures to be taken to give effect to this Charter shall be determined in a flexible manner, having in mind the needs and wishes, and respecting the traditions and characteristics of the group which use the language concerned.*

The flexible character of the EChRML has to be underlined because it appears that, according to Article 3, member states can determine to which languages spoken on their territory the Charter will apply. Furthermore, not all provisions have to be implemented – albeit some minimum requirements are specified in Article 2.[67] To verify the impact of the EChRML on the rights of minorities it should be seen whether more states actually ratify it.[68] To date, only a few countries have recognised Romanes as a minority language in accordance with the Charter.[69]

2.8. Conclusions

As this chapter has shown, the Roma do not always match all the various criteria established to ascertain whether a group is a minority, as invoked by the working definitions of a number instruments. This frustrates efforts to improve their situation through the implementation of the rights of minorities and has brought a number of monitoring bodies, such as the

[67] Article 2 paragraph 2 states: *"In respect of each language specified at the time of ratification, acceptance or approval, in accordance with Article 3, each Party undertakes to apply a minimum of thirty-five paragraphs or sub-paragraphs chosen from among the provisions of Part III of the Charter, including at least three chosen from each of the Articles 8 and 12 and one from each of the Articles 9, 10, 11 and 13."*

[68] To date, 25 countries have ratified the EChRML. *See* http://conventions.coe.int/Treaty/Commun/ChercheSig.asp?NT=148&CM=8&DF=&CL=ENG, last visited Mar. 20, 2012.

[69] As of today, the countries which included the Romanes among their minority languages upon signing the EChRML are Austria, Germany, Hungary, the Netherlands, Slovakia and Sweden. *See* Castangia, *supra* note 60, at 206.

HRC and the ACFC, to explicitly state that the Roma are to be recognised as a minority by their member States. Better results would be achieved if instruments were adopted that specifically targeted the needs of the Roma, such as the proposed Charter of Romani Rights. However, in a Europe that is experiencing a populist backlash against immigrants and multiculturalism policies,[70] this is not foreseeable in the near future; Roma will have to make do with existing instruments. Therefore, the need for an internationally accepted definition of minority is even greater because in this way, states would be prevented from unilaterally deciding which groups living in their territory are minorities and discriminating between similar groups, thus frustrating their international obligations. This is currently done in States such as Italy (used as a case study), in which some groups have been officially recognised as minorities whereas others, such as the Roma, although considered minorities by a number of international bodies such as the HRC and the ACFC despite not straightforwardly fulfilling their working definitions of minority, have been excluded from the benefits that would derive from recognition. A clear definition of minority would remove the possibility of invoking an alleged lack of clarity on the subject from states to justify their discriminatory policies.

Because a definition of minority is still missing and because the status of the Roma in many European countries is still a matter of controversy (and they are often not officially recognised as a minority), it might be suggested that the best way to protect the Roma would be through a full application of the principle of non-discrimination. The right not to be discriminated against has the advantage that it is applicable to everybody, and its application – as opposed to the application of minority rights – does not raise controversial definitional issues. Conversely, although association with a national minority is recognised as grounds for discrimination by Article 14 of the ECHR, this right is normally meant to be applied to individuals or to members of groups, rather than groups themselves, and thus, according to Article 34 of the ECHR, only individuals or *groups of individuals* can claim their rights in front of an international tribunal.

In my opinion, anti-discrimination laws are not enough to advance the status of the Roma. The wide-spread stigmatisation and prejudice and the social and political exclusion of which they are victims cannot be targeted by only allowing claims against discrimination by individuals or groups of

[70] Kymlicka, *supra* note 2.

individuals. The individual right not to be discriminated against is not programmatic in nature, but, like other individual human rights, depends on assertion by individuals: if the members of a disadvantaged minority have no instruments to access justice, there is little way that they can assert their rights by petitioning international bodies. Provided that they manage to bring a claim to an international body and that the claim is successful, it is doubtful that the matter would be solved at the group level.[71] The right to non-discrimination as enshrined in the ECHR, although a good instrument to protect individuals who bring a complaint to the ECtHR, does not protect the culture of the minority group or its cultural identity. Indeed, when a complaint is brought to the ECtHR, the main purpose of the complaint is to remove the situation creating discrimination. However, the Court rarely looks at the general situation that causes suffering to the group and often seems to ignore that the problems referred to it through complaints by members of a minority are the expressions of larger issues involving the whole group and rarely expresses itself outside the strict boundaries of the case.[72]

I fear that the mere application of a non-discrimination principle to protect the rights of the Roma would result in favouring the abandonment of the traditional lifestyle, culture and language of those who did not want to be the target of discrimination. As will be seen in chapter 3, individual rights do not easily enable the creation of the conditions necessary to protect the identities of minorities. The best way to advance the rights of minorities is to ask states to act in positive ways to protect and promote their identities. Instruments dealing with minorities and their cultural identities, if applied to Roma communities across Europe, would ensure a much more extensive protection and promotion of their rights, especially if combined with affirmative action.

For this reason, I support the idea that only through a collective right to cultural identity will full protection and promotion of the rights of minorities such as the Roma be achieved.[73] In addition, a precise and legally accepted definition of minority is needed to render the identification of the Roma among the minority groups of the various European countries a

---

[71] The jurisprudence of the European Court of Human Rights (ECtHR or Court) shows that only recently the Court has been able to establish a link between issues involving the Roma and the protection of the cultural identity of the individual and the community. *See*, for example, the case of *Chapman v. the United Kingdom* (2001) 33 EHRR 18, decided on January 18, 2001.

[72] The jurisprudence of the ECtHR will be reviewed in chapter 3.

[73] This aspect will be further analysed in chapter 4.

more straight-forward task and not a decision to be made by the state unilaterally (as has been the case of Italy, which unilaterally decided to exclude the Roma from the number of minorities it recognised).

On a positive note, it should be pointed out that in 1993, the Parliamentary Assembly of the Council of Europe adopted recommendation 1203 'on Gypsies in Europe,' in which it was stated that *"one of the aims of the Council of Europe is to promote the emergence of a genuine European cultural identity"* and, more specifically, it argued that the Roma, because they are a minority without territory, *"are a true European minority"* and largely contribute to cultural diversity in several ways: with their language, music and traditional activities.[74] Despite not fitting neatly in the theoretical paradigma for minority recognition, the Roma are a European minority,[75] as was pointed out by Leuprecht, former Deputy Secretary General for the Council of Europe in his address to the Human Dimension Seminar on Roma in the CSCE Region, in which he stated:

> *Let us not hide behind legal hair-splitting as to whether this or that definition of minorities applies to the Roma. Let us be honest. We all know that the Roma are a minority and a particularly vulnerable one.* [76]

Furthermore, the situation is gradually improving thanks to the work of the ACFC, which has sought assurances from states that Roma are recognized as a minority;[77] in addition, even the European Union is focusing on the protection of the Roma as a specific non-territorial, European minority.[78]

---

[74] Council of Europe, Parliamentary Assembly, Recommendation 1203 (1993) 'on Gypsies in Europe', adopted on 2 February 1993, para. iii, paras. 1–2.

[75] O'Nions, *supra* note 4, at 62.

[76] Consolidated Summary of CSCE Human Dimension Seminar on Roma in the CSCE Region, Opening Speech by Mr. Peter Leuprecht, Deputy Secretary General of the Council of Europe, Warsaw, Sept. 20, 1994, at 9.

[77] O'Nions, *supra* note 4, at 62.

[78] E.U. Network of Experts on Fundamental Rights: the Situation of Roma in an Enlarged European Union 2004 European Commission. The European Parliament's intention is to apply all the definitions regarding non-territorial languages to Roma minorities. On May 22, 1989 the Council and the Ministers of Education of the European Community adopted Resolution 89/C 153/02, *on school provision for gypsy and traveller children* in which it recognised that Roma's *"culture and language have formed part of the Community's cultural and linguistic heritage for over 500 years."* This is an important recognition that could result in the formal admission of the Roma language among the minority languages of the European Union; it is also a step toward the recognition of the Roma as a European minority.

CHAPTER THREE

THE PROTECTION OF MINORITY RIGHTS THROUGH INDIVIDUAL HUMAN RIGHTS

3.1. Introduction

After WWII, the concept of a general, universal protection of human rights evolved. The U.N. General Assembly proclaimed the U.N. Charter as a common standard of achievement for all peoples and all nations, and it was generally believed that the interests of minority groups would be protected through the prohibition of discrimination,[1] to which all the main international human rights instruments refer. In universal human rights law, only one provision of the International Covenant on Civil and Political Rights (ICCPR) specifically addresses minorities. Regionally, only Europe has addressed the issues of minorities in a binding treaty – the Framework Convention for the Protection of National Minorities (FCNM) – but this treaty is cast in general terms and states have a wide margin of appreciation in its implementation.[2]

Human rights instruments have a clear focus on the rights of the individual, despite some recognition that the individual can only fully develop in the context of a community (for this reason, a variety of social relationships are protected, such as family and religious groups).[3] Article 27 of the ICCPR makes specific reference to minorities by stating:

> *In those States in which ethnic, religious or linguistic minorities exist, persons belonging to such minorities shall not be denied the right, in community with the other members of their group, to enjoy their own culture, to profess and practise their own religion, or to use their own language.*

Nevertheless, the right to petition the Human Rights Committee (HRC or Committee) is only available to the individual rights holder, who can act either in his own capacity as a victim or in that of representative of a

---

[1] H. O'Nions, *Minority Rights Protection in International Law. The Roma of Europe* (United Kingdom, Ashgate: 2007), at 67 [hereinafter O'Nions].

[2] Compliance with the FCNM is monitored by the ACFC through States parties' reports.

[3] O'Nions, *supra* note 1, at 67.

group of individuals and no concept of justiciable collective rights exists (Article 1, Optional Protocol 1).

The European Court of Human Rights (ECtHR or Court), conversely, accepts applications from groups of individuals claiming to be the victims of a violation of their rights (Article 34 of the European Convention for Human Rights and Fundamental Freedoms, ECHR, or Convention); petitions can also be filed by NGOs. Minority groups can thus qualify as victims and bring applications to the Court *qua* group.[4] However, the ECHR does not contain a specific provision on minority rights similar to that of Article 27 of the ICCPR. Article 14 is the only Article that makes reference to minorities by stating that "*the enjoyment of the rights and freedoms set forth in this Convention shall be secured without discrimination on any ground such as* [...] *association with a national minority* [...]."[5] Article 14 is to be read in conjunction with other Articles because it has an accessory character.[6] Thus, the protection afforded by Article 14 is rather limited and

---

[4] G. Gilbert, 'The Burgeoning minority rights jurisprudence of the European Court of Human Rights' 24 *Human Rights Quarterly* 736 (2002), at 739. [hereinafter Gilbert (2002)] In *Muonio Saami Village v. Sweden*, resolved by a friendly settlement, the village, not the villagers, was the applicant. *See Case of Muonio Saami Village v. Sweden,* application No. 28222/95, Eur. Ct. Hum. Rts. (First Section) 15 February 2000. In *Metropolitan Church of Bessarabia* the applicant was the Church. *See Case of Metropolitan Church of Bessarabia and Others v. Moldova,* application No. 45701/99, Eur. Ct. Hum. Rts. (former First Section), 13 December 2001. [hereafter *Metropolitan Church of Bessarabia*] In both cases, the group that brought the claim to the ECtHR was a victim in its own right. In complaints in which this was not the case, the Court found that the group had no standing to bring a complaint contesting a measure that would affect its members. For example, in *Noack and Others v. Germany*, with regard to the DOMOWINA (an organisation defending the interests of the applicants), the Court observed *"that an association does not have standing to lodge an application contesting a measure that affects its members, since it cannot claim to be a victim for the purposes of Article 34 of the Convention." See Noack and Others v. Germany*, Eur. Ct. Hum. Rts, Application number 46346/99, 25 May 2000, para. 1, at 9 [hereafter *Noack and Others v. Germany*].

[5] As seen in chapter 2, neither a definition of minority in international law exists, nor a definition of national minority under Article 14. However, having admitted in *Gorzelik and others v. Poland* that *"the formulation of* [...] *a definition* [*of national minority*] *would have presented a most difficult task, given that no international treaty* [...] *defines the notion of "national minority,""* the ECtHR was ready to review a legal process which was seen as arbitrary because it did not define the terms "ethnic" or "national" minority and *"did not provide for any procedure whereby minorities could seek legal recognition." See* the *Case of Gorzelik and others v. Poland,* (2004) 38 EHRR 4 paras. 45 and 62 [hereafter *Gorzelik and others v. Poland*]. *See also* Gilbert (2002), *supra* note 4, at 738.

[6] Article 1 of Protocol 12 of the ECHR (entered into force in 2005), conversely, provides a self-standing right to non-discrimination. Protocol 12 has not been adopted by the majority of the members of the CoE. As of 18 June 2009, 20 countries have signed it, but of these, only 17 have ratified it. Italy has signed the Protocol but has not ratified it. So far, only the *Case of Sejdić and Finci vs Bosnia and Hercegovina*, communicated in March 2008, has been presented for a violation of Article 1 Protocol 12.

if one complains of a violation, this has to be part of the field of application of one of the other Articles of the Convention. Therefore, members of minority groups have no direct way of claiming minority rights as such in front of the Court, to the point that some authors believe that Article 14 cannot be used by and for minorities and is not suitable for "modern minority protection" because its purpose is not to guarantee minority rights but to prohibit discrimination in the enjoyment of the rights protected by the Convention.[7] Conversely, the Court has held in *Denizci v. Cyprus* that states are under an obligation to uphold *"international standards in the field of protection of human rights and minority rights."*[8] Moreover, it is argued that without the rights included in the ECHR, the existence of special measures of minority protection would be meaningless and that it is important not to underestimate the value of the Convention with regard to minority protection.[9]

Prohibition of discrimination is important for members of minorities, especially because of its possible connection with the right to identity. However, it is only the first pillar and one dimension of the equality principle necessary for the protection of minorities, at the same time being the condition for the second pillar – the "special measures" for (members of) minorities.[10] Even the International Covenant for the Elimination of All Forms of Racial Discrimination (ICERD), designed to protect racial groups, is used for the protection of ethnic or linguistic groups.[11]

However, I believe that non-discrimination is not a sufficient method of support of minority cultures and that approaching minority issues merely through non-discrimination and individual human rights leads to inadequate results. It has been pointed out that *"existing human rights standards are simply unable to resolve some of the most important and controversial questions relating to cultural minorities."*[12] The prohibition of

---

[7] A. Baka, 'The Convention and the Protection of Minorities Under International Law,' in R. St. J. Macdonald et al. (eds), *The European System for the Protection of Human Rights* (Dordrecht : M. Nijhoff, 1993), pp. 875–888, at 883.

[8] *Case of Denizci v. Cyprus*, Eur. Ct. Hum. Rts., Application number 25316-25321/94 and 27207/95, 23 August 2001. *See also* Gilbert (2002), *supra* note 4, at 737.

[9] A. Spiliopoulou Åkermark, *Justification of Minority Protection in International Law* (The Hague: Kluwer Law International, 1997), at 215.

[10] K. Henrard, *Devising and Adequate System of Minority Protection* (The Netherlands: Kluwer Law International, 2000), at 56. [hereinafter Henrard] The notions of special measures and affirmative action will be discussed at the end of the chapter.

[11] But not religious groups. *See* P. Thornberry, *International Law and the Rights of Minorities* (Oxford: Oxford University Press, 1991), at 263–264 [hereinafter Thornberry].

[12] W. Kymlicka, 'Introduction,' in *The Rights of Minorities Cultures*, W. Kymlicka, (ed.) (Oxford: Oxford University Press, 1995), pp. 1–27, at 18 [hereafter Kymlicka (1995)].

discrimination does not guarantee the achievement of substantive equality, which is essential for members of minorities[13] who are generally treated as individuals and detached from their culture,[14] history and traditions. Nonetheless, identity is fundamental for individuals and communities.[15] Cultural identity gives groups their unity and specificity, it characterises their social relationships, ways of life and collective memories. Depriving individuals and groups of their cultural identity means depriving them of their history, which in turn, means depriving them of their right to existence: only through the protection of their identities are minorities allowed to exist.

For these reasons, it is contended that a proper system of minority protection requires at least the prohibition of discrimination and substantive equality,[16] as well as special measures aimed at the promotion and protection of the separate cultural identity of minorities[17] even from interference by the state, which can entail and justify differential treatment for minorities, at times in the form of positive intervention.[18]

The Permanent Court of International Justice (PCIJ), in its advisory opinion on *Minority Schools in Albania*,[19] underlined that the essence of the protection of minorities is the protection of their separate identity, basing its argument on the principles of equality and non-discrimination and on the need to actively support minority cultures. It thus emphasized that the aim of minority treaties is to allow minorities to live in peace with the rest of the population of a state and ensure preservation of their

---

[13] Henrard, *supra* note 10, at 142. Thus, the avenue of individual human rights and the prohibition of discrimination give little support to the minorities' crucial right to identity. *See* Gilbert, G. 'The Legal Protection Accorded to Minority Groups in Europe' *Netherlands Yearbook of International Law* Vol. 23 (1992) 67, at 90 [hereinafter Gilbert (1992)].

[14] The concepts of culture and cultural identity are analysed in chapter 1.

[15] Y. Donders, *Towards a Right to Cultural Identity?* (Antwerp: Intersentia, 2002), at 1 [hereinafter Donders].

[16] It is indeed contended that issues related to minorities are better dealt with through collective rights. The issue of collective rights will be reviewed in chapter 4. The issue of equality will be further analysed in the next section.

[17] Similarly, according to Thornberry *"the right to an identity must remain a key element in any overall system to protect minorities"* to the point that it is sometimes regarded as constituting the whole of minority rights. *See* Thornberry, *supra* note 11, at 141. *See also* Hannum, H., 'The Limits of Sovereignty and Majority Rule: Minorities, Indigenous Peoples and the Right to Autonomy,' in Lutz, E. et al (eds.), *New Directions in Human Rights*, (Philadelphia: University of Pennsylvania Press, 1989), pp. 3–24, at 20. [hereafter Hannum (1989)] The right to identity is explicitly mentioned in the UN Declaration on Minorities, in the FCNM and the Copenhagen Document of the OSCE.

[18] Henrard, *supra* note 10, at 142.

[19] *Advisory Opinion regarding Minority Schools in Albania*, 6 April 1935, 1935 PCIJ (ser. A/B) No. 64 [hereinafter *Minority Schools in Albania*].

characteristics and separate identity. The PCIJ concluded that to achieve both objectives, the best way was to ensure perfect equality between members of minorities and the other nationals of the state and to preserve the traditions, peculiarities and characteristics of protected groups.[20] In other words, it suggested the need to adopt special measures for the protection of the cultural identities of minorities.

A number of rights are important for the protection and promotion of the identity of minorities, whether they have an explicit collective dimension or not. The most important are the right to life, the prohibition of torture and inhuman or degrading treatment and the right to liberty and security of persons. Indeed, members of minorities tend to be the natural victims of violations of these rights[21] due to their vulnerable position in society, which can be related to the numerical and non-dominant position:[22]

> *recent world history provides plenty of evidence that minority peoples are indeed under constant pressure from the dominant society, so that not only their cultural survival but sometimes even their physical existence is endangered.*[23]

Freedom of expression, allowing the expression of ideas and convictions of minorities, and freedom of association, which is the legal foundation for the creation of a group and joint political action allowing the continuation of the distinctive character and way of life, are fundamental for the protection and promotion of the separate identity of minorities.[24] Although primarily individual prerogatives, they can be exercised in the name of or to favour a collective identity and they can enable the realization of collective aspirations.[25]

Cultural rights are essential to the needs of minorities because they aim at the protection and promotion of their separate identities. Freedom of thought, conscience and religion, generally considered an individual right,

---

20 Minority Schools in Albania, *supra* note 19, at 17.
21 Henrard, *supra* note 10, at 63.
22 Id.
23 R. Stavenhagen, 'Human Rights and Peoples' Rights: The Question of Minorities' *NJHR* 16 (1987), at 21.
24 Henrard, *supra* note 10, at 63.
25 S. Gutwirt, 'Het Harlekijnspak en het Vale Ezelsvel. Individuele Vrijheden in de Greep van het Recht op Zelfbeschikking van Volken, het Nationalisme en andere Aanspracken op een Collectieve Identiteit', in N. Sybesma and J. Vanbellingen (eds.), *Naar een Nieuwe Interpretatie van het Recht op Zelfbeschikking?* (Brussels: VUB, 1995), at 76, as cited in Henrard, *supra* note 10, at 63–64.

is crucial for the protection of religious minorities and also applies to ethnic minorities because of the broad sphere of application of the concepts of "thought" and "conscience." Similarly, language and education play a key role in the preservation of minorities' cultural identities[26] because they are the means through which culture is transmitted.[27] An essential right for minorities is therefore the right to establish and administer private education institutions in line with their specific minority identity.

Finally, the right to vote, and more generally the right to political participation, are of special relevance for members of minorities because they potentially enable minorities to have some influence on the elaboration of laws that might have an impact on their existence,[28] and their participation in public affairs is crucial to make the guaranteed rights effective.[29]

In balancing the interests of the individual's culture and human rights with the collective interests of the state, such as the need to protect public order or security, the individual stands alone against the state/society. As a result, the interests of different or "outsider" cultures are presented as at odds with the dominant culture and the emphasis on the individual cannot by itself redress this disparity.[30] Is an individualist focus strictly centred on prohibition of discrimination adequate to protect the right to cultural identity of groups such as the Roma? After having reviewed the principles of equality and non-discrimination and their implications for the protection of minorities, this chapter analyses the limitations of the individualistic approach to human rights when dealing with the protection of minorities. In particular, the contribution of individual human rights to minority protection is assessed through the provisions of the European Union (EU), ICERD, ICCPR, ECHR and the FCNM, which are relevant for (members of) minorities and the jurisprudence, interpretations and opinions of the relevant monitoring body or Court.[31] The interrelation between those rights and the protection and promotion of the

---

[26] H. Hannum, *Autonomy, Sovereignty and Self-Determination: The Accommodation of Conflicting Rights* (Philadelphia: University of Pennsylvania Press, 1990), at 65–66.

[27] Id., at 111.

[28] Henrard, *supra* note 10, at 68.

[29] C.H. Williams, 'The Cultural Rights of Minorities: Recognition and Implementation' in J. Plichtová (ed.), *Minorities in politics: cultural and languages rights: Bratislava Symposium, November 13–16, 1991* (Bratislava: Czechoslovak Committee of the European Cultural Foundation, 1992), pp. 107–120, at 109. The extent to which these rights actually make a difference depends on the structure of the electoral system or other mechanisms that ensure political participation. *See* Henrard, *supra* note 10, at 68.

[30] O'Nions, *supra* note 1, at 95–96.

[31] The main focus is on instruments ratified by Italy and thus applicable to it.

cultural identities of minorities will be underlined with a clear focus on those which are closely related to the right to identity, so as to demonstrate that prohibition of discrimination and an individual human rights approach are not sufficient to protect minorities' cultural identity and the consequent need to address the issue from the perspective of collective rights.[32]

3.2. The Principles of Equality and Non-Discrimination as a Full Realisation of the Rights of Minorities

Equality and non-discrimination concern the recognition of diversity and the right to be different. It is widely accepted that equality and non-discrimination are positive and negative statements of the same principle.[33] In other words, equality means the absence of discrimination, and upholding the principle of non-discrimination between groups will produce equality.[34] Holmes pointed out that it is common to speak of anti-discrimination law as "equality law" and to refer to constitutional anti-discrimination provisions as "equality provisions". She underlined that "equality" has simply taken on a technical legal sense in which it means "anti-discrimination."[35] Having equal rights is not the same as being treated equally: equality and non-discrimination imply that equal situations should be treated equally, but unequal situations should be dealt with unequally. As one of the principles at the basis of the protection and promotion of the identities of minorities, it is important to discuss what equality is and what it implies.

The relevance of the principles of equality and non-discrimination for minorities and minority protection cannot be denied.[36] They are essential foundations to the realisation of human rights and to any recognition of minority-based rights, to the point that *if* they were fully realised they

---

[32] *See also* Henrard, *supra* note 10, at 63.

[33] A.F. Bayefsky, 'The principle of Equality or Non-discrimination in International Law', 11 (1990) *Human Rights Quarterly* 1, at 5.

[34] L. Weiwei, 'Equality and Non-Discrimination Under International Human Rights Law,' *Research Notes 2003/2004, Norwegian Centre for Human Rights*, at 7 [hereinafter Weiwei].

[35] E. Holmes, 'Anti-Discrimination Rights without Equality', 68 (n. 2, March 2005) *The Modern Law Review* 175 [hereinafter Holmes].

[36] K. Henrard, 'Non-discrimination and Full and Effective Equality,' in M. Weller (ed.), *Universal Minority Rights* (Oxford University Press: Oxford, 2007), pp. 75–147, at 76 [hereinafter Henrard (2007)].

would make the need for minority-based rights protection redundant;[37] they imply that human rights are universally applicable and that no human being is entitled to more rights than another. The prevalence of equality and non-discrimination provisions in international law shows that they have reached customary international law status and are in fact proclaimed as official policy in virtually every state, although only prohibition of *racial* discrimination can be considered as part of customary international law (and also a norm of *jus cogens*), as has been stated by Judge Tanaka in his dissenting opinion in the *South West Africa Case*;[38] it is still unclear whether prohibition of discrimination on other grounds has achieved the same status.[39]

The ICCPR contains three non-discrimination provisions. Article 2(1) is a general comprehensive non-discrimination and equality clause which guarantees everyone in the jurisdiction of member states the enjoyment of the rights set forth in the ICCPR without distinction of any kind; Article 3 provides equality between the sexes and Article 26 equality before the law and equal protection of the law without discrimination. Articles 2, 3 and 26 all contain a positive obligation to promote equality and a negative one of non-discrimination. Article 2, similar to Article 14 of the ECHR, requires states to respect and ensure *"the rights recognised in the present Covenant, without distinction of any kind."*[40] In other words, it does not prohibit discrimination *per se* but only discrimination in the enjoyment of the rights guaranteed by the ICCPR. However, if one reads Article 2 in conjunction with Article 26, the potential of the ICCPR is far greater than that offered by the ECHR. In fact, Article 26 provides equal treatment before the law and could cover a wide range of situations in

---

[37] O'Nions, *supra* note 1, at 68. *See also* J. Packer, 'On the Definition of Minorities' in J. Packer and K. Myntti (eds.), *The Protection of Ethnic and Linguistic minorities in Europe* (Ebo/Turku: Ebo Akademi University, 1993), pp. 23–65.

[38] Judge Tanaka's Dissenting Opinion in the *South West Africa Case*, (1966) *ICJ Reports* 3, at 293. Because customary international law is formed through a combination of State practice and *opinio juris*, it can be seen that in the case of prohibition of discrimination, virtually all countries have adopted laws and policies which strongly prohibit discrimination on racial grounds, but the actual practice is different. However, the strong rejection by States of the accusation that their practices might be discriminatory reinforces the view that they see the norms prohibiting discrimination on racial grounds as customary international law.

[39] For example, discrimination on grounds of gender is prohibited by the International Convention on the Elimination of Discrimination Against Women (ICEDAW), but this has been subjected to a large number of reservations upon ratification.

[40] Although the English text uses the expression "without distinction of any kind," which seems to imply a broader prohibition than the wording "without discrimination on

which discriminatory treatment has occurred as a result of the unequal application of the law.[41] "Equality before the law" implies that everyone is entitled to the impartial application of the law, whatever that law may be. Therefore, the principle of equality before the law does not guarantee equality in terms of the content of the legislation. Gerards correctly suggests that it is unavoidable that each legislative act distinguishes between groups or cases because the very act of legislating inevitably results in a distinction between groups or cases that fall under the scope of the legislation and those that do not. Substantive equality will then concern the reasonableness of such distinctions.[42]

The "equal protection" formulation has a much broader application. It means that the substantive provisions of the law should apply to everyone equally. This does not mean that everyone should be treated in exactly the same way but that they should not be treated differently on irrational, arbitrary grounds.[43]

According to General Comment 18 on Article 2,

> *the term "discrimination" as used in the Covenant should be understood to imply any distinction, exclusion, restriction or preference which is based on any ground such as race, colour, sex, language, religion, political or other opinion, national or social origin, property, birth or other status, and which has the purpose or effect of nullifying or impairing the recognition, enjoyment or exercise by all persons, on an equal footing, of all rights and obligations.*[44]

Furthermore, the HRC stated that:

> *While Article 2 limits the scope of the rights protected against discrimination to those provided for in the Covenant, Article 26 does not specify such limitations* [...] *Article 26 does not merely duplicate the guarantee already provided for in Article 2 but provides in itself an autonomous right. It prohibits discrimination in law and in fact in any field regulated and protected by public authorities.*[45]

Importantly, the anti-discrimination clauses enshrined in the ICCPR not only prohibit discrimination by state agencies and laws, but also entail a

---

any ground" of Article 14 of the ECHR, the scope of both provisions seems to be the same. The enumerated grounds in both treaties are not exhaustive. *See* Henrard, *supra* note 10, at 72.

41 O'Nions, *supra* note 1, at 70.

42 J. Gerards, Equality as a Legal Argument, available at http://ivr-enc.info/index.php?title=Equality_as_Legal_Argument, last visited Mar. 20, 2012 [hereinafter Gerards].

43 Weiwei, *supra* note 34, at 15.

44 U.N. Human Rights Committee, 'General Comment 18, Non-discrimination,' U.N. Doc. HRI/GEN/1/Rev.1 at 26 (1994), para. 7 [hereinafter General Comment 18].

45 Id., para. 12.

duty on states parties "to ensure" that individuals are protected against discrimination by private actors.[46] The Committee also stated that identical treatment is not appropriate in every instance and that affirmative action may be necessary to diminish or eliminate conditions which perpetuate discrimination.[47]

Various opinions exist regarding what model of equality should be employed in modern democratic states.[48] As was already discussed, one distinction that needs to be made is between "equality before the law," which refers to the status of persons under the law and thus includes procedural aspects and is linked to demands of formal equality (and which, in any case, does not have the same meaning for everyone[49]) and "equal protection of the law," which, conversely, deals with the implementation of the law and is related to the principle of substantive equality.[50] As Gerards pointed out, in the legal discourse, formal inequality means that two cases are treated unequally, whereas formal equality means that two cases are treated equally (the value of formal equality, then, lies in its ability to protect against defects being introduced into the decision-making process and ensuring that irrational and unfair decisions based on arbitrary criteria are kept out[51]). Whether the concrete cases show any substantive differences or similarities does not seem to be of any significance to the legal notion of formal equality. Conversely, substantive inequality means that

---

46 General Comment 18, *supra* note 44, para. 9.

47 Id., paras. 8 and 10.

48 The Ideas of Equality and Non-Discrimination: Formal and Substantive Equality, available at http://www.equalrightstrust.org/ertdocumentbank/The%20Ideas%20of%20Equality%20and%20Non-discrimination,%20Formal%20and%20Substantive%20Equality.pdf, last visited Mar. 20, 2012 [hereinafter The Ideas of Equality and Non-Discrimination].

49 J. Marko, 'Constitutional Recognition of Ethnic Difference–Towards an Emerging European Minimum Standard?,' in A. Verstichel et al. (eds.), *The FCNM: A Useful Pan-European Instrument?* (Antwerpen: Intersentia, 2008). [hereinafter Marko] Marko pointed out that if the official language for communication with state authorities has to be, for example, German, all German native speakers can communicate with state bodies on a natural basis, whereas all others who have a different native language need a privilege to be put in the same position as the majority speaker, or what would be an additional right to use their different minority language in communication with state bodies. This privilege, which is in fact "affirmative action", would then be needed to put the members of the minority in the same position as the majority and should not be considered an exemption from the principle of individual equality before the law which warrants special justification. The topic of affirmative action will be further analysed in the following.

50 Henrard, *supra* note 10, at 61. Marko argued that "equal protection of the law" implies that *"ethnic differences have to be taken seriously and thus be treated differently in order to avoid assimilation." See also* Marko, *supra* note 49.

51 The Ideas of Equality and Non-Discrimination, *supra* note 48.

substantively unequal cases are treated in the same way. Substantive inequality obviously does not imply a formal difference in treatment – the cases are, after all, treated the same. Still, formal equal treatment can sometimes constitute inequality: inequality as a result of insufficient account being taken of the differences that exist between groups, persons or situations. For this reason, substantive equality is often termed equality in result, whereas formal equality might be described as equality in treatment.

Justice L'Heureux Dubé of the Supreme Court of Canada, writing extra judicially, defined substantive equality (as opposed to formal equality) as reflecting:

> [...] *the underlying goal of achieving an equality of outcome or substance among all members of society, regardless of their differences.* [...] *This ideal can be contrasted with the concept of "formal equality" of sameness of treatment in the law, which does little to overcome patterns of social disadvantage and indeed, may perpetuate them.*[52]

In *Minority Schools in Albania*, the PCIJ held that:

> *Equality in law precludes discrimination of any kind, whereas equality in fact may involve the necessity of different treatment in order to attain a result which establishes an equilibrium between different situations.*[53]

As Holmes suggested, critics of "formal equality" find it frustrating that the law's main preoccupation is with how people are treated as opposed to the ("substantive") situation that results. For these critics, it is pointless to have more equal treatment in the world or to require people to always treat each other equally, if they nevertheless do not end up equally situated. The concept of "formal equality" is seen as too simplistic because it tends to ignore the personal characteristics of an individual altogether. For example, in respect to racial discrimination, advocates of formal equality would proscribe a colour-blind rather than a colour-conscious approach.[54] "Equality laws," a category which is thought at least to include anti-discrimination laws, should be aimed at "correcting disadvantage" and the failure of anti-discrimination laws to do this is attributed to the fact that they are "based on a flawed concept of equality."[55]

---

52 C. L'Heureux Dubé, 'Making a Difference: The Pursuit of Equality and a Compassionate Justice,' 13 *South African Journal on Human Rights* 335 (1997), at 338.

53 *Minority Schools in Albania, supra* note 19, at 20.

54 The Ideas of Equality and Non-Discrimination, *supra* note 48.

55 Holmes, *supra* note 35, at 178–179.

Another important legal concept is that of procedural equality, which is closely related to the concept of equal opportunities. The concept of equality of opportunities is partially based on the idea that measures have to be taken to rectify past discrimination, because to fail to do so would leave people and groups at different starting points. It thus aims at ensuring an equal starting point and is different from equality of results, which conversely aims at ensuring the same outcome. Unlike formal equality, procedural equality takes some account of the differences that exist between individuals, more specifically: of their differences in opportunities. Unlike substantive equality, however, complete equality is not the sought-after goal. Even if people start from the same position and have equal opportunities, the final results that they achieve can differ. Indeed, procedural preferential treatment policies aim at removing social and practical barriers and at combating persistent and negative forms of stereotyping. Such policies might contribute to a particular objective by placing different individuals on an equal footing, but not necessarily so because other obstacles might stand in the way of complete substantive equality.[56]

Major differences of opinion exist regarding the exact meaning and implications of the equality principle and its various dimensions. The generally accepted formulation of the equality principle is the one given by Aristotle: *"treat equally what is equal and treat differently what is unequal, but to the extent of inequality."*[57] A differential treatment only amounts to prohibited discrimination when no reasonable and objective justification for it exists. Article 14 of the ECHR prohibits direct discrimination – meaning a difference in treatment between two persons or groups of persons – in the enjoyment of the rights set forth in the Convention. The ECtHR has expanded on the definition of discriminatory differentiation by stating in *Fredin v. Sweden,*[58] *Belgian Linguistics,*[59] *Petrovic v. Austria*[60] and *Larkos v. Cyprus*[61] that a breach of Article 14 of the ECHR

[56] *See* Gerards, *supra* note 42. *See also* S. Fredman, 'Combating Racism with Human Rights: The Right to Equality,' in S. Fredman (ed.), *Discrimination and Human Rights: The Case of Racism* (Oxford: Oxford University Press, 2001), pp. 9–44, at 19–21 [hereinafter Fredman].

[57] Aristotle, *Politica*, as cited in Henrard, *supra* note 10, at 58.

[58] *Case of Fredin v. Sweden* (1991) 13 EHRR 784.

[59] *Case Relating to Certain Aspects of the Laws on the Use of Languages in Education in Belgium,* 1 Eur. Hum. Rts. Rep. 252 (1968), para. 10 [hereinafter *Belgian Linguistics*].

[60] *Case of Petrovic v. Austria*, application No. 20458/92, Eur. Ct. Hum. Rts., 23 March 1998, para. 30.

[61] *Case of Larkos v. Cyprus*, application No. 29515/95, Eur. Ct. Hum. Rts., 18 February 1999, para. 29.

occurs when individuals are treated differently in relevantly similar or analogous situations, without any objective or reasonable justification for the distinction. But in *Belgian Linguistics*, the Court also pointed out that:

> [...] *Article 14 does not forbid every difference in treatment in the exercise of the rights and freedoms recognised.* [...] *The competent national authorities are frequently confronted with situations and problems which, on account of differences inherent therein, call for different legal solutions; moreover, certain legal inequalities tend only to correct factual inequalities.*[62]

In other words, the Court left a degree of discretion to the state to accommodate domestic factors.[63]

In *Cyprus v. Turkey* the Court found that discrimination against the Greek Cypriot community in northern Cyprus was so severe that it amounted to inhuman and degrading treatment and constituted a violation of Article 3.[64] It is also acknowledged that under Article 14, even indirect discrimination – measures that are at first sight neutral but have a disproportionate effect on a person or group of persons, without any objective or reasonable justification – is prohibited. Similarly, in *Thlimmenos v. Greece* the Court found that:

> *the right not to be discriminated against* [...] *is also violated when states without an objective and reasonable justification fail to treat differently persons whose situations are significantly different.*[65]

I believe that equality as described in this section is only one way to fully achieve the equality principle. Applying the principle of non-discrimination can have adverse assimilative effects because treating everyone the same way might deny the existence of different identities. Hence, the need is present to protect from direct as well as indirect discrimination[66] and to adopt not only affirmative action policies, but also

---

[62] *Belgian Linguistics, supra* note 59, para. 10.

[63] *See also* Gilbert (2002), *supra* note 4, at 741. The state's margin of appreciation under Article 14 is not unlimited, and in particular, it needs to be read in light of Article 18 which provides that *"the restrictions permitted* [...] *to the said rights and freedoms shall not be applied for any purpose other than those for which they have been prescribed."*

[64] *Case of Cyprus v. Turkey*, application No. 25781/94, Eur. Ct. Hum. Rts., 10 May 2001, para. 309 [hereinafter *Cyprus v. Turkey*, Eur. Ct. Hum. Rts.].

[65] *Case of Thlimmenos v. Greece* (2000) 31 EHRR 411, para. 44 [hereinafter *Thlimmenos v. Greece*].

[66] Indirect discrimination principles were first introduced into the law of many countries from the mid-1970s onward. At the time, they were seen as a partial solution to the limitations of direct discrimination principles and as bearing a relationship to a more "substantive" principle of equality than that to which direct discrimination was related (e.g. "equality of results"). Their introduction was seen as an attempt to address the

special measures,[67] collective rights and positive obligations[68] for minority groups, as well as the right to maintain and protect the minority language, culture, traditions and religious practices and cultural identity in general.

3.3. The Protection of Minorities in the European Union

Human rights – including the protection of minorities – have gradually become part of the agenda of the EU, although only from an individualist perspective. However, much of the focus on human rights and minorities has been directed at new member states and applicant states. Respect for minorities as inspired by the Copenhagen criteria (a set of economic and political conditions to be met by new candidate countries, as decided in a European Council meeting held in Copenhagen in 1993) has been a fundamental value during the enlargement process,[69] but it is absent from the list of values for internal development. In other words, minority clauses applied to new members prior to their accession to the EU are not applicable to old members, including Italy – a founding member. De Witte has commented that, *"so far the Union considered the minority protection as an export Article which is not suitable for its domestic use."*[70] It appears to be assumed that, once a country is accepted for EU membership, its minority problems are resolved.[71]

"redistributive and restructuring goals of equality" and to "reduce the degree of exclusion" of certain groups. *See* Fredman, *supra* note 56. Principles forbidding indirect discrimination merely forbid discrimination on certain grounds. However, they expand the relevant range of grounds. Therefore, a ground which would not otherwise be a forbidden ground of discrimination (such as physical strength) becomes forbidden because it bears a certain relationship to the prohibited ground of distinction (sex). *See* Holmes, *supra* note 35, at 184.

[67] The issues of affirmative action and special measures will be discussed later in this chapter.

[68] In human rights law, positive obligations indicate States' obligations to engage in activities aimed at securing the effective enjoyment of a fundamental right. Negative obligations, conversely, imply the obligation to abstain from human rights violations.

[69] K. Topidi, 'European Union Standards and Mechanisms for the Protection of Minorities and the Prevention of Discrimination,' in *Mechanisms for the implementation of minority rights* (Strasbourg: Council of Europe Publishing, 2004), pp. 183–202, at 196 [hereinafter Topidi].

[70] B. De Witte, 'Politics versus law in the EU's approach to ethnic minorities,' in J. Zielonka (ed.) *Europe Unbound. Enlarging and Reshaping the Boundaries of the European Union* (London: Routledge, 2002), pp. 137–160, at 139.

[71] B. De Witte, 'The constitutional resources for an EU Minority Protection Policy' in G. Toggenburg (ed.) *Minority protection and the enlarged European Union: the way forward* (Budapest: OSI/LGI, 2004), pp. 109–124.

Neither a specific EU concept of "minority" exists, nor a general framework of minority protection. Among the few instruments dealing with minority issues, a 1994 resolution of the European Parliament builds on the provisions of the EChRML and emphases the importance for member states to recognise and protect linguistic minorities.[72]

> *Until the Amsterdam Treaty there had been no provision in the primary law, except the general prohibition of discrimination, that would have guaranteed the minorities specific rights and specific protection. The reluctance of the member states to commit themselves to the minority protection was reflected also in the Amsterdam Treaty*[73]

Which incorporated in Article 6(1) all the requirements coming from the Copenhagen criteria, with the exception of the very requirement – protection and respect of national minorities – which is absent from the treaty.[74]

The prevention of discrimination and the protection of equality are now of central importance for the EU, but this was not always the case. Initially, the EU's main focus was the prohibition of discrimination on grounds of nationality (limited to that of member states) and gender. These grounds are not directly relevant for minority protection purposes. The Treaty of Amsterdam[75] contributed to the broadening and strengthening of EU principles of equality because the EU was given competence to combat discrimination on the basis of, among others, racial or ethnic origins and religion, which are grounds of special relevance for minorities.

---

[72] Resolution *on linguistic and cultural minorities in the European Community* A3-0042/94, at D. The Council of the European Union adopted a declaration on 29 June 1991 stating that respect and promotion of human rights were essential for co-operation and relations with third countries and underlining the need to protect, inter alia, minorities. In December 1999, the Council asked to give full attention to the "[…] *improvement of the situation of those groups which do not form a majority in any State, including the Roma/Gypsies."* *See* the Helsinki Conclusions of the EU Presidency, 11 December 1999, Press Release Nr 00300/1/99, available at http://ue.eu.int/ueDocs/cms_Data/docs/pressdata/en/ec/ACFA4C.htm, last visited Mar. 20, 2012, para. 65.

[73] I. Pospíšil, *The Protection of National Minorities and the Concept of Minority in the EU Law*, a paper presented at the ECPR 3rd Pan-European Conference, Bilgi University, Istanbul, 21–23 Sept. 2006, at 4 [hereinafter Pospíšil].

[74] Id., at 4. *See also* J. Hughes and G. Sasse, 'Monitoring the Monitors: EU Enlargement Conditionality and Minority Protection in the CEECs,' *in Journal on Ethnopolitics and Minority Issues in Europe*, Issue 1/2003, at 12 [hereinafter Hughes and Sasse].

[75] Treaty of Amsterdam Amending the Treaty on European Union, the Treaties Establishing the European Communities and Certain Related Acts, available at http://www.europarl.europa.eu/topics/treaty/pdf/amst-en.pdf, last visited Mar. 20, 2012.

Two directives were adopted after the coming into force of the Treaty of Amsterdam. The "Race Directive"[76] underlines the importance of the right to equality, which extends to education, housing, healthcare and other social advantages and refers to both direct and indirect discrimination. Article 5 provides for positive action with a view to ensure full equality and to compensate for disadvantage attributed to previous inequality. However, it does not provide or impose positive obligations on states in this respect and no specification of the special measures that members are allowed to implement exists. This omission is problematic and reflects the overall approach which seems aimed at procedural rather than substantive equality.[77] It is doubtful that substantive equality can be realised in the case of the Roma in the absence of a positive duty on states to remedy past disadvantage and entrenched discriminatory perceptions.[78] Furthermore, it should be observed that the Race Directive has not provided for a systematic monitoring of implementation, and indeed the EU tends to rely on proxies (primarily external bodies such as the Council of Europe, Organisation for Security and Cooperation in Europe (OSCE), and NGOs) to perform the monitoring functions.[79] The other Directive (2000/78)[80] addresses, inter alia, discrimination on the basis of religion.

The development of the jurisprudence of the European Court of Justice (ECJ) and the clarifications provided by the directives will allow a better understanding of the concepts of indirect discrimination and affirmative action, which are relevant to minorities. The ECJ has so far only addressed the aspect of minority-majority relations relating to non-discrimination. Minority rights have a long way to go before being formally and directly recognised before the ECJ.[81]

---

[76] Council Directive 2000/43/EC *implementing the principle of equal treatment between persons irrespective of racial or ethnic origin*, Official Journal L 180, 19 July 2000 P, 0022–0026.

[77] O'Nions, *supra* note 1, at 90.

[78] Id. In view of the difficult situation faced by the Roma across the EU, the European Parliament adopted a resolution condemning episodes of racial discrimination and violent attacks against the Roma and invited EU members to join their efforts in fighting anti-Gypsyism and in developing a common strategy for the integration of the Roma. *See* European Parliament resolution *on a European strategy on the Roma*, P6_TA(2008)0035, 31 January 2008. Despite the resolution, little effort has been made to combat discrimination against Roma in Italy, as will be seen in chapter 5.

[79] Hughes and Sasse, *supra* note 74, at 13. One of them is the EU Fundamental Rights Agency, which started its work on 1 March 2007. *See* http://fra.europa.eu/fraWebsite/about_us/about_us_en.htm, last visited Mar. 20, 2012.

[80] Council Directive 2000/78 of 27 November 2000, *establishing a general framework for equal treatment in employment and occupation*, Official Journal L 303/16 (2000).

[81] Topidi, *supra* note 69, at 186.

Full recognition of minority rights is not evident in the Charter of Fundamental Rights, part of the 2007 Treaty of Lisbon designed to streamline the workings of the EU. The Treaty came into force on 1 December 2009, and thus the Charter has also been adopted and has become legally binding.

The Charter of Fundamental Rights was first proclaimed during the Nice European Council in December 2000 as a non-binding document. A proposal for its incorporation by reference in Article 6 (ex-Article F) of the Treaty of the EU was opposed by several members. The Charter was adapted on 12 December 2007 so as to be included in the Treaty of Lisbon; its 55 Articles list political, social and economic rights. It intends to make sure that EU regulations and directives do not contradict the ECHR, ratified by all EU members (and to which the EU as a whole would accede under the Treaty of Lisbon). It contains three Articles relevant to the protection of the rights of minorities and non-discrimination. The preamble, on paragraph 3, makes a reference to respect for cultural diversity. Article 20 on equality before the law contains a general equality clause that stipulates that 'everyone is equal before the law.' More specific to ethnic and national minorities is Article 21(1), which draws on Article 14 of the ECHR and prohibits *"any discrimination based on any ground such as* [...] *membership of a national minority* [...]" and applies to all the other rights enshrined in the EU treaties, not only to the ones contained in the Charter.

Like many other international documents on human rights, the Charter does not contain any specific minority rights provisions which might be enforced by the ECJ or other competent bodies. According to Pentassuglia, the reason the Charter does not reach out to "minority rights," despite proposals for a minority provision submitted during the drafting stage mostly lies in the fact that the text draws from the ECHR, with a view to making the respective rights, as stated in the preamble, "more visible in a Charter."[82]

If, on the one hand, it can be said that the EU, as an actor in the international scene, has evolved toward more serious consideration for human rights and, to a certain extent, minority rights; it should, on the other hand, be observed that no clear minority rights provisions exist and that the instruments used to guarantee the rights of ethnic or national minorities are based on non-discrimination, which is insufficient to cover the special

---

[82] G. Pentassuglia, *Minorities in International Law* (Strasbourg: Council of Europe Publishing, 2002), at 151.

rights required by ethnic or national minorities and is not suitable for the protection of their identity.[83]

3.4. The United Nations Instruments and their Jurisprudence

3.4.1. *The International Convention on the Elimination of All Forms of Racial Discrimination*

The ICERD does not contain any specific provision on minorities: its main objective is that of promoting *de facto* and *de jure* equality.[84] It has been ratified by a large number of countries,[85] which indicates that the principles it strives to promote are widely recognised in different political cultures. It appears that the Committee on the Elimination of Racial Discrimination (CERD) regards equality of result as the main objective of the Convention. This goal can be perceived in a number of provisions of the ICERD, but cannot be inferred from the given definition of racial discrimination, which limits the prohibited distinctions to those that lead to the denial or impairment of human rights on an equal footing. Indeed, Article 1 defines racial discrimination as:

> *any distinction, exclusion, restriction or preference based on race, colour, descent, or national or ethnic origin which has the purpose or effect of nullifying or impairing the recognition, enjoyment or exercise, on an equal footing, of human rights and fundamental freedoms in the political, economic, social, cultural or any other field of public life.*

This definition is quite broad and includes ethnic and national origin, thus making it also relevant for ethnic and national minorities.

Evidence that the ICERD aims at achieving *de facto* equality can be inferred from the Preamble, which in paragraph 2 notes the enjoyment of certain rights "without distinction of any kind" and in paragraph 7 mentions discrimination between human beings on grounds of race; as well as by the enumeration in Article 5 of a number of rights, which include the right to equality before the law. Furthermore, if one reads the expression "on an equal footing" as per Article 1(1) together with Article 1(4), which allows distinctions for the purpose of affirmative action to ensure groups

---

83 Topidi, *supra* note 69, at 197.

84 Under Article 1(3) ICERD does allow certain distinctions, such as those between citizens and non-citizens, or nationals and aliens, *"provided that such provisions do not discriminate against any particular nationality."*

85 As of 20 March 2012, 175 countries have ratified the ICERD.

or individuals the equal enjoyment of human rights, as well as Article 2(2) which asks parties to take certain affirmative action measures, it can be seen that the ICERD promotes racial equality and not just colour neutral values;[86] not simply *de jure* but also *de facto* equality, designed to allow the various ethnic, racial and national groups the same social development.[87]

According to Article 7:

> *States parties undertake to adopt immediate and effective measures, particularly in the fields of teaching, education, culture and information, with a view to combating prejudices which lead to racial discrimination* [...].

In its report on the implementation of Article 7, the CERD pointed out that:

> *Although the Convention applies to everyone without exception, it is concerned particularly with certain minority groups which have, historically, suffered the greatest social exploration and deprivation.*[88]

Thanks to the broad field of application of the ICERD, state parties are allowed, and in certain circumstances are obliged, to take special measures[89] in favour of disadvantaged racial groups. This proves that the ICERD implicitly[90] recognises and protects the group dimension (and in

---

[86] T. Meron, 'The Meaning and Reach of the International Convention on the Elimination of All Forms of Racial Discrimination," Vol. 79 (n. 2) (April 1985) *The American Journal of International Law* 283, at 288 [hereinafter Meron].

[87] 37 UN GAOR Supp. (No. 18), UN Doc. A/37/18 (1982), para. 468.

[88] U.N. CERD, *Implementation of the ICERD, Article 7: Teaching, Education, Culture and Information as means of Eliminating Racial Discrimination* (New York: United Nations, 1985), at 9. [hereinafter *Implementation of the ICERD*] The Special Rapporteur on contemporary forms of racism, racial discrimination, xenophobia and related intolerance has also brought up minority issues in his report to the Commission of Human Rights. *See* G. Alfredsson, 'Minority Rights: A Summary of Existing Practice' in A. Phillips and A. Rosas (eds), *Universal Minority Rights* (London: Minority Rights Group International 1995), pp. 77–86, at 84. Furthermore, the Secretary of the Committee on the Elimination of Racial Discrimination, during the second session of the UN Working Group on Minorities, observed that *"Article 1 ICERD clearly showed that the Convention was of applicability to persons belonging to national and ethnic minorities." See* U.N. Working Group on Minorities, *Report on its Second Session*, UN Doc. E/CN.4/Sub.2/1996/28, 8 July 1996, at 16. *"It is obvious that the Roma are considered to fall within the ambit of the Convention, with the Committee criticising the treatment of Roma in a variety of countries* [...]*." See* O'Nions, *supra* note 1, at 71–72. *See*, for example, the Concluding Observations on Hungary in which the Committee pointed out the persistent marginalisation of the Roma and the discrimination experienced in most aspects of their life. *See* U.N. CERD, Concluding observations: Hungary, CERD/C/304/Add.4, 28 March 1996 para. 14.

[89] The issue of special measures will be analysed further in the course of this chapter.

[90] Contrary to ICERD, the non-binding UNESCO Declaration on Race and Racial Prejudice includes a more explicit appreciation of the right to maintain minority identity

this sense, also minority identity), especially due to its focus on culture and groups.[91] Article 5 contains an enumeration of certain fundamental rights (including participation in cultural activities) and freedoms which should be guaranteed without distinction based on race, colour, national or ethnic origin: these are the kind of rights which allow everyone to lead their life according to their convictions. Article 5 is framed in individual terms; however, it is evidently relevant for the right to identity of minorities, especially because it provides for the adoption of special measures for certain groups.[92]

On a number of occasions, the CERD has dealt with cases presented by persons of Romany origins. For example, in *Koptova v. Slovak Republic*,[93] the applicant (a Romany woman) complained of a violation of, among others, her right to freedom of movement, following several national resolutions "[...] *which expressly forbade the Romany families from settling in the village and threatened them with expulsion should they try to settle there.*"[94] The CERD recommended the state party to "*take the necessary measures to ensure that practices restricting the freedom of movement and residence of Roma under its jurisdiction are fully and promptly eliminated.*"[95] The importance of ensuring the freedom of movement and residence of the Roma is the only indirect reference to the need to protect their cultural identity, of which movement might be considered a feature. In any case, the issue was not fully analysed because the discriminatory resolutions had been withdrawn.

Reports and individual complaints submitted to CERD show that non-discrimination and equality provisions are of some benefit for minorities, but they have had remarkably little effect for the Roma[96] because they do

---

in Article 1(3). Article 5 calls for the respect of "*the right of all groups to their own cultural identity and the development of their distinctive cultural life within the national and international context.*" It further adds that every minority group has the right to decide to which extent it desires to preserve and develop its own culture or join the dominant one. *See* UNESCO Declaration on Race and Racial Prejudice, available at http://www.unhchr.ch/html/menu3/b/d_prejud.htm, last visited Mar. 20, 2012. The explanatory report specifies that the right to be different is intended as enabling all individuals and groups to lead their lives without needing to abandon their essential identity. *See* UNESCO Declaration on Race and Racial Prejudice, Explanatory Report, Doc 20/C/18 annex, at 4–5. The Declaration can be considered as an example of the increasing importance given to the recognition of the right to cultural identity, even for minorities. *See* Henrard, *supra* note 10, at 203.

91 Henrard, *supra* note 10, at 199.

92 Id.

93 *Koptova v. Slovak Republic*, Communication n. 13/1998, Slovakia 01/11/2000, CERD/C/57/D/13/1998 [hereinafter *Koptova v. Slovak Republic*].

94 Id., para. 2.3.

95 Id., para. 10.3.

96 O'Nions, *supra* note 1, at 72.

not address greater issues of identity protection which are at the core of minority protection. Indeed, the ICERD lacks a proper enforcement procedure and although it allows for special measures to be introduced to favour disadvantaged groups, the introduction of such measures is ultimately left to the discretion of the state (see, for example, the case of *Koptova* in which the CERD "recommends" the adoption of several measures and legislation) and the CERD has proven quite cautious in its suggestions for improvements.

On a more positive note, the CERD has recognised the uniqueness of the situation faced by the Roma and thus adopted its first thematic recommendation in 2000. This recommendation is intended to allow the CERD to apply a more structured analysis of the treatment of Roma by state parties; it addressed several issues, including racial violence (also at the hands of the police) and discrimination in education, living conditions, public life and the media.[97] This is a clear step toward the recognition that issues pertaining to the Roma should be dealt with in a more comprehensive manner that also addresses their cultural identity.

3.4.2. *The International Covenant on Civil and Political Rights and the Human Rights Committee's Interpretation of Article 27*

As was already noted, prohibition of discrimination is a necessary but not a sufficient condition for the protection of minorities. The HRC clearly stated that the mere application of the principles of equality before the law and non-discrimination are not sufficient guarantees for the equal and effective enjoyment by persons belonging to ethnic, religious or linguistic minorities of the rights set out in the Covenant.[98] Thus, the ICCPR tends to offer better protection of minorities – including the Roma, who fall under the scope of the application of Article 27[99] – than the ECHR, because Article 27 explicitly deals with rights for members of minorities.[100]

---

[97] U.N. Committee on the Elimination of Racial Discrimination, General Recommendation 27, *Discrimination against Roma,* 57th Session, 16 August 2000, document A/55/18 annex V.

[98] U.N. Human Rights Committee, *Concluding Observations of the Human Rights Committee: France,* CCPR/C/FRA/CO/4, 31 July 2008, para. 11 [hereinafter *Concluding Observations on France*].

[99] *See* chapter 2.

[100] Henrard, *supra* note 10, at 72. On the terminology used in Article 27 and on its collective dimension, *see* chapter 4. Regarding the HRC's interpretation of who can be considered members of minorities under Article 27, *see* chapter 2. In *Ballantyne, Davidson, McIntyre v. Canada* the Committee concluded that Article 27 only applies to minorities

Before reviewing the jurisprudence of the HRC under Article 27, as well as the views it expressed in its General Comment 23(50), it should be observed that its views are not legally binding on state parties, despite having a considerable degree of authority. The publicity received by the views of the HRC is an incentive for states to abide by them.

> *Legally, the views [...] are not binding on the state party concerned which remains free to criticize them. Nonetheless, any state party will find it hard to reject such findings in so far as they are based on orderly proceedings during which the defendant party had ample opportunity to present its submissions. The views [...] gain their authority from their inner qualities of impartiality, objectiveness and soberness. If such requirements are met, [they] can have a far-reaching impact, at least vis-à-vis such Governments which have not outrightly broken with the international community and ceased to care anymore for concern expressed by international bodies. If such a situation arose, however, even a legally binding decision would not be likely to be respected.*[101]

The following analysis will mostly focus on the degree to which the HRC recognises the protection of identity and the group dimension of Article 27 ICCPR. It should also be underlined that for as many cases that the Committee dealt with, many others were declared inadmissible for a number of reasons. For example, all cases against France were declared inadmissible due to France's interpretative declaration according to which no minorities exist in France.[102] Indeed, following ratification of the ICCPR, France submitted a declaration on Article 27 according to which, because the French Constitution prohibits all distinctions between citizens on grounds of origin, race or religion, no minorities exist in France (and as such, Article 27 is not applicable).[103] In 1989, the HRC concluded that this

---

within a state and not to minorities in a province. However, some HRC members expressed difficulties with the interpretation of a minority merely on the basis of the number of members of the community in the whole state and considered that persons should not necessarily be *"excluded from the protection of Article 27 where their group is an ethnic, linguistic or cultural minority in an autonomous province of a State, but is not clearly a numerical minority in the State itself, taken as a whole entity." See Ballantyne, Davidson, McIntyre v. Canada,* Communications nos. 359/1989 and 385/1989, UN Doc. CCPR/C/47/D/359/1989 and 385/1989/Rev.1 (1993).

[101] C. Tomuschat, 'Evolving Procedural Rules: The United Nations Human Rights Committee's First two Years of Dealing with Individual Communications,' in *Human Rights Law Journal* Vol. 1, No. 1 (1980), pp. 249–257, at 255.

[102] *See* for example the case *T. K. v. France,* Communication No. 220/1987, decision of 8 November 1989 [hereinafter *T. K. v. France*].

[103] For the text of the French declaration, *see* http://treaties.un.org/Pages/ViewDetails.aspx?src=TREATY&mtdsg_no=IV-4&chapter=4&lang=en#EndDec, last visited Mar. 20, 2012. The French state-nation concept, which is based on the republican tradition of 1789, does not allow for any differentiation. The ethnically indifferent "citoyens" form the nation.

declaration should be considered as a binding reservation in accordance with the Vienna Convention on the Law of Treaties, Article 2(1). It held that France clearly intended to modify or exclude the legal effect of this provision and thus it did not consider itself competent to examine cases directed against France concerning alleged violations of Article 27.[104] Dissenting, Judge Higgins held that the French declaration should be regarded precisely as a declaration, and not a reservation, because it was incompatible with the Committee's interpretation of Article 27: the HRC had several times rejected the idea that the existence of minorities would be dependent on a form of discrimination and that minorities also exist in states that apply principles of equality and non-discrimination.[105]

I agree with Higgins' view that Article 27 of the ICCPR is intended to protect minorities and their culture even from interference from the state. The easiest way for a state to interfere with minority rights is to deny the existence of minorities in their territory.[106] This would imply that no need for special measures of protection of such minorities exists because they would automatically be assimilated – which goes against the principles set out in Article 27.[107]

In any event, the HRC implicitly clarified its intention to ignore the position of those members who argued that no minorities were present in their territories or who have not recognised certain minorities. Indeed, it observed that the existence of minorities is a question of fact and that although some states claim that, because they do not discriminate on grounds of ethnicity, language or religion, they have no minorities, *"the existence of an ethnic, religious or linguistic minority in a given state party does not depend upon a decision by that state party but requires to be established by objective criteria."*[108] In view of this, Italy has been criticised

---

Thus, from a political and constitutional perspective, no possibility to differentiate between majority and minority exists and thus, no need to recognise differences of any kind or grant privileges or exemptions to persons or groups exists. *See* Marko, *supra* note 49. Marko believes that the French model leads to the suppression of cultural pluralism and the exclusion and marginalisation of old and new minorities.

[104] *T. K. v. France*, *supra* note 102, para. 8.6.

[105] Id., Appendix I.

[106] Donders, *supra* note 15, at 186.

[107] It is vital that states do not make reservations or interpretative declarations on Article 27, or take other measures that would give them the exclusive right to establish whether a community constitutes a minority under Article 27. *See* Donders, *supra* note 15, at 186–187. However, most states do officially recognise minorities in their territory. So did Italy, which has excluded the Roma from the list of recognised minorities.

[108] U.N. Human Rights Committee, 'General Comment 23(50), Article 27,' UN Doc. CCPR/C/21/Rev.1/Add.5, 1994, paras. 4 and 5.2. [hereinafter General Comment 25(50)] On this aspect, *see also* chapter 2.

for its decision not to include the Roma amongst the recognised minorities[109] and indeed the Roma, according to the HRC, should be the subject of special measures to ensure their participation in mainstream society at all levels.[110]

Quite exceptionally, in *Hopu and Bessert v. France*, the Committee circumvented Article 27, which could not have been applied in this case due to the French reservation, and addressed the claims under Articles 17 (privacy, family and home) and 23 (rights of the family), by pointing out that relationships with ancestors are an important element of identity and a defining role in family life.[111] Dissenting members, however, disagreed on stretching the legal interpretation of family and privacy.[112] The creative approach used by the HRC in this case would imply that France, regardless of its reservation, could not avoid dealing with cases concerning cultural aspects of minority rights.

Article 27 is clearly intended to protect the right to identity for minorities.[113] The HRC has stated that *"the protection of these rights is directed to ensure the survival and continued development of the cultural, religious and social identity of the minorities concerned* [...]."[114] There is thus broad agreement on the fact that Article 27 contains an absolute prohibition of forced assimilation. Although the prohibition of assimilation appears to focus mostly on negative state obligations, a broader interpretation of Article 27 shows that it requires more far reaching obligations. In this sense, when the religion, language and culture of the majority is strongly dominant, merely leaving a minority to its own devices could amount to a form of forced assimilation.[115] For these reasons, on a number of occasions, Article 27 has been interpreted by the Committee as imposing positive obligations to favour minority groups.

The HRC pointed out in its concluding observations on Romania that measures should be adopted to ensure the rights of the Roma in the public

---

[109] U.N. Human Rights Committee, *Concluding Observations of the Human Rights Committee: Italy*, CCPR/C/ITA/CO/5, 24 April 2006, para. 22. [hereafter *Concluding Observations on Italy*] The HRC has observed that the Roma are to be considered a minority protected under Article 27. Concern was also expressed over the fact that Roma are still considered "nomads." On the labelling of Roma as nomads, *see* chapter 5.

[110] Id., para. 21.

[111] *Hopu and Bessert v. France*, Communication number 549/1993, 29 July 1997, paras. 4.3 and 4.4.

[112] *Hopu and Bessert v. France*, Individual opinion by Committee members David Kretzmer and Thomas Buergenthal, cosigned by Nisuke Ando and Lord Colville.

[113] Indeed, the HRC sees way of life as one of the expressions of culture.

[114] General Comment 23(50), *supra* note 108, para. 9.

[115] Henrard, *supra* note 10, at 164.

and the private sector, particularly in respect to access to education and support for the Roma language.[116] The need to adopt measures to ensure integration of minorities has also been underlined by the HRC in its concluding observations on Italy, with special reference to the Roma.[117] Similarly, in its concluding observations on Bulgaria the HRC highlighted the need for positive action to fully implement the rights enshrined in Article 27.[118] Having stressed the value of culture for minorities, the Committee also emphasised the importance to take actions intended to preserve their cultural identity, whether these are measures to ensure the end of racial segregation in housing and schooling (the HRC reiterated the need to take into account the cultural identity of minorities when assessing the specific educational needs of minorities[119]), or effective consultation with them on issues that closely regard them,[120] such as appropriate access to services and employment, or the use of language in the public and the private sector. In *Ominayak and the Lubicon Lake Band v. Canada* the HRC further observed that a state not only has a duty of non-intervention regarding activities by the members of a minority, but can also be required to adopt measures that would actually assist a minority. It therefore established a link between economic and social activities and the culture of a community.[121]

---

[116] U.N. Human Rights Committee, *Concluding Observations of the Human Rights Committee: Romania,* CCPR/C/79/Add.111, 28 July 1999, para. 6. Similarly, in its views on Slovakia, the HRC pointed out that efforts should be made to allow the Roma to use their language in official communications. *See* U.N. Human Rights Committee, *Concluding Observations of the Human Rights Committee: Slovakia,* CCPR/CO/78/SVK, 22 August 2003, para. 16 [hereinafter *Concluding Observations on Slovakia*].

[117] *Concluding Observations on Italy, supra* note 109, para. 21.

[118] U.N. Human Rights Committee, *Concluding Observations of the Human Rights Committee: Bulgaria,* CCPR/C/79/Add.24, 3 August 1993, para. 9.

[119] U.N. Human Rights Committee, *Concluding Observations of the Human Rights Committee: Czech Republic,* CCPR/C/CZE/CO/2, 9 August 2007, para. 17. In this case, the Committee was particularly referring to the Roma.

[120] The enjoyment of cultural rights under Article 27 might require states to take measures to ensure the effective participation of members of minorities in decisions which concern them. *See* General Comment 23(50), *supra* note 108, para. 9.5. *See also Apirana Mahuika v. New Zealand,* in which the Committee found no breach of Article 27 because the government had engaged in thorough consultations on the use or control of fisheries with the Maori. *See Apirana Mahuika v. New Zealand,* Communication n. 547/1993, UN Doc. CCPR/C/70/D/547/1993 27 October 2000, paras. 9.3–10 [hereinafter *Apirana Mahuika v. New Zealand*].

[121] *Ominayak and the Lubicon Lake Band v. Canada,* Communication n. 167/1984, UN Doc A/45/40, Vol. II, App. A (1990), para. 33. [hereinafter *Lubicon Lake Band v. Canada*] In his individual opinion, Ando argued that land issues do not necessarily fall within the scope of the enjoyment of culture. *See Lubicon Lake Band v. Canada,* Appendix I. However, the HRC has supported the view that Article 27 is designed to protect and promote the

In addition, in certain circumstances, the Committee underlined the need not only for positive measures of protection against the acts of the state, but also against acts of private persons within the state.[122] Positive measures are needed to correct conditions that prevent or impair the enjoyment of the rights guaranteed by Article 27, and to protect the identity of a minority and *"the rights of its members to enjoy and develop their culture and language and to practise their religion in community with the other members of their group."*[123] Indeed, *"although the rights protected under Article 27 are individual rights, they depend in turn on the ability of the minority group to maintain its culture, language or religion* [...]."[124] However, it is not clarified whether these measures should be temporary. In his study on Article 27, Capotorti observed that:

> [...] *To enable the objectives of this Article to be achieved, it is essential that states should adopt legislative and administrative measures.* [...] *The implementation of* [*the rights under Article 27*] *calls for active and sustained intervention by states. A passive attitude on the part of the latter would render such rights inoperative.*[125]

The importance of adopting measures to assist minorities is also suggested by the HRC in its various concluding observations, in which it stressed the need to be provided with statistical information that would allow the empirical assessment of effective access to employment, public services, and political participation by persons belonging to racial, ethnic, religious or national minorities and concluded that the absence of this information might mask problems of *de facto* discrimination and impede the design of appropriate and effective public policies to combat discrimination.[126]

---

culture of a minority, and in other cases (such as *Ilmari Länsman* et al *v. Finland*, Communication No. 511/1992, UN Doc. CCPR/C/52/D/511/1992 [hereinafter *Ilmari Länsman* et al *v. Finland*]) has held that land and land use are important aspects of culture and way of life and should thus be protected.

[122] General Comment 23(50), *supra* note 108, para. 6.1. No example of such positive measures against private persons exists.

[123] Id., paras. 6.1 and 6.2.

[124] Id., para. 6.2. The reference to minority identity has been interpreted as an acknowledgment of the collective dimension of Article 27 by the HRC. *See* General Comment 23(50), *supra* note 108, para. 5.1 This issue is further discussed in chapter 4.

[125] F. Capotorti, *Study on the Rights of Persons belonging to Ethnic, Religious and Linguistic Minorities,* UN Doc. E/CN.4/Sub.2/384/Rev. 1, 1979, at 37.

[126] *Concluding Observations on France, supra* note 98, para. 12. In its concluding observations on Bosnia and Herzegovina, the HRC pointed out the importance of having detailed information on the measures implemented to give effect to the linguistic and educational rights of the Roma, thus underlining the need to adopt measures of support, protection and promotion of minority cultures and languages and, by extension, identities. *See* U.N. Human Rights Committee, *Concluding Observations of the Human Rights Committee:*

In *Sandra Lovelace v. Canada*,[127] the HRC showed that it attaches great importance to cultural identity and its value for the protection of minorities and had the difficult task of balancing the interests of the individual against those of the minority group. It observed that not every limitation to rights in Article 27 would cause its violation because states have a certain margin of discretion regarding its application.[128] Indeed, limitations to the rights protected by Article 27 are permissible when reasonable and objectively justifiable and consistent with the rest of the ICCPR,[129] especially when they are intended to protect the identity of the group.[130]

The HRC has commented that:

> *With regard to the exercise of the cultural rights protected under Article 27,* [...] *culture manifests itself in many forms, including a particular way of life associated with the use of land resources, especially in the case of indigenous peoples. That right may include such traditional activities as fishing or hunting and the right to live in reserves protected by law.* [...][131]

Similarly, in *Kitok v. Sweden*,[132] the Committee held that the economic activity of an ethnic minority is an essential element of its culture and should thus be protected under Article 27. Furthermore, limitations to Article 27 are objectively justifiable and necessary for the continued viability and welfare of the minority as a whole.[133] The collective component

---

Bosnia and Herzegovina, CCPR/C/BIH/CO/1, 22 November 2006, para. 24. Similar views were expressed on Hungary and on Slovakia. *See* U. N. Human Rights Committee, *Concluding Observations of the Human Rights Committee: Hungary*, CCPR/CO/74/HUN, 25 September 2002, para. 7, and *Concluding Observations on Slovakia, supra* note 116, para. 19.

127 *Sandra Lovelace v. Canada*, Communication n. R.6/24 (29 December 1977), U. N. Doc. Sup. N. 40 (A/36/40) at 166 (1981) [hereinafter *Lovelace v. Canada*].

128 Id., para. 15. In this sense, *see also Ilmari Länsman* et al *v. Finland, supra* note 121, para. 7.13.

129 *Lovelace v. Canada, supra* note 127, para. 16. The criterion of "reasonable and objective justification" corresponds to that of "necessary in a democratic society" used by the ECtHR and is acceptable and correct, and this vague standard allows for the specific circumstances of the case to be taken into account. *See* Henrard, *supra* note 10, at 176 and 184.

130 In this sense, *see also* Henrard, *supra* note 10, at 177. Interestingly, the justification of the Canadian government for its legislation was, at least in part, the need to protect the identity of the group.

131 General Comment 23(50), *supra* note 108, para. 7. In other words, the HRC has adopted a broad concept of culture, according to which economic activities also fall within the field of application of the Article, as long as they concern an essential component of a traditional culture. That residence on a reserve is important for the experience of culture and as such falls under the term "enjoyment of culture" was also reiterated in *Lovelace v. Canada*.

132 *Ivan Kitok v. Sweden*, Communication No. 197/1985, CCPR/C/33/D/197/1985 (1988) [hereinafter *Kitok v. Sweden*].

133 Id., para. 9.8.

of Article 27 is, in this case, recognised in a more persuasive manner than in *Lovelace v. Canada*.[134] Indeed, although the guiding criterion to decide this case was the ratio decidendi of *Lovelace v. Canada*, in *Kitok v. Sweden* more emphasis was placed on the group dimension and on the interests of the minority.[135]

In *Ilmari Länsman* et al *v. Finland*, the HRC held that for a minority, it is essential to practise traditional activities as a way to preserve its culture and identity. It reiterated that economic activities can fall within the field of application of Article 27, as long as they represent essential elements of the culture of an ethnic community.[136] It also made an important remark which clarified and assured that the rights in Article 27 would neither entail that the development of a minority culture be halted nor lead to the artificial preservation of completely outdated cultures, traditions and ways of life:[137] in other words, according to the HRC culture is not static and adaptation of traditional activities to modern techniques does not mean that such activities would not fall under the term "culture." Furthermore, it found that *"measures that have a certain limited impact on the way of life of persons belonging to a minority will not necessarily amount to a denial of the right under Article 27."*[138]

The jurisprudence of the HRC also helped clarify the scope of Article 1 of the ICCPR, which grants peoples the right to self-determination and is often invoked by members of minorities. Issues under Article 1 and Article 27 often overlap. In *Apirana Mahuika*, the Committee held that *"the provisions of Article 1 may be relevant in the interpretation of other rights protected by the Covenant, in particular Article 27."*[139] However, the HRC feels that it has no competence under the individual complaints procedure to

[134] Henrard, *supra* note 10, at 179.

[135] In *Kitok*, it was the economic interest of the community that was taken into account.

[136] *Ilmari Länsman* et al *v. Finland*, *supra* note 121, para. 9.2.

[137] Id., para. 9.3. In his individual opinion on *Lubikon Lake Band*, Ando argued that *"the right to enjoy one's own culture should not be understood to imply that* [*a*] *traditional way of life must be preserved intact at all costs"* and concluded that *"outright refusal by a group* [...] *to change its traditional way of life may hamper the economic development of the society as a whole." See Lubicon Lake Band v. Canada*, Appendix I. The Committee's dynamic approach to culture was also confirmed in *Apirana Mahuika v. New Zealand. See Apirana Mahuika v. New Zealand*, *supra* note 120. Minority rights are not intended to freeze cultures and would not require that authentic forms from centuries ago are preserved or even resuscitated. *See* Henrard, *supra* note 10, at 182 and 232. Minority groups generally want *"to preserve their existence as a culturally distinct group – always adapting and transforming their culture, of course, but resisting the pressure to abandon entirely their group life and assimilate into the larger society." See* Kymlicka (1995), *supra* note 12, at 8.

[138] *Ilmari Länsman* et al *v. Finland*, *supra* note 121, para. 9.4.

[139] *Apirana Mahuika v. New Zealand*, *supra* note 120, paras. 9.3–10.

pronounce itself on Article 1 because this contains group rights: whenever an individual complaint is based on Article 1, it is considered inadmissible.[140] Indeed, in *Lubicon Lake Band v. Canada*, the HRC stated that under the Optional Protocol, it would accept claims by individuals or group of individuals for alleged violations of rights contained in Article 6 to 27.[141]

The analysis of the jurisprudence, the General Comment 23(50) and concluding observations of the HRC show that the ICCPR has proved to be a useful instrument for minorities, in particular because it specifically recognises the right to enjoy culture in community with other members of the group, a right which is quite similar to a right to cultural identity (and the understanding of culture is quite broad), rather than only having a more general prohibition of discrimination. Furthermore, the Committee also has the function of an adjudicating body and has proved willing to protect the cultural identity of minorities, especially in those cases in which this might be in jeopardy.

In addition, the HRC has determined that Article 27 implies that states have positive obligations toward minorities, thus widening the scope of obligations under it. It would be better to have even clearer provisions for minorities rather than having the Committee interpret Article 27 on a case by case basis[142] but, considering the reluctance of states to accept potentially far-reaching obligations regarding minority protection, the prospects for such a document are not promising, and even less so for a legally binding one.[143]

3.5. The European Convention on Human Rights and the Framework Convention for The Protection of National Minorities

The various cases taken to the ECtHR reveal that for a long time, the Court has preferred to avoid issues of indirect discrimination – a trend that is now changing[144] – which is, however, potentially more harmful than direct

---

140 General Comment 23(50), *supra* note 108, para. 3.1. In *Kitok v. Sweden*, it was stated that *"the author, as an individual, could not claim to be the victim of a violation of the right of self-determination enshrined in Article 1"* because this *"deals with rights conferred upon peoples, as such." See Kitok v. Sweden, supra* note 132, para. 6.3.

141 *Lubicon Lake Band v. Canada*, *supra* note 121, para. 32.1.

142 Henrard, *supra* note 10, at 184.

143 Id.

144 *See*, for example, the *Case of D. H. and Others v. the Czech Republic* (Grand Chamber) Eur. Ct. Hum. Rts., Application number 57325/00, 13 November 2007 [hereinafter *D. H. and Others v. the Czech Republic* (Grand Chamber)].

discrimination for members of minorities.[145] ECtHR's weak equality jurisprudence was due to the limitations of ECHR, judicial procedure, and a formal conception of equality. As previously stated, Article 14 of ECHR only applies in respect to the enjoyment of Convention rights: *"The enjoyment of the rights and freedoms set forth in this Convention shall be secured without discrimination on any ground* [...]." With respect to complaints, only alleged victims can lodge them, and they must first exhaust domestic remedies in the member state. Furthermore, as an evidentiary matter, the ECtHR has been reluctant to draw inferences of discrimination from statistics.[146] By far, the most limiting factor, however, was the ECtHR's *formal* notion of discrimination, which focused on direct discrimination. As O'Connell pointed out, the Court has had difficulty with cases involving covert discrimination or disparate impact discrimination (indirect discrimination).[147] Furthermore, when a violation of an Article of the Convention is established, the Court generally finds it unnecessary to determine whether there has also been a violation of that Article in conjunction with Article 14. So, in *Airey v. Ireland*, the Court held that an examination of whether Article 14 had been violated "[...] *is not generally required when the Court finds a violation of* [*other Articles*] *taken alone.*"[148] In *Dudgeon v. United Kingdom*, the Court, having found a violation of Article 8, thought that there was *"no useful legal purpose to be served in determining whether* [*the applicant*] *has in addition suffered discrimination.*"[149] If the differential treatment was an essential aspect of the case and the Court decided to ignore it, there would be the risk to not sanction certain forms of discrimination against members of minorities as such, which, in turn, would mean losing the chance to create a better system for minority protection under the ECHR.[150]

The interpretation of Article 14 has been restrictive even in cases which concerned deprivation of life or inhuman or degrading treatment. In *Velikova v. Bulgaria*[151] and *Anguelova v. Bulgaria*,[152] the Court could not

---

145 Henrard, *supra* note 10, at 143.

146 R. O'Connell, 'Substantive Equality in the European Court of Human Rights?', 107 *Mich. L. Rev. First Impressions* 129 (2009).

147 Id.

148 *Case of Airey v. Ireland*, Eur. Ct. H. R., 9 October 1979, Series A n. 32, para. 30 [hereinafter *Airey v. Ireland*].

149 *Case of Dudgeon v. United Kingdom*, Eur. Ct. Hum. Rts, 22 October 1982, Series A No. 45, para. 69.

150 Henrard, *supra* note 10, at 78.

151 *Case of Velikova v. Bulgaria*, Eur. Ct. Hum. Rts, Application number 41488/98, 18 May 2000.

152 *Case of Anguelova v. Bulgaria*, Eur. Ct. Hum. Rts, Application number 38361/97, 13 June 2002 [hereinafter *Anguelova v. Bulgaria*].

establish a violation of Article 14 as proof of racial discrimination 'beyond all reasonable doubt,' and thus decided that the breach of Article 2 *might* only have occurred in conjunction with a breach of Article 14.[153] Following criticism of *Anguelova*, in *Nachova and others v. Bulgaria*,[154] the Court shifted the burden of proof onto the state, thus imposing a positive obligation to investigate every arguable claim of a violation of Article 14 without requiring the applicant to provide proof of discriminatory intent.[155]

The Court has often been restrictive in the assessment of claims put forward by members of minorities[156] and has not been keen to use the clause of Article 14 "association with a national minority." However, this trend has recently changed and in the last few years, the Court started adopting a more substantive concept of equality. For example, in *D. H. and others v. Czech Republic*, the Grand Chamber[157] found that as a result of their history and situation, the Roma had become a specific type of disadvantaged and vulnerable minority which required special protection, and even more so in the sphere of education. The position of the Grand Chamber in *D. H. v. Czech Republic* shows that the capacity of the Court and of the ECHR to protect minority rights has strenghtened considerably. The rights with a special connection to identity features, which help to distinguish minorities from the rest of the population, such as language, religion, education and rights of political participation have traditionally been interpreted narrowly,[158] and the Court has generally accepted that

---

[153] In his dissenting opinion, Judge Bonello suggested that ample evidence existed of Bulgarian police hostility toward the Roma in this case and in previous ones. He observed that *"frequently and regularly the Court acknowledges that members of vulnerable minorities are deprived of life or subjected to appalling treatment* [...]*; but not once has the Court found that this happens to be linked to their ethnicity. Kurds, coloureds, Muslims, Roma and others are again and again killed, tortured or maimed, but the Court is not persuaded that their race, colour, nationality or place of origin has anything to do with it."* In addition, the burden of proving discrimination in relation to the particular Convention right was too onerous, and *"*[...] *when a member of a disadvantaged minority group suffers harm in an environment where racial tensions are high and impunity of State offenders epidemic, the burden to prove that the event was not ethnically induced shifts to the government." Anguelova v. Bulgaria, supra* note 152 above, Dissenting Opinion of Judge Bonello, paras. 2–3 and 18.

[154] *Case of Nachova and others v. Bulgaria*, Eur. Ct. Hum. Rts, Application number 43577/98 and 00043579/98, 26 February 2004.

[155] O'Nions, *supra* note 1, at 79. Pleşe, commenting on *Nachova*, concluded that *"the Court has now lived up to its own mandate to provide a remedy to those in greatest need and assert its authority as a defender of the disadvantaged and vulnerable." See* B. Pleşe, 'Strasbourg Court finally redresses racial discrimination,' 1 *Roma Rights Quarterly* 109 (2004), available at http://www.errc.org/cikk.php?cikk=1851, last visited Mar. 20, 2012.

[156] Henrard, (2007), *supra* note 37, at 100.

[157] *D. H. and Others v. the Czech Republic* (Grand Chamber), *supra* note 146.

[158] Henrard, *supra* note 10, at 144.

states have a wide margin of appreciation in such matters. However, the Court has recently shown a clear trend toward recognising the centrality of identity to the person and private life and toward restricting the state's margin of appreciation in cases in which identity is at stake, such as *Goodwin v. the United Kingdom*.[159]

Indirect protection by the ECHR for members of minorities has clearly proven to be inappropriate: the jurisprudence of the Court and the Commission has demonstrated that an additional protection is needed for vulnerable groups such as minorities that goes above and beyond individual rights.[160] The reluctance of the Court to act in favour of the preservation of minorities' identity is even more regrettable in view of the importance of a democratic society in the ECHR framework, because such a society is characterized by pluralism, tolerance and broadmindedness.[161]

The lack of a specific minority provision aimed at protecting minorities' identities in the ECHR means a partial and indirect protection for members of minorities as such, available only through the channel of non-discrimination provisions and only for the rights enshrined in the ECHR, or through the protection of the right to respect for private and family life.[162] Additionally, the Court has been reluctant to establish a clear link between the individual and the collectivity, and thus – as will be seen further in this section – has generally remained silent on the vindication of rights, such as the enjoyment of the traditional way of life and consequently the protection of identity, which most closely affects minority groups such as the Roma.[163] This suggests that minorities can only receive partial protection through the ECHR because, as has already been seen, in

[159] *Case of Christine Goodwin v. the United Kingdom,* Eur. Ct. Hum. Rts., Application number 28957/95, 11 July 2002 [hereafter *Goodwin v. the United Kingdom*].

[160] Fenet, A., 'Europe et les Minorités' in Fenet, A. et al (eds.), *Le Droit et les Minorités. Analyses et Textes* (Bruxelles: Bruylant, 1995), pp. 83–195, at 97, as cited in Henrard, *supra* note 10, at 142.

[161] The hope is that with the renewed attention for minority issues and rights as exemplified by the adoption of the FCNM, there might be some changes in favour of a better protection of the identity of minorities. *See* Henrard, *supra* note 10, at 143. In view of this, the adoption of the EChRML is welcomed as an example of an "instrumental" response to the failures of the ECHR and ECtHR in safeguarding language rights. *See* M. Malik, 'Communal Goods as Human Rights,' in C. Gearty and A. Tomkins (eds.), *Understanding Human Rights* (London: Mansell, 1996), pp. 138–169, at 165.

[162] As will be seen in the following, Article 8 offers the chance to better protect aspects of a particular lifestyle or cultural identity.

[163] *See*, for example, the cases of *Buckley v. the United Kingdom* ((1997) 23 EHRR 101) (decided on 25 September 1996) [hereinafter *Buckley v. the United Kingdom*, Eur. Ct. Hum.

my view, full protection of minorities can only be achieved through the protection of a separate minority identity.

The group dimension of an individual complaint is too often not taken into account by the Court, despite the crucial importance for cases concerning members of minorities.[164] A dissenting judge in *D. H.* noted that the Court dealt with one specific issue in the Czech Republic but failed to address the more serious problem of many more Roma children in Europe who would not receive any formal education. The decision of the Court would do nothing to assist these young Roma. The inevitable consequence of an individualist approach is the absence of a proper enquiry into the particular situation of the group in society. For example, a strict legalistic approach might allow a state to escape wider criticism for failing to address the root causes of discrimination in society.[165] This has clearly been the case in *Buckley*, in which the ECtHR was unwilling to examine the situation of the Roma minority in the United Kingdom outside the strict boundaries of the case.[166] Such a narrow legal reasoning can lead to great injustice and for this reason, the use of other mechanisms, such as the state reporting system are important to hold members accountable.[167]

Conversely, the fact that a community might have standing in front of the ECtHR[168] opens up various possibilities for protecting minority groups, although no explicit minority rights provision is present in the Convention: the ECHR is a human rights instrument, but because groups can claim to be victims, discrimination in the enjoyment of the rights as between the minority group and the majority, or even as between different minorities,

---

Rts.], *Chapman v. the United Kingdom* ((2001) 33 EHRR 18) [hereinafter *Chapman v. the United Kingdom*], *Beard v. the United Kingdom* ((2001)33 EHRR 19) [hereinafter *Beard v. the United Kingdom*], *Coster v. the United Kingdom* ((2001) 33 EHRR 20), *Lee v. the United Kingdom* ((2001) 33 EHRR 29) and *Jane Smith v. the United* ((2001) 33 EHRR 30) (all decided on 18 January 2001), in which a violation of Article 8 of the ECHR (right to enjoy private and family life) was complained in connection with Article 14. Conversely, the former Commission has seemed willing to find Article 8 as including a guarantee for a minority group to live according to its lifestyle. In this sense, *see G. and E. v. Norway* (Eur. Comm. Hum. Rts., DR 9278 & 9415/81, 35 DR 30, at 35–36 (1983) [hereinafter *G and E v. Norway*]) and, similarly, *Buckley v. United Kingdom* ((1995) 19 EHRR CD20) [hereinafter *Buckley v. the United Kingdom*, Eur. Comm. Hum. Rts.]. All these cases will be further analysed in the course of this chapter.

164 Henrard, *supra* note 10, at 144.

165 O'Nions, *supra* note 1, at 95.

166 The case of *Buckley* will be further reviewed in the course of this chapter.

167 O'Nions, *supra* note 1, at 95.

168 *See infra*.

might give rise to a violation by the state, which is justiciable before the Court.[169]

The Court's jurisprudence can cause changes within the state to protect minority interests.[170] For example, the Greek government presented proof of having responded positively to the judgement of *Sidiropoulos and others v. Greece*.[171] Such responses from Greece show the value of pleading minority issues before the Court, as well as when the government acknowledges its obligation to abide by the decision in the individual case and to take steps to rectify a situation of breach and prevent future violations.[172] However, as has already been seen, the Court does not always look into patterns of discrimination against members of minorities, and its rulings are not always in favour of members of minorities when it finds that violations of their rights have been due to discrimination; when they are in minorities favour, this does not necessarily cause the adoption of policies that favour the recognition and protection of minorities' identities but most of the time, just the eradication of the specific situation causing discrimination. In addition, it should be pointed out that the Court will only express its views on cases that are referred to it, meaning that it has to wait for a complaint before actually determining whether a specific situation is the cause of discrimination. In areas in which individuals have little access to the justice system, the Court might never be able to evaluate a situation and demand that a state changes its policies and laws.

The following sub-sections aim at assessing and evaluating the extent to which the rights and freedoms protected by the ECHR, as interpreted by the Court and the Commission, contribute to the protection of minorities' identities, despite the fact that most cases brought before the Court involve claims by individuals rather than groups. An analysis of the Articles – and relevant jurisprudence – of the ECHR which protect rights that might contribute to the preservation of a separate identity of ethnic minorities will be provided. It will thus be assessed how the various Articles of the ECHR, without having an explicit reference to identity and despite clearly focusing on the individual, can contribute to the protection of minorities' identities, depending on the interpretation given by ECtHR through its jurisprudence. It will also be considered whether the ECHR, with its clear focus on individual rights, is a valuable instrument in

[169] Gilbert (2002), *supra* note 4, at 740.
[170] Id., at 754.
[171] *Case of Sidiropoulos and others v. Greece*, Eur. Comm. Hum. Rts., Report of 11 April 1997 [hereinafter *Sidiropoulos and others v. Greece*].
[172] Gilbert (2002), *supra* note 4, at 755.

protecting minorities and their identity. The Articles that have a clear impact on the extent to which members of minorities can preserve their identity are: Article 10, on freedom of expression; Article 11, on freedom of assembly and association; Article 9, on freedom of religion; Article 3 of Protocol 1 on the right to free elections; Article 2 of Protocol 1, on the right to education; Article 8, on the right to privacy, respect of family life, home and correspondence, which can be important for the protection of the ways of life, culture and identity of minorities. At the end of each section, a brief overview of the standards set by the FCNM will also be provided.

3.5.1. *The Right to Freedom of Expression*

Exposure of different groups to the languages, cultures and concerns of others and increased coverage reflecting the cultures and concerns of persons belonging to minorities in the media is an important instrument for the promotion of tolerance, intercultural understanding and peaceful coexistence,[173] as well as for the promotion and protection of minorities' cultural identities. Minorities often seek such coverage in the hope that this will lead to more balanced and non-prejudicial reporting: increased participation of persons belonging to minorities in the media can lead to a better understanding of cultural diversity.[174]

The right to freedom of expression, protected by Article 10 of the ECHR, is linked to pluralism, democracy and tolerance and incorporates the expression of differences and ideas, even those that shock or disturb;[175] it is essential for the respect of other fundamental rights and freedoms. In *United Communist Party v. Turkey*, the Court stated that it:

> *considers one of the principal characteristics of democracy to be the possibility it offers of resolving a country's problems through dialogue, without recourse to violence, even when they are irksome. Democracy thrives on freedom of expression.*[176]

---

[173] J. Packer and S. Holt, 'Article 9,' in M. Weller (ed.) *The Rights of Minorities in Europe* (Oxford: Oxford University Press, 2005), pp. 263–300, at 296 [hereinafter Packer and Holt].

[174] Id., at 296–297.

[175] *Case of Handyside v. the United Kingdom,* Eur. Ct. Hum. Rts., Application number 5493/72, (Series A No 24), 7 December 1976, para. 49 [hereinafter *Handyside v. the United Kingdom*].

[176] *Case of United Communist Party* (*TBKP*), Eur. Comm. Hum. Rts., Application number 19392/92, 28 October 1996. [hereinafter *United Communist Party and Others v. Turkey*] The case to the Court is the *Case of United Communist Party and Others v. Turkey*, Eur. Ct. Hum. Rts., Application number 133/1996/752/951, 30 January 1998, para. 57.

Limitations to the right to freedom of expression exist, which are imposed for a number of reasons, including the protection of national security, territorial integrity or public safety and the protection of the reputation or the rights of others. The Court and the former Commission underlined that freedom of expression is a "super-freedom,"[177] and limitations to it should be strictly supervised.[178] Freedom of expression also includes the right to pluralistic information, which entails positive obligations:[179] a state would be obliged to actively intervene in relations between media so as to counter too strong media concentrations[180] because that could limit the right to pluralistic information.

The recognition of the importance of pluralism for a democratic society entails a potential, although indirect, protection for members of minorities[181] because it implies the right of members of minorities to communicate in their language and to disseminate opinions through the media;[182] it enables minorities to express their divergent ideas and convictions, something considered *"essential for safeguarding the cultural identity of minorities."*[183] Furthermore, freedom of expression protects minorities against too hurtful statements pertaining to aspects of their own, separate identity.[184] Regulations on media ownership designed to further pluralistic societies by accommodating its population diversity have positive effects for members of minorities because they allow them to establish

---

177 Henrard, *supra* note 10, at 90.

178 *See*, among others, *Handyside v. the United Kingdom, supra* note 175.

179 G. Cohen-Jonathan, 'Article 10,' in L.E. Pettiti et. al. (eds.), *La Convention Européenne des Droits de l'Homme. Commentaire Article par Article* (Paris: Economica, 1995), pp. 365–408, at 367–368.

180 Id., at 373.

181 Henrard, *supra* note 10. *See*, for example, the *Case of Özgür Gündem v. Turkey,* Eur. Ct. Hum. Rts., Application number 23144/93, 16 March 2000, the *Case of Erdogu v. Turkey*, Eur. Ct. Hum. Rts., Application number 25723/94, 15 June 2000 and the *Case of Sener v. Turkey*, Eur. Ct. Hum. Rts., Application number 26680/95, 18 July 2000, which all concern the existence and acceptance of a minority through acknowledgement in newspapers and political parties – and only indirectly the protection of the cultural identity of minorities.

182 *Case of Informationsverein Lentia and others v. Austria*, Eur. Ct. Hum. RtS., Series A n. 276, 24 November 1993 [hereafter *Informationsverein Lentia and others v. Austria*].

183 F. Benoit-Rohmer, *The Minority Question in Europe: Towards a Coherent System of Protection for National Minorities* (Strasbourg: Council of Europe, 1996), at 46.

184 Henrard, *supra* note 10, at 90. *See also* the *Case of Otto Preminger Institute v. Austria*, Eur. Ct. Hum. Rts., Series A no 295-A, 20 September 1994, and the *Case of Murphy v. Ireland*, Eur. Ct. Hum. Rts, Application number 44179/98, 3 December 2003. In *Wingrove v. the United Kingdom*, it was reiterated that freedom of expression also implies the obligation to avoid as much as possible statements that are offensive to the profound convictions of others. *See* the *Case of Wingrove v. the United Kingdom*, Eur. Ct. Hum. Rts., 25 November 1996, para. 52.

radio and television stations, although they do not imply an obligation for the state to contribute financially; however, after authorities decide to subsidize or support persons or institutions imparting information, they have to do so without discrimination.

Despite finding a violation of Article 10 due to the state monopoly of radio and television channels,[185] in *Informationsverein Lentia and others v. Austria*, the Commission did not find that the system discriminated against any particular minority and the Court did not find it necessary to consider Article 14. Had the Court considered the alleged violation of Article 14, this would have offered the opportunity to use the principle of non-discrimination in favour of minorities.[186] An obligation to regulate in a pluralistic way is not necessarily sufficient to convince states that the separate culture, language and religion of minorities should enjoy appropriate coverage in the media, regardless of the fact that they might be privately supporting this initiative.[187] In other words, states should have a positive obligation to guarantee minorities the possibility of having access to the media to express their views and support their identity.

The balancing act between freedom of expression and its limitations seems to be a difficult one when the Court has to keep in mind the particular needs of minorities in terms of preserving and promoting their identity. In *Otto Preminger Institute v. Austria*, the Court acknowledged that religion may be crucial to the identity of minorities and argued that amongst the duties and responsibilities connected to freedom of expression, an obligation exists to avoid expressions that are offensive to others and that do not contribute to public debate.[188] This position of the Court implies a measure of minority protection – especially when looking at the importance of religion for members of religious minorities.[189]

As was already stated, freedom of expression is important for members of minorities who wish to express their opinion on policies adopted by the state. In *Ibrahim Aksoy v. Turkey*,[190] the Court emphasised the value of freedom of the press and of the right of the public to have access to different opinions, not just to those generally accepted. Furthermore, the Court also underlined the importance of political parties and their programmes

---

185 *Informationsverein Lentia and others v. Austria, supra* note 182, paras. 43 and 39.

186 Henrard, *supra* note 10, at 94.

187 Id.

188 *Informationsverein Lentia and others v. Austria, supra* note 182, para. 49.

189 Henrard, *supra* note 10, at 96.

190 *Case of Ibrahim Aksoy v. Turkey*, Eur. Ct. Hum. Rts., Application number 28635/95, 10 October 2000.

in a democratic society, even if these call for a change of the organisation of the state – as long as they do not damage the democracy itself. In *Incal v. Turkey*,[191] the Court was prepared to protect the freedom of expression of members of minorities and to place the facts presented into the context of the country – that of terrorism; it rejected the idea that the perceived danger of terrorism was a reason to limit freedom of expression.

It cannot be deduced from the Turkish cases that the Court might be more accommodating toward identity-related claims of members of minorities, but the enhanced protection of the political freedom of member of minorities does provide the necessary foundation for the pursuit of further claims which are also identity related.[192] The Turkish cases show that deference of the Court and the Commission in front of institutional structures would not go as far as allowing state fears to erode human rights of members of minorities or other population groups.[193]

3.5.1.A. *Freedom of Expression in the Framework Convention for the Protection of National Minorities*

The FCNM is the only multilateral instrument which directly addresses the right of persons belonging to national minorities to establish media in their languages. The right to freedom of expression is protected by Articles 7 and 9: Article 7 refers to the protection of linguistic freedom – viewing language as a vehicle of communication; Article 9 further specifies other provisions of the FCNM on the importance of promoting conditions for the maintenance and development of identity and culture, tolerance and intercultural dialogue. Article 9 recognises that majoritarian attitudes and contexts often exist which constrain minority cultures, so that minorities are not able to freely express their views and promote their identity. Its challenge is to ensure the necessary space and facilities for the breadth of ideas, opinions and cultures existing in societies, including those of persons belonging to minorities, to be expressed and enjoyed freely. In this respect, the media has special importance as a vehicle of communication and as a carrier of culture;[194] it can contribute to pluralism by reflecting existing diversity and promoting tolerance and social attitudes of respect.[195] Article 9 requires parties to adopt measures to promote tolerance and permit cultural pluralism; it asks for the removal of obstacles to

---

[191] *Case of Incal v. Turkey*, Eur. Ct. Hum. Rts., Application number 41/1997/825/1031, 9 June 1998.

[192] Henrard, *supra* note 10, at 100.

[193] Id., at 144.

[194] Packer and Holt, *supra* note 173, at 264.

[195] Id.

the expression of members of minorities, also by facilitating their access to the media. It builds on Article 10 of the ECHR, but makes specific reference to information and ideas imparted in the minority language.

Article 9(3) contains both a positive and negative obligation for states, which are obliged not to hinder the creation and use of media by minority members, but rather must ensure that persons belonging to minorities have the possibility to create and use their own media. The Advisory Committee on the Framework Convention (ACFC) has confirmed the obligation of state parties to take active measures to support minority language media, including that of the creation of private media companies. In some instances, it has even stated that authorities should establish facilities to be run by the minority in question and should provide them with the training to do so. However, a shortage of financial resources exists, which prevents minorities – especially dispersed ones – from establishing private media.[196] Furthermore, positive action might be needed by states to ensure that minorities receive broadcasting from abroad in their language.[197] The ACFC has also paid much attention to the promotion of a spirit of tolerance and intercultural dialogue, with specific suggestions on how to achieve this goal and reconcile competing interests with international obligations.[198]

3.5.2. *The Right to Freedom of Assembly, Association and the Registration and Recognition of Minorities*

The rights to freedom of association and assembly are essential for the preservation of the identity of persons belonging to national minorities because they imply that they can unite and associate to express their interests and their identity. Minorities highly value the possibility of maintaining their identity. Failure to accommodate the special needs and interests of minorities has often led to calls for self-determination and secession, which leads states to fear that recognition of minorities might pose a threat to their sovereignty and territorial integrity. Thus, the issues of minority recognition and registration intersect with political considerations, in which some states, in an attempt to control independentist movements, refuse to accord recognition of minority status.[199]

---

196 Packer and Holt, *supra* note 173, at 279–281.

197 Id., at 269.

198 Id., at 299.

199 Z. Machnyikova, 'Article 7,' in M. Weller (ed.) *The Rights of Minorities in Europe* (Oxford: Oxford University Press, 2005), pp. 193–224, at 208 [hereafter Machnyikova, 'Article 7'].

Although individual rights sensu strictu, freedom of assembly and association can only be exercised in a group because they are geared toward people uniting and associating to express and protect their interests. The realisation of these rights is pivotal to the full realisation of individual rights such as freedom of expression and religion, as well as minority-based rights.[200] The major international[201] and regional instruments all contain proclamations of the right to peaceful assembly and association. Article 11 of the ECHR contains the basic right to freedom of association and assembly, on which restrictions can be imposed when they are prescribed by law, have a legitimate purpose and are necessary in a democratic society (paragraph 2). The necessity test requires a balance between the interests of the individual and those of the state in deciding whether the measures are proportionate to the legitimate aim pursued.[202]

Article 11 is indisputably important to members of minorities because it implicitly recognises – although in a limited way – a collective dimension. However, its application in the preservation and protection of minority identity has been limited. Indeed, the question has been raised whether minorities should be considered "associations," thus opening the spectre of collective rights for minorities, and the Court's jurisprudence toward the recognition of minorities as associations has not appeared realistic. The former Commission has been reluctant to allow for the idea of collective rights for minorities on the basis of Article 11.[203] I contend that although these rights are important for minority protection purposes because they protect the group dimension (a crucial aspect of minority issues), their contribution to the right to identity for minorities is not that extensive.[204]

In *Sidiropoulos and others v. Greece*,[205] the Court established a link between freedom of association and the protection and promotion of the cultural identity of minorities by finding that by not allowing the registration and association of the "Home of Macedonian Civilization," the Greek

---

[200] O'Nions, *supra* note 1, at 84.

[201] *See* the Universal Declaration on Human Rights (UDHR), Article 20 and ICCPR, Article 21.

[202] This test was first adopted by the Court in *Handyside v. the United Kingdom, supra* note 175.

[203] Henrard, *supra* note 10, at 83–84. *See also* Gilbert (1992), *supra* note 13, at 88.

[204] Id., at 84 *et seq.*

[205] *Sidiropoulos and others v. Greece, supra* note 171, para. 55 and *Case of Sidiropoulos and others v. Greece*, Eur. Ct. Hum. Rts., Application number 26695/95, 10 July 1998 [hereinafter *Sidiropoulos and others v. Greece* Eur. Ct. Hum. Rts.].

authorities would also stop the promotion of the culture of a region as well as that of a minority.[206]

In *United Communist Party (TBKP) v. Turkey*[207] and *Freedom and Democracy Party (ÖZDEP) v. Turkey*,[208] following the dissolution of the parties by the Turkish authorities, the Court recognised the importance for minorities to take part in the democratic process of a country (which is, as has already been seen, fundamental for the preservation of their identity and expression of their views).

The issues of registration and self-identification are connected with freedom of assembly and association, and indeed, one of the problems faced by minority groups within a state is registration.[209] Registration requirements are obviously important for religious minorities because states often use the registration process to deny the right to exercise freedom of religion to certain groups which do not belong to the mainstream religious denomination or have only a few members. Nothing prevents a state from requiring registration,[210] and, if this is the case, the refusal of registration does not prevent the organisation or group freely associating and having standing from bringing a case to the ECtHR, as has been proven by a number of cases.[211]

In *Gorzelik and others v. Poland*, the ECtHR, despite having pointed out that it was not its task to formulate a definition of national minority, underlined the importance of the right to freedom of association for minorities, especially when no legal procedure exists at the domestic level through which a national or other minority can seek recognition and registration, as an association is the only indirect way to obtain recognition.[212] This is obviously vital for all minorities which are not directly recognised by the state, especially because through association, they can pursue the preservation of their identity (through, for example, religion or language),

206 *Sidiropoulos and others v. Greece, supra* note 171, para. 41.

207 *United Communist Party and Others v. Turkey, supra* note 176.

208 *Case of Freedom and Democracy Party (ÖZDEP) v. Turkey*, Eur. Ct. Hum. Rts., Application number 23885/94, 8 December 1999.

209 Gilbert (2002), *supra* note 4, at 750.

210 Id.. Indeed, most countries adopt policies of official recognition of minorities, through which they establish the criteria for the recognition and are able to exclude certain groups – thus, also excluding them from a series of benefits to which they would otherwise be entitled. However, the HRC and the ACFC have pointed out that the existence of minorities in a country is a question of fact. *See*, for example, General Comment 23(50), *supra* note 108.

211 Id.

212 *Gorzelik and others v. Poland, supra* note 5, para. 62.

which is at the core of their existence. In this sense, the case of *Metropolitan Church of Bessarabia and Others v. Moldova* is emblematic in showing the connection between freedom of association, recognition, registration and minorities' identities. In this case, the Court held that the refusal of the authorities to recognise the Metropolitan Church of Bessarabia infringed the freedom of religion and association of the applicants[213] because it deprived the Church of legal personality, which in turn would stop it from bringing legal proceedings to protect its assets. Furthermore, the lack of authorisation made it impossible for the applicants to practice their religion.

Restrictions on the registration and association of parties and other institutions are only allowed for compelling reasons.[214] The fact that its' members are also members of a minority or are devoted to the protection and promotion of the minority identity and interests, are, obviously, not considered compelling reasons. On the contrary, minority representation is immediately protected by the relevant provisions – even in the case of minorities advocating self-determination or secession. Of course, this is not the case if the party concerned calls on the use of violence or on the imposition of a non-democratic system of governance.[215] The same considerations apply to associations which are not political parties: minority representative organizations have the right to form and exhibit minority culture and to work toward the enhancement of the status of the relevant group. Again, restrictions should be applied only when the association is dedicated to violence or to overthrow a democratic government.[216]

3.5.2.A. *Freedom of Assembly, Association and the Registration and Recognition of Minorities in the Framework Convention for the Protection of National Minorities*

The rights to freedom of assembly and association, as well as freedom of expression and religion, are protected by Article 7 of the FCNM. The fact that this Article contains a number of fundamental freedoms has resulted in states providing only very general information in their reports to the

[213] *Metropolitan Church of Bessarabia, supra* note 4, para. 2.

[214] *See* for example the cases *United Communist Party and Others v. Turkey, supra* note 176, para. 46; and *Sidiropoulos and others v. Greece*, Eur. Ct. Hum. Rts., *supra* note 205, para. 40.

[215] M. Weller, 'Effective Participation of Minorities in Public Life,' in M. Weller, (ed.), *Universal Minority Rights*, (Oxford: Oxford University Press, 2007), pp. 477–516, at 516 [hereafter Weller (2007)].

[216] Id.

ACFC, which conversely has not had a strong voice in giving comprehensive comments on the implementation of Article 7.[217] Only a few members have so far treated Article 7 as a substantive provision requiring a detailed review of domestic legislation and administrative practice.

On the contrary, the connection between the detailed standards of the ECHR and Article 7 provides a good basis for its interpretation. The content of the rights of the ECHR should serve as the focal point for states parties when identifying their obligations on the enjoyment of these freedoms by persons belonging to national minorities. Full implementation of Article 7 would thus require states to ensure justiciable rights in their domestic legal order with respect to the fundamental freedoms that Article 7 intends to protect.[218] Ensuring the freedoms included in Article 7 requires specific positive obligations: states parties must not only abstain from acts infringing on the enjoyment of the freedoms set forth in Article 7, but also have an obligation to stop third parties from engaging in such acts. In practice, parties should provide evidence of their best efforts to ensure that private parties acting within their jurisdiction do not prevent persons belonging to national minorities from enjoying these rights. The obligation, thus, goes well beyond simply combating discrimination: state parties must take the necessary measures to create an environment in which minorities can maintain and develop their distinct identities.[219]

The importance of Article 7 lies in the fact that the ECtHR rarely examines violations of Article 14 if it has established that another substantive right has been violated. The monitoring of the ACFC could thus contribute to the identification of practices that result in direct and indirect discrimination in the enjoyment of these freedoms by people belonging to national minorities.[220] Furthermore, Article 7 is interconnected with other principles of the FCNM: to maximise the benefit of the protection offered by Article 7 to persons belonging to national minorities, states parties should examine it in light of other principles of the FCNM to determine the extent of their obligations. In particular, they should take into account the requirement to promote the conditions necessary for persons belonging to national minorities to maintain and develop their culture and preserve the essential elements of their identity, as set out in Article 5(1).[221]

---

217 Machnyikova, 'Article 7,' *supra* note 199, at 222–223.
218 Id., at 222.
219 Id., at 224.
220 Id., at 223.
221 Id., at 224.

3.5.3. *The Right to Freedom of Thought, Conscience and Religion and the Religious Life of Minorities*

Religion and identity are closely intertwined: religious tradition is often the core of a minority's distinct identity and safeguarding its practice in community with other members of a minority is a vital means for preserving the minority's common consciousness[222] and identity. In a number of cases brought to the ECtHR by Jehovah's Witnesses against Greece, the Court established an interesting idea on the value of religious pluralism, including religion as a factor of individual identity, the limited margin of appreciation that states have in relation to religious affairs and non-discrimination in relation to religion.[223] As the jurisprudence of the Court and the Commission reveals, this right has a wide field of application because it is applicable to all of an individual's convictions, including political or moral ones. The case of *Cha'are Shalom ve Tsedek v. France*,[224] in which the Court found that ritual slaughtering constituted a rite and as such would fall under the protection of Article 9, shows the link between religious rituals and the identity of minorities. The collective dimension of this right[225] implies an additional protection for minorities.

In *Kokkinakis v. Greece*, the Court pointed out that freedom of religion is *"one of the most vital elements that go to make up the identity of believers and their conception of life"*[226] and thus, is a fundamental element to a person's cultural identity. Although it does not protect particular creeds or confessions from all forms of criticism[227] (unless it reaches a level that might cause danger to the freedom of religion), Article 9 should be regarded as guaranteeing religious tolerance, which implies an obligation to secure religious peace in a pluralistic society. Such positive obligations are especially important for members of minorities because they have the most to fear from religious intolerance.[228]

---

[222] Z. Machnyikova, 'Article 8,' in M. Weller (ed.) *The Rights of Minorities in Europe* (Oxford: Oxford University Press, 2005), pp. 225–261, at 229 [hereinafter Machnyikova, 'Article 8'].

[223] *See also* Donders, *supra* note 15, at 272.

[224] *Case of Cha'are Shalom ve Tsedek v. France*, Eur. Ct. Hum. Rts., Application number 27417/95, 27 June 2000.

[225] This is indeed a "community right" because one needs a like-minded community to exercise it effectively. *See* M. Nowak, *UN Convention on Civil and Political Rights: CCPR Commentary* (Strasbourg: N.P. Engel, Kehl, 1993), at 313.

[226] *Case of Kokkinakis v. Greece*, Eur. Ct. Hum. Rts., Application number 14307/88, 25 May 1993, para. 31.

[227] *Case of Church of Scientology & 128 of its members v. Sweden*, Eur. Comm. H. R., Application number 8282/78, 12 July 1980, D.R. 21, para. 109.

[228] Hernard, *supra* note 10, at 112.

One aspect of freedom of religion which is important for religious minorities and for the protection of the identities of minorities is the possibility for parents to educate and bring up their children in accordance with their religious, philosophical and moral convictions. In *Hoffman v. Austria*, the Commission observed that to consider that a minority will automatically be socially marginalized is in itself a denial of the principle of a pluralistic society.[229] The Court concluded that no disadvantages or advantages should be related to association with a particular religious community.[230] If the Court confirms this argument in the future, this will obviously have positive repercussions for members of minorities because one could deduce from such jurisprudence that a state with a pluralistic society can have certain positive obligations regarding minorities; if anything, the prevention of their marginalisation.[231]

Religious minorities normally aspire to live in accordance with customs which are based on their beliefs and traditions, representing their specific characteristics as a community. In view of this, the extent to which the manifestation of their faith is protected plays a fundamental role. The recognition of the collective aspect of the right to manifest religion and beliefs provides minority groups with the means of preserving their unique characteristics and way of life.[232] In *X. v. the United Kingdom*, the Commission held that the right to manifest religion in community with others is an essential part of the right to freedom of religion, and the alternatives "either alone or in community with others" should not be considered mutually exclusive or leave the authorities any choice in the protection guaranteed.[233] The Court further articulated the importance of the community dimension of Article 9 in *Hasan and Chaush v. Bulgaria*, in which it affirmed that participation in the life of a community is a manifestation of one's religion and thus falls within the ambit of application of Article 9 and that religious communities traditionally exist in the form of organised structures and abide by rules which are thought to have a divine origin.[234]

229 *Case of Hoffman v. Austria,* Eur. Comm. Hum. Rts., Report of 16 January 1992, Series A no 255-C, para. 68.

230 *Case of Hoffman v. Austria,* Eur. Ct. Hum. Rts., 23 June 1993, Series A no 255-C, para. 36.

231 Henrard, *supra* note 10, at 113–114.

232 Z. Machnyikova, 'Religious Rights,' in M. Weller (ed.) *Universal Minority Rights* (Oxford University Press: Oxford, 2007), pp. 179–202, at 189.

233 *Case of X. v. the United Kingdom,* Eur. Ct. Hum. Rts, Application number 8160/78, 12 March 1981, at 34.

234 *Case of Hasan and Chaush v. Bulgaria,* Eur. Ct. Hum. Rts., Application number 30985/96, 26 October 2000, para. 62.

In these cases, the ECtHR has formulated some key principles on the protection of cultural identity under Article 9. As was already stated, the Court considers religion an important aspect of the identity of a person, and sees freedom of religion as one of the fundaments of a democratic society. Therefore, the states' margin of appreciation with regard to freedom of religion is limited. Article 9 implies states' abstention and respect, because freedom of religion means that states have no discretion in determining whether a religion or its expressions are legitimate.[235] With regard to the positive state obligations that would stem from Article 9, these are aimed at enhancing the effectiveness of the rights concerned, an issue surely important for minorities.

The Court also values religious pluralism and has indeed stated that to remove possible tensions between groups, states should not eliminate pluralism by bringing the various groups under a single leadership, but should make sure that they tolerate each other.[236] In other words, different religious communities and sub-communities can exist next to each other and the state should interfere with their free development as little as possible. It seems that the Court values religious pluralism as a factor or consequence of freedom of religion, whereby it acknowledges a collective dimension.[237]

Religion is one aspect of cultural identity; therefore, these considerations are important for the protection of the cultural identity of a community.[238] Indeed, *"it is in the context of protecting minority rights that Article 9 may have its greater part to play."*[239] It is predicted that in the future, the Court will deal with more cases in which individuals and religious groups claim protection under Article 9 for non-traditional and/or non-western beliefs and practices and their manifestation. Many of these claims will also involve other Articles of the ECHR, such as Article 2 of Protocol 1, which protects the parents' right to ensure their children are educated according to their religious and philosophical convictions.[240]

---

[235] Donders, *supra* note 15, at 278.

[236] *Case of Serif v. Greece*, Eur. Ct. Hum. Rts., Application number 38178/97 14 December 1999, para. 53 and *Metropolitan Church of Bessarabia, supra* note 4, para. 116.

[237] Donders, *supra* note 15, at 278.

[238] Id.

[239] D.J. Harris, M. O'Boyle and C. Warbrick, *Law of the European Convention on Human Rights* (London: Buttersworth, 1995), at 370 [hereinafter *Law of the European Convention*].

[240] D. Gomien, D.J. Harris and L. Zwaak, L., *Law and Practice of the European Convention on Human Rights and the European Social Charter* (Strasbourg: Council of Europe, 1996), at 271. *See* for example the *Case of Hasan and Eylem Zengin v. Turkey,* Eur. Ct. Hum. Rts.,

3.5.3.A. *The Right to Freedom of Thought, Conscience and Religion in the Framework Convention for the Protection of National Minorities*

Freedom of thought, conscience and religion and the right to establish religious institutions are protected by Article 8 of the FCNM. The true value of this Article lies in the promotion of full and effective equality for persons belonging to national minorities in the enjoyment of their religious freedoms.[241] Through the monitoring mechanism of the FCNM and in particular the monitoring of the implementation of Article 8, it can be observed that state parties normally do secure the free and peaceful exercise of manifestation of religion. It has been highlighted that states parties have an obligation to pay attention to the situation of national minorities in their activities involving religious communities living in their territories and to ensure that persons belonging to national minorities are not subjected to discrimination in the enjoyment of this right. Parties should take effective measures to encourage mutual respect and understanding among different religious groups living on their territory. Minorities should be able to pursue their religious beliefs and customs, establish places of worship and religious institutions and organise their religious affairs, and they should be able to do so without being discriminated against (which requires positive and preventive steps) as well as on an equal footing with other people residing in the country. For this reason, as Machnyikova noted, the ACFC has often called for adjustments of the laws and administrative practices of various states to ensure that national minorities are treated on equal footing; for example, when the state provides support for religious communities or accommodates religious beliefs or practices in the public system.[242]

Article 8 *per se* does not contain an obligation to fund religious activities. However, if a country makes support available only to one religion – through direct funding from income tax or church tax – then particular attention must be paid to other religions so that persons belonging to national minorities have their rights under Article 8 guaranteed.[243]

Application number 1448/04, 9 October 2007, and the *Case of Folgerø and Others v. Norway*, Eur. Ct. Hum. Rts., Application number 15472/02, 29 June 2007.

[241] Machnyikova, 'Article 8,' *supra* note 222, at 260.

[242] Id.

[243] Council of Europe, Advisory Committee on the Framework Convention for the Protection of National Minorities, *Opinion on Finland*, ACFC/INF/OP/I(2001)002, 22 September 2000, para. 29.

3.5.4. *The Right to Effective Participation in Public Life*

In democratic states, public policy is determined by majority decision, and when the legal framework is thus determined by majority rule, this might have adverse effects for minorities[244] because they could face structural discrimination from the state. Minorities not only need to be able to preserve and promote their identity, culture and institutions, but also to participate in the political life of the state, in particular with respect to matters affecting their culture, identity and institutions.[245] One way of ensuring minorities full access to decision-making includes the facilitation of representatives' access to elected bodies at the local, regional and state level; for example, by relieving minority parties from the obligation to be registered throughout the state if they are only present in a particular area or by waiving minimum clauses for representation in parliament. Another way might be that of ensuring that persons belonging to minorities are fully represented in the executive.[246]

Exclusion from participation in the political processes of the state is contrary to the democratic principles that the CoE wishes to defend, as well as to those crystallised in the ECHR. Elections, as the ECtHR stated in *Mathieu-Mohin and Clerfayt v. Belgium*, are the *'basis for a democratic society.'*[247] Article 3 of Protocol 1 to the ECHR, which does not have a linguistic component so that certain restrictions to voting rights are legitimate according to the Court and the former Commission, [248] prescribes free elections at reasonable intervals by secret ballot. Jurisprudence from the Court and the Commission shows that states are free to provide a system of governance and that no specific election system is required so that a majority as well as a proportional representation system would be compatible with it.[249]

States are given a wide margin of discretion in regulating the right to vote and the right to run for elections – challenged when denied arbitrarily

---

244 Weller (2007), *supra* note 215, at 477.

245 Id., at 479.

246 Id.

247 *Case of Mathieu-Mohin and Clerfayt v. Belgium*, Eur. Ct. Hum. Rts, Application number 9267/81, 2 March 1987, para. 47.

248 Id., para. 52.

249 *See*, for example, *Mathieu-Mohin and Clerfayt v. Belgium*, para. 54. Although it would not be unfair to state that Article 3 of Protocol 1 is not violated by an election system that puts certain political parties at a disadvantage, it would be a different matter if every effective influence of minorities was systematically excluded. *See Law of the European Convention, supra* note 239, at 555.

and as such denying the free expression of the opinion of people.[250] People can thus express their opinion, including minorities who satisfy the (not unreasonable) conditions for the right to vote (but no special guarantees for members of minorities exist).[251] In any event, it is clear that minority identity, or the fact that the candidate stands for minority interests, cannot preclude the right to stand for elections. This applies even when the existence of the minority identity claimed by the candidate is denied by the state or when the candidate is committed to advancing the cause of the minority despite resistance by the state.[252]

In *Podkolzina v. Latvia*, the Court observed that states are free to establish the criteria for the status of members of parliament, including those for declaring someone ineligible. The criteria vary in accordance with historical and political factors specific to each state. Electoral legislation must thus be assessed in the light of the political evolution of a country, but the states' margin of appreciation "*is limited by the obligation to respect the fundamental principle of Article 3, namely "the free expression of the opinion of the people in the choice of the legislature."*[253] In *Aziz v. Cyprus*, the Court added that the existence of rules that take into account the historical and political factors of a country should not be such as to exclude certain people or groups of people from participating in the political life and, in particular, in the choice of the legislature, a right guaranteed by the ECHR and the Constitutions of all members.[254] In *Buscarini and Others v. San Marino*, it was observed that:

> [*it*] *would be contradictory to make the exercise of a mandate intended to represent different views of society within parliament subject to a prior declaration of commitment to a particular set of beliefs.*[255]

The Commission held in a number of cases that the condition to submit a minimum number of signatures for a candidature to be acceptable is a

---

250 Weller (2007), *supra* note 215, at 515.

251 Henrard, *supra* note 10, at 129.

252 Weller (2007), *supra* note 215, at 515–516.

253 *Case of Podkolzina v. Latvia*, Eur. Ct. Hum. Rts., Application number 46726/99, 9 April 2002, para. 33.

254 *Case of Aziz v. Cyprus*, Eur. Ct. Hum. Rts, Application number 69949/01, 22 June 2004, para. 28.

255 *Case of Buscarini and Others v. San Marino*, Eur. Ct. Hum. Rts., Application number 24645/94, 18 February 1999, para. 39. Contrary to *Buscarini*, the Court found *McGuinness v. the United Kingdom* inadmissible because the applicant was not required to affirm allegiance to any particular religion and would be able to retain his republican views and pursue them in parliament. *See* the *Case of McGuinnes v. the United Kingdom*, Eur. Ct. Hum. Rts., Application number 39511/98, 8 June 1999, admissibility decision.

legitimate method to verify whether the intentions are serious enough.[256] It is important to point out that obviously, such a requirement is harder to comply with by minorities, but, as acknowledged in *Lindsay and Others v. the United Kingdom*, an election system which takes the special situation of a minority into account would eventually make it easier for the "people" as a whole to express its opinion freely and for this reason, would be in conformity with the ECHR.[257] In other words, according to the Commission, to enhance the democratic participation of minority groups, states can "discriminate."

3.5.4.A. *Effective Participation in Public Life in the Framework Convention for the Protection of National Minorities*

According to Article 15 of the FCNM, members have to take a lot of measures to ensure full and effective participation of minorities in cultural, social and economic life and in public affairs, especially including – but not only – those affecting them. Because a great abundance of ECtHR jurisprudence does not exist on the topic, Article 15 of the FCNM has fostered a great deal of implementation practice.[258] States have generally reported seriously and extensively on their efforts to encourage effective participation, showing that they all regard effective participation of persons belonging to national minorities as an essential and mandatory component of a peaceful and democratic society.[259] The ACFC has stated that:

> [...] *different solutions can be applied to different national minorities as well as to different situations prevailing in the state parties. Measures taken in some state parties have been considered* [...] *as an adequate implementation* [...]. *Yet, it is important to recall that a measure that leads to effective participation in one State party does not necessarily have the same impact in another context. State parties therefore need to assess, in the light of their own domestic situation, the applicability and effectiveness of measures that have, elsewhere, resulted in increased participation of national minorities.*[260]

---

256 *See*, for example, the *Case of X, Y, Z v. FRG*, Eur. Comm. Hum. Rts., Application number 6850/74, 18 May 1976.

257 *Case of Lindsay and Others v. the United Kingdom*, 8 March 1979, D.R. 15 (247), at 251.

258 Weller (2007), *supra* note 215, at 514.

259 M. Weller, 'Article 15,' in M. Weller (ed.) *The Rights of Minorities in Europe* (Oxford: Oxford University Press, 2005), pp. 429–461, at 456 [hereinafter Weller, 'Article 15'].

260 Council of Europe, Advisory Committee on the Framework Convention for the Protection of National Minorities, *Commentary on the Effective Participation of Persons Belonging to National Minorities in Cultural, Social and Economic Life and in Public Affairs*, ACFC/31DOC(2008)001, 27 February 2008, para. 148 [hereinafter ACFC Commentary on Effective Participation].

It also added that measures which can be considered satisfactory in given circumstances and at a given moment of the monitoring process do not necessarily ensure compliance with the standards set by the FCNM in the future.[261] Finally, the ACFC observed that the situation of minorities and majorities is in constant evolution and new issues might arise, some of which in the field of participation in socio-economic life.[262]

It is now clear that state structures should not exclude persons belonging to national minorities from the democratic process. The ACFC has underlined the need of ensuring that the necessary structural guarantees exist so as to allow effective participation of persons belonging to national minorities in the political process.[263] With regard to parliamentary representation, the ACFC has gone beyond the insistence that governments only meet the targets that they have established themselves.[264] Bearing in mind the need for governments to avoid inequality to the detriment of majority populations, the ACFC has unambiguously underlined the need to facilitate access of persons belonging to national minorities to positions of power.[265] This may require special measures in terms of electoral systems design or procedures, at least when there are large numbers of persons belonging to national minorities – no formal requirement of proportionality exists, but states have to demonstrate that adequate representation exists in elected bodies.

One issue that the ACFC has not properly addressed yet is that of the quality of representation of persons belonging to national minorities. Although it is clear that governments have the obligation to establish mechanisms for effective participation, organisations wishing to represent minorities should also demonstrate their genuine representativeness and the transparency of their democratic and financial practices.[266] Furthermore, another issue that needs to be addressed is the exclusion of persons belonging to national minorities from positions in areas connected to justice and security, such as the police and the army.

---

261 ACFC Commentary on Effective Participation, *supra* note 260, para. 149.

262 Id., para. 150.

263 Council of Europe, Advisory Committee on the Framework Convention for the Protection of National Minorities, *Opinion on Albania*, ACFC/INF/OP/I(2003)004, 12 September 2002, para. 72.

264 *See*, for example, Council of Europe, Advisory Committee on the Framework Convention for the Protection of National Minorities, *Opinion on Hungary*, ACFC/INF/OP/I(2001)004, 22 September 2000.

265 Council of Europe, Advisory Committee on the Framework Convention for the Protection of National Minorities, *Opinion on Armenia*, ACFC/INF/OP/I(2003)001, 16 May 2002, para. 77.

266 Weller, 'Article 15,' *supra* note 259, at 458–459.

3.5.5. *The Right to Education*

Education is central in preserving a minority's language, cultural heritage and cultural identity.[267] The right to education, contained in Article 2 of Protocol 1 to the ECHR, includes elements of recognition for the minority group.[268]

> *Education underpins all other elements of culture since it provides for the culture's preservation and promotion horizontally and vertically: it informs other groups in society and passes on the culture to succeeding generations.*[269]

The fact that education has a central role with respect to minority culture is reflected in the inclusion of provisions on the right to education in all major standard setting international documents in this field.[270] The development of minorities' specific educational institutions is the best guarantee of maintaining distinct identities, and this right goes some way toward facilitating the expression of cultural and religious pluralism.[271]

The *Belgian Linguistics* case contains the first judgement of the ECtHR in relation to education and shows the link between this and language and thus with cultural identity. In this case, the Court held that Article 2 of Protocol 1 does not impose any positive obligations on states to establish or finance a particular type of education in a certain language,[272] and the contracting states would, in general, have no obligation to finance private educational institutions. Instead, individuals merely have a right to use the means of instruction existing at a given time.[273] The Court also added that the duty on states to respect the right of parents to ensure education and teaching in conformity with their religious and philosophical

---

[267] *See also* U.N. Committee on Economic, Social and Cultural Rights, *General Comment 21, Right of Everyone to Take Part in Cultural Life*, E/C.12/GC/21, 21 December 2009, para. 2, where the CESCR stated that *"The right of everyone to take part in cultural life is also intrinsically linked to the right to education (arts. 13 and 14), through which individuals and communities pass on their values, religion, customs, language and other cultural references, and which helps to foster an atmosphere of mutual understanding and respect for cultural values."*

[268] Gilbert (2002), *supra* note 4, at 761. *See also* Y. Dinstein, 'Cultural Rights' *Israel Yearbook on Human Rights* 58 (1970), at 68 [hereinafter Dinstein].

[269] G. Gilbert, 'The Cultural and Political Autonomy of Minorities,' *L'Observateur Des Nations Unies* 2007–2, Vol. 23, pp. 225–250, at 242 [hereinafter Gilbert (2007)].

[270] Id., at 242.

[271] P. Thornberry, 'Article 14,' in M. Weller (ed.) *The Rights of Minorities in Europe* (Oxford: Oxford University Press, 2005) pp. 393–406, at 404.

[272] *Belgian Linguistics*, *supra* note 59, para. 3 (The Law, B).

[273] Id., para. 31. The use of the wording "at a given time" might imply that the scope of Article 2 Protocol 1 may vary between states and may be subject to developments. *See* Donders, *supra* note 15, at 272.

convictions would not imply that states have an obligation to accommodate the linguistic preferences of the parents.[274] However, it also claimed that the right to education would be meaningless if it did not imply the right to receive education in the official language or of one of the official languages.[275] In this sense, it held that this provision might impose positive obligations to ensure the equal enjoyment of the right to education.

As seen, the ECHR does not recognise the right to mother tongue education. The Court reiterated this view in *Skender v. Former Yugoslav Republic of Macedonia*, in which it held that:

> [...] *a right to education in a particular language or a right to obtain from the state the creation of a particular kind of educational establishment cannot be derived from Article 2 of Protocol No. 1. This provision does not require of states that they should, in the sphere of education or teaching, respect parents' linguistic preferences, but only their religious and philosophical convictions.*[276]

The Commission[277] and the Court[278] were of a different opinion in *Cyprus v. Turkey*, in which they held that it might be a violation in certain circumstances to deny such education even at the secondary school level.[279]

Article 2 of Protocol 1 not only contains the right to education, but also provides that the state will respect the right of parents to ensure education for their children that is in conformity with their religious and philosophical convictions. The meaning of "religious and philosophical convictions" has been explained by the ECtHR in a number of cases, such as *Campbell and Cosans v. the United Kingdom*, in which it was held that:

---

274 Belgian Linguistics, *supra* note 59, para. 3, para. 32. The Commission had reached a different conclusion, as it contended that the Belgian regulation which was the object of the complaint had the goal to prevent the spread, if not the maintenance, in one region, of the language and culture of the other region as well as that of assimilating minorities against their will into the language of the surroundings. *See Belgian Linguistics*, Eur. Comm. Hum. Rts., Series A No. 6, at 48. Measures of assimilation of members of minorities are prohibited by international law and contradict the basic values of pluralism and tolerance inherent in a democratic society. For example, Article 27 of the ICCPR enshrines the right to identity for minorities and a prohibition of forced assimilation – it is still contested whether Article 27 is customary international law, but it should be pointed out that the ICCPR has been widely ratified. *See also* Henrard, *supra* note 10, at 121.

275 *Belgian Linguistics*, *supra* note 59, para. 32.

276 *Case of Skender v. Former Yugoslav Republic of Macedonia*, Eur. Ct. Hum. Rts., Application number 62059/00, 22 November 2001, at 9.

277 *Case of Cyprus v. Turkey*, Eur. Comm. Hum. Rts., Application number 24781/94, 4 June 1999, paras. 474–479.

278 *Cyprus v. Turkey*, Eur. Ct. Hum. Rts., *supra* note 64, para. 278.

279 However, this decision might be particularly related to the situation in Northern Cyprus. *See* Gilbert (2002), *supra* note 4, at 762.

> *"philosophical convictions" in the present context denotes, in the Court's opinion, such convictions as are worthy of respect in a "democratic society"* [...] *and are not incompatible with human dignity*[280]

Considering this broad interpretation, linguistic preferences could fall under the heading of "philosophical convictions:" the desire of parents to educate their children in their native language might correspond to a vision of life, and that language might entail a certain philosophy and thus reflect cultural identity.[281] Therefore, if the views of the Court in *Belgian Linguistics* and *Skender* were analysed in light of *Campbell and Cosans*, it could be argued that the desire of parents to have their children educated in their mother tongue should be accepted as a philosophical conviction.[282]

The question remains as to whether states have an obligation to support or finance education in a preferred language. In principle, states are obliged to respect the wishes of minorities to set up language education or education in a certain language by their own means, as long as this education complies with the general criteria of education.[283] The issue is more complex when it comes to positive obligations. Of course, a state cannot comply with all the individual preferences of parents, and these matters ought to be dealt with on a case-by-case basis, taking the circumstances into account.[284] It is suggested that the principle of non-discrimination of minority interests should be applied. In other words, minorities should be entitled to access the same facilities as the rest of the population; however, to achieve factual equality, they should receive support by the state. Furthermore, it goes without saying that, if a certain minority receives

---

[280] *Case of Campbell and Cosans v. the United Kingdom,* Eur. Ct. Hum. Rts., Application numbers 7511/76 and 00007743/76, 25 February 1982, para. 36.

[281] Donders, *supra* note 15, at 271.

[282] *See also* Henrard, *supra* note 10, at 120.

[283] The PCIJ in *Minority Schools in Albania* found that *"Albanian nationals belonging to racial, linguistic or religious minorities* [*have*] *the right to maintain, manage and control* at their own expense *or to establish in the future* [...], *schools and other educational establishments, with the right to use their own language* [...]*"* (emphasis added) *See Minority Schools in Albania, supra* note 19, at 22. According to Dinstein *"ethnic, religious and linguistic minorities have a special right* [...] *to establish schools. This right stems from their cardinal interest* [...] *to preserve their separate and independent cultural identity.* [...] *Private schools are indispensable to enable the minority to enjoy the same treatment as the majority, not only in law but also in fact. The abolition of these institutions, which alone can satisfy the special requirements of the minority groups, and their replacement by government institutions, would destroy this equality of treatment, for its effect would be to deprive the minority of the institutions appropriate to its needs, whereas the majority would continue to have them supplied in the institutions created by the state." See* Dinstein, *supra* note 268, at 68 and 72.

[284] Donders, *supra* note 15, at 272.

funds for education, according to the principle of non-discrimination, other comparable minorities should be treated in the same way.[285]

The cases of *D.H. v. Czech Republic*,[286] *Sampanis and Others v. Greece*[287] and *Orsus and Others v. Croatia*[288] represent a major breakthrough in the guarantee of the right to education and prohibition of discrimination. They challenged systemic racial segregation in education. In *D. H.* and in *Sampanis*, the Court found a violation of Article 14 of the ECHR in conjunction with Article 2 of Protocol 1,[289] and determined that the applicants had been assigned to special schools as a result of their Roma origin, following tests which were not designed specifically, but applied education policies and approaches that allegedly did not take into account the Roma ethnicity, language and cultural identity. This led to indirect discrimination. Both governments argued that the parents of the pupils had given consent to place their children in special classes, but the Court found that the right not to be subject to racial discrimination cannot be waved, and doubted that the consent of the parents was truly genuine. Indeed, the parents belonged to a disadvantaged community and no evidence existed that they were presented with detailed information about the options available or the effects of their choices. The absence of consent was even more evident in *Sampanis*, in which the consent to send children to a separate building was given under the pressure of demonstrations by a large number of local parents who opposed the attendance of Roma children in mainstream schools.

---

[285] Donders, *supra* note 15, at 272. In conformity with the principle of non-discrimination, if states subsidized the education of one group, they would be obliged to consider subsidizing others. *See* P. Thornberry, 'Article 13,' in M. Weller (ed.) *The Rights of Minorities in Europe* (Oxford: Oxford University Press, 2005), pp. 393–406, at 405. Consider also *Waldman v. Canada*, in which the HRC observed that although the ICCPR does not oblige states to fund schools established on a religious basis, if a state party decides to provide funding to religious schools, it should make this funding available without discrimination. *See Waldman v. Canada*, Communication number 694/1996, UN Doc A/55/40, CCPR/C/67/D/694/1996, para. 10(6).

[286] *D. H. and Others v. the Czech Republic* (Grand Chamber), *supra* note 144.

[287] *Case of Sampanis and Others v. Greece,* Eur. Ct. Hum. Rts., Application number 32526/05, 5 June 2008.

[288] *Case of Orsus and Others v. Croatia* (Grand Chamber), Eur. Ct. Hum. Rts., Application number 15766/03, 16 March 2010 [hereinafter *Orsus v. Croatia*].

[289] In *Orsus*, the Croatian government successfully justified discriminatory treatment. The ECtHR accepted that the applicant children had difficulties with the language and they were only attending preparatory classes, run in mainstream schools, and only until the point when they would be ready to be transferred to regular classes. *See Orsus v. Croatia, supra* note 288.

These cases show that if the state wishes to avoid violations of Article 14, it must consider the impact of policies and procedures on different groups, because although the intent might not be discriminatory, the result might be. States might have to adopt different policies that take into account the needs of different groups in the provision of goods such as education by, for example, allowing minorities to receive education in their language or to establish their own educational institution.[290]

3.5.5.A. *The Right to Education in the Framework Convention for the Protection of National Minorities*

Protection and promotion of culture and cultural autonomy for minority groups is better served by the FCNM because its concept of education and its role are more progressive.[291] Indeed, in its opinion on the second report of the Czech Republic, the ACFC stated that the ECtHR has a too narrow view of the proper response in a case of indirect discrimination and as such it is not an effective tool to protect and promote the culture of minority groups.[292]

The FCNM guarantees the right to education in its Articles 12, 13 and 14. The ACFC visualizes the rights encompassed in Article 12 as requiring sustained and consistent attention by state authorities, including attention to all manifestations of exclusion from and lack of access to schools.[293] With regard to access to school, the situation of the Roma is dire.

---

[290] These cases are also interesting from a procedural point of view because the Court showed a pragmatic attitude toward the requirement of the exhaustion of domestic remedies. So in *D. H.*, the Court stressed the need to take into account the circumstances of the applicant and the general context of the state. Thus, it demanded proof that domestic remedies were not only available, but also effective. In addition, a number of organisations represented the applicants in these cases, and the Court has proved willing to hear the non-governmental organisations (such as the European Roma Rights Centre, which has a history of litigating Roma cases) and their legal advisers. This flexibility meant that individual victims, who may otherwise lack the possibility of having appropriate legal advice and would thus be subject to more pressure, would have proper representation (not to mention the fact that in this way the Court might be able to hear about issues that go beyond the sole scope of the case). Finally, lacking resources to carry out its own fact finding missions, the Court also availed itself of the reports by a series of non-judicial institutions such as the European Commission Against Racism and Intolerance (ECRI).

[291] Gilbert (2007), *supra* note 262, at 243.

[292] Council of Europe, Advisory Committee on the Framework Convention for the Protection of National Minorities, *Second Opinion on the Czech Republic*, 24 February 2005, ACFC/INF/OP/II(2005)002.

[293] P. Thornberry, 'Article 12,' in M. Weller (ed.) Weller, M. (ed.) *The Rights of Minorities in Europe* (Oxford: Oxford University Press, 2005), pp. 365–393, at 392 [hereinafter Thornberry, 'Article 12'].

> *The lack of attention to Romani language and culture in educational processes leads to the situation where many Roma communities are deprived of the means to develop cultural self-confidence through cultural and linguistic self-knowledge, as well as of the basic skills and knowledge needed to succeed in the general society. The emergence of so-called special schools is a symptom of a wider failure to address Roma education.*[294]

Article 14 expressly requires members to have regard to the need to provide mother tongue education. With regard to separate education for children of minorities, the ACFC observed its appreciation of supportive pre-school classes if aimed at enabling the children to follow the regular curriculum, but, at the same time, indicated that a dangerous grey zone exists between segregating special classes and supportive/remedial classes. In its opinion on Sweden, the ACFC considered that even when initiatives such as placing children in special classes are designed as a form of support for the pupils,

> *specific classes devoted to one national minority as such (rather than [...] to the teaching in/of their language and of their culture) risk placing the children concerned at a disadvantage and harming the implementation of Article 12 and the principle of intercultural dialogue contained in Article 6 of the Framework Convention.*[295]

However, in its Commentary on Education under the FCNM, the ACFC suggested that occasionally a separate teaching, in whole or in part may be more appropriate, or even the only possible solution.[296]

3.5.6 *The Right to Respect for a Particular Lifestyle under Article 8 of the ECHR*

Together with Article 11 (in an expanded interpretation), Article 8 of the ECHR may entail the protection of a particular lifestyle or culture. The EComHR was willing to find that Article 8 includes a guarantee of protection for the lifestyle of a minority group.[297] In *G. and E. v. Norway*, the Commission considered that disrespect for a particular lifestyle of

---

[294] Thornberry, 'Article 12', *supra* note 293, at 392.

[295] Council of Europe, Advisory Committee on the Framework Convention for the Protection National Minorities, *Opinion on Sweden*, ACFC/INF/OP/I(2003)006, 25 August 2002, para. 53.

[296] Council of Europe, Advisory Committee on the Framework Convention on National Minorities, *Commentary on Education under the Framework Convention for the Protection of National Minorities*, ACFC/25DOC(2006)002, 2 March 2006, at 14.

[297] Gilbert (2002), *supra* note 4, at 778.

a minority might raise an issue under Article 8 and that *"a minority group is, in principle, entitled to claim the right to respect for the particular life style it may lead as being "private life," "family life" or "home.""*[298] Article 8 was thus connected with the protection of a particular lifestyle or cultural identity.

The Commission made it clear that *"Article 8 does not guarantee a* right *to a particular lifestyle, it considered that the Article might guarantee the* right to respect *for a particular lifestyle, if it came within one of the categories specified in Article 8."*[299]

In some cases, the ECtHR has been prepared to accept that the duty to "respect" may entail a positive obligation on the part of the state. For example, in *Airey v. Ireland*, it stated that:

> *although the object of Article 8 is essentially that of protecting the individual against arbitrary interference by the public authorities, it does not merely compel the State to abstain from such interference:* [...] *there may be positive obligations inherent in an effective respect for private or family life.*[300]

A number of cases, however, seem to show that the Commission and the Court have often been reluctant to accept claims by members of minorities for the recognition of rights which would facilitate the protection of their separate identity. Indeed the Court identified a conflict between the rights under Article 8 and the interests of the community (the rights of other persons). The Court's main criterion was whether the interference with the applicant's claimed right was "necessary in a democratic society"[301] and has generally given states a wide margin of appreciation in assessing whether the measures taken, which may have an adverse effect on members of minority groups, were proportionate to the legitimate aim pursued.

Such considerations were taken into account in *Noack and Others v. Germany*,[302] in which the Court observed that, for the purposes of Article 8, a minority's way of life is, in principle, entitled to the protection guaranteed for an individual's private life, family life and home (as stated by the Commission in *G. and E. v. Norway*, *Buckley v. United Kingdom* and

---

298 *G and E v. Norway*, *supra* note 163, para. 35.

299 C. Marquand, 'Human Rights protection and Minorities,' *PL* 359 (1994) at 364.

300 *Airey v. Ireland*, *supra* note 148, para. 32.

301 L. Hannikainen, 'Legal Nature of Minority Rights as Part of Human Rights, Limitations, Derogations, Reservations, and Interpretative Statements,' in M. Weller (ed.), *Universal Minority Rights* (Oxford University Press: Oxford, 2007), pp. 27–48, at 37.

302 *Noack and Others v. Germany*, *supra* note 4.

Chapman v. United Kingdom). The Court considered that transferring the population of a village raised a problem under Article 8 because it affected the private lives and homes of the people concerned. However, it concluded that no violation of Article 8 had occurred because the interference, although painful, was not disproportionate to the legitimate aim pursued.[303] This case is a good example of how minority rights should be affected within the state and that a balancing exercise necessarily exists, supposing that the minority group has a voice in the decision-making process.[304]

The decision in *Buckley v. the United Kingdom* is emblematic of the limited protection of cultural identity under Article 8 and of the need for greater awareness of the importance of minority identity when balanced against the planning interests of the state.[305] In *Buckley*, the applicant was a Roma who had occupied her own land in caravans with her family, without planning permission and after having submitted two retrospective planning applications. The local authority attempted to evict her and fined her for breach of the planning regulations when she refused to move. The local authorities indeed argued that she had alternative places to reside, in particular a caravan site nearby. She alleged a breach of Article 8, together with Article 14, of the ECHR. The Commission, following the reasoning of *G. and E. v. Norway*, held that the traditional lifestyle of a minority may attract the guarantees of Article 8,[306] that Roma following a traditional lifestyle required a special consideration in planning matters because the fact that they followed a traditional lifestyle reduced the options open to them[307] and that, in this case, a proper balance between the interest of the community and that of the applicant had not been achieved.[308]

303 With regard to *Noack and Others v. Germany*, the ACFC suggested that "[…] *As the forced dissolution of municipalities in which members of national minorities traditionally reside is undeniably likely to make the preservation of their identity more difficult, it is essential, for such an action to be compatible with Article 5* […]*, that it is taken only as a last resort, when there is no alternative.* […] *The Advisory Committee considers it to be indispensable that* […] *the Sorbian inhabitants concerned can continue to enjoy the rights and facilities they have enjoyed thus far in the cultural and linguistic field.* […]" Council of Europe, Advisory Committee on the Framework Convention for the Protection of National Minorities, *Opinion on Germany*, ACFC/INF/OP/I(2002)008, 1 March 2002, para. 32.

304 Gilbert (2002), *supra* note 4, at 780.

305 O'Nions, *supra* note 1, at 81.

306 *Buckley v. the United Kingdom*, Eur. Comm. Hum. Rts., *supra* note 163, paras. 64–65.

307 Id., paras. 74 and 79–84.

308 Id., paras. 71–73.

The Court, on the contrary, found that the balance between the interests of the applicant and that of the community had been properly taken into account,[309] and only investigated whether Article 8 was violated in view of the right to respect for one's home and declared it unnecessary to assess whether this case also dealt with the right to respect for one's private and family life.[310] It did not say anything on the possibility that Article 8 would imply the right of minorities to respect for their traditional way of life. The Court did not link private and family life to culture, and indeed, the reduction of the case's scope by the Court is a first indication that it is rather reluctant to clarify the requirements implied by the Convention regarding members of minorities.[311] The Court seemed to ignore that the individual case of Ms. Buckley was in reality just the expression of a larger problem involving the Roma minority as a group and the indirect discrimination claim faced; it failed to look at the cumulative effect of the legislation facing Roma in the United Kingdom (which it refused to review), resulting in making the establishment of family and private life near impossible.[312]

Dissenting judges showed a greater appreciation of the issues faced by Roma people and gave greater weight to this aspect of identity when balanced against the state's margin of appreciation. They suggested that some kind of affirmative action was necessary to favour the Roma minority to ensure better protection of their cultural heritage and achieve equality in fact.[313] Judge Lohmus referred to a CoE resolution on the cultural identity of nomads[314] and observed that *"living in a caravan and travelling are vital parts of gypsies' cultural heritage and traditional lifestyle."*[315] He suggested that to treat the applicant, a Gypsy, as having the same rights and duties as other members of the community would fail to take into account the particular situation of the Gypsy minority and that:

> *It may not be enough to prevent discrimination so that members of a minority receive equal treatment under law. In order to establish equality in fact, different treatment may be necessary to preserve their special cultural heritage.*[316]

---

309 *Buckley v. the United Kingdom*, Eur. Ct. Hum. Rts., *supra* note 163, para. 84.
310 Id., para. 55.
311 Henrard, *supra* note 10, at 102.
312 O'Nions, *supra* note 1, at 82.
313 *Buckley v. the United Kingdom*, Eur. Cts. Hum. Rts., *supra* note 163, at 136.
314 Council of Europe, Committee of Ministers, Resolution (75) 13 Containing Recommendations on the Social Situation of Nomads in Europe, Adopted by the Committee of Ministers on 22 May 1975 at the 245th meeting of the Ministers' Deputies.
315 *Buckley v. the United Kingdom*, Eur. Cts. Hum. Rts., *supra* note 163, at 136.
316 Id.

Judge Pettiti pointed out that the Convention could provide a remedy for the disrespect and non-recognition of the Roma culture by imposing positive obligations on states to ensure that fundamental rights were guaranteed without discrimination. He believed that Roma were discriminated against and suffered from disproportionate government measures. He concluded by stating that:

> *The European Court had [...] an opportunity to produce [...] a critique of national law and practice with regard to gypsies and travellers in the United Kingdom that would have been transposable to the rest of Europe, and thereby partly compensate for the injustices they suffer.*[317]

There have been several other cases brought by Roma involving planning issues which reached conclusions similar to *Buckley*. The question of legitimate differentiation in the treatment of different groups arose again in *Chapman v. the United Kingdom*, in which the Court referred, among other instruments, to Recommendation 1203 (1993) of the Parliamentary Assembly of the Council of Europe on Gypsies in Europe, according to which Roma, as one of the few non-territorial minorities in Europe, need special protection, in particular with regard to their language and culture.[318] It recognised that the vulnerable position of Gypsies as a minority meant that some special consideration should be given to their needs and their different lifestyle, both in the relevant regulatory planning framework, and in reaching decisions in particular cases. In this sense, a positive obligation is imposed on states by virtue of Article 8 to facilitate the lifestyle of Gypsies.[319] Pointing out the difficulties that would be raised under Article 14 if a Gypsy, who had unlawfully stationed a caravan site at a particular place, was treated differently from non-Gypsies in the same circumstances, the Court observed that:

> *belonging to a minority with a traditional lifestyle different from that of the majority does not confer an immunity from general laws intended to safeguard the assets of the community as a whole, such as the environment.*[320]

The Court thus stated that it would only depart from the position it held in *Buckley* if compelling reasons required it to do so[321] and found no violation of Article 8 because this does not imply the right to be provided with

---

317 *Buckley v. the United Kingdom*, Eur. Cts. Hum. Rts., *supra* note 163, at 142.
318 *Chapman v. the United Kingdom*, *supra* note 163, paras. 55–67.
319 Id., para. 96.
320 Id.
321 Donders, *supra* note 15, at 297.

a home nor does it create positive obligations for the state.[322] The dissenters, conversely, thought that the Court should be aware of the new developments within members which might make a new view desirable.[323]

In *Beard v. the United Kingdom*, the Court, following the argument of *Chapman*, expressed the view that Article 8 of the Convention should not be interpreted as to create any positive obligation of general social policy on the contracting parties.[324] It clearly admitted:

> [...] *that the applicants' occupation of their caravan is an integral part of their ethnic identity as gypsies, reflecting the long tradition of that minority of following a travelling lifestyle. This is the case even though* [...] *many gypsies no longer live a wholly nomadic existence* [...]. *Measures which affected the applicants' stationing of their caravan* [...] *also affected their ability to maintain their identity as gypsies and to lead their private and family life in accordance with that tradition.*[325]

However, in *Beard*, the Court was not prepared to go as far as to accept that recognition of identity meant that a state must exempt travellers from the general law governing planning, and added:

> *to accord to a gypsy who has unlawfully established a caravan site at a particular place different treatment from that accorded to non-gypsies who have established a caravan site at that place or from that accorded to any individual who has established a house in that particular place would raise substantial problems under Article 14 of the Convention.*[326]

In *Connors v. the United Kingdom*, finally departing from the position held in all other Roma cases, the Court observed that the vulnerable position of Roma as a minority meant that some special consideration had to be given to their needs and their different lifestyle, to the point that a positive obligation exists to contracting parties to facilitate the Roma way of life.[327] The serious interference with the applicant's rights under Article 8 required, according to the Court, particularly strong reasons of public interest as a way of justification. The importance of the decision of *Connors*

---

322 *Chapman v. the United Kingdom, supra* note 163, para. 99.

323 Id., Joint Dissenting Opinion of Judges Pastor Ridruejo, Bonello, Tulkens, Strážnická, Lorenzen, Fischbach and Casadeval. *See also* Donders, *supra* note 15, at 297.

324 *Beard v. the United Kingdom, supra* note 163, para. 109. *See also Coster v. the United Kingdom, Lee v. the United Kingdom* and *Jane Smith v. the United Kingdom.*

325 Id., para. 84.

326 Id., para. 106.

327 *Connors v. the United Kingdom,* Eur. Ct. Hum. Rts., Application numbers 66746/01, 27 May 2004, para. 84.

is quite obvious. A narrow reading would suggest that the government of the United Kingdom would need to rethink its policy on security of tenure on Roma sites. However, a wider reading has implications for the Roma of Europe, suggesting that states will have to demonstrate that they are respecting their obligation to enable the Roma way of life. The margin of appreciation has been considerably narrowed when the Roma lifestyle is undermined.

As seen, Article 8, under the heading of private life, family life and home offers the chance to better protect aspects of a particular lifestyle or cultural identity. Although in the Roma cases the Court did not make any direct reference to cultural identity, it became obvious that the issues involved concerned the protection of the cultural identity of the individual and the community. By referring to minorities, culture and identity, the Court recognised that the individual rights under Article 8 might have a community dimension. However, although the jurisprudence of the ECtHR might suggest that the Convention can protect minority rights in a variety of circumstances, it should be recalled that it is not designed to protect minority identity.[328] Conversely, it should be pointed out that the Court has recognised the significance of identity to the person and private life.[329]

The Court has proved that it is not insensitive to the changes that have occurred, especially at the regional level, and in its latest judgments has indeed referred to various European instruments on minorities and Roma to determine whether any consensus exists on the treatment of minorities. The fact that the Court in particular has been referring to the FCNM[330] – which in Article 5 requires states parties to promote the conditions necessary for persons belonging to national minorities to maintain and develop their culture and to preserve the essential elements of their identity – gives this an extra value. Conversely, it was observed that no international agreement on the concrete action to be taken by states has been reached and that the FCNM only provides a general framework without agreement on its implementation. However, the ACFC held that efforts aimed at supporting the culture and identity of persons

---

328 Gilbert (2002), *supra* note 4, at 780.
329 *See*, for example, *Goodwin v. the United Kingdom*, *supra* note 159.
330 *See*, for example, *Chapman v. the United Kingdom*, *supra* note 163.

belonging to national minorities are essential for an integrated society and that such measures should receive an increasing attention.[331]

3.6. Conclusions: *De Facto* Equality, Affirmative Action and Special Measures as Ways to Protect Minorities

Despite the increased attention for certain minority issues in the most recent jurisprudence of the ECtHR, traditional standards of individual human rights as currently interpreted by the Court are not sufficient to address the most controversial problems of minorities and minority protection.[332] Additional measures are needed to reach substantive equality.[333] It should, however, be pointed out that, as a result of the individualistic approach, special measures greatly depend on the political will of states and in this sense, a relevant factor will be the popularity of the group in question. In the absence of provisions protecting the identity of groups and of obligations to support the interests of minorities, little exists to actively promote the maintenance of minority identity,[334] and it is quite obvious that states rarely show such concern, especially when the minority is small or unpopular with the electorate.[335] Hence, it is easy to understand the state's unwillingness to consider affirmative action policies when there are a few votes to be won and many to be lost,[336] such as in the case of the Roma in Italy.

I argue that affirmative action, special measures and collective rights are the only effective way to achieve *de facto* equality and thus protect the identity of minorities. Indeed, laws which appear to be ethnically neutral have indirect discriminatory effects and an adverse impact on members of a particular minority. Furthermore, many people do not regard themselves merely as individuals: minority issues have a collective dimension and as such, a system for minority protection should be more geared toward that

---

[331] Council of Europe, Advisory Committee on the Framework Convention for the Protection of National Minorities, *Opinion on Estonia,* ACFC/INF/OP/I(2002)005, 14 September 2001, para. 27.

[332] Henrard, *supra* note 10, at 145–146.

[333] Id., at 146.

[334] Id., at 96.

[335] For example, the Roma minority is smaller than other minorities in most countries, with the exception of Romania and Bulgaria. Furthermore, in most cases Roma are geographically dispersed and lack a political organisation which makes them particularly vulnerable to assimilationist policies.

[336] O'Nions, *supra* note 1, at 95.

dimension. An emphasis on individual rights will not be enough to redress the undervalued cultures of minorities, but together with a more collective approach to minority issues, special measures are needed to achieve this goal.[337]

This section focuses on the issues of *de facto* equality, affirmative action and special measures to favour minorities. The rationale behind such policies is that past acts of discrimination have led to systemic patterns of discrimination in many societies, to the point that the present effects of past discrimination may still be felt, continued and even exacerbated by facially neutral policies or practices that, although technically neutral and not purposely discriminatory, perpetuate the consequences of prior discrimination.[338]

As of today, an international consensus still does not exist regarding the use of special measures to advance the status of minorities.[339] Several authors who support the idea of using special measures rely on the views of the PCIJ in *Minority Schools in Albania*, in which two main ideas were recognised as especially necessary to ensure minority protection:

> *The first is to ensure that nationals belonging to racial, religious or linguistic minorities shall be placed in every respect on a footing of perfect equality with the other nationals of the state. The second is to ensure for the minority elements suitable means for the preservation of their racial peculiarities, their traditions and their national characteristics. These two requirements are indeed closely interlocked, for there would be no true equality between a majority and a minority if the latter were deprived of their own institutions, and were consequently compelled to renounce that which constitutes the very essence of its being a minority.*[340]

The goal of effective equality thus necessitates that members of minorities are granted equivalent rights adjusted to their specific situation.[341] Indeed, special measures are not only necessary to realise real and effective equality, but also to satisfy the requirement to respect the separate identity of minorities.[342]

> *International law does recognise that equal treatment may result in unequal consequences and this has led to the recognition of affirmative action strategies. Special measures for minority groups can be defined as the requirement to*

---

337 The issue of collective rights is further analysed in chapter 4.
338 Meron, *supra* note 86, at 289.
339 Henrard, *supra* note 10, at 220.
340 *Minority Schools in Albania*, *supra* note 19, at 17.
341 Henrard, *supra* note 10, at 228.
342 Id.

> *ensure suitable means, including differential treatment, for the preservation of minority characteristics and traditions which distinguish them from the majority of the population.*[343]

Already in 1970, it was observed that *"certain distinctions are legitimate if they are special measures designed to achieve rather than to prevent equality in the enjoyment of rights."*[344] The 1978 World Conference to Combat Racism and Discrimination expressed itself in favour of special measures, saying that they:

> [...] *should include appropriate assistance to persons belonging to minority groups, to enable them to develop their own culture and to facilitate their full development, in particular in the fields of education, culture and employment.*[345]

Special measures are permitted under Article 27 of the ICCPR. The HRC observed that:

> [...] *as long as [special] measures are aimed at correcting conditions which prevent or impair the enjoyment of the rights guaranteed under Article 27, they may constitute a legitimate differentiation under the Covenant, provided that they are based on reasonable and objective criteria.*[346]

The objective of the ICERD is the attainment of equality. Hence, facially neutral policies that have an adverse impact on some racial groups should be prohibited, even if no discriminatory motive is intended. The ICERD allows for special measures, and in Article 1(4) defines them as measures:

> *taken for the sole purpose of securing adequate advancement of certain racial or ethnic groups or individuals requiring such protection as may be necessary in order to ensure such groups or individuals equal enjoyment or exercise of human rights and fundamental freedoms.*

It further states that, in given conditions, they do not constitute discrimination, but these shall be discontinued as soon as the objective for which they were taken is achieved.[347] The CERD has also emphasised that:

---

343 G. Alfredsson and A. de Zayas, 'Minority Rights Protection by the United Nations' (1993) *Human Rights Law Journal*, Vol. 14, No. 1, pp 1–9, at 2.

344 W.A. McKean, 'The Meaning of Discrimination in International and Municipal Law' (1970) *BYIL* Vol. 44, pp. 177–192, at 180.

345 World Conference to Combat Racism and Discrimination UN Doc. A/33/262 (1978), at 20–1.

346 General Comment 23(50), *supra* note 108, para. 6.2.

347 Similarly, the CESCR has stated that *"in order to eliminate substantive discrimination, States parties may be, and in some cases are, under an obligation to adopt special measures*

> *Special measures should not be confused with specific rights pertaining to certain categories of person or community, such as, for example the rights of persons belonging to minorities to enjoy their own culture, profess and practise their own religion and use their own language, [...]. Such rights are permanent rights, recognised as such in human rights instruments, including those adopted in the context of the United Nations and its agencies. States parties should carefully observe distinctions between special measures and permanent human rights in their law and practice. The distinction between special measures and permanent rights implies that those entitled to permanent rights may also enjoy the benefits of special measures.*[348]

The CERD has also specified that:

> *The term "special measures" includes also measures that in some countries may be described as "affirmative measures," "affirmative action" or "positive action" in cases where they correspond to the provisions of Articles 1(4) and 2(2) of the Convention* [...].[349]

Positive action implies targeted assistance to people so that they can take full and equal advantage of particular opportunities. Positive discrimination means explicitly treating people more favourably on a series of grounds.[350] When talking about minorities, affirmative action policies refer to positive steps taken to increase the representation of members of minorities in areas such as employment, education, business, political representation, and in general all areas from which they have been historically excluded. Affirmative action measures are temporary and often have a specified time limit. As soon as the goal has been achieved, the measures cease, even in cases in which the beneficiary of the measures is

---

to attenuate or suppress conditions that perpetuate discrimination. Such measures are legitimate to the extent that they represent reasonable, objective and proportional means to redress de facto discrimination and are discontinued when substantive equality has been sustainably achieved. Such positive measures may exceptionally, however, need to be of a permanent nature, such as interpretation services for linguistic minorities and reasonable accommodation of persons with sensory impairments in accessing health care facilities." See United Nations, Committee on Economic, Social and Cultural Rights, *General Comment No. 20, Non-Discrimination in Economic, Social and Cultural Right,* E/C.12/GC/20, 10 June 2009, para. 9.

348 U.N. Committee on the Elimination of Racial Discrimination, *General Recommendation 32, The meaning and scope of special measures in the International Convention on the Elimination of Racial Discrimination,* Seventy-fifth session, August 2009, para. 15.

349 Id., para. 12.

350 Department for Communities and Local Government, 'Discrimination Law Review, A Framework for Fairness: Proposals for a Single Equality Bill for Great Britain, a consultation paper,' 2007, at 61. It should be noted that, according to the CERD, *"The term "positive discrimination" is, in the context of international human rights standards, a contradictio in terminis and should be avoided."*

a traditional minority group. The temporary aspect thus differentiates affirmative action policies and minority rights, in which the latter are the rights that minorities have *qua* minorities.[351] Article 2(2) demands that members engage in affirmative action policies in the social, economic, cultural and other fields, when the circumstances require so,

> [...] *to ensure the adequate development and protection of certain racial groups or individuals belonging to them, for the purpose of guaranteeing them the full and equal enjoyment of human rights and fundamental freedoms.*[352]

It is rather difficult for state parties to avoid the reach of Article 2(2). Indeed, the view of the CERD is that Article 2(2) unequivocally applies when a state party is ethnically diverse.[353] It would seem that states parties whose population is homogeneous are exempt, but the CERD has interpreted the concept of "homogenous" in such a narrow way that exemptions are rare. The population of a state party is regarded as non-homogeneous if it includes Roma,[354] certain religious ethnic groups;[355] any group with common interests unable to represent itself before the government;[356] any indigenous or minority group still disadvantaged due to past discrimination;[357] and groups whose economic and social development are much lower than that of the rest of the population.[358]

---

[351] *See also* M.A. Javonic, 'Recognizing Minority Identities Through Collective Rights,' 27 Vol. 2 (2005) *Human Rights Quarterly* 625, at 638–639 [hereinafter Javonic].

[352] It is striking that it is not just individuals, but "individual members of racial groups" as well as "groups" as such that are mentioned as the object of protection. This acknowledgement of the group dimension is a step toward the explicit recognition of collective rights. *See* Henrard, *supra* note 10, at 149. In this sense, the ICERD goes further than Article 27 of the ICCPR, by providing specifically for affirmative action in the interests of protection of group identity. O'Nions, *supra* note 1, at 75–76. *See also* T. Meron, *Human Rights Law Making in the United Nations: A Critique of Instruments and Process* (Oxford: Clarendon, 1986), at 37. Group identity is also recognised by Article 14 of ICERD, which allows groups as well as individuals to petition the Committee.

[353] 38 U.N. GAOR Supp. (No. 18), U.N. Doc. A/38118 (1983), at 114 para. 478 [hereinafter U.N. GAOR Supp.].

[354] U.N. Committee on the Elimination of Racial Discrimination, 26th Sess. (577th mtg.) U.N. Doc. CERDIC/SR.577 (1982), at 29.

[355] U.N. GAOR Supp., *supra* note 353, at 46 para 181.

[356] U.N. Committee on the Elimination of Racial Discrimination, 30th Sess. (685th mtg.) U.N. Doc. CERD/C/SR.685 (1984), at 120 para. 48.

[357] U.N. Committee on the Elimination of Racial Discrimination, 30th Sess. (678th mtg.), U.N. Doc. CERDIC/SR.678 (1984), at 28 para. 11.

[358] U.N. Committee on the Elimination of Racial Discrimination, 22nd Sess. (486th mtg.) U.N. Doc. CERDIC/SR.486 (1980), at 73 para. 46. Even refugees and migrant workers have been included in the mandate of Article 2(2). The feeling among the CERD seems to be that in most states, parties current circumstances "now warrant" the implementation of Article 2(2). *See* D. Mahalic and J.G. Mahalic, "The Limitation Provisions of the International Convention on the Elimination of All Forms of Racial Discrimination," Vol. 9, No. 1 (Feb., 1987) *Human Rights Quarterly* 74, at 83–84.

The objective of Article 2(2) is that of ensuring the integration of groups into the societies in which they live, without leading to assimilation. Integration is seen as securing the economic and social development of minority groups without leading to the loss of traditions and cultural identity. Assimilation, conversely, would promote economic and social development without regard for, or even in an attempt to destroy the cultural identity of minority groups, and would therefore be incompatible with Article 2(2).

Article 2(3) specifies that special measures should not lead to the maintenance of unequal rights and should only be temporary.[359] These measures go beyond the narrow application of prohibition of discrimination and have the final aim of ensuring substantive equality for disadvantaged groups or members of these groups in relation to the rest of the population.[360]

The CERD emphasised that Article 7 calls for positive action to ensure equal enjoyment and development of the different cultures existing in a state. It also underlined that:

> *protection of the cultural identity of each people should not be taken to extremes* [...] *It* [*is*] *all a matter of balance, in which each culture* [*has*] *to adapt to the development requirements but without being expected or required to relinquish its individuality.*[361]

The views of the CERD reflect a balanced position, which takes into account the right to identity of minorities and its implications and the need for certain uniform national rules. Indeed, although Article 2(2) does not require states to aid the preservation of cultural identity, the reference to the cultural field and to "protection" rather than just "development" suggests that at least the spirit of the ICERD would be violated by measures that, by promoting adequate development of all groups in social, economic, cultural and other fields, constitute assimilationist policies and

---

359 The demand that special measures should only be temporary can be judged in a negative way. *See* Henrard, *supra* note 10, at 198. In this sense, Capotorti observed that *"the aim of the special measures is to restore the balance between the respective positions of the various groups, including minority groups, but the ultimate objective of the convention is* [*the*] *uniform treatment of individuals* [*regardless*] *to whatever group they belong.* [...]*" See* F. Capotorti, 'Protection of Minorities under Multinational Agreements on Human Rights,' *Italian Yearbook of International Law* (1976) 3, at 9.

360 Henrard, *supra* note 10, at 198.

361 *Implementation of the ICERD, supra* note 88, at 7.

may cause the loss of a group's cultural identity.[362] The determination of the limits of special measures will depend on the specific circumstances.[363] The obligations of states to resort to special measures and affirmative action should be determined by the degree of the group's access to political and economic resources.[364]

The ECtHR has acknowledged the possibility of using special measures to achieve substantive equality. Therefore, introducing distinctions in law to remedy inequalities does not contravene the prohibition of discrimination. Positive measures favouring minorities are sometimes considered reasonable and objectively justifiable and the Court would refrain from interfering on behalf of a majority in which the state took steps to promote the interests of the minority group.[365] This view was confirmed in *Belgian Linguistics*, in which it was held that not all cases of differential treatment violate Article 14 of the ECHR and that *"certain legal inequalities tend only to correct factual inequalities"*[366] and in *D.H. and Others v. Czech Republic*, in which the Court found that:

> [...] *Article 14 does not prohibit a member State from treating groups differently in order to correct "factual inequalities" between them; indeed in certain circumstances a failure to attempt to correct inequality through different treatment may in itself give rise to a breach of the Article.*[367]

This idea, however, does not imply a general obligation for contracting parties to take measures of affirmative action, but simply allows for the possibility of doing so. There would be an obligation to such forms of affirmative action on the basis of Article 14 in combination with another Article of the Convention only if the latter Article imposed a positive obligation on states.[368] In addition, formal unequal treatment of substantively

---

362 Meron, *supra* note 86, at 309. Meron also wonders if a state could be accused of perpetuating policies of racial discrimination if it carried out its integrationist policies so far that they might constitute assimilation, causing the loss of traditions and cultural identity. In this sense, the CERD has warned member states that when they take measures to promote the development of ethnic groups, they must make sure that these do not turn into assimilation.

363 *See also* Henrard, *supra* note 10, at 199.

364 Meron, *supra* note 86, at 308. Meron pointed out that although Article 2(2) of the ICERD does not provide standards for determining when the circumstances of a group warrant special measures, the text suggests that the test is whether the group requires the protection and aid of the state to attain a full and equal enjoyment of human rights.

365 Gilbert (2002), *supra* note 4, at 750.

366 *Belgian Linguistics*, *supra* note 59, para. 10.

367 *D.H. and Others v. the Czech Republic* (Grand Chamber), *supra* note 144, para. 175.

368 Henrard, *supra* note 10, at 77.

different things is demanded to obtain real, concrete equality.[369] *"Accommodation of differences is the essence of true equality,"* and this seems to be related to the wish of minorities to hold onto their own, separate identity.[370]

Although international law recognises the need of positive measures to achieve substantial equality, obstacles and criticism to affirmative action exist because it is not a universally popular strategy for remedying past injustice and present inequality – this will not be overcome unless there is an acceptance of the failure of individual rights to support and promote minority identity.[371] One argument against equality policies as an instrument to ensure full realisation of the rights of minorities is that because most societies are multicultural, granting extra rights to members of specific groups might diminish the rights of other individuals and cause resentment, which is incompatible with the ultimate goal of preventing discrimination. The only way to prevent discrimination would then be to remove the opportunity to discriminate, and – through punishment – to show that discriminatory behaviour is socially unacceptable.[372] Furthermore, collective rights might be seen to exaggerate and promote group difference and eventually deepen ethnic conflict.[373] A criticism often voiced in connection with collective rights is that to categorize the population along certain identity features would further obstruct the integration of the groups concerned in society instead of facilitating it. Such categorization would then confirm and maybe even freeze the differences and carry the risk of antagonising the rest of the population.[374] Such a technique can be criticized because it uses and therefore reinforces the categorisation one tries to eliminate to achieve a "non-racial society."[375] Similarly, it can be said that:

> *The practice of reverse discrimination undermines the foundation of the very ideal in whose name it is advocated, it destroys justice, law, equality, citizenship and replaces them with power struggles and popularity contests.*[376]

---

369 *See Thlimmenos v. Greece, supra* note 65.

370 W. Kymlicka, 'Individual and Community Rights,' in J. Baker (ed.), *Group Rights* (Toronto: University of Toronto Press, 1994), pp. 17–33, at 24 [hereinafter Kymlicka (1994)]

371 O'Nions, *supra* note 1, at 77.

372 Mack and Duster, as cited in O'Nions, *supra* note 1, at 68–69.

373 O'Nions, *supra* note 1, at 69.

374 Henrard, *supra* note 10, at 148.

375 Id.

376 L. Newton, 'Reverse Discrimination as Unjustified' (1973) *Ethics* 83, at 112.

Another problem with granting special rights to certain groups is that of determining which groups ought to be the subject of special measures.[377] A marginalised group may be further stigmatised by its designation as needing special treatment and this, in turn, might encourage a feeling of resentment amongst other groups. In addition, the beneficiaries may feel that they have been awarded a particular position as a token rather than as a merit.[378]

Marko believes that special measures for (members of) minorities should always be geared toward a situation of substantive equality between the members of the minority and the rest of the population. They are not privileges but nothing more than a necessary legal instrument to counteract the assimilative consequences of the nation-state concept.[379] These measures are concerned with the preservation and promotion of the separate identity of minorities.

Kymlicka based his argument in favour of special measures on the demand of substantive equality in combination with the importance of cultural membership. Starting from the premise that members of a minority culture are disadvantaged compared with the rest of the population, he noted that *"inequality in circumstances faced by members of minority cultures generates legitimate claims,* [...] *which can be met through certain forms of minority rights"*[380] so as to avoid loss of cultural membership.[381] As such, these measures would not violate the prohibition of discrimination but would help *"reduce the vulnerability of minority communities to the decisions of the larger society."*[382] The question would then be how to ensure that support for a particular group is provided fairly and that a proper balance is achieved between the various situations of the distinctive population groups when trying to preserve a group's identity. In this respect, forms of support for particular national and ethnic groups should be provided fairly and should not privilege some groups and disadvantage others.[383] When existing policies support the language, culture

---

377 O'Nions, *supra* note 1, at 69.

378 Id., at 77.

379 Marko, *supra* note 49.

380 W. Kymlicka, *Liberalism, Community and Culture* (Oxford: Clarendon, 1989), at 4 [hereinafter Kymlicka 1989].

381 Id., at 151.

382 Kymlicka (1994), *supra* note 370, at 20.

383 W. Kymlicka, *Multicultural Citizenship: a Liberal Theory of Minority Rights* (Oxford: Oxford University Press, 1995), at 115 [Hereafter Kymlicka (1995)].

and identity of dominant groups, equality would imply that similar support is provided to minority groups.[384]

Hannum supports the idea of granting minorities the right to protect and promote their cultural identity, which implies also the right to use their own language and to provide minority language education, the right to maintain traditional religions, and the preservation of some sort of political, environmental and economic control.[385] This enumeration contains certain forms of autonomy, which points to a connection between minority protection and the right to internal self-determination.[386]

As seen, positive obligations favouring minorities could be justified by the requirement of substantive equality: state intervention would be necessary to bring members of minorities to equal conditions with the majority population in a variety of fields. In this sense, the collective dimension is fundamental because the actuation of special measures for minorities leads to the implicit acceptance of the existence of a separate group.[387] Special measures may thus include the granting of a separate legal status to linguistic, religious or ethnic groups, which might involve measures to ensure territorial autonomy or participation in the public and political life of the country. Therefore, according to Kymlicka, special measures, contrary to affirmative action, are not necessarily temporary because, as members of minorities are constantly faced by the threat of losing cultural membership, temporary affirmative action would not be sufficient to obtain real or substantive equality and collective rights might be needed.[388]

One aspect of affirmative action is the use of quotas, over which a heated debate is taking place:

> *According to one view, reservations and quotas were a fundamental means of promoting equality in law and in fact for persons who had been victims of discrimination but others believed that it would be preferable to make special facilities available to backward groups in order to enable them to meet the general standards of merit.*[389]

---

[384] Kymlicka (1995), *supra* note 383, at 115.

[385] Hannum (1989), *supra* note 17, at 20–21.

[386] Henrard, *supra* note 10, at 231.

[387] Marko, *supra* note 49.

[388] Kymlicka (1989), *supra* note 380, at 190. Kymlicka is not an ardent proponent of collective rights as such, although favouring a more explicit recognition of the group dimension of the minority phenomenon. *See* Kymlicka (1994), *supra* note 370, at 23. On collective rights, *see* chapter 4.

[389] W. Mc Kean, *Equality and Discrimination under International Law* (Oxford: Clarendon Press, 1985), at 100 [hereinafter Mc Kean].

In the *Regents of University of California v. Bakke*[390] case, the dilemma of protecting an individual right to equality when a group of individuals is automatically given certain benefits which are not available to others was analysed by the United States Supreme Court. Here, the plaintiff, Bakke, challenged the special admissions program of the Medical School at the University of California at Davis, which reserved 16 percent of places in its entering class for members of specified minority groups, or 'economically and/or educationally disadvantaged' applicants, whose applications were considered separately from the mainstream of applications. The terms of consideration were similar to the mainstream ones, but applicants were not as summarily rejected, nor were they rated or compared with the general applicants: the 16 percent of places reserved to members of minority groups or "economically and/or educationally disadvantaged" applicants were filled regardless of how the applicants compared with the general applicants. Bakke's application was rejected despite the fact that several applicants under the special entry programme had grade point averages and admission test scores significantly lower than his. He thus claimed that the special admissions program tried to exclude him on the basis of his race, which would cause a violation of his rights under the Equal Protection Clause of the XIV Amendment.

Bakke argued that he was discriminated against under the "affirmative action" policy of the Medical School, and this was done on ground of his race. It could be argued that members of minority groups had a greater chance, because it might be thought that more places were open to them (against fewer applicants) and different criteria were applied. Conversely, it should be seen that members of minority groups did not in fact have a better chance because they were likely to have had less opportunities in life, be less qualified and so on.

The Supreme Court sustained that although affirmative action systems are constitutional, a quota system based on race is unconstitutional. In particular, Justice Powell observed that:

> *The guarantee of equal protection cannot mean one thing when applied to one individual and something else when applied to a person of another colour. If both are not accorded the same protection, then it is not equal.*[391]

---

390 *Regents of the University of California v Bakke*, 438, US 265 (1978).

391 Id., at 280.

In general, it is suggested that quotas should be of a temporary nature and maintained no longer than it is necessary to achieve the objectives for which they are imposed.[392] This analysis implies a negative attitude toward the use of quotas outside the specific domain of affirmative action.[393] An outright dismissal of the use of quotas, either as a form of affirmative action or as a more general form of "special" measure for minorities would be too radical.[394]

Minority rights imply positive, possibly even financial obligations for states. In view of the increasing recognition of positive obligations on the basis of individual human rights and the need to make these rights effective, similar obligations for minority rights could not and should not be denied. Indeed,

> *the fact that members of minorities do not have the power and ability to protect and promote their distinctive identity sufficiently, arguably enhances the need for their rights (as guaranteed) to be effective and also for genuine positive state obligations.*[395]

I believe that affirmative action, positive obligations and special measures[396] are all necessary to protect minorities and ensure their full integration, to avoid not fully understanding the problems certain groups face and the ongoing discrimination to which they are subjected, thus not allowing the possibility of remedying its effects. Special measures for minorities are needed to put minorities in a position equal to that of the majority population. The analysis of the individual approach to minorities' issues and of the jurisprudence based on individual rights' claims has proved that a strictly individualistic approach to minority issues, based on the prohibition of discrimination, is not enough to ensure protection of minorities' identities. Indeed, as was already noted throughout this chapter, inherent limitations exist when protecting individuals through rights that have to be asserted in litigation as opposed to thinking in terms of duties on the part of the state and proactive programmes of action. For this reason, affirmative action and special measures, together with the recognition of collective rights for minorities,[397] are the best ways to redress

---

392 Mc Kean, *supra* note 389, at 100.

393 Henrard, *supra* note 10, at 150.

394 Id.

395 Id., at 151.

396 *See infra.*

397 Collective rights are seen as permanent. Eide emphasized the fact that collective rights are intended *'to allow for a lasting manifestation of difference.' See* A. Eide, 'Minority

a situation of protracted disparity and discrimination and to end the opposition between minority groups and the majority society by ensuring their empowerment, integration and full participation in the life of the country in which they live.

Protection and World Order: Towards a Framework for Law and Policy,' in *Universal Minority Rights,* A. Phillips, and A. Rosas (eds.) (London: Minority Rights Group International 1995), pp., at 87 and 101 *"Therefore, once certain specific legal arrangements for the minority protection are introduced in a domestic legal system, that state is no longer allowed to abolish, restrict, or diminish the scope of these rights, for they are treated as acquired minority rights." See* Javonic, *supra* note 351, at 639.

CHAPTER FOUR

INDIVIDUAL V. COLLECTIVE RIGHTS

4.1. Introduction

It is my view that protection of the right to cultural identity of minorities such as the Roma is better achieved through collective rights rather than only individual rights. Before embarking on a discussion about their value, it is important to define what is intended by the expression "collective rights."

In the context of the debate between individual and collective rights, human rights have been divided into "three generations."[1] The first generation consists of civil and political rights, derived from Western capitalist ideas and based on the concept of (negative) freedom. The second generation is that of economic, social and cultural rights, based on the notion of equality and first introduced by socialist and communist states. Collective rights are the third generation of human rights, formulated thanks to the pressure coming from Third World countries and based on the third element of the slogan of the French revolution, "fraternity" or "solidarity."

Group rights are seen as varieties of the rights of individuals to associate in pursuit of particular interests. In other words, they are the rights to public goods which are important for the well-being of a group of individuals and as such, require a set of convergent individual interests.[2]

---

[1] The term "generation" has encountered strong criticism because it suggests that one generation of rights precedes the other whereas, in fact, all generations are supposed to support and mutually strengthen each other. I hold that it should not be termed generations of rights, but more appropriately "kinds" of human rights, which are not, however, to be considered as neatly distinguishable from each other. In fact, all rights are intertwined, indivisible, integrated and dependent on each other, in the sense that the protection of one right cannot be fully achieved if another one is ignored or violated. Furthermore, I believe that all kinds of rights are needed to ensure a meaningful and dignified life to everyone. The indivisibility of human rights is discussed in the preliminary report of the Special Rapporteur Danilo Türk, *Realisation of Economic, Social and Cultural Rights*, UN Doc. E/CN.4/Sub.2/1989/19. This idea is also expressed in the 1993 Vienna Declaration, which, in section I(5) stated that *"All human rights are universal, indivisible and interdependent and interrelated. The international community must treat human rights globally in a fair and equal manner, on the same footing, and with the same emphasis.* [...]*" See* Vienna Declaration and Programme of Action, A/CONF.157/23, 12 July 1993.

[2] N. Torbisco Casals, *Group Rights as Human Rights: A Liberal Approach to Multiculturalism* (Springer: Doordrecht, 2006), at 53.

These refer to rights given to individuals but in their capacity as members of a certain group because they would be meaningless if exercised alone. Group rights are also seen as the sum of the rights of the individual members of the group, and thus asserted by the organisations that represent the groups and best suited to search for affirmative action. They have been distinguished from solidarity rights, which are human rights belonging to all humans threatened by war, pollution or societal inadequacies.

Collective rights (different from group rights and solidarity rights) are considered *"claims based not on shared human traits but on cultural distinctiveness and membership in a community defined by this distinctiveness."*[3] In this sense, collective rights transcend the individualistic framework, they are of a non-reducible collective nature and they cannot be *"analyzed adequately and without loss of meaning in terms of individual rights."*[4] Collective rights are the rights of groups that have goals that go beyond the ending of discrimination against their members. Such groups are called collectivities and their members are joined together not only by external discrimination, but also by internal cohesiveness: collectivities seek to maintain and protect their cultural characteristics; they seek group survival.[5] In the case of collective rights, *"their subjects do not come into being by way of association but are simply given [and] in order for them to be capable of bearing rights, they need to be officially recognized by the state."*[6] According to Van Dyke, groups are collective entities *"that exist as units and not*

[3] P. Juliver, 'Are Collective Rights Anti-Human? Theories on Self-Determination and Practice in Soviet Successor States' in *Netherlands Quarterly of Human Rights* Vol. 11, n. 3 (1993), pp. 267–282, at 268–269.

[4] K. VanderWal, 'Collective Human Rights: a Western View' in J. Berting, P.R. Baehr, J.H.Burgers, C. Flinterman, B. de Klerk, R. Kroes, C.A. van Minnen and K. VanderWal (eds.) *Human Rights in a Pluralist World* (London: Meckler, 1990), pp. 83–98, at 88.

[5] D. Sanders, 'Collective Rights' *Human Rights Quarterly* 13:3 (1991), pp. 368–386, at 369–370. [hereinafter Sanders] It should be pointed out that some confusion exists concerning the use of the expressions "collective rights" and "group rights," with several authors using one of the two expressions to indicate the same concept. For example, Henrard mentioned collective rights as the rights for members of a group, as members, and saw group rights as rights which are granted to the group as such. *See* K. Henrard, *Devising an Adequate System of Minority Protection* (The Netherlands, Kluwer Law International, 2000), at 153. [hereinafter Henrard] Kymlicka refered to collective rights as the rights of the group as such and as the rights which belong to certain people individually but in their capacity of members of a certain group. *See* W. Kymlicka, 'Individual and Community Rights,' in J. Baker (ed.), *Group Rights* (Toronto: University of Toronto Press, 1994), pp. 17–33, at 17–18 [hereinafter Kymlicka (1994)].

[6] J. Kis, 'Beyond the Nation State,' 63 *SOC. RES.* 191 (1995), at 221. The idea that collectivities have to be recognised to exercise their rights is particularly important, especially for minorities and even more so for minorities which have not been recognised – *see*, for example, the case of the Roma in Italy.

simply as aggregations of individuals."[7] A sense of solidarity, a we/they sense and a sense of sharing a common heritage and a common destiny which are distinct from those of others must exist.[8] Lador-Lederer, in a similar manner, noted that groups are those to which individuals belong for better or for worse, to the extent that their destinies can be dissociated only artificially. In this case, even if it is the individual who might be the object of protection, the fundamental element is the group because the individual is endangered by his belonging to that group. Such groups are permanent and not occasional groups, in which membership can be easily changed.[9]

Jones suggested that:

> *A right is a group right only if it is borne by the group* qua *group. If the individuals who form a group hold rights as separate individuals, their several individual rights do not add up to a group right. [...] In the same way, a right may have a content that relates to a collectivity without its being a group right. An individual can have a right to join a group, such as a trade union, only if there is a group for him to join. Having joined the group, that individual may have rights that he possesses only as a member of the group. In both instances, however, these typically will be rights held in an individual capacity rather than rights that belong to the group.*[10]

Jones also distinguished between group rights in the collective conception and group rights in the corporate conception. The collective conception of group rights implies that the interests of the individual members of the group do not necessarily have to be represented as interests that they might have as independent and unrelated individuals. The collective conception ascribes moral standing only to the individuals who jointly hold the group right.[11] The corporate conception, conversely, ascribes moral standing to the group as such and therefore the holder of the right is the group conceived as a single, integral entity. As Jones noted, *"The right is*

---

[7] V. Van Dyke, 'Collective Entities and Moral Rights: Problems in Liberal-Democratic Thought,' 44 *The Journal of Politics* (1982) 21, at 23.

[8] Id., at 32.

[9] Examples of occasional groups are, according to Lador-Lederer, prisoners of war, stateless persons, refugees. *See* J.J. Lador-Lederer, *International Group Protection: Aims and Methods in Human Rights* (Leiden: A.W. Sijthoff, 1968), at 15.

[10] P. Jones, 'Human Rights, Group Rights, and Peoples' Rights, 21 (1999) *Human Rights Quarterly* 80, at 82. [hereinafter Jones] It should be pointed out that Jones used the expression "group right" in the same way I use the expression "collective right" and vice versa, he referred to collective rights in the way I refer to group rights.

[11] Id., at 85.

held not jointly by the several individuals who make up the group, but by the group as a unitary entity: the right is "its" right rather than "their" right."[12]

In other words, Jones called the "collective conception of group rights," what I would call "group rights," whereas what he called "corporate conception of group rights" are, in my view, "collective rights." Indeed, I view collective rights as the rights of collectivities as such, which are granted to the collectivity as a moral entity. In this sense, the subject of rights would be the collectivity, and this would also have legal standing before courts.[13]

It is suggested that collective rights include the right to peace, the right to communicate, the right to a clean environment[14] and the right to self-determination.[15] Supporters of collective rights then add the right to cultural identity – considered to be of such a collective nature that individual human rights norms would not be sufficient to protect it properly. For example, it is argued that the right to preservation of one's cultural identity is a paradigm of a collective right.[16] A separate right to cultural identity should therefore be developed because the existing human rights system, with its individual character and underdevelopment of cultural rights, does not meet the claims of communities with regard to the recognition and protection of their cultural identity.

Researchers contend that demands for better protection of the rights of the Roma must come from the Roma and, to be more effective, they must involve affirmative action, special measures and recognition of collective rights. Some might think that advocating collective rights to redress the rights of the Roma might be inappropriate or ineffective, but as shown in

---

[12] Jones, *supra* note 10, at 86.

[13] According to Marko, we can only speak of group rights in the narrow sense when groups are no longer considered to be the object of protection, but when they become bearers of subjective rights or entitlements and thus also have legal standing before courts. Marko wrote of "group rights" in the same way that I write of "collective rights." *See* J. Marko, "Constitutional Recognition of Ethnic Difference – Towards an Emerging European Minimum Standard?", in Annelies Verstichel et al. (eds.), The FCNM: A Useful Pan-European Instrument?, (Antwerpen, Intersentia, 2008) [hereinafter Marko].

[14] K. Vasak, 'Pour une troisième génération des droits de l'homme,' in C. Swinarski (ed.), *Essays on International Humanitarian Law and Red Cross Principles in Honour of Jean Picket* (The Hague: Martinus Nijhoff, 1984), pp. 837–850, at 839–840.

[15] As seen in chapter 3, under Article 1 of the ICCPR the right to self-determination can only be claimed by peoples and not by individuals. The presence of the right to self-determination in the ICCPR indicates that this right is a fundamental prerequisite for the realisation of individual human rights.

[16] M. Galenkamp, *Individualism versus Collectivism – The concept of collective rights* (Gouda Quint: Deventer, 1998), at 15 [hereinafter Galenkamp (1998)].

chapter 3, so far, individual emphasis has done little to preserve them, and individual rights have often proved inaccessible for the Roma.[17]

In my opinion, the best way to protect the rights of the Roma and to ensure their full integration into European and Italian society is mainly through the recognition of collective rights, which ought to be used together with – and not in opposition to – the principles of equality and non-discrimination (as articulated both in terms of individual rights and associative rights), as well as with group rights. I contend that individual and collective rights are not exclusive of each other but reinforce one another. Individual rights may require a collective dimension to be effective. The two are to be seen as a parallel, in the sense that collective rights, and in particular a collective right to cultural identity, are the necessary precondition for the full integration and recognition of certain groups within society, only after which more individualistic claims should become plausible. Collective rights, together with appropriate economic and social policies addressing the disadvantage experienced by the Roma, can bring an end to their marginalisation and allow their full integration.

This chapter will discuss the recognition of collective rights as a way to better advance the rights of minorities. After showing what the added value of collective rights is, the protection of collective rights granted by international instruments which might be applicable to Roma communities in Europe and Italy will be reviewed. The focus will then be on the debate between supporters and opponents of collective rights. Finally, it will concentrate on cultural rights and on the collective right to cultural identity,[18] which I deem to be the best way to protect the identity of minorities.

---

[17] An example of the difficulty of defending Roma through individual rights is the case of *D.H. and Others v. the Czech Republic*: the practice of placing Roma children in special classes, although it might seem to be a benevolent way to ensure education to those who cannot cope with the demands of regular schooling and thus to be compatible with human rights standards, is in reality discriminatory. The ECtHR has been unable to address the pattern of discrimination at the root of this practice because it is constrained by the language of individual rights. It should be observed that in this case, the Grand Chamber of the ECtHR eventually reversed a previous judgement and held that there had been a violation of Article 14 of the Convention, together with Article 2 of Protocol 1. *See* H. O'Nions, *Minority Rights Protection in International Law. The Roma of Europe* (United Kingdom: Ashgate, 2007), at 266. [hereinafter O'Nions] *See also* the *Case of D.H. and Others v. the Czech Republic,* Eur. Ct. Hum. Rts., Application number 57325/00, 7 February 2006; and the *Case of D.H. and Others v. the Czech Republic* (Grand Chamber) Eur. Ct. Hum. Rts., Application number 57325/00, 13 November 2007: both are discussed in chapter 3.

[18] The issues of culture and cultural identity are fully analysed in chapter 1.

4.2. The Added Value of Collective Rights

International law grants rights to members of minority groups rather than groups *per se*, and thus the extent to which the group could demand the resources necessary to improve the situation of its members is poorly developed. Although collective rights are not entirely alien to the language of international human rights, they are hardly accepted as desirable.[19] The need for collective rights in a situation in which individuals – even those belonging to minorities – have already been granted human rights is questioned. Furthermore, it is assumed that individuals who are members of minorities have been granted the protection of Article 27 of the International Covenant on Civil and Political Rights (ICCPR) and this, together with other propositions of international law, puts emphasis on the need to press for equal rights for any individual who is a member of a minority; after this is done, minority groups do not need any additional facilities for the protection of their group identity.[20] No positive right exists for minorities to enjoy their identity. Article 27 of the ICCPR mentions individuals "in community with other members of the group," and is framed in negative terms, stating that members of minorities "shall not be denied the right" to enjoy their culture or practice their religion, and so on.

Chapter 3 has demonstrated that the individual emphasis on human rights advocated by international law barely meets the needs of communities as disadvantaged as the Roma because it hardly takes into consideration the importance of communal values for the individual rights-bearer. Although, on the one hand, it must be admitted that collective rights are hardly justiciable and as such a straightforward answer to the issue of the protection of the rights of the Roma does not exist, on the other hand, collective rights are possibly the only feasible solution to the problems of discrimination of minorities.

I maintain that equal treatment of individuals is not always sufficient to eliminate inequalities. As seen in chapter 3, a number of rights have a strong group dimension (such as the right to freedom of association, the right to manifest one's religion and the right to education); however, the protection these rights provide, although surely positive for minorities, is not enough to protect, preserve and promote the separate identity of

---

19 O'Nions, *supra* note 17, at 269.

20 M. Galenkamp, *Collective Rights,* SIM (Netherlands Institute of Human Rights) special, No. 16, 1995, pp. 53–106, at 75 [hereinafter Galenkamp (1995)].

minorities. The needs of certain groups are not sufficiently addressed by individual human rights:

> *it has become increasingly clear that existing human rights standards are simply unable to resolve some of the most important and controversial questions relating to cultural minorities, [which] have been left to the usual process of majoritarian-decision making within each State.*[21]

The result has thus been that cultural minorities have become increasingly vulnerable to significant injustice at the hands of the majority.[22]

The arguments in favour of collective rights can be summed up in five main points:

> *First, the adoption of collective rights regimes reaffirms the international community's commitment to the preservation of ethnic minorities and their culture. Second, collective rights regimes may serve the goals of preserving minority cultures and protecting the human rights of members of minority groups generally. Third, collective rights guarantees are needed to overcome the effects of past discrimination. Fourth, ethnic minorities may need additional rights beyond those granted to the majority, merely to be placed on an equal footing in society. Finally, the effectiveness of present collective rights legislation and the successful explicit adoption of collective rights measures in various nations to the benefit of their national minorities, are perhaps the strongest testimony to the value of collective rights.*[23]

The starting point is therefore a belief in the value of cultural membership to the individual.

> *Membership of such groups is of great importance to individual well-being, for it greatly affects one's opportunities, one's ability to engage in the relationships and pursuits marked by the culture. Secondly, [...] the prosperity of the culture is important to the well-being of its members. If the culture is decaying, or it is persecuted or discriminated against, the options and opportunities open to its members will shrink, become less attractive, and their pursuit less likely to be successful.*[24]

---

[21] W. Kymlicka, 'Introduction,' in W. Kymlicka (ed.), *The Rights of Minorities Cultures* (Oxford: Oxford University Press, 1995), pp. 1–27, at 18 [hereinafter Kymlicka (1995)].

[22] Id.

[23] M. Geroe and T. Gump, 'Hungary and a New Paradigm for the Protection of Ethnic Minorities in Central and Eastern Europe,' 32 *Columbia Journal of Transnational Law* (1994–1995), pp. 673–705, at 681–682. A number of collective rights measures have been adopted in Central and Eastern Europe countries. *See*, for example, the 1993 Hungarian Act on the Rights of National and Ethnic Minorities, which unequivocally supports collective rights in Article 15, and the reference to collective rights in the Czech Republic Constitution.

[24] A. Margalit and J. Raz, 'National Self-Determination,' in W. Kymlicka (ed.), *The Rights of Minority Cultures* (Oxford: Oxford University Press, 1995), pp. 79–92, at 87.

Thus, collective rights, not reducible to individual rights, should be recognised if it is acknowledged that:

> *the identity and well-being of the members of the group and the identity and well being of the group are linked. Members of the group identify themselves – explain who they are – by reference to their membership in the group; and their well being or status is in part determined by the well being or status of the group.*[25]

I maintain that recognition of cultural communities is essential and (collective) minority rights must be recognised so that the culture can flourish. As specified by the Permanent Court of International Justice (PCIJ) in the *Minority Schools in Albania* case, the system of minority protection used to be such:

> *to secure for certain elements incorporated in a State, the population of which differs from them in race, language or religion, the possibility of living peaceably alongside that population and co-operating amicably with it, while at the same time preserving the characteristics which distinguish them from the majority.*[26]

The importance of the full recognition and enjoyment of collective rights shall be underlined, especially in the case of minorities. Indeed, I contend that it is mainly through membership to a particular group that individuals who belong to minorities can better express their own cultural identity. The cultural dimension of identity is important to individual notions of self, and even more so for disadvantaged minority groups such as the Roma. The identity of the individual Roma is strictly linked to that of the group:

> *The individual is that which his belonging to a given group makes him. He is neither known nor recognised as an individual, but by the situation within the group, which determines his identity both for himself – his self-designation – and for others: the ways in which he will be seen by them, and see them in turn. Hence the significance, when people meet, of employing linguistic and cultural elements and designations, enabling the individuals in question to define themselves and each other, to differentiate themselves and yet feel a common bond.*[27]

---

[25] O.M. Fiss, *Groups and the Equal Protection Clause,* (1976) 5 Philosophy and Public Affairs 107, as quoted in D. Johnston, 'Native Rights as Collective Rights: A Question of Group Self-Preservation' in W. Kymlicka (ed.), *The Rights of Minorities Cultures* (Oxford: Oxford University Press, 1995), pp. 179–201, at 183 [hereinafter Johnston].

[26] *Minority Schools in Albania,* 1935 PCIJ (ser. A/B) No. 64 at 17 (April 6) [hereinafter *Minority Schools in Albania*].

[27] J.P. Liégeois, *Roma, Gypsies and Travelers* (Strasbourg: Council of Europe Publishing, 1994), at 63.

The community has always been a vital unit of Romany organisations, and collective rights recognition is therefore essential if the community interests are to be preserved and developed.[28]

Treating the rights of members of minority groups exclusively as individual rights might thus mean not providing protection for the collectivity as such and in particular for its identity because of the collective dimension of the minority reality.[29] I argue that the individualist bias of human rights instruments, that is, not giving enough weight to the importance of cultural identity, may thus lead to misrecognition of minorities and to the denial of their existence.[30] Misrecognition, conversely, can lead members of minorities such as the Roma to seek to distance themselves from their culture. To preserve cultural differences and eliminate inequalities, it is necessary to protect the specific identity of a minority group through policies of preferential treatment (affirmative action or special measures[31]), rather than by attempting to secure equal treatment to the individual members of that group:[32] if collective rights are not forthcoming, discriminatory patterns are likely to persist and the achievement of equal rights by minorities becomes less likely.[33] Collective rights are therefore important because they imply the acknowledgement of the existence of the group; they are needed against assimilationist policies of states that want to be unitary because they entail the preservation, fostering, strengthening and passing on of the minority identity.

Measures such as granting certain forms of autonomy to a minority, establishing and possibly financing minority schools and determining the language rights of (members of) linguistic minorities in their communications with public authorities, although all issues closely linked to protection and preservation of the identities of minorities,[34] cannot be treated

---

[28] O'Nions, *supra* note 17, at 64.

[29] Henrard, *supra* note 5, at 240.

[30] The case of Italy, in which Roma have been excluded from the recognised minorities, is emblematic in this sense. The misrecognition of the Roma minority in Italy will be fully reviewed in chapter 5.

[31] Henrard sees collective rights as a sub-category of special measures for minorities. *See* Henrard, *supra* note 5, at 241.

[32] This is what Galenkamp calls the "added value of collective rights:" the capacity to protect interests – such as the preservation of one's group identity – that cannot by definition be individualised. *See* Galenkamp (1995), *supra* note 20, at 76.

[33] G. Alfredsson, 'A Frame an Incomplete Painting: Comparison of the Framework Convention for the Protection of National Minorities with International Standards and Monitoring Procedures,' (2000) *International Journal of Minority and Group Rights* Vol. 7, n. 4, pp. 291–304, at 292.

[34] Henrard, *supra* note 5, at 241.

and decided on a purely individual basis because several factors beyond the individual should be taken into account to delineate these rights appropriately. A stronger recognition of the collective dimension of the minority phenomenon is thus necessary and desirable to properly realise minority protection, in the sense that the collective aspect should be taken into account more explicitly when minority rights are elaborated:[35]

> *the collective element of minority rights must be assumed, because it corresponds better to both reality and to the aim of minority protection. For example, cultural traditions, as well as educational and religious institutions are – and can be – maintained by a community only on a collective basis. In addition, the collective enjoyment of culture, the joint practice of religion, and the use of language are vital to the very identity of minorities. Identity is, in turn, what subjectively determines the existence of a minority.*[36]

It should also be noted that although it can be claimed that individual members of minorities have a right to equality (and thus could assert their rights through the channel of individual rights), discrimination almost always occurs because the individual is a member of a group with specific characteristics.[37] The targets of many of the worst human rights violations since 1945 have been ethnic groups as such, and violations have often been conceived by the perpetrators and perceived by the victims in collective terms. Victim groups often plausibly believe that such collective problems require collective solutions and because the problem is due to hostile attitudes toward groups, the solution requires the promotion of the dignity of groups.[38] For these reasons, *"from the 1980s onwards, many scholars have argued that the individualistic approach to human rights based on the principles of equality and non-discrimination no longer meets the present global issues concerning* [...] *the needs of communities."*[39] Communities

---

[35] Henrard, *supra* note 5, at 241.

[36] J. Pejic, 'Minority Rights in International Law,' 19 (No. 3) *Human Rights Quarterly* 666 (1997), at 674.

[37] Sanders, *supra* note 5, at 368. Similarly to Sanders, Lerner pointed out that *"usually, discrimination is based on grounds of group membership and not on specific qualities or defects of an individual.* [...] *it is membership in the group that engenders discrimination, namely distinctions on grounds of natural or social categories, which cannot be linked to individual capacities or merits or to the actual behaviour of the individual." See* N. Lerner, *Group Rights and Discrimination in International Law* (Dordrecht: Martinus-Nijhoff, 2003), at 33.

[38] M. Freeman, 'Are there collective human rights?' *Political Studies* Vol. 43 Special Issue (1995), 25–40, at 32–33 [hereinafter Freeman].

[39] Y.M. Donders, *Towards a Right to Cultural Identity?* (Antwerp: Intersentia, 2002), at 4 [hereinafter Donders].

have therefore been recognised as an important factor in creating a valuable life for individuals, and thus they should be protected by collective rights. Indeed,

> *Cultural minorities seek more than the right of their individual members to equality and participation within the larger society. They also seek distinct group survival. Because economic and social forces, as well as State policies, tend to promote assimilation, the leaders of cultural minorities often look to the State for support. They seek either protection or autonomy as the means to ensure that their collectivities can survive and develop.*[40]

There is an intricate link between group identity and individual rights, which makes individual rights without a collective dimension meaningless for many people. The primacy of the individual over his community can be seen as an attractive approach in which all people are given equal opportunities and have equal access to education. But for many people born into unequal, disadvantaged situations – such as the Roma – the primacy of individual rights does not represent the reality. Individual human rights are simply unable to meet the challenges presented by the Roma[41] and without collective rights, there can be no real protection of individual rights.[42]

4.3. The Protection of Collective Rights in International Instruments

In current international law, only a few provisions that confer rights to collectivities exist, and most are not legally binding. It was immediately after WWII that two instruments for the protection of human rights were adopted – one, widely recognised but not legally binding *per se* and thus of limited use, is the Universal Declaration of Human Rights (UDHR or Universal Declaration); the other is the U.N. Charter (or Charter), which, although legally binding, is not exclusively a human rights instrument.

---

[40] Sanders, *supra* note 5, at 370.

[41] This has been understood by some Eastern European States, such as Hungary, in which the minority government system aims to increase the participation of specific minorities, including the Roma, from a collective dimension. *See* O'Nions, *supra* note 17, at 64–65.

[42] O'Nions, *supra* note 17, at 32–33. Indeed, *"the respect of human individual rights may entail also the satisfaction of collective needs and vice-versa certain collective interests and ideals do require satisfaction, if the individual is to be really protected." See* R. De Nova, 'The International Protection of National Minorities and Human Rights' *Howard LJ* 11 (1965) 275, at 284–285.

The Charter's primary objective, as underlined in the preamble, was to save *"succeeding generations from the scourge of war"* and *"to reaffirm faith in fundamental human rights, in the dignity and worth of the human person."* Article 1(2) states that one of the main purposes of the U.N. is *"to develop friendly relations among nations based on respect for the principle of equal rights and self-determination of people* [...]." Article 55 makes a similar reference by stating:

> *with a view to the creation of conditions of stability and well being which are necessary for peaceful and friendly relations among nations based on respect for the principle of equal rights and self-determination of peoples* [...].

Article 1 of the UDHR asserts that *"all human beings are born free and equal in dignity and rights."* The Charter and the UDHR do not mention the rights of minorities, and they have very few collective features (although the preamble to the Charter starts with the inscription *"we the peoples"*) which are limited, for example, to the recognition that individuals have the right to participate in collective practices (Articles 21 and 27 of the UDHR). However, the idea of collectivity is expressed in the form of duty of the individual toward the community, which is recognised as vital for the development of the person. Article 29(1) of the UDHR asserts that *"everyone has duties to the community in which alone the free and full development of his personality is possible."*

The limited presence of collective features in the UDHR is due, according to many, to the fact that it reflects a Western perception of human rights and that it is the product of Western cultural imperialism.[43] Indeed, *"were the Universal Declaration of Human Rights to be debated again in the General Assembly, the final draft would be significantly different from that which was adopted in 1948."*[44] To Africans and Asians, the idea that people would possess a non-community-linked human identity (which is a basic principle of the UDHR) is absolutely inconceivable. In fact, in the African and Asian mind, the human being *"is not the Lockean "man" and in this view lies the essence of the difference between the Third World and the First World."*[45] Furthermore,

---

[43] It should, however, be underlined that the UDHR was approved with the votes of a number of non-Western countries, such as Saudi Arabia and India. Conversely, it must be pointed out that, before the end of the colonial rule, many non-Western scholars were Western-educated.

[44] E.J.M. Zvobgo, 'A Third World View' in D.P. Kommers and G.D. Loescher (eds.), *Human Rights and American Foreign Policy* (Notre Dame: University of Notre Dame Press, 1979), pp. 90–107, at 95.

[45] Id., at 93.

> *one critical difference between the African and Western traditions concerns the importance of the human individual. In the liberal democracies of the Western world the ultimate repository of rights is the human person. The individual is held in a virtually sacralized position. There is a perpetual [...] concern with the dignity of the individual, his worth, personal autonomy and property. [...] If Africans were the sole authors of the Universal Declaration of Human Rights, they might have ranked the rights of communities above those of individuals, and they might have used a cultural idiom fundamentally different from the language in which the ideas are now formulated.*[46]

The Convention on the Prevention and Punishment of the Crime of Genocide gives protection from genocide to all persons and groups living within a state, as defined by national, racial, ethnic and religious criteria (strangely enough not by any linguistic ones). Article 2(1) defines genocide as "[...] *any of the following acts committed with intent to destroy, in whole or in part, a* [...] *group as such.*" Paragraph 2 specifies that genocide also extends to the infliction of mental and bodily harm and the deliberate infliction of conditions of life calculated to bring about the physical destruction of all or part of a group. The Convention does not specifically state the right of a population to exist, but formulates it negatively by prohibiting the destruction of a group.

The International Covenant for the Elimination of All Forms of Racial Discrimination (ICERD), in its Articles 1(4) and 2(2), provides for the possibility of preferential treatment of racial or ethnic groups or of members of such groups to ensure their advancement and their enjoyment of human rights and fundamental freedoms.

The International Covenant for Economic Social and Cultural Rights (ICESCR) and the ICCPR state in Article 1 (identical for both covenants) that:

> *All peoples have the right to self-determination. By virtue of that right they freely determine their political status and freely pursue their economic, social and cultural development. All peoples may, for their own ends, freely dispose of their natural wealth and resources without prejudice to any obligations arising out of international economic cooperation, based upon the principle of mutual benefit, and international law. In no case may a people be deprived of its own means of subsistence.*

---

[46] A. Legesse, 'Human Rights in African Political Culture' in K.W. Thompson (ed.), *The Moral Imperatives of Human Rights: A World Survey* (Washington: University Press of America 1980), pp. 123–128, at 124 and 128.

It should be underlined that Article 1 of the ICESCR and of the ICCPR is a right for "peoples" and not minorities. Furthermore, as explained by the Human Rights Committee (HRC),

> *the right of self-determination is of particular importance because its realization is an essential condition for the effective guarantee and observance of individual human rights and for the promotion and strengthening of those rights.*[47]

Article 27 of the ICCPR holds that:

> *In those States in which ethnic, religious or linguistic minorities exist, persons belonging to such minorities shall not be denied the right, in community with the other members of their group, to enjoy their own culture, to profess and practice their own religion or to use their own language.*

The formulation of the Article makes it evident that although this minority right has a collective aspect, it is not granted to minorities as such, but to individual members of these groups;[48] a view confirmed by the HRC, which pointed out that Article 27 *"confers rights on persons belonging to minorities which 'exist' in a state party."*[49] These persons should have a culture[50] or a religion or a language in common.[51] Conversely, in several of

---

[47] U.N. Human Rights Committee, *General Comment 12, The Right to Self-Determination of Peoples,* 13 March 1984, para. 1. The CESCR recognises that *"all indigenous peoples* [...] *have the right to the full enjoyment, as a collective or as individuals, of all human rights and fundamental freedoms as recognized in* [...] *international human rights law." See* U.N. Committee on Economic, Social and Cultural Rights, *General Comment 21, Right of Everyone to Take Part in Cultural Life*, E/C.12/GC/21, 21 December 2009, para. 7 [hereinafter *General Comment 21*].

[48] The original text of Article 27 was phrased in terms of "minorities" rather than "persons belonging to... minorities." The change occurred because of the fear of states to grant legal personality to groups via the recognition of collective rights, which would encourage secessionist groups and ultimately lead to the territorial break-up of the state. *See* Henrard, *supra* note 5, at 172. The language used in Article 27 is therefore a compromise solution between the wish of minorities for collective rights, on the one hand, and the fear of states that the recognition of such rights would stimulate secession, on the other hand. *See* F. Benoit-Rohmer, *The Minority Question in Europe: Towards a Coherent System of Protection for National Minorities* (Strasbourg: Council of Europe, 1996), at 19 [hereinafter Benoit-Rohmer].

[49] U.N. Human Rights Committee, 'General Comment 23(50), Article 27': U.N. Doc. CCPR/C/21/Rev.1/Add.5, 1994, para. 5.2 [hereinafter General Comment 23(50)].

[50] One of the many manifestations of culture is the way of life, as stated in the General Comment 23(50), para. 7. Unlike the ECtHR, the HRC has been keen in recognising the right of members of minorities to enjoy their culture. *See*, for example, the cases of *Kitok v. Sweden*, Communication No. 197/1985 (10 August 1988): CCPR/C/33/D/197/185, and *Ominayak, Chief of the Lubicon Lake Band v. Canada,* Communication No. 167/1984 (10 May 1990): CCPR/C/38/D/167/1984.

[51] General Comment 23(50), *supra* note 49, para. 5.1.

its views under the individual complaint procedure, the HRC seemed to accept more or less explicitly that Article 27 has a collective and an individual focus. General Comment 23(50) also emphasises the necessity to protect the separate identity of minorities, so that the reference to the identity of minorities can be understood as an acknowledgement of the collective dimension. Indeed, it states that:

> *although the rights protected under Article 27 are individual rights, they depend in turn on the ability of the minority group to maintain its culture, language or religion. Accordingly, positive measures by States may also be necessary to protect the identity of a minority* [...].[52]

The hybrid character of Article 27 is underlined by pointing out that although it is framed in terms of individual rights, it implies a certain recognition of the collective dimension of the minority phenomenon, which:

> [...] *would result not only from the protection of the collective exercise of the rights, namely in community with the other members of the group, but also from the attribution of these rights to individuals in their capacity as members of a minority group.*[53]

The rather general and thus vague formulation of Article 27, in combination with its *ratio legis* – the protection of minorities' right to identity – seems to generate the possibility to argue for a more positive evaluation of the need for collective rights under this Article. Indeed, the expression "right to identity of minorities" already points in the direction of a stronger recognition of the collective dimension of minority rights.[54]

One recognition of collective rights comes from the Committee on Economic Social and Cultural Rights (CESR), which makes reference to the communal exercise of the rights recognised in the ICESCR. This, in its General Comment 17 and in General Comment 21, underlines that cultural rights can be exercised alone or in association with others or as a community.[55]

The U.N. Declaration on the Right to Development formulates the right to development as a right to which individuals and peoples are entitled. For example, Article 1(1) provides that:

---

52 General Comment 23(50), *supra* note 49, para. 6.2.

53 Henrard, *supra* note 5, at 172.

54 Id., at 173.

55 *See* U.N. Committee on Economic, Social and Cultural Rights, General Comment 17 *The right of everyone to benefit from the protection of the moral and material interests resulting from any scientific, literary or artistic production of which he or she is the author (Article 15, paragraph 1 (c), of the Covenant)*, E/C.12/GC/17, 12 January 2006, at para. 8 and *General Comment 21, supra* note 47, at para. 15.

> *the right to development is an inalienable human right by virtue of which every human person and all peoples are entitled to participate in, contribute to and enjoy economic, social, cultural and political development, in which all human rights and fundamental freedoms can be fully realised.*

Article 2, however, specifies that individuals must be regarded as the main subject of development.

The 1992 U.N. Declaration on the Rights of Persons Belonging to National or Ethnic, Religious or Linguistic Minorities maintains the spirit of Article 27 of the ICCPR. Both the title and Article 2 refer to *"persons belonging to* [...] *minorities."* The Working Group on Minorities, which drafted the Declaration, has thus purposely approached the issue of minority rights only from the individual rights' point of view, avoiding the issue of collective rights.[56] The individualistic approach of Article 2 is softened by Article 3, which provides that:

> *persons belonging to minorities may exercise their rights, including those set forth in this Declaration, individually as well as in community with other members of their group, without any discrimination.*

Furthermore, the Declaration introduces a new element of minority protection in its Article 1(1), by stating that:

> *States shall protect the existence and the national or ethnic, cultural, religious and linguistic identity of minorities within their respective territories and shall encourage conditions for the promotion of that identity.*

Individual-oriented language also occurs in Article 2(5) of the Declaration, which gives members of minorities a three-fold right: they have the right to maintain contacts within the group itself, to hold contacts with other minority groups living in the same country and to have contacts across borders with members of minorities to which they are related. The wording of this paragraph in strictly individual terms is not completely suitable to the context. Only by interpreting Article 2(4) (right to maintain and establish associations) and 2(5) together does it become evident that the scope of paragraph 5 is not only that of contacts between individuals, but also that of contacts between minority associations.[57]

The 1993 Vienna Declaration and Programme of Action contains a minority provision in the spirit of Article 27 of the ICCPR, and indeed

[56] G. Alfredsson, 'Minority Rights: A Summary of Existing Practice' in A. Phillips and A. Rosas (eds), *The UN Minority Rights Declaration* (Turku/London: 1993), pp. 73–79, at 78.

[57] A. Spiliopoulou Åkermark, *Justification of Minority Protection in International Law* (The Hague: Kluwer Law International, 1997), at 185.

refers to persons belonging to minorities, who, among others, have the right to enjoy their own culture. Article I(10) on the right to development emphasises that the individual is the bearer of this right.

UNESCO has adopted two declarations with regard to collective rights. One is the UNESCO Declaration of the Principles of International Cultural Cooperation of 1966 and the other is the UNESCO Declaration on Race and Racial Prejudice of 1978. In its Article 1, the first states that *"every people has the right and duty to develop its culture."* Article 5 adds that *"cultural cooperation is a right and a duty for all peoples and all nations."* The main importance of the 1978 declaration lies in the fact that it grants groups the right to be different, by declaring in Article 5(1) that they all have a right *"to their own cultural identity and the development of that distinctive cultural life."*

The 1989 International Labour Organisation (ILO) Convention 169 concerning Indigenous and Tribal Peoples in Independent Countries gives in Article 5 *"recognition and protection of the social, cultural, religious and spiritual values and practices of interested populations, both as groups and as individuals."* The U.N. Declaration on the Rights of Indigenous Peoples has a collective focus, whereas in Article 1, indigenous peoples are granted the right to enjoy human rights and fundamental freedoms *"as a collective or as individuals."* A right to autonomy is also recognized in Article 4. This refers to internal and local affairs; however, contrary to the text of the Draft Declaration which in Article 31 made specific reference to autonomy with regard to internal and local affairs, *including* culture, it does not specify what internal and local affairs might imply.[58] The collective focus of ILO Convention 169 is undeniably important, as well as that of the Declaration on the Rights of Indigenous peoples.[59]

The European Convention for Human Rights and Fundamental Freedoms (ECHR) maintains an individualistic approach and does not mention collective rights. Conversely, the initial proposal for the Council of Europe Framework Convention for National Minorities (FCNM), as set out by the Commission for Democracy through Law (Venice Commission), contained clear references to collective rights. The protection of identity

[58] The Draft Declaration had a much stronger focus on collective rights, and indeed stated in Article 34 that *"Indigenous peoples have the* collective *right to determine the responsibilities of individuals to their communities."* This, in the text of the Declaration, became Article 35, but the word "collective" has been deleted from the text.

[59] *See* chapter 2. It should be underlined that even if ILO Convention 169 was applicable to the Roma, this would have no effect to the Roma living in Italy because Italy has not ratified it.

was included as a collective right in Article 3 of the proposal, according to which minorities had the right "[...] *to the respect, safeguarding and development of their ethnical, religious or linguistic identity.*"[60] However, it is clear that the FCNM intends to protect individuals. Indeed, although the title speaks of "national minorities," the preamble refers to "persons belonging to national minorities," terminology adopted to emphasise the fact that the FCNM protects individual rights enjoyed in community with others, rather than collective rights enjoyed by groups.[61] This formulation reflects that of other international instruments, such as the ICCPR, and given its repeated invocation throughout the substantive provisions, it would be misleading to evince from the shorter title that the FCNM endorses collective rights.[62] The Explanatory Report highlights that Article 1 refers to the protection of national minorities and of the rights and freedoms of persons belonging to national minorities.[63] Apparently the reason for rejecting the idea of collective rights was the fear felt by many countries of secessionist demands.[64] To overcome these fears, the FCNM acknowledged that the protection of a national minority group could be achieved through the protection of the rights of the individuals belonging to that group. But this does not imply the recognition of collective rights.[65] Another reason for this approach might be the willingness of persons belonging to national minorities to hold on to liberal fears that collective rights would endanger the primacy of individual rights.[66]

However, the departure point of the FCNM does not solve the problems emerging from the consistent collective character of minorities. Many persons belonging to national minorities advocate the protection of their group identity (including the right to organise themselves as a group).

---

[60] The other proposal was contained in the Council of Europe, Parliamentary Assembly, Recommendation 1201 (1993) *on an additional protocol on the rights of national minorities to the European Convention on Human Rights,* adopted on 1 February 1993. The proposal of the Venice Commission is reproduced in *Human Rights Law Journal,* Vol. 12, 1991, No. 6–7, pp. 269–273.

[61] T.H. Malloy, 'Title and Preamble,' in M. Weller (ed.), *The Rights of Minorities in Europe* (Oxford: Oxford University Press, 2005), pp. 49–73, at 50.

[62] Id., at 50.

[63] Council of Europe, Preparatory Work of the Ad Hoc Committee for the Protection of National Minorities (CAHMIN), *Explanatory Report to the Framework Convention for the Protection of National Minorities,* CAHMIN H(1995)010, para. 31 [hereinafter FCNM Explanatory Report].

[64] H-J. Heintze, 'Article 1,' in M. Weller (ed.), *The Rights of Minorities in Europe* (Oxford: Oxford University Press, 2005), pp. 77–96, at 85 [hereinafter Heintze].

[65] FCNM Explanatory Report, *supra* note 63, para. 13.

[66] W. Kymlicka (1995), *Multicultural Citizenship: a Liberal Theory of Minority Rights* (Oxford: Oxford University Press, 1995), at 4–9 [hereinafter Kymlicka (1995a)].

For this reason, they demand the right to use their language, to practise their culture, to influence the content of the education of their children and to participate in political action affecting them.[67] Furthermore, in certain circumstances the protection of national minorities can only be guaranteed through collective action.[68] For this reason, the FCNM requires that persons belonging to national minorities should exercise their minority rights "in community with others," thus recognising a collective dimension within its ambit.

The Organisation for Security and Cooperation in Europe (OSCE), whose commitments are politically rather than legally binding, originally maintained an individualistic approach to human rights, as shown in the Helsinki Final Act of 1975. A change occurred in 1989, when the Concluding Document of the Vienna Meeting was adopted. In this, Principle 19 underlines that participating states:

> *will protect and create the conditions for the promotion of the ethnic, cultural, linguistic and religious identity of national minorities on their own territory. They will respect the free exercise of rights by persons belonging to such minorities and ensure their full equality with others.*

This Principle shows that the OSCE has a mixed approach toward collective rights because it is the members of minority groups and not minority groups as such who are the subjects of the rights conferred.

The 1990 Document of the Copenhagen Meeting of the Conference on the Human Dimension of the OSCE reiterates the mixed approach. Again, as Principle 32 points out, it is individual members of national minorities who:

> *have the right freely to express, preserve and develop their ethnic, cultural, linguistic or religious identity and to maintain and develop their culture in all its aspects, free of any attempts at assimilation against their will.*[69]

Generally speaking, it seems that the Copenhagen Document attributes rights to "members" of national minorities, which is especially shown in

---

[67] Heintze, *supra* note 59, at 86.

[68] *"Under the Framework Convention this question is somewhat academic because there is no directly applicable enforcement mechanism, but, were one to exist, it is arguable that the minority group could assert its need for protection through that mechanism." See* G. Gilbert (1996), 'The Council of Europe and minority rights' 18.1 *Human Rights Quarterly* 160 (1996), at 178 [hereinafter Gilbert (1996)].

[69] As it will be seen, this principle is particularly relevant with regard to the Roma because in many countries, attempts are made to assimilate them to the way of life of the majority society.

the last phrase of Principle 32, which states that *"Persons belonging to national minorities can exercise and enjoy their rights individually as well as in community with other members of their group* [...]*."* Protection of minority groups as such is better shown in Principle 33, which declares that *"the participating states will protect the ethnic, cultural, linguistic and religious identity of national minorities on their territory and create conditions for the promotion of that identity."*

Principle 35 ensures the right of members of national minorities to participate in public affairs, including those related to the protection and promotion of their identity. In fact, it affirms that:

> *the participating states will respect the right of persons belonging to national minorities to effective participation in public affairs, including participation in the affairs relating to the protection and promotion of the identity of such minorities. The participating states note the efforts undertaken to protect and create conditions for the promotion of the ethnic, cultural, linguistic and religious identity of certain national minorities by establishing, as one of the possible means to achieve these aims, appropriate local or autonomous administrations corresponding to the specific historical and territorial circumstances of such minorities and in accordance with the policies of the state concerned.*

Principle 35 could thus be considered the first step toward the recognition of collective rights and toward forms of self-determination for minorities: *"the provision adopts the view that individual rights can only be properly protected where the groups have political control over their own affairs."*[70] The reference to autonomy underlines the importance of political rights to give effects to other rights granted to (members of) minorities and of a certain degree of "internal self-determination" to lead to the preservation and the development of a separate minority identity.[71] In this sense, political rights and autonomy shall be viewed only as some of the steps on a path toward the full preservation and promotion of minorities' identities.

Governments might accede to the needs of minorities on an ad hoc basis, but only institutionalised protection will lead to the protection of the identity of minorities.[72] For minority rights to be effective, states must provide funding; however, the invocation of individual human rights

---

[70] G. Gilbert, 'The Legal Protection Accorded to Minority Groups In Europe,' *Netherlands Quarterly of Human Rights* Vol. 23 (1992) 67, at 95 [hereinafter Gilbert (1992)].

[71] Henrard, *supra* note 5, at 254–255.

[72] J. Wright, 'Minority Groups, Autonomy and Self-determination' *Oxford Journal of Legal Studies* 1999 19 (605), at 614 [hereinafter Wright].

standards might render this task particularly difficult. Therefore, to fulfil their cultural aspirations, minority groups depend on the democratic process and thus, exercise autonomy over matters of particular concern to them and secure control over their collective life through participation in the democratic process.[73] Furthermore,

> *in order for the whole people to be represented in government without "distinction as to race, creed or colour," minority groups should have some measure of autonomy over the matters of particular relevance to their ethnic, cultural, religious or linguistic identity, thus achieving de facto parity with the dominant group who, by the fact of numerical domination, control those matters (relating to ethnic, cultural, religious, and linguistic identity) affecting them.* [...] *In the absence of participation/representation in government, the minority group may simply be oppressed by the majority in relation to the cultural aspect of their lives.*[74]

Even the 1991 Report of the CSCE Meeting of Experts on National Minorities proves the OSCE mixed approach toward collective rights because it reiterates that rights are granted to members of minority groups and that the OSCE states will actively protect and promote the specific identity of minority groups.

4.4. The Debate Between Supporters and Critics of Collective Rights

The next two sub-sections will provide a summary and analysis of the main positions and arguments of supporters and opponents of collective rights. Before embarking on the analysis of the main positions, it should be underlined that most of the debate is based on the notion of a dichotomy of individual versus collective rights, in the logic of "either-or."[75] However, as Marko correctly pointed out, comparative constitutional law provides evidence that this is an erroneous dichotomy, mainly based on ideological assumptions. The first assumption comes from the history of the Cold War, in which individual rights became equated with democratic

---

[73] Wright, *supra* note 72, at 609.

[74] Id., at 614. Autonomy does not mean separation, but simply "[...] *control, and the methods of achieving control, and the degrees of control, will vary from group to group.*" In this sense, territorial autonomy might be an inappropriate tool for many groups, such as those geographically dispersed. *"Autonomy may be achieved through participation in central government."*

[75] Marko, *supra* note 13.

systems and collective rights with communist authoritarian systems. The second assumption is based on the ideological presumptions of strict individualism; any special rights for members of minority groups are seen as a privilege or exemption from the equality principle. Finally, any form of cultural or territorial autonomy is seen as going against the principle of national sovereignty and as such, as a threat to the territorial integrity of a state.[76] As I will also conclude,[77] Marko advised that individual and group-related rights can be combined.

4.4.1. *Only Individuals can be Bearers of Human Rights*

Critics of group rights maintain that individual rights, especially the right to freedom of association, offer sufficient protection for minorities. The recognition that membership in a community is important for the shaping of individual identities does not mean that special rights should be attached to such communities.[78] Indeed, the protection of cultural differences should be based on the individual right to freedom of association: the claim of minorities to live according to their cultural characteristics does not have to be respected because cultures are entitled to protection, but because individuals have the freedom to associate – they are free to form communities and live according to the cultures of such communities.[79] It would thus follow that collective rights could hinder or even violate the rights of individuals – in most cases, we see individuals crushed by society but rarely do we see society crushed by the exercise of individual human rights.

Enforcing collective over individual identity is thus seen as a violation of human rights, whereas enforcing individual rights over collective rights ordinarily is not. Even when the exercise of individual rights may threaten or destroy the group, individual human rights should be given priority. If the group is eroded or transformed by the free exercise of the human rights of its members, *"such an outcome is likely to be morally and politically acceptable, and often even desirable."*[80] This view has been strongly

[76] Marko, *supra* note 13.
[77] *See* further below in this chapter.
[78] C. Kukathas, 'Are There Any Cultural Rights?' in W. Kymlicka (ed.), *The Rights of Minorities Cultures* (Oxford: Oxford University Press, 1995), pp. 228–256, at 231–232 [hereinafter Kukathas].
[79] Id., at 238–239.
[80] J. Donnelly, *Universal Human Rights in Theory and Practice* (Ithaca: Cornell University Press, 1989), at 151 [hereinafter Donnelly (1989)].

criticized: it seems that because no coherent theory of individual and collective rights exists, the concept of collective rights is rejected altogether, deeming it especially dangerous when proposed as a prerequisite for other human rights. Indeed, it cannot possibly be denied that collective preconditions exist for the protection of individual human rights, and although collective rights might be dangerous for individual human rights, it is important to recognise them because they are the precondition for other human rights and are therefore needed to protect them – their *ultimate* purpose is not the protection of the group in itself, but of the individuals who compose it.[81]

Another problem is that:

> *some ethnic and national groups are deeply illiberal, and seek to suppress rather than support the liberty of their members. Under these circumstances, acceding to the demands of minority groups may result in gross violations of the most basic liberties of individuals.*[82]

Thus, the individual should not only be able to associate, but should also be free to dissociate from such communities to which he or she belongs.[83]

I agree that individuals should have the choice to leave a community in which they feel their rights are being violated; I also feel that for the members of certain groups, no real alternative exists but to decide to abandon their community, due to external circumstances rather than to the practices of the group to which they belong. For this reason, it is my belief that the collective right to cultural identity ought to be protected – if only to give individuals the choice of whether they want to live according to the customs of their minority group. In fact, an exclusive focus on individual rights is not sufficient for advancing the protection of the rights of certain groups. The wide-spread stigmatisation and prejudice and the social and political exclusion of which some groups (such as the Roma) are victims cannot be targeted by allowing only individual claims against discrimination. Provided that the individual claims are successful, the matter would not be solved at its source, at the level of the group.[84] The mere

---

[81] Freeman, *supra* note 38, at 32. Emphasis added.

[82] Kymlicka (1995a), *supra* note 66, at 75.

[83] Kukathas, *supra* note 78, at 238–239. In addition to these criticisms, the fear also exists that the proclamation of collective rights may threaten the territorial integrity of states.

[84] The jurisprudence of the ECtHR shows that only recently has the Court been able to establish a link between issues involving the Roma and the protection of the cultural identity of the individual and the community. *See*, for example, the case of *Chapman v. the*

application of the principle of non-discrimination to protect the rights of discriminated groups such as the Roma would end up favouring the abandonment of the traditional lifestyle, culture and language by those who did not want to be the target of discrimination. In this sense, collective rights in general and the collective right to cultural identity in particular, together with the use of the rights of minorities and affirmative action, if applied to Roma communities across Europe, would ensure a much more extensive protection and promotion of their rights.

4.4.2. *Collectivities as the Bearers of Rights*

Several provisions in international law, although intended to protect the rights of individuals, also guarantee the interests (and by extension, the rights) of the collectivity, either as society in general, or as a group within society (for example, a minority group). At the same time, limits to the enjoyment of the rights of individuals are placed to protect the interests of society in general, and, more specifically, the rights of other individuals. So, for example, the ECHR, although strictly maintaining an individualistic approach and making no mention of the rights of collectivities, places a limit on the rights of individuals to respect for private and family life, freedom of thought, conscience and religion and freedom of expression (as expressed in Articles 8, 9 and 10) in the interest of public safety, for the protection of public order, health and morals and for the protection of the rights and freedoms of others. Similarly, the ICCPR places a limit on the right to freedom of expression as stated in Article 19, to protect, amongst others, the rights and reputation of other individuals.

The proclamation of human rights has led to a heated debate over the nature, the meaning and the justifiability of collective rights, including whether or not these are compatible with individual human rights.[85] Supporters of collective rights point out that the proclamation of collective rights finally does justice to the criticism coming from Third World countries, according to which existing human rights standards have too much of an individualistic nature. Furthermore, they argue that the fact that collective rights have not been articulated to a high degree of specificity is not a sufficient reason to reject them in advance, because many individual rights are vague and undetermined too.[86] Moreover, the fact that

United Kingdom (2001) 33 EHRR 18, decided on 18 January 2001 [hereinafter *Chapman v. the United Kingdom*].

[85] Galenkamp (1995), *supra* note 20, at 66.

[86] Id., at 67.

tension exists between individual and collective rights that may be invoked to justify the violation of individual human rights cannot be considered a decisive argument against collective rights.[87]

Collectivities *can* be the bearers of rights, although sometimes it is argued that they *should not* be granted rights because they might misuse them and threaten individual rights. However, it should be underlined that all rights can be misused, including individual rights. If we were to be consistent, *"we would have to deny the latter as well, and that is absurd."*[88] Indeed, if collective rights can be used to oppress individuals, individual rights too can be used to damage and destroy communities. Moreover, some collective rights protect individual rights and empower their bearers because organised groups are better able to defend the rights of their members than they can do individually.[89] I am of the opinion that it is thanks to collective rights, group rights and collective action that progress has been achieved in the protection of individual rights. One example could be that of trade unions which have fought for more humane conditions of work and succeeded in protecting the rights of all workers.

Individual freedom is tied to membership in a community and therefore, collective rights could actually enlarge the freedom of individuals.[90] In addition, collective rights could promote equality between the minority and the majority.[91]

I feel that minority groups can and should be integrated while they should also maintain a distinct entity. Indeed, integration does not and should not necessarily lead to assimilation. By integration of a minority group, I mean its full participation in the life of a state as well as the achievement of full equality of the rights held by the majority society, without foregoing its identity and culture, or its language, religion and values. Assimilation, conversely, is the accomplishment by the minority group of the same rights as the rest of the society through the abandonment of its identity, culture, values, and so on. This consideration might be of particular importance when assessing the status of Roma communities in countries such as Italy.

---

[87] Galenkamp (1995), *supra* note 20, at 68.

[88] B. Parekh, *Rethinking Multiculturalism – Cultural Diversity and Political Theory*, (Basingstoke: Macmillan Press, 2000), at 216 [hereinafter Parekh].

[89] Parekh, *supra* note 88, at 216.

[90] Kymlicka (1995a), *supra* note 66, at 52. Kymlicka disagrees with those insisting that minority rights are inherently in conflict with liberal principles of individual liberty and universal rights.

[91] Id.

Human communities too can have moral dignity or status, and thus become the bearers of rights, *"for they give meaning and a sense of rootedness and belonging to their members, which is why the latter are often prepared to give up their lives for them."*[92] Two criteria have been identified for communities to be rights holders. One is that the community must be an entity by itself – thus, having a different and separate identity from that of its members and being more than just the sum of its members. The second criterion has to do with the interdependence of the members and the community, whereby the first should be directly linked to the identity of the community.[93]

The main question that must be asked is which collectivities should have what rights under what conditions. The question can only be asked in terms of consideration of human well-being and cannot be defined in the abstract because although some collective rights can claim universal validity, others vary from society to society.[94] It has been stated that a collectivity has a *prima facie* claim to its rights if it meets one of six conditions. First, it has to mean a great deal to its members, enjoy a moral status in their eyes, and they must wish to preserve it. Second, its existence is fundamental to the interests of its members, which can only be promoted through the exercise of collective action by the community. Third, a community is deeply insecure and cannot and would not integrate into mainstream society without certain guaranteed rights. Fourth, a community has been subjected to long oppression, lacks the confidence and ability to compete with the rest of society and needs to be equalized with the latter by affirmative action. Fifth, a community has the potential to make a valuable and unique contribution to the wider society and can only do so if it has the right to preserve its identity. Sixth, some communities are based on shared doctrines of which they see themselves as custodians and can

---

[92] Parekh, *supra* note 88, at 215. It is also thought that the bearers of collective rights are specific kinds of communities – which are inclusive, "natural" communities. McDonalds believes that "natural groups" are *"peoples with a language, history, culture or set of beliefs in common." See* M. McDonald, 'Should Communities Have Rights?' in A.A. An-Na'im (ed.) *Human Rights in Cross-Cultural Perspectives* (Philadelphia: University of Pennsylvania Press, 1992), pp. 133–161, at 150. Kymlicka noted that natural groups are *"genuinely distinct societal cultures."* By "societal culture" the author meant *"a culture which provides its members with meaningful ways of life across the full range of human activities, including social, educational, religious, recreational, and economic life, encompassing both public and private spheres. These cultures tend to be territorially concentrated, and based on a shared language." See* Kymlicka (1995a), *supra* note 66, at 80 and 76.

[93] Johnston, *supra* note 25, at 181–183.

[94] Parekh, *supra* note 88, at 217.

only function or contribute to the well-being of their members and of those of the wider society when endowed with appropriate rights.[95]

Others conclude that collective rights ought to have three conditions, the first being that they need to be a non-reducible collective agent. This means that the rights are ascribed to a collectivity as such which cannot be reduced to the sum of its members (such as in the case of freedom of association), and which do not apply to individuals as members of a community (such as in the case of freedom of religion). The second condition is that the constitutive agent has to be of a constitutive kind and have a distinctive group identity: in addition, the community should have a collective interest or a collective identity which needs to be protected by collective rights. Furthermore, the community should have a certain internal structure that leads to a representative body that could legitimately speak on behalf of the whole community.[96]

I contend that a community can, and ought to be, the subject of collective rights if it meets at least some minimum conditions. First, its members must identify themselves in terms of the community – a strong sense of belonging must exist that brings the members of the community to differentiate themselves from mainstream society;[97] in addition, the customs, culture and language that the community carries on must have significant meaning to its members and they must wish to preserve it. Second, the community has a long history of discrimination and oppression, has not so far been able to compete with the majority society and needs special measures to reach full equality with it. Third, the community cannot integrate into mainstream society; it is not confident regarding its possibilities and capabilities, and it risks being singled out, excluded and discriminated against; its members are discriminated against because they belong to the community and, most importantly, the community as a whole is discriminated against and becomes the target of racial profiling.[98] These conditions are surely met by Roma communities living in

---

95 Parekh, *supra* note 88, at 217–218.

96 M. Galenkamp, 'Collective Rights: Much Ado About Nothing' *Netherlands Quarterly of Human Rights* Vol. 9, No. 3 (1991), pp. 291–307, at 296–299. [hereinafter Galenkamp (1991)] Subjects of this kind might be minorities or indigenous peoples.

97 *See*, for example, the Roma, who call any non-Roma "gadjè."

98 A good example would be that of the Roma minority of Italy, in which the whole community is singled out, excluded and criminalised for the criminal behaviour of a few of its members: it appears that, among the majority society, no concept of individual criminal responsibility exists and the whole community is held accountable for the acts of only a few of its members.

Europe and Italy, and it could thus be concluded that they should be the bearers of collective rights.

The argument according to which rights presuppose the capacity for agency and reciprocity which only individuals possess has been rejected by pointing out that even animals and children can have rights, although they do not possess the capacity for agency and reciprocity – we simply grant them rights if we feel it is desirable to do so and then authorise adults to exercise them on their behalf.[99] Furthermore, collectivities have their decision-making procedures and representatives which can act on their behalf.[100] Against those critiques of collective rights which state that rights can only be given to those who exist or are real, it is argued that it is not true that only individuals exist and collectivities do not: the latter exist in the form of consciousness, beliefs, rituals and so on of their members and persist over time when these are institutionalised. They are made up of individuals who are equally shaped by them and neither can be reduced to the other or declared self-subsistent or fictitious.[101] I support the same view, and I also point out how in many cases, people define themselves through their membership to a particular group, which at the same time is shaped by its members. For instance, some people define themselves in terms of political beliefs and through being part of a political party, whereas, at the same time, the programme, scope and mode of action of the party is decided by its members.

---

[99] Jones noted that people, when asking whether collectives may be right holders, actually do so in the same way they ask whether fetuses, animals, and future generations may be right holders. The dilemma would then be whether *"we should ascribe moral standing to groups in the way that we ascribe moral standing to individual persons. If the answer is yes, then we can conceive a group, as we can conceive an individual, as an irreducible right-bearing entity."* *See* P. Jones, 'Human Rights, Group Rights, and Peoples' Rights, 21 (1999) *Human Rights Quarterly* 80, at 86. In the *Reparations* case, the International Court of Justice affirmed a variety of models of personality and asserted the power of the international community *"to bring into being an entity possessing objective international personality and not merely personality recognised by them alone, together with capacity to bring international claims."* *See Reparation for Injuries Suffered in the Service of the United Nations,* International Court of Justice, Advisory Opinion, April 11, 1949, ICJ Reports 1949, at 174. Commenting on this case, Lautherpacht underlined that the range of subjects of international law is not rigid and immutable but is capable of modifications and development in accordance with the will of states. *See* H. Lauterpacht, *International Law, Collected Papers,* Vol. 1 (1970). In the *Western Sahara* decision, the International Court of Justice left open for groups (whether composed of states, tribes or individuals) the claim to be a legal entity distinct from its members. *See Western Sahara,* International Court of Justice, Advisory Opinion, 16 October 1975, *ICJ Reports* 1975, at 63.

[100] Parekh, *supra* note 88, at 214.

[101] Id., at 215.

The idea that only human beings have interests and can suffer or prosper is also rejected. Some interests are individual in nature, but others are shared with and pertain to people as members of the community and can only be pursued together – for example, we want our political community to continue to exist. These,

> *are either our interests as a community and in that sense our collective interests, or form the shared background or precondition of our individual interests, and hence our common interests. In either case they may be rightly called the interests of the community.*[102]

Granting rights to collectivities, according to supporters of collective rights, is necessary to ensure a life of dignity and respect for the individual members of some groups.[103] People are not merely individuals, but also members of groups, and by adopting collective rights, we may do justice to the social nature of individuals. Indeed, human beings are social beings and better exist in relation to one another. When people are born, they are all the same – they *"share the same language, religion, culture and political philosophy."*[104] Through membership in a group, individuals define their identity and lead a more meaningful and dignified life.[105] In other words,

---

102 Parekh, *supra* note 88, at 215. A common sense of belonging among citizens is fundamental for the survival and stability of a multicultural society. However, a multicultural society is too diverse to base its sense of belonging on shared cultural or ethnic characteristics; thus, this must be based on a shared commitment to the political community – in which members are bonded to each other by ties of common interest and attachment, *"through their mediating membership of a shared community"* and not by reasons of ethnicity, religion, culture or other characteristics. A political community does not even involve commitment to common goals, because its members might deeply disagree on these, or to its form of government, of which they might have different views; let alone, a commitment to its dominant "cultural ethos" of which some might disapprove. Commitment or belonging are reciprocal in nature, and thus citizens cannot be committed or belong to a political community unless it is committed and belongs to them. This implies that the political community shall value all its members equally and reflect that value in its structure and conduct of public affairs. *See* B. Parekh, *What is multiculturalism*, available at www.india-seminar.com/1999/484/484%20parekh.htm, last visited Mar. 20, 2012.

103 Galenkamp (1995), *supra* note 20, at 67.

104 J. Packer, 'On the Definition of Minorities' in J. Packer and K. Myntti (eds.), *The Protection of Ethnic and Linguistic minorities in Europe* (Ebo/Turku: Ebo Akademi University, 1993), pp. 23–65, at 43 [hereinafter Packer].

105 Although individuals might not necessarily be protected against discrimination by their community; indeed they might be discriminated against by it because there might be competition for resources within a group. *See*, for example, the case of *Lovelace v. Canada* in which the applicant, a Canadian woman of Indian origin, lost her Indian status and access to special programmes, such as those on education, housing and social assistance, because she married outside her community. *See Sandra Lovelace v. Canada*, Communication n. R.6/24 (29 December 1977), UN Doc. Sup. N. 40 (A/36/40) at 166 (1981).

"human beings are conceived and born by social acts."[106] Individual human beings today see their personal identity as defined in significant measure by membership to a group:

> *Even in the modern West, where individualism seems to have reached the pinnacle of its historical development, few people define themselves entirely as individuals: the isolated, atomised individual is the exception rather than the rule. Most Westerners still define themselves as part of a family* [...]. *Many individuals define themselves in significant measure by their religion.* [...] *The same is true for many ethnic minorities.*[107]

The collective aspect becomes important when linked to membership of certain groups – such as linguistic minorities. Many contemporary nation-states contain minorities and collectivities bound by values which are different from those of the majority. These groups may require special rights to achieve "equal citizenship."[108] These rights may be collective but the claims of the groups are usually met with the implementation of the individual right to be free from arbitrary discrimination and appropriate measures of positive discrimination,[109] which however, as seen in chapter 3, are not sufficient to protect the cultural identities of minorities.

Although no special set of collective rights exists, all human rights have a social dimension, which is recognised even in international law provisions. For example, the formulation of Article 27 of the ICCPR is such that although not granting collective rights, it admits that the rights of individuals are premised on the existence of a community. The rationale behind giving full recognition to collective rights lies in the fact that most social and political problems today are collectivity-related and therefore draw attention to the collective dimension of human existence. Only through the promotion of collective rights can real protection of minorities be achieved.

4.5. Collective Rights and Cultural Identity

Cultural rights in general and the right to cultural identity in particular have a special position in the discussion on collective rights. Minority

---

[106] Packer, *supra* note 104, at 43.

[107] J. Donnelly, 'Human Rights, Individual Rights and Collective Rights,' in J. Berting, P.R. Baehr, J.H.Burgers, C. Flinterman, B. de Klerk, R. Kroes, C.A. van Minnen and K. VanderWal (eds.) *Human Rights in a Pluralist World* (London: Meckler, 1990), pp. 39–62, at 49–50 [hereinafter Donnelly (1990)].

[108] Freeman, *supra* note 38, at 26.

[109] Id., at 26.

protection is often justified by referring to the protection of culture, and culture has an intrinsic relation to the right to identity of minorities. The next sub-section will focus on cultural rights and on the collective right to cultural identity.

4.5.1. *Cultural Rights*

In the context of the discussion on culture and on a collective right to cultural identity, it is important to define what cultural rights are.[110] This sub-section aims at briefly reviewing the concepts of cultural rights in international law and in legal theory and their relation to the protection of minorities, considering the significance they have for the protection and promotion of their culture and way of life.

As highlighted by the U.N. independent expert in the field of cultural rights:

> *cultural rights are pivotal to the recognition and respect of human dignity, as they protect the development and expression of various world visions - individual and collective - and encompass important freedoms relating to matters of identity.*[111]

The main sources of cultural rights in international law are Article 27 of the UDHR, Article 15 of the ICESCR, Article 27 of the ICCPR and regional instruments such as the American Declaration on the Rights and Duties of Man (Article 13) and the Additional Protocol to the American Convention on Human Rights in the Area of Economic, Social and Cultural Rights (Article 14). Article 5(e)(vi) of the ICERD expresses the right to equal participation in cultural activities. Similar to this is Article 17 of the African Charter which also contains, in Article 29, a provision on the duty to preserve African cultural traditions. UNESCO has also taken part in the creation of additional standards related to the individual and collective rights in the field of culture.

Article 27(1) of the UDHR reads: *"Everyone has the right to freely participate in the cultural life of the community, to enjoy the arts and to share the scientific advancements and its benefits."* This is the only provision of the UDHR that specifically refers to culture and thus has a link with the protection of cultural identity. The Travaux Préparatoires of Article 27 show

---

[110] Culture and cultural identity have already been defined and analysed in chapter 1.

[111] *Report of the independent expert in the field of cultural rights, Ms. Farida Shaheed, submitted pursuant to resolution 10/23 of the Human Rights Council*, A/HRC/14/36, 22 March 2010, at 3–4.

that the main idea when drafting the Article was to include a reference to culture in the UDHR, without clearly defining the concepts of culture, participation and community. At the time Article 27 was drafted, culture was considered in a rather narrow sense, including mainly cultural materials such as art and literature.

The ICESCR is the first legally binding document that contains an explicit reference to "cultural rights" in the title. Although it does not contain a specific provision which directly addresses the issue of the protection of minorities comparable to Article 27 of the ICCPR, the ICESCR has some provisions which are important for minority protection – such as Article 15, which is also the only one which refers to culture and which, in a similar way to that of Article 27 of the UDHR reads "*1. The State parties to the present Covenant recognise the right of everyone: (a) to take part in cultural life* [...]." Article 2 contains an obligation for member states to take steps, to the maximum of their abilities, to achieve the progressive realisation of the rights it contains, including Article 15. This, in its paragraph 2, specifies that the steps to be taken should include those necessary for the conservation, the development and the diffusion of science and culture. In other words, by obliging the state to respect the freedom to assert and develop cultural orientation, Article 15 gives persons belonging to minorities or indigenous groups the right to express and develop their culture, including language (a carrier of culture), religion, traditions and customs.[112] The interplay between Article 15 of the ICESCR and Article 27 of the ICCPR thus shows a close link and interdependence between civil and political rights and economic, social and cultural rights. Limits to the rights set forth in Article 15, as laid down in Article 4, are permissible only if determined by law and compatible with the nature of these rights and for the purpose of promoting the general welfare in a democratic society. States also have a duty to promote awareness and enjoyment of the cultural heritage of national ethnic groups and minorities and of indigenous peoples – including through communication through the media.[113]

---

[112] A. Eide, 'Cultural Rights and Individual Rights' in A. Eide et al. (eds.), *Economic, Social and Cultural Rights* (Netherlands: Kluwer Law International, 2001), pp. 289–301, at 293.

[113] The importance of the right to freedom of expression (including access to and adequate coverage in the media) for the preservation of minorities' identities should not be underestimated. It is indeed a guarantee for the reproduction of a certain culture (which is once more related to the right to identity of minorities) and it implies the right to communicate in one's language and to disseminate opinions through the media. *See* the *Case of Informationsverein Lentia and others v. Austria*, Eur. Ct. Hum. RtS., Series A n. 276, 24 November 1993. Freedom of expression enables minorities to express their divergent

In 1992 and in 2008, the CESCR held a day of general discussion on Article 15 during which the members acknowledged that culture has a broad meaning that also includes "way of life," which entails that states have an obligation to take active measures to protect and promote minorities' cultures and ways of life.[114] Contrary to Article 27 of the ICCPR, Article 15 of the ICESCR imposes positive obligations, in the sense that contracting states are required to take measures to ensure that everyone's right (including that of members of minorities) to participate in cultural life is fully realised.[115] The CESCR also emphasised the importance of a "cultural infrastructure," including cultural centres, museums, libraries and theatres.

Article 27 is the only Article of the ICCPR that refers directly to the right to enjoy culture – which, however, is not considered a universal right, but a specific right for members of ethnic, religious or linguistic minorities. Culture is linked with religion and language and with a collective dimension, as expressed in the phrase "in community with other members of their group." In his study on Article 27, Capotorti asserted that "[...] *the objective to be attained is the preservation and natural development of the cultural identity of minorities: the State is therefore called upon to adopt all necessary means to end.*"[116] However, it should be underlined that compared to Article 15 of the ICESCR, Article 27 of the ICCPR establishes not only the right to participate in cultural life in general terms, but also, in more specific terms, that of the common enjoyment of a specific culture, seen in rather broad terms by the HRC.[117]

---

ideas and convictions, something considered *"essential for safeguarding the cultural identity of minorities." See* Benoit-Rohmer, *supra* note 48, at 46. Furthermore, it protects them against hurtful statements pertaining to aspects of their own, separate identity. *See* Henrard, *supra* note 5, at 90. The (individual) right to freedom of expression is fully analysed in chapter 3.

[114] R. O'Keefe, 'The "Right to Take Part in Cultural Life" under Article 15 of the ICESCR' *ICLQ* 1998 (904), at 917–918.

[115] According to the CESCR, Article 15 *"requires from the State party both abstention* (i.e., *non-interference with the exercise of cultural practices and with access to cultural goods and services*) *and positive action* (*ensuring preconditions for participation, facilitation and promotion of cultural life, and access to and preservation of cultural goods*)." *See General Comment 21, supra* note 47, para. 6. Many scholars and experts have agreed that cultural rights imply negative as well as positive obligations for states and can be enjoyed by the individual alone as well as jointly with others. *See* Donders, *supra* note 39, at 71.

[116] F. Capotorti, *Study on the Rights of Persons belonging to Ethnic, Religious and Linguistic Minorities,* UN Doc. E/CN.4/Sub.2/384/Rev. 1, 1979, para. 599.

[117] *See* chapter 1.

The HRC observed that the protection of cultural rights:

> *is directed to ensure the survival and continued development of the cultural, religious and social identity of the minorities concerned, thus enriching the fabric of society as a whole. Accordingly, the Committee observes that these rights must be protected as such and should not be confused with other personal rights conferred on one and all under the Covenant.*[118]

It has been suggested that cultural rights are privileges enjoyed by groups to maintain their way of life,[119] which include the right of members of communities such as minorities to preserve their distinctive culture against the state and the majority community.[120] Cultural rights are seen as a residual category because they have received less attention and they are less developed than civil and political and economic and social rights, a development that might be due to the vagueness of the term "culture."[121] The fact that cultural rights might be residual does not mean that they are not essential, as a community's distinctive way of life generally has an important value for its members and participation in culture is essential for a life of dignity.[122]

I strongly disagree with the idea that cultural rights might be a residual category: surely the fact that cultural rights have not received as much attention as other rights, or that their meaning and implications have not been fully clarified, does not mean that they are less important than other rights, especially when considering that the survival of the identity of minority groups might depend on respect for cultural rights. Furthermore, taking into account the aforementioned idea that all human rights are intertwined, indivisible, integrated and dependent on each other, it is dangerous to categorise a specific type of rights – in this case cultural rights – as residual. Too often, violations of cultural rights have led to the oppression and enforced assimilation of minorities. Furthermore, many minorities are still victims of discrimination and intolerance today, and they will not be able to reach full equality with the majority society unless their cultural rights are fully respected. In this sense, the protection of cultural rights (and of cultural identity) is a fundamental element for the survival of minorities.

---

118 General Comment 23(50), *supra* note 49, para. 9.

119 Y. Cohen, 'From National State to International Community,' in *Cultural Rights as Human Rights* (Paris: UNESCO, 1970), pp. 76–87, at 77.

120 Protecting a way of life might require more than just mere non-discrimination, but also special policies of support that would help to avoid social homogenisation. *See* Donnelly (1990), *supra* note 107, at 56.

121 Id., at 54–55 and Donders, *supra* note 39, at 2–3.

122 Id., at 55.

It has been emphasised that when speaking of cultural rights, it is not always clear which form of culture is being referred to: a distinction should be made between general cultural rights (such as the right to education, the right to participate in cultural life and rights related to the protection of a specific culture) and rights related to cultural resources which are of universal importance as part of the cultural heritage of humankind.[123] Apart from individual cultural rights which are essential to the development of cultures, new collective claims have been added, such as the collective right to the protection of cultural identity. Two groups of collective cultural rights have thus been distinguished. On the one hand, rights relating to cultural identity, such as the right to preserve and develop a culture, the right to respect for cultural identity and the right not to have an alien culture imposed on one's own culture exist; on the other hand, rights to cultural heritage, such as the right of a people to its own cultural heritage also exist.[124]

The content of cultural rights depends on the definition of culture. If culture is considered to be the accumulated material heritage of humankind, then cultural rights would mean the right of equal access to this cultural capital and the right to cultural development. If, conversely, culture is mainly considered from the creative perspective (meaning the process of artistic creation), cultural rights would mean the rights of individuals to create freely and to have free access to these creations in museums, theatres and libraries. Finally, culture can be considered to be a way of life, the sum of material and spiritual activities and products of a social group, including a system of values, symbols and practices that distinguish it from another group. Cultural rights then imply the right of a community to maintain and develop its own culture or the right to cultural identity.[125] The last, collective approach toward cultural rights is generally the preferred one.[126] I endorse the collective approach toward cultural rights, viewing culture in an encompassing way, consisting of, among other

---

123 H.L.V. Prott, 'Cultural Rights as Peoples Rights' in J. Crawford (ed.), *The Rights of Peoples,* (Oxford: Clarendon, 1988), pp. 93–106, at 101.

124 Id., at 95–97.

125 R. Stavenhagen, 'Cultural Rights: A Social Science Perspective,' in A. Eide, C. Krause, and A. Rosas (eds.), *Economic, Social and Cultural Rights – A textbook* (Martinus Nijhoff Publishers: Dordrecht, 2001), pp. 85–110, at 89–92.

126 Many authors emphasise that cultural rights have both an individual and a collective component. Meyer-Bisch emphasised the intermediate role of cultural rights between the rights of individuals and the rights of peoples and the importance of cultural rights for communities. Marie saw cultural rights as a bridge between individual rights and collective rights because many cultural rights have an individual as well as a collective dimension.

things, language, religion, customs (including way of life), traditions and beliefs, as well as art. Indeed, it is believed that many of these rights can only be enjoyed by individuals together (as also prescribed by Article 27 of the ICCPR), and several are meant to give communities the possibility of developing, protecting and preserving their cultural identity. Cultural rights will then be considered to be the rights related to the protection, development and expression of cultural identity as well as of a distinctive culture.

4.5.2. *The Right to Cultural Identity*

The value of cultural identity was first recognised by the PCIJ in its advisory opinion on the case of *Minority Schools in Albania*, in which it pointed out that minority treaties had two main purposes: perfect equality for the members of the minorities protected and the preservation of their peculiarities, traditions and characteristics.[127]

Cultural identity is laid down as a general value to be protected by states in Article 1 of the 1992 U.N. Declaration on the Rights of Persons Belonging to National or Ethnic, Religious and Linguistic Minorities (which is not legally binding). This, in paragraph 1, declares that *"States shall protect the existence and the national or ethnic, cultural, religious and linguistic identity of minorities within their respective territories and shall encourage conditions for the promotion of that identity."* A similar obligation to that of Article 15 of the ICESCR[128] is expressed in the Declaration's Article 2,

He mentioned the individual right to participate in cultural life, which makes no sense without, and indeed can only be enjoyed within, a community. *See* B. Marie, 'Le Droits Culturels: Interface entre les Droits de l'Individu et les droits des Communautés' in P. Meyer-Bisch (ed.), *Le Droits Cultures, une catégorie sous-développée de droits de l'homme, Actes du VIIIe Colloque interdisciplinaire sur le droits de l'homme* (Switzerland: Editions Universitaires Fribourg Suisse, 1993), pp. 197–213. Wilhem pled for respect for the collective dimension of cultural identity. *See* M. Wilhem, 'L'Entendue des Droits a L'Identité a la Lumiére des Droits Autochtones' in P. Meyer-Bisch (ed.), *Le Droits Cultures, une catégorie sous-développée de droits de l'homme, Actes du VIIIe Colloque interdisciplinaire sur le droits de l'homme* (Switzerland: Editions Universitaires Fribourg Suisse, 1993), pp. 212–244, at 236–237.

[127] *Minority Schools in Albania, supra* note 26, at 17.

[128] Which, as stated in General Comment 21 of the CESCR, *"includes the right of minorities and of persons belonging to minorities to take part in the cultural life of society, and also to conserve, promote and develop their own culture. This right entails the obligation of states parties to recognize, respect and protect minority cultures as an essential component of the identity of the states themselves. Consequently, minorities have the right to their cultural diversity, traditions, customs, religion, forms of education, languages, communication media (press, radio, television, Internet) and other manifestations of their cultural identity and membership." See General Comment 21, supra* note 47, para. 32.

which, in a similar fashion to that of Article 27 of the ICCPR declares that *"persons belonging to national or ethnic, religious and linguistic minorities* [...] *have the right to enjoy their own culture* [...]." However, contrary to Article 27 of the ICCPR, Article 2 is formulated positively in the form of "have the right" rather than "shall not be denied." Like Article 4 of the ICESCR, Article 2(3) of the Declaration imposes a limit to the enjoyment of the right to participation in cultural life, by using the expressions "where appropriate" and "in a manner not incompatible with national legislation." Article 4(2) of the Declaration proclaims the right of minorities to practice their culture, but specifies that this cannot occur *"*[...] *where specific practices are in violation of national law and contrary to international standards."*

Article 5 of the FCNM obliges states parties to promote the conditions necessary for persons belonging to national minorities to maintain and develop their culture and preserve their essential elements of identity – among which traditions and cultural heritage. It does not include an explicit right to cultural identity or to the protection of cultural identity, but simply obliges states to "promote the conditions necessary" for the development of culture and the preservation of elements of identity. It is not cultural identity of the members of minorities that is protected as such, but the *essential elements* of this – religion, language, tradition and cultural heritage. Article 5 imposes not only states' abstention for the respect of culture, religion, cultural heritage and language, but also positive obligations, as reflected in the use of the verb "to promote" in paragraph 1.

Paragraph 2 provides that parties should refrain from policies aimed at the assimilation of persons belonging to national minorities against their will and should protect these persons from any action aimed at such assimilation.[129] During the drafting of this Article, the ad hoc Committee for the Protection of National Minorities (CAHMIN)[130] agreed that the explanatory report to the FCNM would elaborate on the details of this provision, and in particular on the fundamental elements of cultural

---

[129] It would be for individual members of the minority group to enforce the rights contained in Article 5 of the FCNM on an individual basis: *"Article 5 goes to the very root of a convention on the protection of national minorities and, if justiciable at all, would give locus standi to the group itself to seek a review of government action or inaction. An individual could only seek its enforcement in a representative capacity on behalf of the group, not to preserve his or her own individual rights." See* Gilbert (1996), *supra* note 67, at 183.

[130] Established on 4 November 1993 by the Committee of Ministers, the ad hoc Committee for the Protection of National Minorities (CAHMIN) is made up of experts from the Council of Europe's member states.

identity,[131] but this has not been done. The explanatory report only states that Article 5 is meant to "[...] *ensure that persons belonging to national minorities can maintain and develop their culture and preserve their identity.*" It also adds that the reference to traditions does not imply the acceptance of practices that are contrary to national and international standards and that voluntary assimilation is not prohibited.[132]

The CAHMIN extensively discussed the right to cultural identity and whether this should be included in a protocol to the ECHR. First, it recognised that the concept of cultural identity could only be considered in relation to groups of persons, although it stated that this would not imply the acceptance of collective rights.[133] Supporters of a right to cultural identity considered this right a fundamental, universal right which would probably be justiciable and emphasised its symbolic and political value. Other members of the CAHMIN were concerned by the broadness of the concept of cultural identity and the implications it would have for the states involved. They also argued that cultural identity, as such, was too vague a concept and that aspects of cultural identity were in any case covered by Articles 8 to 11 of the ECHR. In addition, they maintained that the inclusion of a right to cultural identity could cause tension within the societies of members: a right to cultural identity could encourage controversial practices such as arranged marriages and the inferior position of women; conversely, disproportionate attention to cultural identity could advocate cultural activism that might lead to separatist tendencies in society.[134] These are important concerns but, in my view, they should not delay the recognition of a right to cultural identity. Indeed, I maintain that although the right to culture of each community should be respected, this does not imply immediate respect for the content of each culture. Cultures that advocate illiberal and discriminatory practices should be pressed for change and deprived of their autonomy.[135] In addition, culture and cultural identity should not be seen as static, but rather as dynamic and open to change.

---

131 CoE Doc. CAHMIN (94)9, Preliminary Draft Framework Convention for the Protection of National Minorities, March 1994.

132 FCNM Explanatory Report, *supra* note 63, paras. 42–44.

133 CoE Doc. CAHMIN (94)35, December 1994, at 12.

134 Id., at 11.

135 Kukhatas argued that because the basis for cultural communities is the individual right to freedom of association, this implies that members are free to leave the community if they wish to do so. Consequently, only communities which respect their members' right to leave have a high degree of power, and cultural communities which persist in illiberal practices are bound to disappear if their members apply their right to leave. *See* Kukhatas, *supra* note 78, at 231–249.

In the end, a protocol was never adopted.[136] However, from the cases taken to the European Court of Human Rights (ECtHR) by Roma families, it appears that Article 8 of the ECHR on the right to respect for private life, family life and home could indeed be seen as an instrument for the protection of cultural identity. Although in *Buckley v. the United Kingdom*,[137] the Court did not try to link private and family life to culture, it did so in *Chapman v. the United Kingdom*[138] by arguing that the identity of Roma and their traditional lifestyle involved respect for private life and family life.[139] Therefore, Article 8, under the heading of private life, family life and home offers the chance to better protect aspects of a particular lifestyle or cultural identity. Although the Court, in the Roma cases, did not make any specific reference to cultural identity, it became obvious that the issues involved concerned the protection of the cultural identity of the individual and the community. By referring to minorities, culture and identity, the Court recognised that the individual rights under Article 8 have a community dimension. It should however be remembered that, although the ECtHR has recognised the significance of identity to the person and private life,[140] as seen in chapter 3, the ECHR is not designed to protect minority identity.[141]

Furthermore, special reference, in the Court's jurisprudence, to the FCNM (and in particular to Article 5) gives this an extra value and shows that the FCNM might serve as a normative framework for the development of minority rights under Articles 8 and 14 of the ECHR.[142]

---

[136] The so-called Fribourg Group was the one working on the additional protocol. When the work for the additional protocol was suspended, the group continued its work and started negotiations with UNESCO in 1998, but the Declaration was never formally adopted. Article 2(b) contains a definition of the terms "cultural identity" according to which *"the expression "cultural identity" is understood as the sum of all cultural references through which a person, alone or in community with others, defines or constitutes oneself, communicates and wishes to be recognized in one's dignity."* Article 3 contains a reference to the right to cultural identity, according to which *"Everyone, alone or in community with others, has the right: a. To choose and to have one's cultural identity respected, in the variety of its different means of expression."* It was precisely the collective approach of the Declaration and its references to communities in the various definitions that led to its rejection. *See* Donders, *supra* note 39, at 78.

[137] *Case of Buckley v. the United Kingdom*, Eur. Ct. Hum. Rts., Application number 20348/92, 25 September 1996.

[138] *Chapman v. the United Kingdom, supra* note 84.

[139] Both cases are reviewed in chapter 3.

[140] *See*, for example, the *Case of Christine Goodwin v. the United Kingdom*, Eur. Ct. Hum. Rts., Application number 28957/95, 11 July 2002.

[141] G. Gilbert, 'The Burgeoning minority rights jurisprudence of the European Court of Human Rights' 24 *Human Rights Quarterly* 736 (2002), at 780.

[142] Donders, *supra* note 39, at 297.

However, the ECtHR has observed that the FCNM only provides a general framework without agreement on its implementation. Conversely, the Advisory Committee on the Framework Convention (ACFC) suggests that efforts aimed at supporting the culture and identity of persons belonging to national minorities are essential for an integrated society and that such measures should receive increased attention.[143]

4.5.3. *A Collective Right to Cultural Identity?*

Cultural rights in general, and in particular the right to cultural identity, have a special position in the discussion on collective rights. Indeed, cultural rights refer directly to individuals as "members" of their communities. They *"protect the individual within the cultural community against the State or other communities and can also protect a cultural community as such."*[144] Cultural rights:

> *protect those essential aspects of personal dignity that are based on membership in a cultural community, much as political and economic rights protect those aspects that rest on membership in political and economic communities.*[145]

When it comes to cultural identity, many questions arise. The first is that of whose cultural identity ought to be protected by the right to cultural identity – that of the individual or that of the community?

Some scholars see the right to cultural identity as collective in nature, as belonging to those groups whose cultural identity is in danger, such as some minorities and indigenous peoples. Its collective nature, they add, is also based on the fact that it belongs to succeeding generations.[146] I consider the right to cultural identity to be a collective one in the sense that the bearers of the right are collectivities as such and not just their individual members. Furthermore, as was previously stated, the collective right to cultural identity is seen as a fundamental right for minorities whose culture and cultural identity is under threat of disappearing. In fact, without this right, their culture is likely to be lost.

---

[143] Council of Europe, Advisory Committee on the Framework Convention for the Protection of National Minorities, *Opinion on Estonia,* ACFC/INF/OP/I(2002)005, 14 September 2001, para. 27.

[144] Donders, *supra* note 39, at 100.

[145] Donnelly (1989), *supra* note 80, at 156.

[146] J.H. Burgers, 'Introduction Item: The Right to Cultural Identity' in J. Berting, P.R. Baehr, J.H.Burgers, C. Flinterman, B. de Klerk, R. Kroes, C.A. van Minnen and K. VanderWal (eds.) *Human Rights in a Pluralist World* (London: Meckler, 1990), pp. 251–253, at 252 [hereinafter Burgers].

It is believed that we have values related to the dignity and worth of human beings as such, which can only be enjoyed within a collective setting; that is, within a historical, structural and cultural context. Certain groups ask that these moral and extra-legal values are transformed into the legal right to cultural identity – these are usually oppressed, suppressed and exploited groups whose identity and survival is being denied by the existing power structures and who perceive the denial of their cultural identity as an act of aggression and as a violation of their human rights.[147] If culture is seen as part of a totality, as a comprehensive way of life, the question arises as to the existence of a right to culture, and then as to whether this right should be considered individual or collective. It is suggested that the conceptions of individual and collective rights are not exclusive of each other; they are not contradictory, but rather mutually reinforcing. *"Collective rights, and in particular the collective rights of cultural groups, are defensible, when they reinforce the enjoyment of individual rights."*[148]

Some believe that if a right to cultural identity is supposed to protect the cultural identity of the individual as part of human dignity, an individual right would be the obvious choice. The cultural identity of the community as such could be protected by a collective right. Therefore, they conclude that in between an individual right and a collective right, there could be the option of an individual right with a collective dimension.[149]

The argument regarding the collective dimension of the right to cultural identity has been explained by dividing the right to culture into various levels, beginning with the right to maintain a comprehensive way of life within the larger society without interference. The second level includes the first and adds the right to recognition of the community's way of life by the general society. The next level includes the previous two levels and adds the right to support for the way of life by the state so that the culture can flourish.[150] The right to culture is thus only available to a community and not to individuals. Although human beings have a right to enjoy their own culture, the concept of culture involved in this right concerns the broad concept of a way of life, which only exists in a community.

---

147 R. Stavenhagen, 'The Right to Cultural Identity' in J. Berting, P.R. Baehr, J.H.Burgers, C. Flinterman, B. de Klerk, R. Kroes, C.A. van Minnen and K. VanderWal (eds.) *Human Rights in a Pluralist World* (London: Meckler, 1990), pp. 255–258, at 256–257.

148 Id., at 258.

149 Donders, *supra* note 39, at 100.

150 A. Margalit and M. Halbertal, 'Liberalism and the Right to Culture' *Social Research*, Vo. 61 n. 3, Fall 1994, pp. 491–510, at 498–499 [Hereafter Margalit and Halbertal].

Thus, a paradox exists: on the one hand, individuals have a right to culture; on the other hand, the content of culture as the way of life can only be attributed to a community, which is a more appropriate subject of a right to culture.[151] This community should meet certain criteria, including the numerical one, and *"in order to demand its right to a culture that constitutes a sufficient reason for obligating others, a group must pass some numerical threshold of right-bearers."*[152]

While claiming that cultural identity is not something that can be provided to individuals by the state or by any other group but something that individuals acquire in their living life, other scholars admit that it can be attacked by the state or other groups or institutions, resulting in serious affronts to human dignity. However, the best way to protect cultural identity is to protect already established civil, political and cultural rights – in particular, cultural identity will be protected when members of culturally distinctive groups are allowed to participate in their culture, both in public and in private, without any fear of discrimination, retaliation or attack by the state or by other groups.[153] In other words, according to this argument cultural identity is already protected by internationally recognised human rights: one already has a right to participate in cultural life and *"minority cultures, whose cultural identity is most likely to be subject to attack, are already specifically protected."*[154] Thus, a right to cultural identity seems hardly a major benefit and the problem is not that of the recognition of a right to cultural identity, but rather that of the full protection of internationally recognised human rights.[155]

The conclusion of this argument is that group identities (or minority identities) are not – and should not become – subject of international human rights protection because it is only individual autonomy that gives rise and value to identities that must be respected by others, and others (whether individually or collectively) have no right to impose any particular identity on a resistant individual or a group. Identity is entitled to protection only when it is an autonomous expression of the rights and values of those who carry it. People should be entitled to develop, express and modify their identities, acting both individually and collectively. No particular identity should be given a special protection as a matter of human

[151] Margalit and Halbertal, *supra* note 150, at 491 and 497–499.
[152] Id., at 500–501.
[153] Donnelly (1990), *supra* note 107, at 58.
[154] Id., at 59.
[155] Id., at 58–59.

rights beyond that which derives from the (individual and collective) choice of its members.[156]

It is also added that:

> *there is a real loss when a community dies out, but if its members freely chose another way of life, we must be prepared to accept that loss. If a group is dissolving or collapsing from within, rarely will it make sense to require that it be kept alive from the outside. If a group's survival requires the systematic denial of the internationally recognised human rights of its members, it is unlikely to deserve even our toleration, let alone our support.*[157]

However, the same argument admits that cultural rights are especially important because they protect individuals in minority communities against the state and the majority community. "[...] *Cultural rights protect those essential aspects of personal dignity that are based on membership in a cultural community* [...]." Cultural rights may require more than just tolerant non-discrimination: protecting a way of life might require special policies of support.[158]

Although certain communities should be granted collective rights to protect their culture and cultural identity, at the same time, they should not impose restrictions on their members: not all cultural activities can be accepted uncritically. However, illiberal cultures should not be eliminated but rather helped to liberalise themselves through an open dialogue.[159] It is also believed that not all existing collective identities should be protected: *"the fact that a group has a specific cultural identity does not automatically imply that this identity is worth preserving."*[160] From a different point of view, interference with a group's culture may be justified only in extreme cases, such as human sacrifice or the withholding of medical treatment to children; otherwise, intrusion in the cultural practices of other groups will undermine diversity.[161] Finally, it is also maintained that

---

156 J. Donnelly, *Universal Human Rights in Theory and Practice* (Ithaca: Cornell University Press, 2003), at 214–215 [hereinafter Donnelly (2003)].

157 Id., at 218.

158 Id., at 219. The issue of special measures in favour minority groups is reviewed in chapter 3.

159 Kymlicka (1995a), *supra* note 66, at 155 and 168.

160 For example, a group with a strong fascist or racist identity should not be protected. *See* Galenkamp (1995), *supra* note 20, at 77. Bearing in mind that a danger is inherent in accepting a rule that allows someone to deem a group and its practices illiberal, it is still unclear who should determine whether a cultural identity is worth preserving or if it is illiberal: issues of cultural relativism would likely arise.

161 W. Galston, *Liberal Pluralism* (United Kingdom: Cambridge University Press, 2002), at 114. The CESCR has stated that *"applying limitations to the right of everyone to take part in cultural life may be necessary in certain circumstances, in particular in the case of negative*

liberalisation of minority cultures should be left to minorities in a climate of tolerance and respect, and that the possibility of illiberal practices are best addressed within the cultural framework of the minority.[162]

The tendency of western societies to get involved in the cultural lives of other communities and push them for change must, however, be kept in mind: cultural communities must be allowed, as much as possible, to change their practices according to their own will.[163] Indeed, no cultural community is devoid of reformist resources and the practices and constitutive beliefs are better changed from within because the outsider is unlikely to be able to fully understand its complexity.[164] The level of intervention will thus depend on the involvement of the community with the wider society: the greater that is, the greater the duty of the wider society to intervene and be concerned with the community's culture and way of life.

Several problems have been denoted with the collective right to cultural identity. First, the collective right to cultural identity might be based on a too narrow and static view of culture.[165] Another problem is that the recognition of a collective right to cultural identity might mean that individuals become locked within their culture. It is likely that the political elite will be determining the identity of a community and to protect its position, such an elite will define the group identity in rather traditional and static terms, which might imply the consolidation of elite values at the cost of minority values; individuals favouring change become trapped in this static culture.[166] Another worry is that by creating communities, great emphasis is placed on the difference between members and non-members. Although, on the one hand, internal solidarity may increase;

---

practices, including those attributed to customs and traditions, that infringe upon other human rights." See General Comment 21, supra note 47, para. 19.

[162] O'Nions, *supra* note 17, at 58.

[163] It has also been pointed out that tolerance of minorities' cultures will facilitate adaptation and evolution within the minority. Sanders, *supra* note 5, at 375. Interestingly, Sanders suggested that tolerance may thus be a sophisticated route to minority assimilation.

[164] *See also* Parekh, *supra* note 88, at 177.

[165] Galenkamp (1995), *supra* note 20, at 76–78; and Galenkamp (1998), *supra* note 16, at 136–146. On culture, *see* chapter 1.

[166] Id., at 77. It is also believed that, because the concept of cultural identity is rather vague, it can be easily manipulated. For example, the apartheid regime in South Africa based its justification on the theory that different cultures needed to be protected from each other's influence. *See* Burgers, *supra* note 146, at 253.

on the other hand, external tolerance may diminish.[167] Finally, it has been argued that collective rights might not be the best way to protect cultural identities.

These dilemmas can be partially overcome if two minimum guarantees are met for the collective right to preserve one's cultural identity. First, the rights of sub-groups within a community should be guaranteed and respected. Moreover, cultural traditions or activities should have the full consent of the individual members of the community: if they are no longer actively supported by the members of the community, they no longer have a right to exist.[168] Another question is that of who should represent the views of the members of the community: it would be impossible for a community to express its views without proper representation. Individuals within a community should be able, regardless of their representatives, to express their views freely – which implies that they should be granted proper participation rights.[169]

Doubts have also been expressed about the desirability and possibility of special collective rights because, according to some scholars, the content and subject of the collective right to cultural identity are generally unclear and it is doubtful that collective rights would be the best way to solve minority problems. In fact, it is unclear to them what value collective rights would bring to the existing human rights: *"it is unclear why respect for the cultural identity of ethnic minority groups requires anything other than the ascription of quite familiar civil and political rights such as freedom of religion."*[170]

Although I agree that a collective right to cultural identity raises many issues that are hard to solve, I am convinced of the necessity of its full recognition in international law, because it represents the best way for minority groups to protect their identity – including religion and language.

---

[167] To strengthen the "we" feeling of a community, individuals who do not easily fit within the group identity and might constitute a threat to the group cohesion can become the target of criticism and can eventually be excluded. Exclusion due to the homogenisation of the community is problematic because it can be the cause of nationalistic fragmentation of multicultural societies which could cause secession from the state and culminate in the creation of new, homogeneous communities. *See* Galenkamp (1995), *supra* note 20, at 78.

[168] Id., at 78–79. In other words, individuals should not be forced to become part of a tradition, and they have the right to opt out of it. In my view, this is a non-point: obviously, aspects of a culture which are not supported by its members are eventually destined to die.

[169] Id., at 80.

[170] Galenkamp (1998), *supra* note 16, at 192–193.

Indeed, although it could be argued that existing international law provides adequate instruments to guarantee the protection of the rights of minorities, the thorough analysis of case law in chapter 3 shows that these are hardly adequate. Furthermore, minority groups who should benefit from those rights often have not received official recognition by the state and thus cannot enjoy them. In fact, although the HRC has pointed out that it is not for the state to determine the existence on its territory of a minority,[171] in practice states have taken over the power to grant recognition to minorities and with this the rights that are implied.[172]

Individual and collective rights are not exclusive of each other and actually do reinforce one another: as I have already stated, I see the two as parallel in the sense that collective rights, in particular a collective right to cultural identity, are the necessary precondition for the full integration and recognition of certain groups into society, only after which more individualistic claims should become plausible. Individual rights may require collective rights to be more effective, and collective rights allow groups to express their history, culture and values in a climate of tolerance and respect for diversity. The complexity of Roma exclusion requires a solution that draws both on individual rights and on the recognition of their collective right to cultural identity. The preservation of cultural identity is the prerequisite to the maintenance of human dignity, which requires special protection that goes beyond that ensured by existing individual human rights. Finally, it is worth repeating that the recognition of a collective right to cultural identity does not necessarily mean the protection of every element of every culture[173] and that this right should not be intended as a denial of the right of individuals to abandon their traditional culture. As stated in Article 3 of the FCNM, individuals should be free to decide whether they want to be part of a cultural community such as a minority and should have the right to choose whether to be members of it. Conversely, protecting the collective right to cultural identity of minorities means ensuring their full equality with the majority society as well as better protection of the individual rights of their members so that they do not feel obliged to leave their community and to renounce their culture to live a more dignified life.

---

[171] General Comment 23(50), *supra* note 49, para 5.1.

[172] Italy is an example of a state which has arbitrarily refused to recognize a minority (the Roma) while granting official recognition to a number of other minorities. The case of Italy will be thoroughly analysed in chapter 5.

[173] As was mentioned earlier, cultures which express extremely racist or violent views should not be supported.

CHAPTER FIVE

THE CASE OF ITALY

5.1. Introduction

Despite the fact that Italy has ratified most international human rights instruments, Roma living in Italy face continued discrimination in most aspects of their lives. Regardless of its alleged efforts, the Italian parliament has so far failed to pass new laws that can better deal with the many issues faced by the Roma. In particular, Roma are still denied the status of national minority as well as that of linguistic minority – a fact that would make the application of national laws and the implementation of international instruments more straightforward. Italy is the only country in Europe which recognises the existence of minorities on its territory, but it does not recognise the Roma and Sinti as a minority – thus, expressly discriminating against one group.

The Roma communities established in the Italian territory differ among themselves with regard to the group to which they belong, to the time and context of their settlement and to their social and cultural characteristics. Regardless of this heterogeneity, all of them face the prejudices and negative stereotypes of the rest of the Italian population on a regular basis. Even the Roma who are Italian citizens are considered "foreigners" and are excluded and discriminated against. Living in the worst conditions are the foreign Roma, in particular those who arrived from Yugoslavia at the end of the 1960s and who lack the necessary documents to legally reside in the country. Added to these are a number of Roma from the Balkans and Romania, who came as a result of wars and persecutions and who claim refugee status.[1]

Negative stereotypes of Roma are common in Italy. Many Italians see them as the archetype of the unwanted criminal immigrant. The most common concept is that they kidnap children, a negative myth that deeply burdens them. Recent polls show that Italians not only do not like Roma,

---

[1] Commissione per le politiche di integrazione degli immigrati, *Secondo Rapporto sull'Integrazione degli immigrati in Italia, Chapter 3.7, Rom e Sinti: un'integrazione possibile,* (Rome: Dipartimento per gli Affari Sociali, 13 December 2000), at 381 [hereinafter *Rom e Sinti: un'integrazione possibile*].

but also fear them. In the region of Piemonte, the Institute for Economic and Social Research (IRES) conducted a research study on 1,521 children between the ages of 8 and 9, asking them what they most feared. Sixty percent admitted their fear was of going outside, and thirty-six percent of those who had this fear cited the danger of meeting drug addicts, Moroccan immigrants and "Gypsies" as the reason for it. Eighty-two percent of the interviewed declared their fears came from information they received from their parents and teachers, directly or indirectly; 92 percent said they feared "Gypsies" because *"they kidnap children."*[2] According to another research commissioned to ISPO (*Istituto per gli Studi sulla Pubblica Opinione*) by the Italian Commission for immigrants' integration policy, Roma are the least popular minority in Italy: only 11.6 percent of Italians find them "nice."[3]

In the course of this chapter, I will only differentiate between Italian and non-Italian Roma when this is also done by existing laws because of the conditions in which all Roma in Italy live, regardless of their legal status as residents, citizens or immigrants. It will also be underlined that almost all of the NGOs reports and international organisations documents consulted only make reference to Roma in general, without differentiating between citizens, European Union (EU) immigrants and extra-EU migrants. Even the Advisory Committee for the Framework Convention (ACFC) tends to ignore the difference between citizens and non-citizens, following the principle that minorities are a matter of fact, not a question of law to the point that exclusionary moves by member states such as Germany – which recognised as a national minority Roma and Sinti who are citizens – are normally ignored.[4] Furthermore, it should be observed that all international NGOs and organisations tend to speak mostly of foreign Roma, as if Italian Roma were not the target of grave violations of their human rights.

The aim is to show that Italy fails to implement its international obligations when it comes to the Roma, whether they are citizens or not: when they are Italian, they do not enjoy the same rights as the rest of the citizens

---

[2] R. Miceli, *Sicurezza e Paura*, Working Paper n. 127, IRES Piemonte, October 1999, p. 54, available at http://213.254.4.222/cataloghi/pdfires/495.pdf, last visited Mar. 20, 2012.

[3] *Rom e Sinti: un'integrazione possibile*, *supra* note 1, at 381.

[4] The ACFC, in its first opinion on Germany, stressed that *"the implementation of the Framework Convention should not be a source of arbitrary or unjustified distinctions." See* Council of Europe, Advisory Committee on the Framework Convention for the Protection of National Minorities, *Opinion on Germany*, ACFC/INF/OP/I(2002)008, 1 March 2002, para. 14.

and are not recognised as a minority (although they should be) by all Italian and international standards; when they are not Italian, they are victims of inequalities and discrimination regardless of whether they are EU citizens. In practice, no matter their status, they face the same problems of extreme discrimination.

After providing some background information on the Roma in Italy, this chapter outlines the position of international human rights law in Italy and the status of ratifications of the various international instruments and gives an overview of the protection of minorities and the prohibition of discrimination as per the Italian Constitution and the Italian legal system. It then analyses the Framework Law of December 15, 1999 which allowed for the official recognition of twelve linguistic and historic minorities living in the territory of the country, but not the Roma and Sinti, and reviews the juridical status of the Roma and Sinti in Italy. It also considers the rise of anti-Roma feelings which lead to an explosion of violence and counter measures taken by the state in June 2008, as well as the concerns expressed by regional and UN bodies over the treatment of Roma and Sinti and the failure of the government to respond. It looks into measures that have been taken to ensure the enjoyment of fundamental rights by the Roma and Sinti and their protection. It finally suggests strategies to end discrimination of Roma and Sinti in Italy and to ensure their integration into the majority society and the full implementation and application of international human rights standards.

5.2. Background Information on the Roma in Italy

No precise data exists regarding the presence of Roma in Italy. Censuses do not disclose information on membership of a linguistic minority (let alone ethnic groups) and no fixed criteria classify a person or a group as *"Gypsies."*[5] According to recent estimates by the National Statistics Institute (ISTAT), some 60 million people currently reside in Italy.[6] Official statistics suggest that between 110,000 and 120,000 Roma and Sinti are living in Italy and that 60 percent of them (around 70,000) are Italian citizens.[7]

---

[5] G.M. Scalia, *Le Comunità "sprovviste di territorio." I Rom, i Sinti e i Camminanti in Italia* (Italy: Ministero dell'Interno, Dipartimento per le Libertà Civili e l'Immigrazione, 2006), at 21. [hereinafter Scalia] My italic, the word "zingari" (gypsies) is the one used in the report.

[6] 'ISTAT: la popolazione in Italia oltre il traguardo dei 60 milioni,' *La Repubblica*, Feb. 26, 2009.

[7] *Rom e Sinti: un'integrazione possibile, supra* note 1, at 381.

However, in 1995, the NGO Minority Rights Group International estimated their number to be between 90,000 and 110,000.[8] Other Italian NGOs believe that between 60,000 and 90,000 Roma have Italian citizenship, and between 45,000 and 70,000 come from other countries or were born in Italy to Roma coming mainly from Eastern Europe – mostly from the former Yugoslavia and Romania – but also from Spain and France.[9] Thus, it is estimated that around 140,000 to 160,000 Roma are living in the country.[10] Only 30 percent of the Roma residing in Italy are still nomads, whereas the rest are sedentary or in the process of becoming such. According to AIZO (*Associazione Italiana Zingari Oggi*), 50 percent of the Roma in Italy are less than 15 years old, 49 percent are older than 30 and only 1 percent is older than 60.[11]

The number of Roma stemming from post-1945 immigration virtually outnumbers that of the descendants of the communities established in Italy since the middle ages.[12] The main distinction among the various Roma living in Italy is based on legal grounds between those with and those without Italian citizenship (other than this, hardly any differences exist in the treatment of the Roma throughout Italy, regardless of whether they are Italian citizens, EU citizens, or "extra-comunitari" – that is, non-EU immigrants). Furthermore, the communities who live on the Italian territory differ among themselves with regard to the group to which they belong, according to the time and context of their settlement and according to their social and cultural characteristics. They began to settle in Italy in the fifteenth century: the Sinti reached the centre-north of Italy coming from the Balkan region, and the Roma crossed the Adriatic Sea from the

---

[8] J.P. Liégeois and N. Gheorghe, *Roma/Gypsies, a European Minority,* United Kingdom, Minority Rights Group International Report, 1995, at 7 [hereinafter Liégeois and Gheorghe].

[9] A. Arlati, 'Gli Zingari in Italia,' 602 *Gli Zingari* 36 (1997), at 37. According to Scalia, the presence of Roma coming from the older members of the EU is practically irrelevant. *See* Scalia, *supra* note 5, at 21.

[10] OsservAzione raises several doubts on the accuracy of these data and points out that they are the result of progressive additions done by public authorities, activists and scholars following the largest arrivals of Roma in the country. The data is thus the result of a number of assumptions. OsservAzione also observes that official authorities often refer to these data: this does not constitute proof of their accuracy and objectivity, but in this way the data become socially and politically relevant. OsservAzione, *Cittadinanze Imperfette: Rapporto sulla discriminazione razziale di Rom e Sinti in Italia* (Italy: Edizioni Spartaco, 2006), at 26 [hereinafter OsservAzione].

[11] C. Osella, *Nomadi incalzati dal consumismo,* Dec. 5, 1999 Zingari Oggi 12 (1999), at 12.

[12] F. Sigona, 'Locating "The Gypsy Problem." The Roma in Italy: Stereotyping, Labelling and "Nomad Camps,"' *Journal of Ethnic and Migration studies*, Vol. 31, No. 4, July 2005, pp. 741–756, at 744 [hereinafter Sigona].

south, settling in the southern part of the country.[13] The Roma and Sinti are then divided into a variety of other subgroups which often take their names from the province or region of the main settlement or from their principal economic activity (e.g. Piedmont Sinti, Circensian Sinti, Abruzzo Roma, Napulengre Roma).[14]

The longest established communities of Roma are those living in the centre-South of Italy who, in historic documents, are referred to as "Egyptians commonly called Gypsies;" and the "Gizi Land" was an area corresponding to today's Molise. The largest group, which is also the best integrated and most active economically, is that of the Abruzzesi Roma, who have been living in the country for several centuries and have spread in many centre-south regions other than Abruzzo.[15] They are sedentary, living in the same area to keep social cohesion. They are traditional tinkers and horse dealers, but today they are mostly merchants and are well-integrated in the majority society. Another important group who has been living in the country for a number of centuries is that of the Calabresi Roma (in the region of Calabria), who used to be ironmongers and as such were particularly appreciated – to the point that in adjacent regions, such as Sicily and Basilicata, it was common practice to see the "village gypsy" for small house-works. The Calabresi Roma are currently suffering from the financial crisis and live in shanty-towns at the margins of cities.[16] Many of the Roma living in the Northern regions are Slovenian and Havati (Croatian) Roma who entered Italy mostly from Friuli-Venezia Giulia after the end of WWII. Today, they have spread across Northern and central Italy. The Vlah Roma originate from the former Habsburg Empire. Of these, the most important group is that of the Kalderasha, but the Chukuresti, Doresti, Lovara and Churara are also present. These Roma arrived around the XIX century and are currently spread across the country.[17]

The Khorakhané Roma (Khorakhai means Turkish and alludes to religion: Khorakhané Roma are Muslims) originate in the former Yugoslavia as a result of the war. Among the Muslim Roma the largest group is the Zergarja (from the word "cera," tent), who are mostly nomads from Bosnia. Other Muslim groups are the Rundasha of Montenegro, the Kaloperja,

---

13 *Zingari Ieri e Oggi*, M. Karpati (ed.) (Rome: Edizioni Lacio Drom, 1993).

14 Sigona, *supra* note 12, at 744.

15 Scalia, *supra* note 5, at 22 and 25.

16 Id.

17 Id., at 23 and 26.

the Giambasha and the Shiftari (from Kosovo). The Arlija are considered the elite of the Muslim Roma (but there are very few in Italy).[18]

Similarly, mostly arriving after WWII as well as after the war in the former Yugoslavia are the Christian-Orthodox Roma called Dasikané or Gagikané from Serbia: the name derives from the word "gadjé" that the Roma use to refer to non-Roma and which alludes to their white skin. The largest group of Christian Roma in Italy is the Lovara, referred to by other Roma as Kanjara (chicken thieves), who come mainly from Macedonia. Also Christian are the Kalderasha of Serbia, the Tamarja and the Banacani. The Rudari Roma, or the Tigani, who speak predominantly Romanian and also Romanes are, again, Christian-Orthodox. The recently arrived Roma (either Muslim or Christian-Orthodox) are evenly spread across the country, mostly living near medium-sized and large cities.[19]

The Sinti are also divided into regional groups. They are normally travelling entertainers (circus artists and owners) and small artisans, most of whom are nomads due to their traditional activities, although recently becoming more sedentary. The Sinti groups usually take their names from the region in which they live. Thus, there are the Piemontesi Sinti in Piedmont; the Lombardi Sinti in Lombardia; the Emilian Sinti in Emilia Romagna; the Estrekhària Sinti (from Österreich, Austria) in South-Tyrol and so on.[20]

Roma in Italy are normally addressed with the terms "zingari" (gypsies) or "nomadi" (nomads). The first has a clear negative connotation, whereas the term "nomads" is used more commonly and considered more politically correct, although based on the wrong assumption that all Roma are nomads. The 1994 *First report on the status of minorities in Italy*, found that 32.9 percent of the Roma were nomads, in the sense that they lived in a mobile habitat and moved up to 50 times a year; 15.7 percent were semi-nomads, as they lived in a mobile habitat but only move at a fixed time of the year or lived in a fixed habitat for part of the year; and 51.4 percent were stationary, not moving even if their habitat might be a mobile one.[21] Historically, nomadism is one of the main characteristics of the lifestyle of the Roma, but that should be seen as a peculiar phenomenon, almost unique compared with other kinds of nomadism. Indeed, this has been

---

[18] Scalia, *supra* note 5, at 23 and 26.

[19] Id., 23–24 and 26.

[20] Id., at 23 and 25.

[21] Ministero dell'Interno, Ufficio centrale per i problemi delle zone di confine e delle minoranze etniche, *Primo rapporto sullo stato delle minoranze in Italia,* 1994, at 374. [hereinafter *Primo rapporto sullo stato delle minoranze in Italia*].

functional to the survival of the group in economic terms (in this sense, the nomadism practiced by the Roma was consequential to the practice of traditional occupations); but it also was a mechanism of self-defence from the hostility of non-Roma. When referring to nomads, one cannot avoid associating them with vagabonds, and the term nomad is often used to refer not only to the traditional culture of Roma, but also, and especially, to a characteristic of their nature which is morally questionable.[22]

Labelling the Roma as nomads indicates that Italian authorities, as well as the majority society, have not realised – or rather, have refused to accept – that there has been a radical change in the traditional lifestyle of Roma. Italian authorities have so far preferred to maintain the traditional image of the Roma as nomads: on the one hand, tolerating the creation of nomad encampments on the outskirts of towns, and on the other hand, creating or institutionalising encampments under the control of local authorities. In this respect, the second report submitted by Italy under Article 25 of the Framework Convention on National Minorities (FCNM), states:

> [...] *nomadism is regarded as a basic element of the Gypsy culture: therefore, the right to nomadism, and consequently to stays, is openly stated. This implies specific provisions envisaging the setting up and the funding of stay and transit areas, appropriately equipped. Furthermore, all mentioned laws envisage the adoption of measures in favour of Gypsies, with the aim of improving their life conditions with regard to health care, housing, education and employment; all of them are respectful of the ethnic and cultural peculiarities of the Gypsy community.*[23]

In its Second Opinion on Italy, the ACFC expressed concern that:

> *the integration model widely called for by the authorities is still based on the life in camps, which is presented as an appropriate way through which Roma, Sinti and Travellers can continue to live as "nomads." In fact, living in such camps isolated from the Italian society renders access to employment, education and health care extremely difficult* [...].[24]

---

[22] C. Marta, 'Le Politiche per i Rom e Sinti in Italia,' in Commissione per le Politiche di Integrazione, Dipartimento per gli Affari Sociali, Presidenza del Consiglio dei Ministri, *Rom e Sinti: un'integrazione possibile. Italia ed Europa a confronto*, Naples, 23–24 June 2000, pp. 43–49, at 43 [hereinafter Marta].

[23] Council of Europe, Advisory Committee on the Framework Convention for the Protection of National Minorities, *Second Report submitted by Italy pursuant to Article 25, paragraph 1 of the Framework Convention for the Protection of National Minorities*, 14 May 2004, ACFC/SR/II(2004)006, at 12 [hereinafter ACFC Second Report by Italy].

[24] Council of Europe, Advisory Committee on the Framework Convention for the Protection of National Minorities, *Second Opinion on Italy*, 24 February 2005, ACFC/INF/OP/II(2005)003, para. 58. [hereinafter ACFC Second Opinion on Italy].

In its Concluding Observations on Italy the Human Rights Committee (HRC) also stated that it was concerned with Italy's policy to consider Roma as "nomads" and by its camp-based policy.[25] Similar concerns were expressed in 1999 by the Committee for the Elimination of Racial Discrimination (CERD), which observed that:

> *in addition to a frequent lack of basic facilities, the housing of Roma in such camps leads not only to a physical segregation of the Roma community from Italian society, but a political, economic and cultural isolation as well.*[26]

In 2005, the Commissioner for Human Rights of the Council of Europe expressed similar concerns in his report on his visit to Italy.[27]

Likewise, deciding on a collective complaint presented by the European Roma Rights Centre against Italy, the Committee of Ministers of the Council of Europe pointed out that the insufficiency and inadequacy of camping sites constitutes a violation of Article 31(1) (right to adequate housing) of the revised European Social Charter taken together with Article E (prohibition of discrimination). According to the Committee, Italy failed to give evidence that:

> *it has taken adequate steps to ensure that Roma are offered housing of a sufficient quantity and quality to meet their particular needs* [...]. *By persisting with the practice of placing Roma in camps, the government has failed to take due and positive account of all relevant differences, or adequate steps to ensure their access to rights and collective benefits that must be open to all.*

The Committee also condemned forced evictions, when carried out in conditions that do not respect the dignity of the persons concerned and when there is no alternative accommodation available. It found that Italy has *"failed to establish that the relevant evictions it carried out satisfy these conditions,"* and that it has *"not provided credible evidence to refute the claims that Roma have suffered unjustified violence during such evictions."*[28]

---

[25] U.N. Human Rights Committee, *Concluding Observations of the Human Rights Committee: Italy*, CCPR/C/ITA/CO/5, 24 April 2006, para. 21 [hereinafter HRC Concluding Observations on Italy].

[26] U.N. Committee on the Elimination of Racial Discrimination, *Concluding observations of the Committee on the Elimination of Racial Discrimination: Italy*, CERD/C/304/Add.68, 7 April 1999, para. 11 [hereinafter CERD Concluding Observation on Italy].

[27] Id. *See also* Council of Europe, Office of the Commissioner for Human Rights, *Report by Mr Alvaro Gil-Robles, Commissioner for Human Rights, On his visit to Italy, 10–17 June 2005, for the attention of the Committee of Ministers and the Parliamentary Assembly*, CommDH(2005)9, Strasbourg 14 December 2005, paras. 210–213.

[28] Council of Europe, Committee of Ministers, Resolution ResChS(2006)4, Collective complaint No. 27/2004, by the European Roma Rights Centre against Italy, *Adopted by the*

Although it is the Roma themselves who, upon arrival, live in encampments, this is not a good reason to have adopted such a system, forcing thousands of people to live in inhumane conditions and, furthermore, not allowing them to integrate into society through jobs and through provision of education, which, as will be seen later in this chapter, implies the impossibility of being granted residency permits. In 2008, the CERD expressed concern that Roma and Sinti still live in conditions of *de facto* segregation in camps. It recommended the development and implementation of policies and projects aimed at avoiding segregation of Roma communities in housing and invited Italy to act firmly against local measures denying residence to Roma or causing their unlawful expulsion and to refrain from placing them in camps outside populated areas that are isolated and without access to health care and other basic facilities.[29]

The label "nomad" is applied indifferently to the whole Roma and Sinti population, regardless of whether they are Italian citizens or foreigners, travellers or sedentary people, refugees or economic migrants.[30] The conflict over the term "nomads" used to identify the Roma is a key issue in the

---

Committee of Ministers on 3 May 2006 at the 963rd meeting of the Ministers' Deputies. The practice of forced evictions continues to be carried out irrespective of any resolution and recommendation taken by international and regional bodies. For example, a Roma camp was dismantled in Rome on October 6, 2008, as reported by AdnKronos in *'Italy: Roma-Gypsy camp dismantled again in capital,'* available at http://www.adnkronos.com/AKI/English/Security/?id=3.0.2548154333, last visited Mar. 20, 2012. Furthermore, in February 2009, the Special Commissioner for the Region of Lombardia adopted a new regulation for the nomad encampments in Milan, establishing norms on who can enter and visit the camps, the length of residencies, and the possibility of dismantling the camps. This has been widely criticised by a number of local organisations for its failure to offer residential alternatives for Roma who do not want to change residency every three years but would prefer to be sedentary – indeed, it only mentions the possibility of Roma living in temporary camps, thus making nomadism a definite solution, in violation of all international norms on freedom of movement, protection of privacy and family life, right to education and possibility of integration. *See* Commissario per l'emergenza nomadi in Lombardia, *Regolamento delle aree destinate ai nomadi nel territorio del Comune di Milano*, available at http://www.interno.it/mininterno/export/sites/default/it/assets/files/16/0845_regolamento20090205.pdf and Osservazioni del Tavolo Rom sul Regolamento delle aree destinate ai nomadi nel territorio del Comune di Milano, available at http://coopofficina.splinder.com/post/19826090, both last visited Mar. 20, 2012.

[29] U.N. Committee on the Elimination of Racial Discrimination, *Concluding observations of the Committee on the Elimination of Racial Discrimination, Italy*, CERD/C/ITA/CO/15, 16 May 2008, para. 14 [hereinafter CERD Concluding Observations on Italy 2008].

[30] Szente observes that *"In Italy, the issue of Roma is reduced to an issue of nomads. This means that the question that the wider populace, the authorities and most of the activists dealing with Roma alike constantly pose themselves is "how to deal with this socially unadapted, nomadic population whose traditional, indigenous lifestyle is incompatible with conditions set by a modern, European society." See* V.L. Szente, 'Field Report: Italy', 3 (1997) *Roma Rights* 51, at 51.

ongoing debate in Italy and Europe over the recognition of the Romani minority and its rights.[31] The labelling of the Roma is even more important considering that:

> *legislation, for its effects, contributes to feed and reinforce those aspects of the image, which are indispensable to itself. [...] The law feeds itself with the image. The image helps to rationalise it. The image is, hence, re-strengthened by it.*[32]

The interconnection between labels, laws and policies can be easily shown in the case of Roma: nomadism is considered a key feature of Roma culture by non-Roma, thus the law turns the stereotype into a label and eventually supports the policy of placing Roma in nomad camps.[33] The "nomad theory" is used to legitimise the marginalisation of Roma, something particularly visible at the regional level, in which regional governments, with the aim of protecting nomadic cultures, support local authorities in building camps. A clear example of this is the number of laws aimed at the protection of the Roma culture that were adopted by ten out of twenty regions of Italy between the 1980s and the early 1990s. Each of these refer to the Roma in a slightly different way – calling them Roma, Sinti, "zingari" and nomads – but all of them acknowledge a number of ways to protect the nomadic culture, the most important of which is the building of nomad camps (so is specified, for example, by law 32/90 of the region of Umbria; law 11/88 of Friuli-Venezia Giulia; and law 299/90 of Lombardia). The main consequence is that the perception that all Roma are nomads and should thus live in camps that segregate them from the rest of Italian society is officially approved.[34] Describing the Roma as nomads also contributes to reinforcing the idea that Roma are not Italians and do not belong in Italy,[35] their status is in-between those of "enemies" and "strangers," where they live in "our" cities yet rarely intermingle with us.[36]

---

[31] Sigona, *supra* note 12, at 745. Roma prefer being identified as Roma, Sinti and, more generally, with the name of the specific group to which they belong.

[32] J.P. Liégeois, 'Il discorso dell'ordine. Pubblici poteri e minoranze culturali', *Lacio Drom*, Vol. 5 (1980), pp. 9–29, at 28.

[33] Sigona, *supra* note 12, at 749.

[34] Id., at 746. In other words, even those Roma who have been sedentary for generations and would prefer to live in houses or flats have no choice but to live in camps which are not properly equipped, regardless of whether they are authorised or unauthorised. The camps are often dismantled and moved following protests by the local population and on allegations that they have not been authorised, and thus the Roma are forced to become nomadic.

[35] That Roma are perceived as foreigners is also shown by the existence of a number of local administrative offices for "nomads and non-Europeans." *See* L. Piasere, *Popoli delle Discariche. Saggi di antropologia zingari* (Rome: CISU, 1991).

[36] Sigona, *supra* note 12, at 747.

Roma camps are built or allowed to exist in areas close to prisons, rubbish dumps or abandoned areas with low economic value. The choice of location reveals a widespread attitude: *"Gypsies must be kept apart from the general population, and the general population would do best to keep their distance from them."*[37] Illegal settlements are nothing more than slums with no running water, sewers or electricity, and their size varies from 40 inhabitants to 1300.[38] Legal camps are usually built *ex novo* by local authorities, or sometimes they are illegal camps which eventually receive official acceptance. Normally called "campi nomadi" (camps for the nomads), lately some local authorities have started using what they consider more politically correct definitions, including "villaggio di accoglienza per Rom" (reception village for Roma).[39] But the change of name has hardly resulted in a change of practice. The structure of legal camps is normally imposed on the Roma with little attention for their social networks and family connections. Former illegal settlements, conversely, normally maintain their seemingly chaotic structure, with limited public intervention that normally consists of the installation of running water and toilets and other hygiene-related facilities. A common feature of legal camps (whether *ex novo* or former illegal settlements) is that they are enclosed and have a guarded entrance so that the movements of anyone entering and leaving the camps can be monitored.[40] The ACFC observed that:

> *the fact that a camp is labelled as "authorised" or "unauthorised" by the authorities does not seem to make a real difference as in both cases the local authorities* [...] *offer limited intervention to equip the camps with minimal shared facilities like toilets or showers.*[41]

A common feature of the various Roma communities living in Italy – whether Italian citizens or not – is the absence of communication with the authorities. There are few associations or NGOs who work to help the Roma, and those who do are seriously under-funded and their offices and help-desks at risk of closure. Thus, the Roma hardly have any way of making their concerns heard at the national level. Furthermore, there is generally a lack of political will by the Italian authorities to do anything to

---

37 N. Solimano and T. Mori, *A Roma Ghetto in Florence,* The UNESCO Courier (June 2000), at 40.

38 Sigona, *supra* note 12, at 748.

39 Id.

40 Id.

41 ACFC Second Opinion on Italy, *supra* note 24, para. 56.

improve the conditions of the Roma and to recognise their right to participate in public life – which would begin with their recognition as full citizens rather than as illegal immigrants or nomads.

At present, Italy does not have specific legislation on the Roma. They, like all residents of Italy, are subject to the penal, civil and administrative laws of the country. As seen, the task of enacting laws that deal more specifically with Roma issues has normally been deferred to the regions.

5.3. The Italian Legal System

5.3.1. *The Position of International Human Rights Law in Italy*

The Italian 1948 Constitution is the primary source of law in Italy.[42] The Constitution is inderogable and cannot be modified by ordinary sources of law but only through a specific procedure which also implies the need to verify the compatibility of the (new) norm with the Constitution. This means that the Constitution is "inflexible".[43] Article 134 of the Constitution gives the Constitutional Court the duty to evaluate the constitutional legitimacy of laws, thus implying that the Constitution has a higher status over other norms. Part of the Constitution contains a body of inalienable moral values (called "nucleo duro") which are fundamental rights (such as those expressed in Articles 13, 14, 15 etc.) and supreme principles of the legal order of the state, as expressed in the Constitution and in sentences of the Constitutional Court. Right below the "nucleo duro" of the hierarchy are EU sources, such as treaties and directives.[44] The rest of the Constitution is third in the hierarchy of sources, and with it are constitutional norms and norms modifying the Constitution. This also includes norms of customary international law. Just below these in the hierarchy, come norms of international law as codified in treaties and then ordinary laws (such as legislative decrees and acts). Article 10 of the Constitution states that Italy is bound by general principles of international law, something reiterated also by Article 117. However, the Constitutional Court has established that only norms of customary international law can override

[42] R. Bin and G. Pitruzzella, *Diritto Costituzionale* (G. Giappicchelli Editore: Torino, 2001), at 319.

[43] F. Sorrentino, *Le Fonti del Diritto Italiano* (Cedam: Italy, 2009), at 88 [hereinafter Sorrentino].

[44] In this sense, *see* Constitutional Court sentence 170/1984, also known and the *Granital Case* [hereinafter *Granital Case*].

the Constitution (save for the "nucleo duro"), whereas norms of international law such as treaties do not.[45] Only in one case has the Constitutional Court recognised that ordinary laws (in the specific case, laws 845/1955 and 881/1977, ratifying the European Convention on Human Rights and Fundamental Freedoms (ECHR) and the International Covenant on Civil and Political Rights (ICCPR)) are a-typical sources and as such cannot be abrogated or modified by other ordinary laws.[46]

Italy adopts a mixed approach with regard to the ratification of norms of international law. There is no absolute clarity whether Italy is a monist system with regard to EU norms because the EU normative system and the Italian one are autonomous and distinct (which would then reflect a dualist system: hence two separate and distinct normative systems), yet coordinated (hence monist: one sovereignty, therefore what is decided in one normative system is automatically applied to the other one as well).[47] Furthermore, as specified by Constitutional Court sentence 183/1973,

> *fundamental exigencies of juridical equality and certainty establish that communitary norms – although not norms of international law, or of foreign law or national law – should have full and direct application in all member states, without the need for ratification and adaptation laws, as acts having law force and value in each country of the Community, so that they can enter into force and be applied equally and evenly in all member states.*[48]

This implies that, when it comes to international law treaties (including international human rights law treaties), these need to be ratified through specific norms and only then can the international treaty have legal effect in the country.

Italy, one of the founding members of the European Union, has signed and ratified all the most important international human rights instruments, including the ICCPR (Law 881/1977), the ICERD (Law 654 of 13 October 1975), the ECHR (Law 845/1955) and its first Protocol (Law 848 of 4 August 1955, and entered into force in Italy on October 26, 1955), the European Social Charter (Law 929 of 3 July 1965, entered into force on 21 November 1965) and the FCNM (which entered into force in Italy on March 3, 1998, following the adoption of Law 302 of 28 August 1997 authorising its ratification and the deposit of Italy's instrument of

---

45 *See* Constitutional Court sentences 188/1990 and 153/1987. *See also* Sorrentino, *supra* note 43, at 134–135.

46 *See* Constitutional Court sentence 10/1993.

47 *See* the *Granital Case*, *supra* note 44.

48 Constitutional Court sentence 183/1973, non-official translation.

ratification on 3 November 1997). As it will be seen in the course of this chapter, norms for the protection against discrimination exist in Italy. In the absence of norms recognising the Roma as a national minority, they are the only ones that can be used for the protection of individual members of Roma communities. As it will be shown, these are generally poorly applied in all fields of discrimination and not just with regard to discrimination on grounds of race because, when it comes to the Roma, norms prohibiting discrimination are even more scarcely applied and, in addition, a range of different laws are put in place, making them the subject of stricter obligations and sanctions in case they fail to abide by these.

To date, the Italian government has yet to establish a national human rights institution to address the numerous pressing concerns related to racial discrimination. In 1997, an Interministerial Committee for Human Rights (CIDU) was set up in the Ministry of Foreign Affairs. This comprises representatives of several ministers and of various public authorities. The Minister of Foreign Affairs also appoints three leading human rights specialists for a period of three years. Civil society is not represented, although the CIDU often consults it. The only Italian governmental entity that clearly addressed issues related to Roma and other minorities was the Office for Ethnic Minorities and Border Problems within the Ministry of Internal Affairs. Established in 1994, this did not have functions of public education and legislative monitoring and ceased to function with the changes of governments that followed. At the moment, the only existing body working on issues related to minorities and non-discrimination is the Office for Civil Rights, Citizenship and Minorities of the Ministry of Internal Affairs, but in the description of its functions, no specific mention of Roma and Sinti is made other than a report on groups with no territorial ties (namely the Roma, although not called as such). However, the website does also mention the existence of offices working on historical and new minorities and the Office for the Promotion of Equal Treatment and the Fight against Discrimination based on Race or Ethnic Origin (UNAR, Ufficio Nazionale Antidiscriminazioni Razziali), working within the Department of Equal Opportunities of the Presidency of the Council of Ministers, which evidently is not an autonomous body.

5.3.2. *General Overview: Minority Protection and Non-Discrimination in the Italian Constitution and Legal System*

Article 2 of the Italian Constitution states that *"the Republic recognises and guarantees the inviolable rights of man, both as individual and as a member of the social groups in which one's personality finds expression* [...]."

In Italy, about 2.5 million people (almost 5 percent of the entire population) belong to a minority group. According to law 482 of 1999 12 recognised minorities exist, all of which are linguistic and historic.[49] In the Italian legal system, the concept of minority is strictly linked to that of language, on the basis of Article 6 of the Constitution, which states that *"the Republic shall safeguard linguistic minorities by means of special provisions."*[50] Article 6 reflects the assumption that all Italian citizens are members of the Italian nation, which is, indeed, a nation of nations. In fact, according to the Italian constitutional tradition, based on the French-derived "citizenship-approach" and avoiding the concept of ethnicity, the Italian "nation" is built up of many linguistic groups.[51] In law then, in Italy no ethnic minorities exist, except linguistic ones.

In 1999, the Office for Ethnic Minorities and Border Problems of the Ministry of Internal Affairs drafted the first report submitted by Italy to the ACFC. In the report, the Office pointed out that in Italy the concept of minority is linked to that of linguistic minority under Article 6 of the Italian Constitution.[52] In its opinion on Italy, the ACFC observed that in the absence of a definition of minority in the FCNM, states should examine the scope of the application to be given to it within their country. It pointed out that although they have a margin of appreciation in this respect, to take the specific circumstances prevailing in their country into account, this must be exercised in accordance with general principles of international law. It also stressed that the application of the FCNM should never be a source of arbitrary or unjustified distinction.[53]

Although other features of minorities, such as race or religion are acknowledged, the media and politicians talk about people of various nationalities, races and religions and the national statistics agencies report on the presence of various nationalities and religions in the territory,

---

[49] Law 482 of 1999 will be further analysed in the course of this chapter.

[50] Article 6 of the Constitution makes no mention of any territory to which the various minorities should be linked, a criterion that has been introduced by the framework law 482 of 1999. This aspect will be further analysed later in this chapter.

[51] Palermo, F., 'A Never-Ending Story? The Italian Draft Bill on the Protection of Linguistic Minorities' in Trifunovska, S. (ed.), *Minority Rights in Europe: European Minorities and Languages* (The Hague: TMC Asser Press, 2000), pp. 55–66, at 61 [hereinafter Palermo (2000)].

[52] Council of Europe, Advisory Committee on the Framework Convention for the Protection of National Minorities, *Report Submitted by Italy pursuant to Article 25, paragraph 1 of the Framework Convention for the Protection of National Minorities,* ACFC/SR(1999)007, at 4 [hereinafter ACFC Report by Italy].

[53] Council of Europe, Advisory Committee on the Framework Convention for the Protection of National Minorities, *Opinion on Italy,* ACFC/INF/OP/I(2002)007, 14 September 2001, paras. 13–14 [hereinafter ACFC Opinion on Italy].

no mention of racial, religious or ethnic minorities exists in the law, whether at the level of the Constitution or in other national norms. These groups are thus given a different protection, mainly through the equality clause of Article 3 of the Constitution, which provides for equality of treatment by conferring equal status and equality before the law on all citizens *"without distinction as to sex, race, language, religion, political opinions, and personal and social conditions."*

The main framework for the implementation of the principle of equal treatment and non-discrimination is represented by the statutory rules contained in chapter IV of the Consolidated Law on Immigration (Testo Unico sull'Immigrazione, hereinafter TU), legislative decree 286/98 of 25 July 1998.[54] This law consolidates in a single text immigration rules along with rules on the legal status and treatment of foreigners. Although the TU is devoted to the legal condition of foreigners, the section prohibiting discrimination applies also to Italian nationals. With regard to the prohibition of discrimination, the TU contains in Articles 43 and 44 norms aimed at preventing discrimination on grounds of race, ethnicity, nationality or religion against Italians or foreigners.[55] Article 43 defines

---

[54] This was modified on 30 July 2002 by the law 189/2002 (also known as Legge Bossi-Fini)

[55] Article 2 of the TU makes a distinction between legal and illegal immigrants – in accordance with Article 10 of the Constitution which states that the Italian juridical system conforms to the norms of international law – granting even to the latter, the fundamental human rights guaranteed by national legislation, international treaties and general principles of international law. In this sense, even migrant workers or visitors in a state party shall not be denied the rights under Article 27 of the ICCPR, in line with General Comment 23(50) of the HRC, which states that the rights conferred by Article 27 should not be denied to persons irrespective of their legal status in a member state – whether they are citizens, nationals or permanent residents. *See* U.N. Human Rights Committee, *General Comment 23(50), Article 27,* UN Doc. CCPR/C/21/Rev.1/Add.5, 1994, para. 5.2. [hereinafter General Comment 23(50)] It should be pointed out that most countries and commentators disagree with this broad definition of minority for the purposes of Article 27 given by the HRC.

Legal immigrants have the same civil rights as Italian citizens. Indeed, according to Section 5 of the TU *"foreigners who have legally entered Italy* [...], *who have been granted a valid stay permit or a valid residence permit* [...], *are entitled to reside on the national territory.*[...]" Among the fundamental rights that can be enjoyed by all immigrants, there are the right to health, family and education, the right to legal defence and the right to a fair trial, the right to asylum and to non-refoulement, the right to liberty and privacy and the right to freedom of religion, opinion and expression.

Article 13(2) of the TU states that foreigners illegally residing in Italy can be expelled when they do not have a residency permit, or when this has expired or has been withdrawn. Therefore, whenever immigrants in an irregular position are detected, *refoulement* provisions envisaged by the aforementioned legislation have to be enforced. *See Second report submitted by Italy, supra* note 23, at 11. Most of the time, the illegal status of immigrants is what is considered relevant, so that they, facing the constant possibility of being expelled, cannot enjoy those fundamental rights which should be granted regardless of

discrimination as every behaviour which, directly or indirectly, causes a distinction, exclusion, restriction or preference based on race, colour, national or ethnic origin or religious beliefs and which has the aim or the effect of compromising the recognition, the enjoyment and the exercise of human rights and fundamental freedom in the political, economic, social and cultural fields and in any other field of public life.[56]

According to Article 44 of the TU, persons who have been victims of racial discrimination can start legal action to stop the prohibited behaviour and possibly be paid damages. The burden of proof is on the victim, who thus has to prove that he has been discriminated against, something which can be quite difficult. This requirement is partially reduced by paragraph 9, according to which, if the alleged discrimination occurred in the employment field, the proof can be deduced from data about employment, payments, duties, movements as well as promotions or dismissals of the employer.[57]

---

social or legal status – which succumb to the need of the authorities to ensure the respect of the norms on the entry and permanence of migrants. It is obvious here that there is little regard for the reasons the legal status of the immigrants might not have been certified yet, and that "illegal" immigrants might not have access to an effective remedy because expulsion orders are presented even before an appeal can be made or a national court has had the chance to express itself on the legality of the expulsion orders. Indeed, although the right to legal defence is guaranteed by the Italian Constitution regardless of the legal status of the person and thus granted also to foreign citizens, whether they are legally residing in the country or not (so that, according to Article 2(5) of the TU even illegal immigrants can apply to the judicial authorities for the recognition of their rights and interests), the new norms on expulsion introduced by the Legge Bossi-Fini make the application of this principle rather complicated because they allow for the immediate escort to the border of illegal immigrants (even those who have applied for asylum), sometimes even before the judiciary has had a chance to review the legality of the decree of expulsion. Deciding on a case on the right to effective remedy for immigrants, the ECtHR has found in *Čonka v. Belgium* that Article 13 on the right to effective remedy would be violated when measures which are possibly contrary to the Convention and whose effects are potentially irreversible are executed before the national authorities have examined whether they are compatible with the Convention. *See* the *Case of Čonka v. Belgium*, Eur. Ct. Hum. Rts, Application number 51564/99, 5 February 2002, para. 79. Conversely, in *Maaouia v. France*, the ECtHR suggested that exclusion orders, which in most of the CoE members can also be issued by administrative authorities, constitute *"a special preventive measure for the purposes of immigration control." See* the *Case of Maaouia v. France*, 33 EHRR 42, 5 October 2000.

[56] Discrimination is also defined by law number 40 of 6 March 1998 on immigration and the status of aliens which provides in Section 41(1) that *"discrimination exists where there is conduct which directly or indirectly gives rise to distinction, exclusion, restriction or preference by reason of race, national or ethnic origin or religious beliefs or practices, the purpose or effect of which is to prevent or jeopardise the recognition, enjoyment or exercise, in conditions of equality, of human rights and fundamental freedoms in the political, economic, social, cultural or other spheres."*

[57] The difficulties in proving discrimination can be deduced by the low number of legal actions started by foreigners since the adoption of the TU.

The protection afforded by the TU is reinforced by EU Directive 2000/43, which establishes the principle of equal treatment regardless of race and ethnicity and which was adopted in Italy with legislative decree 215 of 9 July 2003. This decree does not provide for any kind of affirmative action[58] (which is however provided for in Article 5 of the EU Directive 2000/43) and the intention of shifting the burden of proof on the person accused of discrimination expressed by the EU Directive has not been adopted.[59] The major weakness in the procedural system assisting the anti-discrimination legislation lies in the rule on the burden of proof, in which the legislator continues to be careful. According to Article 4(3) of the decree implementing Directive 2000/43, if a victim of alleged discrimination submits elements of fact suitable to establish "serious, exact and consistent elements" about the existence of a direct or indirect discrimination, including on the basis of statistical data, the judge can evaluate such elements on the basis of the rule of the Civil Code (Article 2729(1)), allowing a "prudent appreciation" of presumptions. In other words, according to Article 2729 of the Civil Code, in cases in which the acceptance of proof by the judge is not provided for by law, this is left to his discretion. In practice, the burden of proof remains entirely on the victim of discrimination.[60] Article 4 of decree 215 of 9 July 2003 has been partially modified by Article 8(6) of law 101 of 6 June 2008[61] to guarantee a more straightforward shift of the burden of proof.

---

[58] Affirmative action is, in principle, legitimate according to the Italian constitutional system, in light of the principle of substantive equality under Article 3(2) of the Constitution. Affirmative action exists and is applied with regard to gender in the field of employment on the basis of Act 125/1991. In the grounds concerned by the EU Directives, affirmative action only applies to disabled persons. As Simoni pointed out, positive actions favouring the Roma do not exist at the national level. Some regional legislation provides the possibility of weak forms of support to integration of Romani groups, but such measures are marginal in the overall picture and usually unimplemented. *See also* A. Simoni, *Report on Measures to Combat Discrimination Directives 2000/43/EC and 2000/78/EC, Country Report Italy,* December 2004, at 25–26 [hereinafter *Country Report Italy*].

[59] A reference is made to burden of proof provision contained in the Italian Civil Code (Article 2729). The burden of proof provisions under civil law are much stricter than those envisaged in the Race Equality Directive, which implies that persons wishing to bring claims of discrimination cannot benefit from the full range of protections which should be available to them in Italy. *See Written Comments* of the European Roma Rights Centre (ERRC), the Centre On Housing Rights and Evictions (COHRE), OsservAzione and Sucar Drom *Concerning Italy for Consideration by the United Nations Committee on the Elimination of Racial Discrimination at its 72nd Session*, at 9. [hereinafter *Written Comments*] The rules on burden of proof are also neglected by the legislative decree 216 of 9 July 2003 implementing Directive 2000/78 on equality of treatment in employment and occupation.

[60] *Country Report Italy, supra* note 58, at 28–29.

[61] *"Conversione in legge, con modificazioni, del decreto-legge 8 aprile 2008, n. 59, recante disposizioni urgenti per l'attuazione di obblighi comunitari e l'esecuzione di sentenze della Corte di giustizia delle Comunità europee."*

Discrimination and hatred on grounds of race, ethnicity, nationality and religion are also condemned by law 205/93 of 25 June 1993, *Misure urgenti in materia di discriminazione razziale, etnica e religiosa*, also known as Legge Mancino by the name of its proponent. It should be underlined that the Italian Criminal Code does not contain any specific provision to combat racism and it is only the legge Mancino (modified by law 85/2006 of 24 February 2006 *Modifiche al codice penale in materia di reati di opinione*) which establishes a criminal framework in this sense. According to this, racial motivation constitutes a special aggravating circumstance, increasing the punishment by one half for all offences committed with the intention to discriminate on the basis of race, ethnicity, or national or religious background. In addition, ex officio investigation and prosecution are prescribed for racially aggravated offences. Finally, the establishment of, participation in, or assistance to organizations, associations, movements or groups aiming to incite racial discrimination or hatred is prohibited. Also prohibited are propaganda advocating racial or ethnic superiority or hatred and instigation to commit or the commission of discriminatory or violent acts on racial, ethnic, national or religious grounds.[62]

Article 6 of the Constitution is devoted to the protection of linguistic minorities but it does not specify if the protection of minorities should be granted through a framework law or by different measures for every (protected) minority. Other Articles in the Constitution supplement the principle of protection of linguistic minorities by stating, on the one hand, the need to adapt the principles and methods of the legislation to the need of autonomy and decentralisation[63] and, on the other hand, by showing the intention of implementing and enforcing in the Italian legal system the general norms of international law on the subject.[64]

Due to the difficulty of drafting a general provision satisfying the needs and requests of all the various minorities and because of the international

---

[62] The amendment introduced in February 2006 to the Mancino law mitigated the punishments attached to the foregoing offences by reducing the initial maximum term of 3 years imprisonment to either a fine of 6,000 euro or 18 months' imprisonment. A proposal to restore more severe punishments is currently under examination. *See* U.N. Human Rights Council, *Report of the Special Rapporteur on contemporary forms of racism, racial discrimination, xenophobia and related intolerance, Doudou Diène. Mission to Italy*, A/HRC/4/19/Add.4, 27 February 2007, para. 11 [hereinafter Report of the Special Rapporteur on contemporary forms of racism].

[63] Article 5 of the Constitution states that "*The Republic* [...] *recognizes and promotes local autonomy; it shall apply the fullest measure of administrative decentralization in services dependent on the State and adjust the principles and methods of its legislation to the requirements of autonomy and decentralization.*"

[64] Scalia, *supra* note 5, at 13.

anchoring of the South Tyrolean minority (due to its geographical and historical link to Austria), a general framework law was only adopted by the parliament in 1999,[65] and the end result has been that every recognised minority enjoys a different treatment. Some saw this as a violation of the equality principle which imposes the same treatment for similar groups enjoying a similar status.[66] This is the usual result in almost all of the European constitutional systems (and now also recognised by the FCNM).[67] The explanation lies in the impact of extra-legal elements (such as the number of the members of the minority group, their political cohesion and the influence of foreign national states).[68] However, in Italy, the differences in the legal conditions of the various minorities are particularly evident. For this reason, it has been claimed that Italy is at the same time a country with a very advanced system for the protection of (some) minorities and one in which other minority groups risk being completely assimilated.[69] The Constitutional Court has invited the parliament to establish at least a minimum standard for all the groups. It accepted however that different protection of minority groups is a feature of the Italian "minority Constitution."[70]

The constitutional principles described should be applied through ordinary laws, which recognise the existing minority rights of certain groups to use their own language in legal proceedings (as under the Civil and Criminal Procedure codes). This right is usually exercised with the aid of an interpreter, with the exception of the Province of Bolzano, in which it is possible to conduct proceedings in the German language; political representation for some minority groups (for instance, in the European elections for South Tyrol and Aosta Valley, Article 12(9), law 18 of 24 January 1979); the possibility to constitute schools in the language of

---

[65] *See* 5.3.3. *infra.* Another important attempt at adopting a framework law on the protection of minorities was that of 1992, with the framework law designed by Lobriola, which obtained the approval of the chamber of deputies but was never converted into law because of the early fall of the government in 1992. *See* F. Palermo, 'Le minoranze linguistiche in Italia dopo la legge generale di tutela,' *Quo vadis Romania? – Zeitschrift für eine aktuelle Romanistik*, Vol. (23), 2004, pp. 35–46, at 37 [hereinafter Palermo (2004)].

[66] S. Bartole, 'Minoranze Nazionali', *Novissimo Digesto Italiano* Appendix V (1982), at 45.

[67] Palermo (2000), *supra* note 51, at 56.

[68] Id.

[69] Id. According to Palermo the reasons are mostly financial – some affirmative rights such as linguistic ones are expensive for the state to implement. In these conditions, some of the smaller groups struggle to survive.

[70] Corte Costituzionale della Repubblica Italiana, Pronunciation Nos. 28/1982, 62/1992 and 15/1996, available at http://www.cortecostituzionale.it/ita/attivitacorte/pronunceemassime/pronunce/filtro.asp, last visited Mar. 20, 2012.

the minorities (in South Tyrol, Friuli-Venezia Giulia and Aosta Valley, Articles 4 and 9, law 477 of 30 July 1973); special provisions for the media (for the German, the French and the Slovenian minority), and many others. All such measures recognize the diversity in the legal status of the various minorities, providing legal recognition to a pre-existing factual situation.[71]

Protected minorities in Italy are normally identified with a territory. The rights connected with minority protection, because they are considered linked to a particular territory and not to the individuals residing in that territory, are not considered personal:

> *the affirmative minority rights are connected primarily to a territory rather than to its inhabitants, so that in the Italian constitutional system, personally related minority rights are rarely recognized; this means, for instance, that a French speaking inhabitant of the Aosta Valley can only make use of his linguistic rights within his region.*[72]

This implies that the belonging of a person to a linguistic minority can result in special rights only in connection to the territory.[73] It should be pointed out that Article 6 of the Italian Constitution makes no distinction between "territorial minorities" and minorities which are spread across the country or even the "new" minorities which are the result of immigration.[74] In addition, belonging to a minority – with a degree of partial exception of the province of Bolzano – is normally based on the free will of the individual.[75] In other words, a person is a member of a minority only if he decides to be so. Finally, only those linguistic minorities which are officially recognised by the state are the subjects of special rights.[76]

As a main criterion for minority protection, the Italian Constitution adopts the territorial autonomy of the regions where such groups live and indeed provides for the territorial autonomy of those regions. In other words, considering the territorial character of the protection granted to minorities by the Italian legal system, the autonomy of the areas where minorities reside is one of the best protection instruments: the more power local and regional authorities have and the more developed

---

[71] Palermo (2000), *supra* note 51, at 56–57.
[72] Id., at 55.
[73] *See infra.*
[74] The "territoriality principle" is strictly a feature of the framework law, which will be analysed in 5.3.3 *infra.*
[75] Palermo (2000), *supra* note 51, at 55.
[76] Palermo (2004), *supra* note 65, at 37.

the self-government, the more chances for the minorities living in that territory to be granted appropriate recognition and protection, because small groups at the national level can have a larger impact at the local level, where they become numerically significant, such as in South Tyrol and in the Aosta Valley.[77] A consequence of this is that protection is more efficient for territorially compact minorities, whereas it is inadequate for groups which are scattered across the national territory,[78] such as the Roma. In practice, the most safeguarded minorities in Italy are the larger linguistic groups, living in border areas adjacent to the respective national states: German speakers along the Austrian border, French speakers along the French border, Slovenian speakers near Slovenia.[79]

Since 1970, when regions with ordinary autonomy were set up, some smaller minorities have also slowly become more safeguarded. Today, many regions have laws on the protection of minorities living in their territory: Piemonte has passed a law in favour of the French-provençal and the Walser speaking group, Veneto for German and Ladin speakers, Molise for Albanians and Croats, Basilicata for the Albanians, Calabria for the Provençal-speaking minority. However, in most of these cases, these laws have been ineffective because they are too general, too utopian or impossible to apply for economic and political reasons.[80]

The end result is that protection of minorities in Italy is rather asymmetrical, both in the sense of the law (some regions have more encompassing laws) and in the sense of the actual protection granted to them. Thus, there are some "strong" minorities and some "weak" ones (besides some non-recognised minorities), depending on the degree of protection they enjoy. The need for a framework law is thus especially evident for small minorities because it ensures a minimum standard of protection and its utility has been stressed by the Constitutional Court on various occasions.[81]

5.3.3. *The Framework Law of 15 December 1999*

A general law on minority protection was adopted on 15 December 1999 (law of 15 December 1999, No. 482, "Norms concerning the protection of linguistic and historical minorities" – *"Norme in materia di tutela delle*

---

[77] Palermo (2004), *supra* note 65, at 37.
[78] Id.
[79] Id.
[80] Id.
[81] Corte Costituzionale della Repubblica Italiana, Pronunciation No. 312/1983.

minoranze linguistiche e storiche," hereinafter the framework law). The framework law is a pre-requisite for the implementation of the FCNM.[82] It aims at putting in practice the normative framework established by Article 6 of the Constitution and by European and international instruments on the protection of minorities,[83] including the FCNM. However, the text of Article 2 of the framework law makes a general reference to the principles laid down by European and international institutions but does not specifically mention any of them. As Article 2 of the framework law states,

> *according to Article 6 of the Constitution and in accordance with the general principles laid down by European and international institutions, Italy protects the language and culture of the Albanian, the Catalan, the German, the Greek, the Slovene and the Croat populations, as well as those speaking French, Provenzial, Friulan, Ladin, Occitan and Sardinian.*

Article 2 thus protects all the small linguistic minorities which are historically living on the Italian territory, but not the new ones (i.e. immigrants), whose legal protection still remains a problem.[84] In addition, it does not protect the Roma and Sinti minorities or their languages, although they have been living in Italy since the XV century. One peculiarity of Article 2 is that it seems to differentiate between "ethnicity" and "language," because it states that Italy protects the language and culture of a number of "populations" and of those "speaking" a number of other languages. The impression is that not all cultural and linguistic groups are a constitutive part of the multicultural Italian nation.[85] What exactly is the difference between the two groups remains unclear – especially in view of the fact that, as has already been stated, in its Constitution, Italy only recognises the existence in its territory of linguistic minorities.

The framework law provides protection on the basis of four main principles: ethnicity, language, history and presence in a specific territory.[86]

---

82 ACFC Second Report by Italy, *supra* note 23, at 4.

83 Including the FCNM, although the text of Article 2 of the framework law makes a general reference to the principles laid down by European and international institutions but does not make specific mention of any of them.

84 The law of 22 July 1998 (provisions for immigrants) does not provide minority rights to immigrants. Palermo pointed out that *"minority protection does not only mean the protection of 'historical' minority groups, but it also safeguards the 'new' immigrant cultures. Minority protection means the protection of those who cannot integrate in society for economic, linguistic and cultural reasons." See* Palermo (2000), *supra* note 51, at 65.

85 Palermo (2004), *supra* note 65, at 39.

86 Scalia, *supra* note 5, at 13. The applicability of these principles to the Roma is covered into 5.4 *infra.*

It grants to the provincial assemblies the competence to identify the geographical areas to which the minority rights can be applied. According to Article 3, the initiative can also be taken by citizens and representatives of the minorities. The rationale behind this provision is that individuals only belong to minorities if they claim to identify themselves with one, and, furthermore, that even citizens who do not belong to a minority might have an interest in its survival and can thus work toward the inclusion of its district within the scope of application of the framework law.[87] As Palermo noted, the competence in this matter should have been transferred to the regional authorities rather than the provincial ones (as provided by the original proposal): indeed, although local authorities have a more direct contact with citizens and are better equipped to understand the real needs of the various situations posed by the presence of minorities, only the regions are political bodies and the protection of minorities is certainly a political issue and not just an administrative one.[88] I agree with this view and also think that, by deferring the power and duty of dealing with minorities to the local authorities, the Italian government fails (and probably refuses) to recognise the real dimension of the problem that the presence of so many groups in the territory poses – especially when some of them, such as the Roma, are scattered across the entire country. This view is also reinforced by the persistent lack of official recognition of a number of groups (such as the Roma) as a minority because they are not connected to a specific territory.

The framework law grants recognised minorities the right to use their language in schools and in the public sector as well as in the media: the rights provided are intended to guarantee the survival of even the smallest linguistic minorities traditionally living in the Italian territory. However, the effectiveness of the framework law in protecting such minorities living

[87] Palermo (2004), *supra* note 65, at 38.

[88] Palermo (2000), *supra* note 51, at 59. One issue that must be considered is that the role of the state has deeply changed in the protection of minorities, even and especially for Italy. Although in the past, the state was the main actor in the protection of minorities, deciding in which cases to grant special rights and thus differentiate among groups, and in which cases to simply apply the principle of equality, today it is only *one* of the players: on the one side minimum international standards need to be met, and on the other side, the regions have acquired more importance with the possibility of adopting their own laws. The role of the state has thus changed from one of intervention to one of regulation: the state now acts as the main control mechanism for the application of the principle of equality and for the correct balance in the application of the principle of differentiation, whereas the regions are the ones to establish the special rights of minority groups. *See* Palermo (2004), *supra* note 65, at 45.

in Italy is quite debatable for a variety of reasons. As was already seen, the first is that only certain linguistic minorities are recognised. Furthermore, the legal condition for the protection of minorities is their official recognition: only officially recognised minorities are granted special rights and special protection; in all other cases, only the equality principle and the principle of non-discrimination can be applied. Last but not least, as was already stated, minority rights are coupled with the territory and not with persons: those belonging to a minority can claim their minority rights only within a certain territory and this, in turn, means that minorities are protected mainly through regional autonomy.

5.4. The Juridical Status of the Roma in Italy

5.4.1. *The Roma as a Minority*

The Italian government was able to implement whatever criteria it considered appropriate to decide which groups would constitute a national minority because a clear, internationally and legally accepted definition of minority was still missing, when adopting the framework law. This has led to the deliberate exclusion of the Roma from the officially recognised minorities of Italy.[89]

Discussing the juridical status of the Roma in Italy is not an easy task because no specific authority exists on the subject, regardless of the long-established presence of Roma in the country. De facto, Roma have no specific juridical status. Furthermore, and as was previously mentioned, the Roma do not have any particularly close link with a specific part of the Italian territory and the Italian society, by which they have always been rejected and have been the object of prejudice at all levels – both institutional and non-institutional. When discussing the issue of recognition of minority groups in Italy, the framework law is an important step because it provides the necessary legal condition for positive action in favour of small minorities.[90] Of the four principles which are at the basis of the framework law, Roma fulfil three: the historic principle, Roma and Sinti have been present on the Italian territory for over 600 years; the ethnic principle, Roma and Sinti all have the same ethnic origins; and the

[89] As it will be seen in the following, the issue of the inclusion of the Roma among the recognised minorities was extensively discussed in the parliament.

[90] Palermo (2000), *supra* note 51, at 62.

language principle, Roma and Sinti all speak Romanes, which has been recognised by several international organisations and linguists as a minority language. It should also be pointed out that the Roma have a strong cultural identity and are thus recognisable for their culture,[91] social behaviour and historical background, but not for their geographic origins or citizenship.

However, as of today, regardless of characteristics easily and widely recognised, Italy has not recognised the Roma as a national minority: although the framework law recognises the presence in Italy of at least 12 different minorities, the government has not found it appropriate to include the Roma within the scope of this law and has thus excluded them from the benefits which would derive from the application of Article 6 of the Constitution. In fact, contrary to previous drafts, such as that of 1992, and contrary to what is stated in the 1994 *First report on the status of minorities in Italy*, which states that the Roma are considered a minority according to the draft of the framework law,[92] the framework law does not provide legal recognition of linguistic and historical minorities such as the Roma and Sinti, which are not linked to a specific territory.[93]

When the framework law was discussed, although Italian authorities admitted the necessity of a comprehensive policy that aims at the full integration of the Roma, the dilemma of whether to recognise the Roma as a minority raised several doubts. The main questions regarded the typology of the minority status to be attributed to the Roma, as well as the identification of individual beneficiaries of specific rights which must be fully guaranteed and protected because of membership to the group in question.[94] In addition, the Roma living in Italy rarely satisfy the elements of citizenship and have difficulties proving a stable residence, which in any case would be insufficient to grant individuals the status of members of a

---

[91] Which, as was seen in chapter 1, can actually be very different among the various Roma groups but which has some common characteristics, allowing for the identification of the whole group in homogeneous terms.

[92] *Primo rapporto sullo stato delle minoranze in Italia, supra* note 21, at 361.

[93] This aspect is again reiterated by the Italian authorities in its latest periodic report to CERD, in which they state that *"Law No. 482/1999 only recognizes the rights of the historical linguistic minorities mentioned in it. Roma, Sinti and Camminanti communities were not included for reasons of non-compliance with the territoriality requirements provided by that law." See* U.N. Committee on the Elimination of Racial Discrimination, *Reports submitted by States parties under Article 9 of the Convention, Sixteenth to Eighteenth periodic reports of States parties due in 2009, Italy*, CERD/C/ITA/16-18, 21 June 2011, para. 131.

[94] U.N. Committee on the Elimination of Racial Discrimination, *Thirteenth periodic reports of States Parties due in 2001, Addendum, Italy*, CERD/C/406/ADD.1, 17 October 2000, para. 232 [hereinafter CERD, Thirteenth periodic reports, Italy].

protected minority under Article 6 of the Italian Constitution. Furthermore, Roma in Italy are hardly linked to a territory, meant as a space in which they act in a unitary way, especially from the political point of view: in this sense, they fail the "territoriality" criterion which is required by the state for the protection of minorities.[95] No norms in the Italian legal system deal with "communities without a territory" and as such, protect their culture and language. It is, however, important to point out that, as was already stated, Article 6 of the Italian Constitution does not differentiate between "territorial minorities" and minorities which are spread across the country. The "territoriality principle" is strictly a feature of the framework law. A question which could be considered concerns the constitutionality of the territoriality principle as expressed in the framework law. The Constitutional Court has not ruled on the issue. According to Italian constitutional law, it is impossible for individuals or groups or NGOs to directly challenge the framework law in front of the Constitutional Court – only a judge deciding on a case related to the framework law could ask the Constitutional Court to pronounce itself on the issue, but this has not happened so far.[96] In my view, the language of Article 6, which merely states that the Republic protects linguistic minorities with appropriate norms, leaves ample room for interpretation. A literal

[95] Thus, in Italy, the Roma and Sinti do have rights as single individuals, by virtue of being citizens of the state (and in this sense, an element of territoriality is present), but not as a minority because they cannot be linked to a specific territory. Other countries, such as Hungary, have included the Roma amongst the recognised minority groups regardless of the fact that they are scattered throughout the territory – *see* the Hungarian Minority Act of 1993. Hungary has been able to achieve better results than Italy through a more innovative policy of integration, of which the formal recognition of the Roma as a national minority was only the first step.

[96] The possibility of challenging the constitutionality of the principle of territoriality of the framework law has not been discussed extensively by scholars yet. It should, however, be pointed out that, in sentence 159/2009, the Constitutional Court interestingly referred to the principle of territoriality of the framework law in a question on the constitutionality of (among others), Article 6 para. 2 of the regional law 29/2007 of Friuli-Venezia Giulia (according to which all offices in the region, and not only in the areas in which linguistic minorities are present, are allowed to use Friulan in their transactions). The Court made reference to the framework law, underlining the validity of the principle of territoriality as expressed in it. It is rather unusual and questionable that the Constitutional Court uses a law which is hierarchically inferior to the Constitution to decide on the compatibility with the Constitution of a regional law. As Palermo suggested, this is a "sought for mistake" which is taken to the extreme consequences. *See* F. Palermo, 'La Corte "applica" il Titolo V alle minoranze linguistiche e chiude alle Regioni,' in Vol. 3 (2009) *Giurisprudenza Costituzionale* 1780, at 1786. [hereinafter Palermo (2009)] The sentence 159/2009 does not leave room for hope that the principle of territoriality as expressed in the framework law is eventually considered incompatible with Article 6 of the Constitution. It remains to be seen whether any other case on the topic arises.

interpretation of Article 6 would surely allow the recognition of the Roma amongst the minorities living in Italy because nothing in it speaks of the principle of territoriality. Furthermore, according to the Constitution, Italy conforms to international norms, and nothing exists in international law that would prevent the Roma from being recognised as a minority: as was already seen, a number of international bodies interpreting international norms have expressed the view that the Roma are to be considered a minority, even in Italy, and have disregarded the fact that the Roma are geographically dispersed.[97]

The fact that the Roma have not been included among the legally recognised minorities and that Romanes has been excluded from the application of Article 2 of the framework law was a matter of extensive public debate in the context of Italy's accession to the FCNM. This background also emerged during the consideration of Italy's first report under the FCNM. In its first report to the ACFC, Italy mentions the *gypsies* as a minority with no connection to any particular territory.[98] The ACFC noted this in its Opinion on Italy and observed that:

> *in its initial State report and its two further reports, the Italian government supplied information on all minorities protected by law No. 482 of 15 December 1999, deeming them covered by the Framework Convention.* [...] *However, there was no detailed information on the Roma minority although the initial State report mentions its presence as a "minority with no connection with any territory" and gives an estimate of its numbers.'*[99]

It further observed:

> *that although the initial draft of law No. 482 on protection of historical linguistic minorities included the Roma minority, it was later excluded at the parliamentary deliberation stage chiefly on the ground of this group's having no association with a given territory. The Advisory Committee is of the opinion that, especially in view of their attested historical presence in Italy, the Roma should also be entitled to the protection afforded by the Framework Convention. The Committee therefore welcomes the clarification given when it visited Rome by the representatives of the Italian government to the effect that the Roma,*

[97] The HRC, specifically referring to the Roma in its Concluding Observations on Italy, pointed out that *"the absence of connection with a specific territory does not bar a community for qualifying as a minority under Article 27 of the Covenant." See* HRC Concluding Observations on Italy, *supra* note 25, para. 22.

[98] ACFC Report by Italy, *supra* note 52, at 34. In short, Italy agreed that the Roma are protected under the FCNM, but when passing the framework law, did not include the Roma among the protected minorities.

[99] ACFC Opinion on Italy, *supra* note 53, para. 12.

> *while not coming under law No. 482 of 15 December 1999, are nonetheless protected by the Framework Convention [but] notes, however, that at present there is no legal instrument at national level granting the Roma comprehensive protection. The many legislative provisions concerning the Roma which have been adopted at regional level may in fact not suffice; often confined to promoting certain cultural aspects or to the pursuit of social aims, they are very disparate and significantly lack coherence.* [...][100]

The principle of territoriality as expressed in the framework law goes against international law obligations, including the 1992 European Charter for Regional or Minority Languages (EChRML).[101] This Charter, in Part I, Article 1(c) recognises "non-territorial languages" as:

> *languages used by nationals of the State which differ from the language or languages used by the rest of the State's population but which, although traditionally used within the territory of the State, cannot be identified with a particular area thereof.*

Indeed, although according to the EChRML, even non-territorial languages such as Romanes or Yiddish are to be protected, as was already shown, only minority languages spoken in a clearly circumscribed territory are granted protection under the framework law in Italy. However, the Charter allows (Article 21) reservations to be made to, among other provisions, also Article 7(5), according to which the principles applied for territorial languages shall be applied also to non-territorial ones. In other words, when ratifying the Charter, Italy could, in principle, make a reservation according to which the provisions of the Charter do not apply to Romanes.[102] Another possible (and probable) reason was a political one because the right-wing parties clearly stated that they would vote in favour

---

100 ACFC Opinion on Italy, *supra* note 53, para. 16. The same was restated in the Second Opinion on Italy, in which it was added "[...] *Such regional legislation often reduces Roma, Sinti, and Travellers' culture to the alleged itinerant way of life of these persons, which tends to be treated as a problem. Even when these regional laws contain useful elements for the promotion of the Roma language and culture, they tend to be regarded as a priority in State policies neither at national nor at regional levels.* [...]" *See* ACFC Second Opinion on Italy, *supra* note 24, paras. 11 and 33.

101 *See also* E. Dell'Agnese and T. Vitale, 'Rom and Sinti, una galassia di minoranze senza territorio,' in G. Amiotti and A. Rosina (eds.), *Tra identità ed integrazione: passato e presente delle minoranze nell'Europa mediterranea* (Milan: Franco Angeli, 2007), pp. 123–145, at 129. [hereinafter Dell'Agnese and Vitale] It should be pointed out that the EChRML has only been ratified in March 2012.

102 This has been already done by Croatia which, when acceding to the Charter, declared that *"in pursuance of Article 21 of the European Charter for Regional or Minority Languages, [...] in respect of the Republic of Croatia the provisions of Article 7, paragraph 5, of the Charter shall not apply." See* List of declarations made with respect to treaty No. 148, European Charter for Regional or Minority Languages.

of the framework law only if Roma and Sinti were not included. Indeed, the issue of the inclusion of the Roma was extensively discussed in the parliament, and the left-wing parties wanted to follow the recommendations of the CoE and thus include the Roma and Sinti in the law, but eventually the view of the right-wing parties prevailed.[103]

It should also be pointed out that the exclusion of the Roma and Sinti from the list of officially recognised historical minorities can be challenged because they have been present in the Italian territory at least since the XV century. The ERRC, the Centre On Housing Rights and Evictions (COHRE), and OsservAzione pointed out to the CERD that:

> *While the ICERD is silent on the matter of recognition of minority status, two issues are noteworthy here: (i) Italian officials have created a particular status and pointedly refused to provide it to persons of one ethnic group; these acts have been undertaken for purely discriminatory reasons, motivated by contempt for Roma as an ethnic group, and concealed within the harmful pretext that "Roma lack historical links to Italy"; (ii) the very fact that the status has, during parliamentary debate, first been discussed and then pointedly withdrawn from offer, has had a damaging and degrading effect on public regard for Roma in Italy.*[104]

In 1998, the Chamber of Deputies[105] proposed a separate specific provision titled "Norms concerning the protection of the Gypsy minority" (*"Norme in materia di tutela della minoranza zingara"*) which deals directly with issues related to the Roma. According to this, the Roma minority would be granted a number of rights, such as the recognition of the nomadic status as an aspect of a specific ethnic group; the right to nomadism and the right to being sedentary; the right to protection of cultural identity; the right to work; the right to health, including the knowledge of all services available in the country; the right to education and protection of children; and the right to participation in the public life of the country. As it was stated in the latest report submitted by Italy to the CERD:

---

[103] Palermo (2000), *supra* note 51, at 62.

[104] *Written Comments, supra* note 59, at 8. Basically, the Roma minority, although fulfilling the criteria set out for official recognition according to Italian law – both the Constitution and the framework law – is being discriminated and as such could lodge a complaint, possibly following the reasoning of the *Belgian Linguistics* case, in which the ECtHR held that discrimination occurs when individuals are treated differently in relevantly similar or analogous situations, without any objective or reasonable justification for the distinction. *See Case Relating to Certain Aspects of the Laws on the Use of Languages in Education in Belgium,* 1 Eur. Hum. Rts. Rep. 252 (1968), para. 10 [hereinafter *Belgian Linguistics*].

[105] The Chamber of Deputies is one of the two bodies constituting the Italian parliament. The other is the Senate. They have the same functions.

> *The formulation of an appropriate legislative measure would enable to equalize the status of half of the approx. 150.000 Roma populations resident in Italy to that of the Italian citizens. As regards the remaining Roma populations – characterized in all cases by nomadism, they already enjoy the right to freedom of movement and circulation while, if composed from citizens of the European Union, they are under the rules regulating the stay of foreigners, if composed from non EU citizens.*[106]

The intention of including the Roma among the minorities recognised by the framework law was also expressed in May 2006, when it was stated that:

> [...] *a draft law for a comprehensive strategy at national level on all issues concerning Roma, Sinti and Travellers is being prepared by the competent Ministries and will hopefully be approved within a reasonable delay* [...]. *Subsequently, the Roma, Sinti and Traveller Community will also be included, taking due account of necessary distinctions, among the historical minorities, whose status is ruled by law 482/99.*[107]

A number of years later and after a change of government and parliament in May 2008, this commitment has not been implemented. Indeed, as of March 2012, no such law has been passed nor, it appears, will it be passed in the near future.[108] Thus, at the moment no specific law exists in the

---

[106] United Nations Committee on the Elimination of Racial Discrimination, *Fifteenth periodic reports of States parties due in 2005 Addendum Italy,* CERD/C/ITA/15, 29 March 2006, para. 172 [hereinafter CERD Fifteenth periodic reports, Italy].

[107] Appendix to Resolution ResChS(2006)4 Information provided by the Permanent Representative of Italy during consideration by the Committee of Ministers of the report transmitted by the European Committee of Social Rights concerning Collective complaint No. 27/2004. Similar intentions were expressed in the comments by the government of Italy after the concluding observations of the HRC, which had pointed out that the Roma would qualify as a minority under Article 27 of the ICCPR despite not being connected to a specific territory. *See* HRC Concluding Observations on Italy, *supra* note 25, para. 22; and United Nations Human Rights Committee, *Comments by the Government of Italy concluding observations of the Human Rights Committee,* CCPR/C/ITA/CO/5/Add.1, 19 February 2007, at 7.

[108] Several law proposals have been presented to the parliament since 2001. These are reported in the UNAR report of 2007 and are Piscitello, "Tutela del diritto al nomadismo e riconoscimento delle popolazioni zingare quali minoranze linguistiche;" Valpiana, De Simone, Mascia, Russo Spena, Vendola, "Riconoscimento e tutela delle minoranze rom, sinte e caminanti;" Danieli and Valditara, "Legge-quadro per favorire l'istruzione, la formazione professionale, l'accesso al lavoro e alla casa degli appartenenti alle comunità nomadi e per disciplinare la loro presenza sul territorio nazionale;" Malabarba, "Disposizioni per il riconoscimento e la tutela delle popolazioni rom e sinti e per la salvaguardia della loro identità culturale." *See* Presidenza del Consiglio dei Ministri, Dipartimento per le Pari Opportunità, UNAR, Ufficio Nazionale Antidiscriminationi Razziali, *L'efficacia degli strumenti di tutela nel contrasto alle discriminazioni razziali,* Relazione 2007, at 63. [hereinafter UNAR Report 2007] Another proposal is that of 3 July 2007 – law proposal n. 2858, "Modifiche alla legge 15 dicembre 1999, n. 482, *per l'estensione*

Italian legal system that allows for the inclusion and recognition of the Roma among historic and linguistic minorities.[109] Indeed, as the ACFC stated in 2008 in its Second Opinion on Italy,

> *Despite* [...] *attempts to tackle the situation of the Roma, Sinti, and Travellers in the legislative sphere at national level, there appears to be no real will amongst main political forces in Italy to carry forward the project of developing a specific piece of legislation to protect the language, culture and identity of these persons,* [...].[110]

Concern was also expressed by the CERD, which, while observing that despite:

> *assurances* [*have been*] *provided by the delegation that the State party would consider the recognition of Roma and Sinti as minorities in national law, on an equal footing with the historical linguistic minorities protected* [...] *no comprehensive national legislation and policies addressing the specificities and needs of Roma and Sinti have been adopted.*[111]

CERD recommended the adoption and implementation of a comprehensive national policy and legislation regarding Roma and Sinti with a view to recognizing them as a national minority and protecting and promoting their languages and culture.[112]

The exclusion of Roma and Sinti from the framework law and the absence of specific legal provisions protecting their identity and their culture at the state level have further resulted in the lack of their political and social participation. As the ACFC has observed:

> *The lack of a comprehensive national strategy to improve their socio-economic situation further complicates efforts to improve the situation in this field. Indeed, sporadic involvement of Roma, Sinti and Travellers in local projects supported by certain municipalities is not sufficient to guarantee the effective participation of this minority in public affairs.*[113]

Most of the action aimed at promoting the rights of the Roma in Italy is taken at the local and regional level, but this mostly refers to Italian Roma

---

delle disposizioni di tutela delle minoranze linguistiche storiche alle minoranze dei rom e dei sinti," currently pending with the Ministry of Internal Affairs. This law proposal will be further analysed in the following.

109 Scalia, *supra* note 5, at 14.

110 ACFC Second Opinion on Italy, *supra* note 24, para. 31.

111 CERD Concluding Observations on Italy 2008, *supra* note 29, para. 12.

112 Id. It is interesting to observe that the views of the CERD were published just a few days before the emanation of a series of legislative decrees targeting the Roma. These will be further analysed in the following.

113 ACFC Second Opinion on Italy, *supra* note 24, para. 142.

and generally aims at regulating the creation of nomad camps. Very few norms aim at the promotion of and respect for the culture and language of the Roma population. The few existing national measures to promote and protect the rights of the Roma in Italy have all admitted the importance of ensuring full implementation of the right to education[114] as a way of empowering the Roma community, but have been insufficient in guaranteeing the integration of the Roma in the majority society and the full respect of their rights and identity.

The result of this situation is the increased resistance to recognition of the rights that are normally granted to citizens for the Italian Roma, or, in the case of foreign Roma, of the rights that are normally granted to foreign citizens. It is the foreign Roma who suffer the most because of this "political indifference."[115] They live in the most precarious conditions and, for the most part, they do not have any possibility of acquiring a legal status.

In the following sections, I will provide an analysis of the consequences of the authorities' lack of interest in the welfare of Roma, to the point that the Roma have even less chance of being juridically visible and the subject of rights.

5.4.2. *The Developments of 2007–2009: The Emergency Decrees*

According to the report submitted by Italy in 2006 to the CERD:

> *The Roma populations cannot be considered as a group which is practically segregated from the rest of the population, since the Italian legislation provides for specific measures in their favour* [...]. *In practical terms, Italian legislation does not provide for any distinction among citizens on the grounds of their ethnic, linguistic or religious origins.*[116]

The Italian authorities also state that Roma who hold Italian citizenship have the same rights and duties as other citizens,[117] whereas those who are

---

114 *See* section 5.5 *infra.*

115 N. Zorzella, 'Gli "zingari" stranieri e i meandri del diritto italiano" in A. Simoni (ed.) *Stato di Diritto e Identità Rom,* (Turin: L'Harmattan Italia, 2005), pp. 140–166, at 141 [hereinafter Zorzella].

116 CERD Fifteenth periodic reports, Italy, *supra* note 106, para. 171.

117 According to Article 1(2) of the ICERD, states are allowed to make distinctions between citizens and non-citizens. Paragraph 3 affirms that nationality, citizenship or *naturalization* provisions should not discriminate against any particular nationality, but does not go any further in establishing specific provisions in this sense. It becomes obvious, then, that a state discriminating on grounds of race may claim to do so in accordance to the principles expressed in paragraph 2, because the distinction is based on citizenship. *See* T. Meron, 'The Meaning and Reach of the International Convention on the Elimination of

EU citizens enjoy full rights of free movement, and non-EU citizens are subject to the norms governing residence in Italy of foreign citizens. In the same report it is admitted that:

> *Those Roma populations who do not have Italian citizenship face some difficulties when applying for the release of stay permit or for their naturalisation. That is why the relevant legislation includes the release of a working contract among conditions and pre-requisites. Therefore, some difficulties are due to getting a job. They may also entail some difficulties as to the access to health-care services and to education. In practical terms, in order to obtain a stay permit, it is necessary to get a job. Thus, when Roma populations face difficulties when applying for the release of a stay permit, this is not a matter of discrimination but of lack of a basic condition, as envisaged by Act No. 189/2002.*[118]

Most of the foreign Roma in Italy come from Romania, a member state of the EU, since the 2007 enlargement.[119] On October 31, 2007, following a brutal crime allegedly committed by a Romanian Roma, the Italian government adopted an emergency decree (decreto legge 181/2007, *Disposizioni urgenti in materia di allontanamento dal territorio nazionale per esigenze di pubblica sicurezza*) for the immediate expulsion of citizens of other EU countries. The temporary decree gave local prefects the authority to expel EU citizens considered a threat to public order, even without a criminal investigation. Although the decree referred to citizens of any EU member state, it was evident that the main target was Romanian Roma. The temporary decree, which came into force on 2 November, was abrogated on 2 January 2008 by decree number 249, "urgent measures in matters of expulsions and removal for terrorism and for imperative reasons of public safety" (*"Misure urgenti in materia di espulsioni e di allontanamenti per terrorismo e per motivi imperativi di pubblica sicurezza"*).[120]

A series of "Pacts for Security" have been signed in Italy,[121] the first one in November 2006 in Naples, then, beginning 19 May 2007, in Rome and

---

All Forms of Racial Discrimination," Vol. 79 (n. 2) (April 1985) *The American Journal of International Law* 283, at 311.

[118] CERD Fifteenth periodic reports, Italy, *supra* note 106, paras. 173–174. This aspect will be further analysed in the course of this chapter. What is not mentioned in the report is the discrimination that Roma face in the field of employment, whether they are Italian or not.

[119] It is estimated that 560,000 Romanians currently live in Italy, making up 1 percent of the entire population and thus being the largest immigrant group; of these, 50,000 are Roma. *See* http://hrw.org/english/docs/2007/11/08/italy17280.htm, last visited Mar. 20, 2012.

[120] The ERRC, COHRE and OsservAzione note that the decree *'further distorts public perceptions of the matters at issue by eliding immigration with international terrorism and other extreme threats to public safety.' See Written Comments, supra* note 59, at 12.

[121] For the various Pacts, *see* http://www.interno.it/mininterno/export/sites/default/it/temi/sicurezza/sottotema010.html, last visited Mar. 20, 2012.

Milan and other major centres around the country. These Pacts – signed by various authorities in the midst of racist statements – foresee the forced eviction of more than 10,000 Roma from their homes in Rome alone.[122]

According to the Rome Pact, starting the week of 23 May 2007, 4,000 Roma were to be placed in four "villages of solidarity." A task force of 150 police officers was set up to limit the security risk to the non-Roma living in the areas close to the camps. The remaining approximately 11,000 Roma living in Rome were forcedly evicted from their homes and had to rebuild unauthorised camps in new areas.[123] In Milan, the Pact aims at reducing

---

[122] In November 2002, the Italian government reached a friendly settlement in the case of *Sulejmanovic & others and Sejdovic & Sulejmanovic v. Italy*, following the application of some Bosnian Roma claiming the violation of Articles 3, 13 and 14 of the ECHR because of their collective forced eviction from the Roma camp Casilino 700 in Rome in March 2000. On that occasion, the government revoked the deportation orders, permitted the families to return to Italy and issued them with leave to remain on humanitarian grounds. It also arranged a temporary site pending a permanent solution and for the children to attend school and receive medical care. *See* the *Case of Sulejmanovic & others and Sejdovic & Sulejmanovic v. Italy*, Eur. Ct. Hum. Rts., Application numbers 57574/00 and 57575/00, 8 November 2002. Furthermore, on 19 May 2005 by judgment no 16571/05 the Italian Court of Cassation quashed a decision of the Milan court that had annulled the expulsion orders of a number of Romanian Roma. The Court of Cassation recalled that under Article 4 of Protocol 4 to the ECHR the term "collective expulsion" indicates expulsion that targets a group of aliens without a reasonable and objective examination of the reasons and of the defence of each of them. It also observed that under Italian law an expulsion may be proscribed on humanitarian grounds or on grounds relating to family cohesion. However, the Court of Cassation struck down the lower court's decision, noting that the sole fact that the expulsion decrees in question had been adopted at the same time using identical wording and reasoning and against persons of the same ethnic origin was not in itself contrary to Article 4 of Protocol 4 to the Convention. *See* Council of Europe Commissioner for Human Rights, *Memorandum by Thomas Hammarberg Commissioner for Human Rights of the Council of Europe Following his visit to Italy on 19–20 June 2008*, Strasbourg, 28 July 2008 CommDH(2008)18, para. 39. *See also* the case of *Hamidovic v. Italy*, concerning a Roma citizen of Bosnia and Herzegovina, mother of three children, who was expelled from Italy in September 2005 while her individual application was pending before the ECtHR and despite the request made by the Court to Italy under its Rule 39 (Interim measures) to suspend the applicant's expulsion while her application was pending before the Court. *Case of Hamidovic v. Italy*, Eur. Ct. Hum. Rts., the application is still pending before the Court (Application number 31956/05).

[123] *See Written Comments*, *supra* note 59, at 10–11. Figures regarding the number of those expelled following the enactment of emergency decrees vary greatly depending on the source, and no official data exist on the ethnicity of those expelled, although a general feeling is present among various NGOs that the vast majority is of Roma origin. The Committee of Social Rights found that the practice of evictions of Roma and Sinti and the violent acts accompanying such evictions constitutes a violation of Article E (non-discrimination) taken in conjunction with Article 31 paragraph 2 (on the reduction of homelessness); that the living conditions of Roma and Sinti in camps, which had worsened following the "security measures," causes a violation of Article E together with Article 31 paragraph 1 (on access to housing of an adequate standard); and that the segregation in camps, resulting

criminality and addressing the problem of unauthorised nomad camps. Within three months of signing the Pact, the responsible authorities were to *"define a strategy in which extraordinary power will be given to the Prefect to implement the strategic plan for solving the Roma emergency in Milan,"* including the power to control the presence of Roma in the city.[124]

In May 2008, following early elections in April, a new government was created. In the election campaign a competing coalition inserted the repression of the presence of unauthorised nomads in its political programme.[125] Capitalising on the fear of Italians regarding Roma, immigrants and security and despite its obligations under international human rights law, the new government has already fuelled harsh sentiment with constant anti-Romani messages widely published in the media.[126] Soon after the election, the government approved a tough "security package" to stem illegal immigration and expel unwanted foreigners,[127] which included the

---

from housing policies which assume Roma to be nomads and fail to meet their needs, violate Article E taken in conjunction with Article 31 paragraph 3 (on affordable housing). *See* European Committee of Social Rights, Decision on the merits, *Centre on Housing Rights and Evictions (COHRE) v. Italy,* Complaint n. 58/2009, 25 June 2010.

[124] *Written Comments, supra* note 59, at 10–11. It should be noted that figures regarding the number of those expelled following the enactment of emergency decrees vary greatly depending on the source, and no official data exist on the ethnicity of those expelled, although a general feeling is present among various NGOs that the vast majority of those expelled are of Roma origin.

[125] *See* A. Simoni, 'Sicurezza, legalità e lo spettro degli "zingari,"' *Reset* 107, May-June 2008. More recently, on September 14, 2008 during the annual meeting of the Lega Nord Party, Mr Giancarlo Gentilini, former mayor and currently vice-mayor of Treviso "proudly" announced that he had dismantled two nomad camps, and suggested that all the "children of the Roma who steal from old people" should be killed. The full video of his speech can be viewed on http://www.youtube.com/watch?v=5sH84Ne3jcA, last visited Mar. 20, 2012. The UNAR has opened an investigation on this case.

[126] Open Society Institute, Center on Housing Rights and Evictions, the European Roma Rights Centre (ERRC), Romani CRISS and the Roma Civic Alliance in Romania, *Security a la Italiana: Fingerprinting, Extreme Violence and Harassment of Roma in Italy*, July 2008, available at http://www.errc.org/db/03/4C/m0000034C.pdf, last visited Mar. 20, 2012, at 15. [hereinafter *Security a la Italiana*] The CERD, in its concluding observations on the latest report submitted by Italy, expressed concern about reported instances of hate speech, including statements targeting foreign nationals and Roma, attributed to politicians. Concern was also expressed for the continued role of mass media in portraying a negative image of the Roma and Sinti communities and for the fact that insufficient measures have been taken to address this situation. *See* CERD, Concluding Observations on Italy, 2008, *supra* note 29, paras. 15 and 22. Concern has also been expressed in this sense by the ACFC. *See* ACFC Second Opinion on Italy, *supra* note 24, paras. 80–81. According to the ERRC, OsservAzione and the COHRE, anti-Romani speech reported in the media amount to a violation of Article 4 of the ICERD. *See Written Comments, supra* note 59, at 4.

[127] When Brussels Trumps Rome, The Berlusconi government is forced to soften its anti-immigration measures, *The Economist*, 23 October 2008.

dismantlement of Romani camps and the expulsion or incarceration of their inhabitants.[128]

On 21 May 2008, the government passed a decree whose title reads *"Declaration of the state of emergency with regard to nomad community settlements in the territories of Campania, Lazio and Lombardia regions."* The state of emergency is, according to the decree, due to the presence of "nomads" residing in urban areas and to the fact that, because of their precarious conditions, their residencies have caused a situation of serious social alarm with grave repercussions to public order and security of the local populations. Although initially the text of the decree makes reference to illegal "extra-comunitari" immigrants in general, it becomes almost immediately clear that Roma are the main target because after the initial references, the text makes explicit allusion only to the nomads, who are thus singled out as the cause of serious social alarm.[129]

According to the decree, the state of emergency was supposed to last until 31 May 2009. But on 28 May 2009, it was extended until 31 December 2010 and to the regions of Piemonte and Veneto; and again on 17 December 2010, a Decree of the President of the Council of Ministers extended the state of emergency until 31 December 2011. In adopting the decree, the Italian government invoked law 225/92, which deals with emergency situations caused by natural disasters. This allows public authorities to practically derogate from every provision of law and other regulations that apply under normal conditions. It makes no mention of situations arising from coexistence between ethnic groups: in practice, the Roma are equated to a calamity and their mere presence creates a situation of emergency.[130]

In its resolution of 10 July 2008 on the census of the Roma on the basis of ethnicity in Italy, the EU Parliament stated that it was:

> *concerned that, owing to the declaration of a state of emergency, extraordinary measures in derogation from laws may be taken by Prefects to whom authority*

---

[128] *Security a la Italiana, supra* note 126, at 16.

[129] Id., at 17. With three different acts (Ordinanza 3677, 3678, 3679), one for each region mentioned in the decree, special commissioners (generally the prefects) were appointed with a mandate to intervene with measures aimed at ending the emergency, which included the monitoring of existing nomad camps by police forces, as well as the designation of unauthorised camps and the identification (through fingerprinting to be done by the police) of people who live there, including children. Quite worryingly, the Prefect of Rome, Carlo Mosca, was replaced following his refusal to fingerprint Roma children living in Rome. *See* 'Prefettura, Mosca lascia il posto a Pecoraro,' *La Repubblica*, Nov. 14, 2008. On fingerprinting, *see infra.*

[130] *Security a la Italiana, supra* note 126, at 18.

> *has been delegated to implement all measures, including the collection of fingerprints, based on a law concerning civil protection in the event of "natural disasters, catastrophes or other events," which is not appropriate or proportionate to this specific case.*[131]

On June 6, 2008 the government announced the intention to conduct a census in Romani camps, including the fingerprinting of the inhabitants. This was deemed a solution for inadequate housing of the Roma and for the rising crime rates. However, strangely enough the census was carried out by police forces and not by ISTAT. It is also quite questionable that people who were questioned for the census had to indicate their nationality, religion and ethnicity; this information appears in official documents from the census carried out in Naples, such as those that can be seen in the report "Security a la Italiana". According to Article 8(1) of the EU Council Directive 95/46/EC on the protection of personal data, *"Members States shall prohibit the processing of person data revealing racial or ethnic origin, political opinions, religious or philosophical beliefs, trade-union membership, and the processing of data concerning health and sex life,"* in the absence of specific laws permitting such, which outline specific aims, processes and guarantees to avoid abuse of such data.

Amid strong international reactions, including reports in various international media,[132] the EU Parliament initially expressed concern for this measure, and indeed in its resolution of 10 July 2008 it urged:

> *the Italian authorities to refrain from collecting fingerprints from Roma, including minors, and from using fingerprints already collected* [...] *as this would clearly constitute an act of direct discrimination based on race and ethnic origin prohibited by Article 14 of the ECHR and furthermore an act of discrimination between EU citizens of Roma origin and other citizens, who are not required to undergo such procedures.*

The EU Parliament also found that

> *such acts would constitute a violation of the prohibition on direct and indirect discrimination, particularly as laid down in Council Directive 2000/43/EC and enshrined in Articles 12, 13 and 17 to 22 of the EC Treaty.*[133]

---

131 European Parliament Resolution *on the census of the Roma on the basis of ethnicity in Italy*, P6_TA-PROV(2008)0361, July 10, 2008 [hereinafter Resolution *on the census of the Roma*].

132 For example, a report was published on 17 August 2008 by the Observer. *See* D. McDougall, 'Why do the Italians hate us?', *The Observer*, Aug. 17, 2008.

133 Resolution *on the census of the Roma*, *supra* note 131.

However, on 4 September 2008 an EU Commission spokesman pointed out that the practice proposed by Italian authorities is only aimed at identifying persons who cannot be identified in any other way and excluded the collection of data relating to ethnic origin or people's religion. He also said that the report submitted by Italian authorities in early August showed that no EU principles of human rights protection or non-discrimination were violated, and that some debatable measures had been changed.[134] It is interesting to observe that no instruments other than EU ones including all the ones Italy has ratified, such as the ECHR and the ICERD – were mentioned by the EU authorities.

According to the ERRC, the COHRE and OsservAzione, as a result of the entirety of the situation described, the Italian government can be seen to have spectacularly failed to uphold its obligations under Article 7 of the ICERD[135]

> *to adopt immediate and effective measures, particularly in the fields of teaching, education, culture and information, with a view to combating prejudices which lead to racial discrimination and to promoting understanding, tolerance and friendship among nations and racial or ethnical groups* [...].'

Serious doubts can be expressed about the legality of the government measures, such as the actual legal grounds for the declaration of a state of emergency. It is debatable whether the situation leading to the declaration of the state of emergency posed a serious threat to the life of the nation or even parts of it, considering that the state of emergency was initially declared for only three regions, a fundamental condition for the declaration of a state of emergency according to Article 15 of the ECHR.

In August 2008, the Ministry of Internal Affairs published the guidelines to put into practice the decrees, with the aim of showing the legality of the measures of fingerprinting and their non-discriminatory character. According to the guidelines, the decrees are aimed at putting an end to

---

134 L. Kubosova, 'EU gives blessing for Italy's Roma fingerprint scheme,' *EU Observer*, Sept. 5, 2008, available at http://euobserver.com/9/26691/?rk=1, last visited Mar. 20, 2012. The census ended on 15 October 2008. Results show that 167 camps were involved, of which 43 were authorised by the city authorities and 124 were illegal and that at present 12,346 Roma people – including 5,436 minors – live in camps around Rome, Naples and Milan. According to the Minister of Internal Affairs Roberto Maroni, who had previously estimated that at least some 10,000 Roma were living in nomad camps around Milan, at least 12,000 Roma fled before the census could take place; hence, the number reported by the authorities is inferior to the expected one. *See* http://www.interno.it/mininterno/site/it/sezioni/sala_stampa/speciali/censimento_nomadi/index.html, last visited Mar. 20, 2012.

135 *Written Comments*, *supra* note 59, at 6.

degrading living conditions and ensuring legality and access to social and health services and education, as well as to safeguard the people living in nomad camps and who were the recent object of violent acts of racism and xenophobia. Furthermore, the guidelines state that the application of the decrees shall take place in the full respect of fundamental human rights and that they shall not target specific groups but anyone living in nomad encampments, regardless of their nationality or religion. With regard to the fingerprinting and census, the guidelines specify that these are intended as a measure aimed at their integration and at the designation of further strategies needed, that the census shall be implemented with respect for fundamental rights and human dignity and as such, will not be including any irrelevant information such as the ethnicity and religion of those interviewed.[136]

Importantly, legal action has been undertaken with the aim of certifying the legality of the measures taken with regard to the "gypsy issue."[137] Four complaints have been placed by various individuals and/or NGOs: two in Rome, one in Mantua and one in Milan. Two of these, those based in Rome, have been rejected because, following the guidelines set by the Ministry of Internal Affairs, the Courts considered that the intent of the decrees was not discriminatory.[138] An appeal was lodged with regard to one of the two, and this was partially accepted by the Court of Appeal, which declared unlawful the emergency decrees of 2008, thus starting a further appeal by the authorities to the Council of the state.[139]

In the complaint lodged in Mantua by the NGOs Sucardrom and ASGI (Associazione per gli Studi Giuridici sull'Immigrazione), it is asked that the decrees be abrogated and the census of the people residing in the

---

[136] Linee guida del Ministero dell'Interno, 17 July 2008, per l'attuazione delle ordinanze del Presidente del Consiglio dei Ministri del 30.5.2008, nn. 3676, 3677 e 3673, concernenti insediamenti di comunità nomadi nelle Regioni Campania, Lazio e Lombardia. It should be underlined that the guidelines have been published without previous consultation with the national authority on the protection of privacy, and that in any case, as various copies of the census documents (fingerprinting) show, the ethnicity, nationality, religion, as well as passport number of the persons who took the census are indicated.

[137] A. Simoni, 'I decreti "emergenza nomadi": il nuovo volto di un vecchio problema,' X Vols. 3–4 (2008) *Diritto immigrazione e cittadinanza* 44, at 46 [hereinafter Simoni (2008)].

[138] The two complaints which failed were presented to the Court of Rome (Tribunale Ordinario di Roma) and to the Administrative Tribunal of Lazio (TAR, Tribunale Amministrativo Regionale per il Lazio, Roma). The first complaint was presented by the NGO Progetto Diritti and was rejected on 13 August 2008. The second complaint, presented by the ERRC, was rejected on 22 October 2008.

[139] This will be further reviewed in the following.

camp not be put in practice. It is argued that the decrees are discriminatory because they violate Article 43 of the TU on prohibition of discrimination and because in the mere presence of persons belonging to "nomad communities" and the existence of nomad camps they identify a reason for the proclamation of a state of emergency. In addition, they force a particular group of persons to be identified on grounds of ethnicity and to abide to a particular juridical system put in place by the derogations. In other words, according to the complaint, the mere belonging (or the suspicion of belonging) to the ethnicity classified as "nomad" is the only assumption for the application of extra-ordinary measures.[140] The complaint concluded that the right to equality and the right to dignity as protected by Articles 2 and 3 of the Italian Constitution were violated, as well as Articles 3, prohibiting degrading treatment, and 8, on right to privacy, together with Article 14 of the ECHR.[141] The judges in Mantua will thus have to decide whether the system introduced by the decrees is discriminatory on grounds of race and ethnicity – in which the discriminated groups are evidently the Roma.[142] Similar allegations appear in the complaint lodged in Milan,[143] which, in addition, also mentions a violation of Article 14 of the Constitution, guaranteeing the inviolability of domicile due to the incursion in the camp of Via Impastato in Milan in the middle of the night. The complaint also makes a clear reference to a number of international human rights obligations which have allegedly been violated, including Articles 1, 8 and 14 of the ECHR; Articles 1 and 3 of the FCNM (in the complaint, it is alleged that the Sinti are a national minority because they are Italian citizens residing in Italy); the ICERD; Articles 2, 8 and 16 of the Convention on the Rights of the Child. It is interesting to point out that the UNAR has neither condemned the developments in

140 Tribunale Civile di Mantova, Ricorso ex artt. 43 e 44 TU d.lgs. 286/98 e art. 11 e ss. d.lgs. 215/2003, at 3–4. The complaint points out that discriminatory intent is already evincible from the fact that the emergency decrees refer to the nomads and in Italy, the word "nomads" is commonly used to refer to Roma and Sinti: the use of the term "nomads" is discriminatory and should be appropriately censored because it violates the right to identity of people of Roma or Sinti origins.

141 Although international instruments such as ICERD and the ECHR can be directly relied upon in the Italian legal system, hardly any organization, association or lawyer presenting a complaint of discrimination to a national court makes reference to the international obligations by which Italy is bound.

142 Simoni (2008), *supra* note 137, at 48.

143 Tribunale di Milano, ricorso ex artt. 44 D.Lgs. N. 286/1998 e 2 D.Lgs. N. 215/2003.

Italy, nor commented on or taken a position with regard to the complaints that have been filed.[144]

Amid the latest legal developments, on July 1, 2008, it was reported that Italy's highest appeal court had ruled that it was acceptable to discriminate against Roma on the grounds that they are thieves. The ruling by the Court of Cassation, which appears to provide judicial backing for the government's policies, was handed down in March but reported only on 30 June.[145] The court reversed the conviction of six defendants, among them Mr Flavio Tosi (who when the facts of the case occurred in 2001, was an official of the anti-immigrant Northern League regional counsel) who was quoted by a witness at his trial as having said: *"The Gypsies must be ordered out because, wherever they arrive, there are robberies."* The Court of Cassation decided that the statement made by Mr Tosi did not show he was a racist, but that he had *"a deep aversion [to Roma] that was not determined by the Gypsy nature of the people discriminated against, but by the fact that all the Gypsies were thieves."* His dislike of them was *"not therefore based on a notion of superiority or racial hatred, but on racial prejudice."*[146] The Court said that if the Roma are thieves, then discrimination against them is legitimate; it also clarified that when dealing with "hot issues" such as that of the safety of citizens, it is important not to accuse politicians of incitement to racial hatred when they simply want to pursue discriminatory initiatives on the basis of the criminal activities of certain groups and not because of racial differences. Discrimination, according to the Court, is that which is found on the diversity of the subject whether he is "black, gypsy or Jewish" and not on his behaviour.[147]

For the first time in a national case, on October 20, 2008, someone (in this case, Mr Tosi and 5 others) was found guilty of incitement to racial

---

144 On a positive note it should be pointed out that in 2011, in an effort to implement the European Commission Communication 173/2011, as a way of enforcing the national strategy for Roma inclusion, a Roma Contact Point was established within the UNAR offices, with the aim of consulting Roma representatives in the development of policies that specifically regard them. *See* http://www.unar.it/, last visited Mar. 20, 2012.

145 Centre on Housing Rights and Evictions, Associazione Studi Giuridici sull'Immigrazione, European Roma Grassroots Organization, European Roma Rights Centre, OsservAzione, National Roma Centrum, Cultural Center "O Del Amenca", Policy Center for Roma and Minorities, Roma Center for Social Intervention and Studies, Roma Women Association in Romania, *Memorandum: Request for Expedited Engagement of Follow-Up Procedure and/or Urgent Action/Early Warning Procedure Concerning Italy ICERD Compliance,* at 9–10.

146 J. Hooper, 'Italy: Court inflames Roma discrimination row,' *The Guardian,* July 1, 2008.

147 'Cassazione, se i nomadi sono ladri è legittima la discriminazione,' *La Repubblica,* June 29, 2008.

hatred against the Roma.[148] However, the interpretation of the Court of Cassation is indicative of the level of racial prejudice against the Roma which is deeply permeated in Italian society, and of the general belief that all the Roma are criminals. On the one hand, it demonstrates that many in Italy have no real understanding of justice or civil or criminal responsibility, and are capable of blaming an entire community if an individual within it is thought to be guilty of a crime – even before being judged by a court of law. On the other hand, it shows that even the Courts are unable to be objective in their judgements and detach themselves from prejudice and slander.

Quite alarmingly, racist and xenophobic speech targeting the Roma in political discourse has not stopped, and during the latest municipal elections in Milan, the use of electoral material – such as posters on walls and vehicles – warning against the risk of the city turning into a "Gypsytown" (*zingaropoli*) was widespread. However, as reported by the Commissioner for Human Rights of the Council of Europe, even outside election periods, anti-Roma attitudes continue to taint political speech. For example, in the context of the expulsions of Romanian and Bulgarian Roma from France during the summer of 2010, the Minister of Interior was reported as expressing regret at the fact that because many Roma and Sinti have Italian nationality *"they have a right to stay and nothing can be done about it."*[149] Similar worries have been expressed by the ACFC in its October 2010 opinion on Italy, in which it stated that it was "deeply concerned" at the increasingly common presence of racially inflammatory public discourse targeting, among others, Roma and Sinti, in the discourse of certain prominent political figures.[150]

In June 2010, the European Committee of Social Rights, deciding on a collective complaint filed against Italy, found that the use of xenophobic political discourse against Roma and Sinti violated Articles E (non-discrimination) and 19(1) of the Revised Charter.[151] The Committee found

---

[148] The CERD noted the small number of cases on racial discrimination in Italy. *See* CERD, Concluding Observations on Italy, 2008, *supra* note 29, para. 21.

[149] L. Salvia, 'Maroni: giusto espellere i Rom. Saremo più duri di Sarkozy,' *Corriere della Sera*, Aug. 21, 2010.

[150] Council of Europe, Advisory Committee on the Framework Convention for the Protection of National Minorities, *Third Opinion on Italy*, adopted on 15 October 2010, ACFC/OP/III(2010)008, 30 May 2011, para. 87. [hereinafter ACFC Third Opinion on Italy].

[151] European Committee of Social Rights, Decision on the merits, *Centre on Housing Rights and Evictions (COHRE) v. Italy*, Complaint 58/2009, June 25, 2010, paras. 136–140 [hereinafter *COHRE v. Italy*].

this to be an aggravated violation, noting that *"the racist misleading propaganda against migrant Roma and Sinti* [*was*] *indirectly allowed or directly emanating from the Italian authorities."*[152]

Finally, on November 16, 2011 the Council of the State has established, with sentence 6050, which rejects the appeal filed by the Presidency of the Council of Ministers, the Ministry of Interior, the Civil Protection unit and the Prefects of Rome, Milan and Naples against the Tribunale Amministrativo Regionale of Lazio sentence of July 1, 2009, that the state of emergency declared in 2008 is illegal, thus making void the nomination of special commissioners for the emergencies and the decrees adopted by them. The sentence further affirms the illegality of the identification measures adopted during the census of the nomad camps.[153]

5.4.3. *Fundamental Rights and the Roma*

In view of what has just been said, the following discussion applies not only to non-EU Roma, but also to those coming from Romania.

Some of the Roma who arrived in Italy as a result of war and persecution are *sans papiers* (undocumented), thus having no legal permits to stay in the country or having only short-term leave to remain on humanitarian grounds and facing many difficulties when trying to renew their permits. These people live in a "legal limbo" which has effects on several aspects of their lives.[154] Italy is indeed one of the many European countries in which Roma are often denied citizenship. The "New norms on citizenship" (law 91 of February 5, 1992) establish precise rules for granting Italian citizenship. These include residency in the territory for a period of at least 3 years and/or having been born in the country. Nevertheless, Roma who have been present in Italy for over 30 years and whose children were born in the country have not been granted citizenship yet but at most only a permit for a limited and usually short amount of time. Indeed, when asked to show proof of their uninterrupted legal residency in the country for at least eighteen years, many Roma face difficulties because the nomad

---

[152] *COHRE v. Italy, supra* note 151, para. 139.

[153] *"Sentenza n. 6050 del 16 Novembre 2011 del Consiglio di Stato, Stato di emergenza dichiarato nel territorio delle Regioni Lombardia, Lazio e Campania in relazione agli insediamenti di comunità nomadi,"* available at http://www.immigrazione.biz/sentenza.php?id=1182, last visited Mar. 20, 2012.

[154] According to OsservAzione, the Romanian Roma living around large cities such as Rome, Milan, Turin, Naples or Florence face the worst hygienic conditions and the continuous threat of being expelled, something that makes them particularly vulnerable to racism. *See* OsservAzione, *supra* note 10, at 27.

camps in which they live, if unauthorised, are not recognised as legal residency or have not been for a number of years. In addition, considering the precariousness which is typical of the lives of many Roma living in Italy, the continuous risk of being forced to migrate due to racist attacks or to move following an order to vacate by the authorities, it becomes clear that many Roma are unable to prove a proper residency.[155] Furthermore, citizenship is by no means synonymous with additional rights. Indeed the Italian government pointed out several times that citizenship *"is insufficient to grant individuals the status of members of a recognised protected minority under Article 6 of the Italian Constitution."*[156] According to the Special Rapporteur on Contemporary Forms of Racism, the fact that many Roma, although born in Italy or having Italian parents, still lack citizenship, is one of the many institutionalised forms of discrimination that Roma face. Even the Commissioner for Human Rights of the Council of Europe, in his 2011 report, underlined that:

> *the situation of stateless Roma persons in Italy is even more precarious today, as a result of the combined effect of [...] the "security package", which criminalised irregular entry into Italy and stay without a valid residence permit, and the "Nomad emergency" legislation, which allowed the carrying out of censuses of the population of Roma settlements. In practice, this has resulted in many Roma and Sinti living in Italy, including Italy-born stateless persons, being liable to criminal prosecution and expulsion.*[157]

Furthermore, as stated by the Special Rapporteur on Contemporary Forms of Racism,

> *these Roma are de facto stateless and should, in the view of civil society, receive special attention from the government and be the subject of special provisions within the citizenship law and other relevant legislation for their regularization and acquisition of citizenship.*[158]

---

155 OsservAzione, *supra* note 10, at 31.

156 CERD, Thirteenth periodic reports, Italy, *supra* note 94, para. 236.

157 *Report by Thomas Hammarberg, Commissioner for Human Rights of the Council of Europe Following his visit to Italy from 26 to 27 May 2011*, CommDH(2011)26, 7 September 2011, para. 37 [hereinafter Report by Thomas Hammarberg].

158 *See* Report of the Special Rapporteur on contemporary forms of racism, *supra* note 62, para. 38. Although the lack of residence permit or Italian citizenship is not an obstacle to obtaining urgent health care in hospitals, it implies the impossibility of joining the state health insurance on an equal footing with other persons. This means that the only possibility of obtaining non-emergency health care for non-residents and non-citizens is by going to private doctors, but as a result of extreme poverty among Romani immigrant groups this might not be a real possibility. Such persons cannot be legally employed. They would also be ineligible for standard state-provided social assistance. *See Written Comments*, *supra* note 59, at 5.

An increasing number of Roma children born in Italy to foreign parents are stateless and face overwhelming obstacles in obtaining a passport at all. The Italian authorities reassured international institutions in 2009 by affirming that a law aimed at granting Italian nationality to children born in Italy to stateless parents when at least one of the parents was in Italy from January 1996 was pending before the Parliament. However, no progress has been achieved in this sense, and although there was a plan to ratify the European Convention on Nationality (without the suggested reservation to Article 6(4)(f) on facilitating the acquisition of nationality by persons who are lawfully and habitually residing on its territory for a period of time beginning before turning eighteen), this has not been ratified yet.[159]

About one-third of the Roma and Sinti population, including both Italian and an estimated 18,500 foreign citizens currently live in authorised or unauthorised camps separated from the rest of Italian society. The numbers might be even higher as a result of the recent immigration flows of Romanian Roma. In the context of the norms on immigration, the Roma find even more difficulties in the enjoyment of their rights. Most of the foreign Roma currently living in Italy come from countries in which they have been and still are being discriminated against in many fields, such as employment, housing and participation in the political life of their country, and are even persecuted. The consequent exodus – accentuated by the war in the Balkans and by the end of communist regimes which, contrary to what was hoped, has led to even more discrimination – has forced many Roma to enter the country either legally or illegally. Regardless of these conditions, Roma hardly have any significant chance of being granted the status of refugees according to the 1951 Geneva Convention Relating to the Status of Refugees (Refugee Convention), which recognises the status of refugees to those who can prove persecution and/or discrimination on personal grounds.

Article 10(3) of the Italian Constitution supposedly has a wider application than the one of the Refugee Convention because it grants the right to asylum to any foreign person who cannot enjoy "democratic liberties" in his country of origin without him having to prove persecution or discrimination on personal grounds. Only a generic requirement of verifying the conditions of lack of liberties or violation of constitutional rights in the country of origin of the asylum seeker is necessary. In this case, the main

[159] Report by Thomas Hammarberg, *supra* note 157, para. 38.

problem is not the difficulty of verifying the situation, but the fact that this possibility is virtually ignored, due to both the lack of information on the subject and the lack of a proper legislation with regard to the right to asylum.[160] The obvious result is that in both cases, the right to asylum is denied to the Roma, despite the objective discrimination and racial persecution to which they are subjected in their country of origin.

Conversely, the risk of persecution and discrimination is rarely an obstacle to repatriation, despite the prohibition of Article 19(1) of the legislative decree 286/98, according to which nobody can be returned to a country in which a risk exists that he might be subject to persecution on grounds of race, sex, language, religion, nationality, political opinion, social status, or even to a country in which a risk exists that he might be sent to another country in which he is not protected against this persecution. So Roma can be and are indeed sent back to countries in which they are subject to discrimination, even in emergency situations such as those in the 1990s, when Kosovo Roma were sent back to Albania or the former Yugoslavia, and despite the principles expressed by the ECtHR in the cases of *Soering* and *Chahal*,[161] according to which no person is to be sent back to a country in which a risk exists that he might be subject to inhuman or degrading treatment or punishment.

Law 390/92, emanated immediately after the beginning of the war in the former Yugoslavia, establishes protection on humanitarian grounds. Furthermore, after the war in Kosovo, the decree of the president of the Council of Ministers of May 12, 1999 has provided for the possibility of granting "humanitarian residency" ("permesso di soggiorno umanitario") to people fleeing Kosovo. Protection on humanitarian grounds has only been sparsely granted to Roma, mostly taking into account the need for the country not to face a mass invasion rather than their need for protection and has resulted in the creation of encampments (most of the time in abandoned areas on the outskirts of big cities rather than in an area with the actual possibility of integration into the local society) in which local authorities barely intervene to guarantee minimum assistance in the search for a job, and in which the situation has often become explosive due to the disastrous sanitary conditions and the intolerance expressed by

160 Previous governments tried to introduce a law on the subject, but they did not make it to the parliament for approval. Articles 31 and 32 of law 189/2002 only refer to political asylum as provided for in the Refugee Convention.

161 *Case of Soering v. United Kingdom*, (1989) 11 EHRR 439 and *Case of Chahal v. United Kingdom*, (1996) 23 EHRR.

the local population.[162] Only rarely have the Roma living in camps been informed of their rights and of the possibility of applying for a residency permit and thus becoming regular immigrants; this usually ends in moving, constantly accumulating expulsion decrees and remaining invisible in front of the law.[163] In any event, after the emergency ended, residency in Italy was only allowed for those who could prove they had a job and had not committed a felony. Once more, the need to guarantee a more productive and "clean" immigration prevailed, and no real attention was given to the continuous risk Roma faced if returned to Kosovo or to the difficulties of integrating into society that they might face in the various countries of the former Yugoslavia.

In this situation, the Roma were the most penalised because hardly any of them could prove to have left former the Yugoslavia or Kosovo as a result of the war (one of the requisites to be granted protection on humanitarian grounds), and their continuous movement – before and after the war – was the cause of the exclusion from the benefits of the law. Similarly, the difficulty in finding an occupation led to the denial of the residency permit after the war ended, thus making de facto illegal a large number of Roma.[164] It should, however, be observed that expulsion has not always been issued for those who lost their permission of residency or for those against which the decree of expulsion had been issued. But this so-called "tolerance" was anything but a benefit because the loss of the residency permit or the existence of a decree of expulsion has not allowed most of those Roma to become legal residents. The consequent juridical invisibility and the political and legal indifference are only some of the reasons the Roma are rarely the subject of institutional actions;[165] this situation is added to the fact that they barely enjoy the civil and social rights guaranteed by Article 2(2) of the TU.

Because most Roma arrive in Italy following migration fluxes as a result of wars and persecutions, they have never benefited from the regularisations which, since 1986, have allowed foreigners illegally residing in the

---

[162] As has been seen already, in cases of friction with the local population, the Roma have been moved from the unauthorised encampments through expulsion decrees; they have either been forced back to their countries of origin or more simply pushed outside of the cities.

[163] Zorzella, *supra* note 115, at 156.

[164] Id., at 151.

[165] Id., at 152. We should be reminded that the few actions taken by the authorities with regard to the Roma are often the result of a so-called "security emergency" following an uprising by the majority society complaining about petty crimes and other illegal activities allegedly committed by Roma.

country to obtain a residency permit if able to prove that they have a job and a place to live. Segregated in encampments, disjoined from the majority society and without any support from the authorities, most Roma have missed the opportunities to gain official legal status. The minority of Roma who manage to get official status have also encountered enormous difficulties in maintaining such status because they have not always been able to prove the permanence of the requisites necessary for the renewal of the residency permit.

Similarly, the protection provided for by the TU is hardly applicable to Roma minors primarily because, aside from a few exceptions, no local projects aimed at the integration of Roma children exist that take into account the peculiar conditions in which they live. For example, it has always been difficult to enrol Roma children in primary schools, and only the TU has diminished the obstacles because Article 38 establishes that foreign children *living in the country*[166] have to attend primary school, and that they are subject to all the existing norms in terms of right to education and participation in the school life. Many children are enrolled in school thanks to the intervention of social services or local authorities, but in general a lack of long-term planning exists, as children barely make it through the entire education system and parents are rarely supported throughout. Aside from the willingness or the concern of the parents to send their children to school, it is often the terrible living conditions which prevent them from caring for their children properly, and these situations are rarely solved with the intervention of local authorities. This issue has also been stressed by the ACFC, which underlined that scarce school attendance at compulsory school and the higher education level is:

> [...] *largely due to their precarious living conditions and, more generally, to the fact that the placement of Roma, Sinti and Travellers in isolated camps is still considered the model to follow by many authorities. Initiatives taken so far by the Italian authorities* [...] *have produced limited results, mainly due to the absence of a comprehensive strategy of integration at national level aimed at improving their situation in various fields of life* [...]. *In its comments on the first opinion, the government indeed recalled the difficulty to find Roma or Sinti language teachers and stressed that equal access to education remained the priority in its action in favour of these persons.*[167]

---

[166] Emphasis added. This implies that it is irrelevant whether the kids are legal or illegal immigrants, and that their mere presence in the territory is enough to enjoy the right to primary education.

[167] ACFC Second Opinion on Italy, *supra* note 24, para. 114.

Generally, it is volunteers who help out and thus the problem, which is clearly a social one, keeps being managed as a private one. The result is that most of the time, Roma children do not complete primary education, or that school attendance does not correspond to actual learning. Another difficulty in guaranteeing foreign Roma children fundamental rights such as the right to education lies in the fact that they, as many other foreign children, do not speak Italian fluently and are thus accused by the parents of Italian children of slowing down the learning process of the rest of the class. The latest report to CERD points out that:

> *In order to promote a relevant attendance at school, the Ministry of Education has allocated specific financial resources for the schools affected by high percentage of immigrants, including Roma students, in order to implement educational activities aiming at favouring their effective integration.*[168]

It should be observed that many Romani children in Italy are in fact Italian citizens.

In October 2008, the government discussed a proposal according to which foreign children shall be enrolled in special classes until it can be proved that they speak and read Italian so that they can attend regular schools. A strong debate is taking place between the majority and the opposition parties, in which the first holds that this would only be a temporary solution in order to guarantee full integration of foreign children in schools, and the latter points out that it is a pedagogical paradox to place all foreign children in the same class for them to learn Italian (because they are more likely to learn through full contact with Italian children) and that no time limits have been placed to this provision.[169] With regard to separate classes for foreign children, it is important to examine the decisions of the ECtHR in the cases of *D.H. and Others v. Czech Republic,*[170] *Sampanis and Others v. Greece*[171] and *Orsus and Others v. Croatia,*[172] (analysed in chapter 3) in which the Court found that placing children in special schools because of their ethnic origins and/or (allegedly) their

[168] CERD Fifteenth periodic reports, Italy, *supra* note 106, para. 177.

[169] 'Classi per stranieri: il no di Veltroni: "Dio ce ne scampi." Alemanno frena,' *Corriere della Sera*, Oct. 15, 2008.

[170] *Case of D. H. and Others v. the Czech Republic* (Grand Chamber) Eur. Ct. Hum. Rts., Application number 57325/00, 13 November 2007.

[171] *Case of Sampanis and Others v. Greece,* Eur. Ct. Hum. Rts., Application number 32526/05, 5 June 2008.

[172] *Case of Orsus and Others v. Croatia* (Grand Chamber), Eur. Ct. Hum. Rts., Application number 15766/03, 16 March 2010.

language constitutes a violation of Article 2 Protocol 1 to the ECHR together with Article 14.

Effective school attendance, in any case, does not prevent the expulsion of foreign children from the Italian territory regardless of Article 19(2(a)) of the TU because such a norm provides for an exception to the norm prohibiting the expulsion of children in cases in which they are meant to follow the parents or guardians who have been expelled.

Foreign children who arrive without their parents, at times following their brothers, as "unaccompanied minors" are granted – at least in theory – more protection from expulsion. Unaccompanied minors have more chances of staying in Italy, at least until they reach adult age (and unless the Committee for Minors intervenes before they do) because the absence of their parents makes them the object of obligatory intervention of social services (by which they might be placed in protected communities or with some relatives living in the territory, and either enrolled in schools or helped in their job search) and of the Tribunal for the Minors. In the case of Roma children, the exception to the norm prohibiting expulsion becomes the rule because they rarely arrive in Italy without their families and therefore are more at risk of being repatriated because the adults they travel with rarely enter the country legally and as such are at a continuous risk of expulsion. Article 31(3) TU provides that the Tribunal for the Minors can temporarily authorize entry and residence in the country of the parents or guardians of a minor if this is in the interest of the child, but this norm is subject to the restrictions posed by strict interpretations, including the suspicion that this Article might be used by the parents to gain legal status in the country through the children.[173] This creates an obvious paradox, considering that one of the fiercest critiques against the Roma is that they do not properly take care of their children, and that, when they try to do so, they are accused of exploiting them. Surely Roma children are the ones suffering the most for the lack of protection, because, although living in dire conditions, they are obliged to share the fate of their parents who are often illegal immigrants, even in the case in which the law should provide for their protection.[174]

Finally, it should be underlined that despite the existing norms and the many international instruments ratified by Italy, it is always difficult for Roma to prove that they have been the object of discrimination, especially in light of the persistent prejudice felt by most of the majority society at all

173 Zorzella, *supra* note 115, at 154–155.

174 Id., at 155.

levels, public and private, institutional and non-institutional. The equality principle which is enjoyed by the majority society has little value for the Roma, either as a group, or as individuals belonging to the group. The Roma in Italy are living in a paradox in which succeeding governments have tolerated and indeed encouraged the creation of camps by the Roma (while guaranteeing other immigrant groups "normal" houses, and which has occurred solely on the basis of their ethnicity and is thus in violation of Article 43(2(a)) and (c) of the TU and of Article 3(1(i)) of legislative decree 215), the very fact that leads to the perpetration of social prejudices against them.[175]

5.5. Measures "In Favour" of The Roma?

As has already been stated, Italy has never adopted any coherent and articulated policy to deal with the issues presented by the Roma communities. The only real efforts at the national level have been those in the field of education, which, although important, should be seen as only a part of the policy of protection and integration of the Roma and Sinti communities. In 1965, the Ministry of Education signed an agreement with Opera Nomadi and the University of Padua according to which 11 special classes for Roma children would be created in various cities across the country. In 1982, the special classes were abolished. On July 16, 1986, the Ministry of Education adopted the circular number 207, which marked the end of any special agreement with Opera Nomadi and the passage of any competence and responsibility regarding the education of Roma children to educational institutions. This circular was based on the fundamental principle that education is compulsory for all Roma children and that the state should do its best to favour this.

At the end of the 1980s, with another circular of the ministry of education (circular number 301 of September 8, 1989), the "intercultural perspective" acquired importance and was indeed consolidated by several pronouncements of the National Council for Public Education. In the pronouncement of June 26, 1993 regarding linguistic minorities, the Roma and Sinti communities were mentioned among the various "linguistic isles."[176] This is particularly important when considering that ten years later, the framework law did not include Roma and Sinti among the recognised

[175] Zorzella, *supra* note 115, at 163.
[176] Marta, *supra* note 22, at 46.

protected minorities. With circular number 73 of March 2, 1994, the Ministry of Education underlined the importance of having an intercultural dialogue and pointed out that the Roma should be recognised as an ethnic group. In practice, intercultural education – and especially the education of Roma and Sinti children – has not caused the radical changes that would have been expected following so many proclamations. Nevertheless, the ACFC observed that:

> *some commendable initiatives, which are often implemented by NGOs and/or social workers, have been taken to ensure better access of Roma, Sinti and Traveller's children to schools. Such initiatives, which include the organisation of public transportation of pupils to schools and the introduction of cultural mediators, are frequently supported from the municipal authorities.*[177]

The Ministry of Interior has always had a great role in shaping the policies dealing with Roma and Sinti issues. In the 1970s, an inter-ministerial commission was created to deal with the "problem of the gypsies," reflecting the view according to which Roma represent issues of public order, and which failed in its duties only a few weeks after starting its works.[178] The same fate has been shared by other similar commissions, the last of which was created in 1994 (the Office for Ethnic Minorities and Border Problems, mentioned in the preceding, and which only drafted one report).

In 1973, the Ministry of Interior sent a circular which asked all mayors of Italy to allow the Roma to camp and to favour them in the registration with local authorities, in the allowance of work permits and in the camping sites and education of children. In 1985, similarly to the one of 1973, another circular (number 151/85 of July 5, 1985) having as its subject the "issue of the nomads" demanded the full recognition of *"a real equality between those belonging to the groups [Roma and Sinti] – who in the great majority of cases, have Italian citizenship – and other citizens"* and that an adequate response was given to:

> *the primary needs of nomadic populations, which is at the same time respectful of the culture and customs of life – which are quite different among each other – of the various ethnicities of which nomadism is made up of.*

The importance of this document is in its direct reference to the Roma ethnicity and culture, elements that should never be forgotten if the problem of the integration of Roma communities into the majority society is to

177 ACFC Second Opinion on Italy, *supra* note 24, para. 113.
178 Marta, *supra* note 22, at 47.

be solved successfully.[179] It is my opinion that this document is yet another proof that the Roma should be considered an ethnic minority, in Italy and in other European countries,[180] and it points out the need for a clear policy to deal with the many issues faced by the Roma communities – both at the Italian and at the European level – whose basis would have to be the recognition of the Roma as an ethnic and cultural minority. This, in turn, emphasizes the value that an internationally accepted definition of minority would have because it would constitute a starting point from which countries could adopt laws that clearly define the status of the various groups living in their territory without much margin for error or interpretation and thus adopt clear and coherent policies for their integration – including affirmative action – and especially for the protection of their rights.[181]

On January 18, 1991, a new circular issued by the Ministry of Interior showed a completely different attitude: although it condemned any episode of intolerance against the Roma expressed "with open and cruel hostility," the circular seemed to almost justify them because of the many practices of the Roma such as persistent begging, chiromancy and in some cases even crimes against property and drug trafficking. The circular thus underlined the need for the concrete control by the police.

In 1994, the Office for Ethnic Minorities and Border Problems published the *First report on the status of minorities in Italy*, which included a chapter on the Roma, which also stated that:

> *the integration of* gypsies[182] *in the national community through a process of slow assimilation, has not worked so far, nor does it have great possibilities of success because we are facing a group with characteristics of behaviour and culture which are different from those of other linguistic minorities. A long process of development within the group is necessary for the gypsies to peacefully face the problem of* socialisation *and of living together with the local communities nearest to them.*[183]

The use of the term "socialisation" is inappropriate because it clearly implies that the Roma are the ones who should adapt to "our" values.[184]

---

179 Marta, *supra* note 22, at 47.

180 For a list of the countries which include the Roma in the protection afforded by the FCNM, *see* chapter 2. For a list of the countries which have recognised the Roma either as a national or ethnic minority, *see* chapter 1.

181 This aspect is further analysed in chapters 2 and 3.

182 Emphasis added: the word "zingari" (gypsies) is the one used in the report.

183 *Primo rapporto sullo stato delle minoranze in Italia, supra* note 21, at 385.

184 Marta, *supra* note 22, at 48.

In the first report to the ACFC of 1999, the Italian authorities stated that a number of regional laws intended to protect the *gypsies*[185] had been adopted and that a number of bills on the protection of *gypsies* were under examination by the parliament.[186] No such bill has been adopted so far.

The legal vacuum that has left the Roma at the mercy of national authorities has been in part filled by regional laws. The recognition of the Roma and Sinti as a minority and the protection of their culture appeared to be the guiding principle at the basis of the many regional laws that have been adopted since the mid-80s. The first of these laws was adopted by the region of Veneto in 1984, followed by Lazio and the autonomous province of Trento in 1985, Sardinia and Friuli-Venezia Giulia in 1988, Emilia Romagna in 1988, Tuscany in 1989, and all the other regions in the years to follow. The progressive "regionalisation" of the protection of minorities should be noted. According to this:

> *the legislation* [...] *for the protection of the Roma ethnic identity has been seen as a vital part of this process, which however has at its foundation a system of protection centred on linguistic minorities having strong territorial ties.*[187]

Regional laws are not enough to guarantee the full protection of the Roma, and in any case, they are hardly applied. Furthermore, as has already been seen, all of them recognise nomadism as a characteristic cultural trait and as such they protect the right to nomadism and to stop in the territory of the region. Although reference is also made to the living conditions of the Roma (in particular health care, education and employment), the main objective of these laws is the establishment of areas for the nomad camps.[188] In practice, regional laws have at their basis the misconception that all Roma are nomads and that they should be treated as such.

Regional laws may also include guidelines for building camps and allocating funding. In reality, the actual decision power is the responsibility of local government. In recent times, city councillors have not been particularly responsive to the cultural arguments presented in the regional laws, but, at most, they only intervened when health and security problems of the illegal settlements came to the attention of the local and national

---

185 Emphasis added.

186 ACFC Report by Italy, *supra* note 52, at 16.

187 A. Simoni, 'Stato di diritto e rom. Breve rassegna storica e comparata su di un problema mai risolto', in I. D'Isola, M. Sullam, G. Baldoni, G. Baldini and G. Frassanito (eds), *Alla periferia del mondo. Il popolo dei rom escluso dalla storia* (Milan: Fondazione Roberto Franceschi, 2003), pp. 54–75, at 73 [hereinafter Simoni (2003)].

188 Marta, *supra* note 22, at 48.

media.[189] The camps are therefore not so much a perennial feature of Roma culture, but rather a ready-made housing solution (at relatively low cost) to what is perceived as a constant state of 'emergency.'[190]

These laws can have some positive effects at the national level, if anything because they are the starting point for a discussion on the living conditions of the Roma in Italy. However, they imply several issues. The first is that these laws are the result of the persistent idea that the Roma are nomadic people: although this might have been true at the beginning of the 1980s, it is no longer the case. In this sense, Tuscany and Emilia Romagna amended the laws to adapt them to the new circumstances, in which the majority of Roma are stationary rather than nomads.[191] In addition, no enforcement mechanism exists for any of these laws[192] and the result is that many municipalities are reluctant to apply regional laws (and to access the funds to do this) and to establish the camps to which the region has agreed to follow EU norms on the matter. The result is that few camps exist with the facilities provided according to the law and instead, many camps exist that are ill-equipped and encourage the ghettoisation of Roma rather than facilitate their integration.[193] The latter have often become the only shelter for the Roma arriving from the Balkans.

When the authorities are missing, the implementation of local strategies is mainly delegated to the voluntary sector, which has the fundamental task of mediating between local government and the Roma. However, as many failed projects which aimed to improve the living conditions and to promote Roma participation have shown, leaving to volunteers and NGOs the task of implementing local strategies implies two main risks: first, volunteers might end up confusing their role of mediator with that of representative; therefore, rather than facilitating the communication of Roma needs, they change roles and begin to speak 'for' them; second,

---

[189] Sigona, *supra* note 12, at 748.

[190] Id.

[191] Marta, *supra* note 22, at 48–49. For example, Tuscany promulgated 3 laws on the Roma: law 17 of 1988, law 73 of 1995 and law 2 of 2000, all recognising the scarce efficacy of previous laws and acknowledging the fact that these only allowed the creation of camps in marginal areas. The current legislation, conversely, allows for the coordination with urban planning and for the creation of small camps for no more than 60 people by also contributing financially to the restoration of living spaces and to the legalisation of working places for artisan activities. *See* UNAR Report 2007, *supra* note 108, at 55–57.

[192] Dell'Agnese and Vitale, *supra* note 101, at 136. The same is also said in the UNAR report of 2007. *See* UNAR report 2007, *supra* note 108, at 55.

[193] Marta, *supra* note 22, at 49.

institutionalising Roma and making them dependent on the mercy of the host society instead of promoting their participation and mobilisation.[194]

The only way for the regional laws to finally work is that they are amended in view of the changing conditions and that they become part of a framework to be coordinated and administered at the national level, a strategy that is still missing in Italy. In addition,

> *the extension of the process of the regionalisation of protection, already questionable with regards to "traditional" linguistic minorities, to a minority which does not have such ties, without a fully standardised language, and, most of all, with such a peculiar history of intolerance is not the best premise for a solution.*[195]

If appropriate norms are missing at the national level, little hope exists for a clear assertion of the rights of the Roma[196] and it is harder to promote *"a discussion of the balance of the (sometimes opposing rights) of the subjects involved."*[197]

5.6. Conclusion and Final Remarks

The Special Rapporteur on Contemporary Forms of Racism observed that although Italian society is not marked by a serious phenomenon of racism, it is facing a disturbing trend of xenophobia and the development of manifestations of racism, primarily affecting the Sinti and Roma community and immigrants and asylum-seekers mostly of African origin but also from Eastern Europe and the Muslim community.[198] Government policies do little to change this situation and the media make political use of and legitimize racism and xenophobia by exploiting the profound process of multiculturalism taking place in Italian society and its consequent identity crisis.[199] Right-wing parties such as the Lega Nord and the Popolo delle Libertà (PDL, formerly known as Forza Italia) continue to promote at the national level and implement their xenophobic and racist platforms at the regional and local levels and, when it comes to the Roma, little is also done by left-wing governments, as the Pacts on Security previously discussed

[194] Sigona, *supra* note 12, at 752.
[195] Simoni (2003), *supra* note 187, at 73.
[196] Dell'Agnese and Vitale, *supra* note 101, at 136.
[197] Simoni (2003), *supra* note 187, at 73.
[198] *Report of the Special Rapporteur on contemporary forms of racism, supra* note 62, para. 58.
[199] Id., para. 59.

and first put in place by the former leftist government demonstrate. Disguising their views as freedom of expression, the media often continue to incite racial and religious hatred. Only too often they report cases of crimes in which the nationality or ethnicity of the person who committed the crime are emphasised, almost implying that their nationality or ethnicity was the reason for which the crime was committed.[200]

According to the Special Rapporteur, the current xenophobic trend is partially a manifestation of the fear resulting from the identity crisis of Italian society and the challenge of multiculturalism, particularly regarding non-European migrants. He underlined how the Italian national identity, historically constructed to promote the nation-state marked by the legacy of the fascist state and impregnated with ethnic and religious connotations, no longer corresponds to the profoundly multicultural dynamics of modern society.[201] Racism and xenophobia are professed because of the need to "defend the national identity" and "protect the national security." No real understanding exists of the concept of individual legal responsibility, in which it is the single person who should be made responsible for the crimes committed, rather than the group to which he belongs. No willingness to exchange values exists, or to open up to other cultures, which are seen as a threat to society and to "Italianness."

As the Special Rapporteur rightly pointed out, racism, discrimination and xenophobia have a deep cultural dimension. A profound lack of knowledge and understanding of the culture and religion of national minorities and migrants is present, in particular regarding Islam and Roma and Sinti culture and value systems, which remain untaught or insufficiently incorporated into school curricula despite their long-standing presence in Italy.[202] Very little school curriculum includes the teaching of Romani

---

[200] This was also noted by the Special Rapporteur, who pointed out that *"When crimes are committed by persons of foreign origin or belonging to the Roma or Sinti community, their nationality or ethnicity is particularly emphasized." See Report of the Special Rapporteur on contemporary forms of racism, supra* note 62, para. 57. A recent example in which the nationality and ethnicity of the person accused of a crime has been strongly underlined is that of the incident caused on November 5, 2008 by a Croatian Roma who, driving drunk and on drugs, hit 13 people who were in line at the bus stop. The first lines of a number of newspaper articles pointed out the driver's ethnicity and nationality, almost as if these were the main reason for the incident, rather than the fact that the driver was drunk and on drugs. *See* 'Roma: nomade ubriaco travolge 13 persone alla fermata del bus', *Corriere della Sera,* Nov. 5, 2008.

[201] Report of the Special Rapporteur on contemporary forms of racism, *supra* note 62, para. 60.

[202] Id., para. 64.

history and culture, even when these are part of Italian history and even within the teaching of the Fascist period, of WWII and of Nazi holocaust, which are otherwise subjects of exhaustive study. Italians are still convinced that the best approach to integration is assimilation, whereby "immigrants have to accept and adapt to our values" and respect our laws. This aspect has also been observed by the Special Rapporteur, who added that demanding immigrants and asylum seekers to divest themselves of their cultural, religious and, if possible, ethnic specificity, *"is not only a rejection of cultural diversity but also the reproduction and recycling of the historical cultural prejudice against the uncivilized non-European"* and thus a reproduction of the pan-European views which negate history as well as geography.[203]

Analysis of Italian laws, policies and practices reveal a lack of political will to include the Roma and allow for their full integration. Roma are scarcely represented at the political level and indeed, they hardly participate in the political process of the country, whether at the local, regional or national level.

> *The participation of Roma and Sinti, both as voters and as candidates, to the last local elections in Italy was extremely limited, nevertheless, compared to past elections, there were some signs of political engagement in the electoral process. This happened despite the absence of institutional initiatives aimed at facilitating and promoting the political participation of these communities to local polity. On the contrary, often local authorities (see for example the resettlement of Roma in rural areas in Rome) implement policies that, directly or indirectly, discourage and obstacle Roma and Sinti participation.*[204]

Little improvement has been observed during the latest political elections in April 2008, when Dijana Pavlovic, a Serbian Roma having Italian citizenship, was a candidate in Milan but only received a few votes after being described by the media as a Romanian nomad.

> *The political debate on Roma and Sinti issues during the electoral period revolved mainly around security, urban regeneration/deprivation and access to/exploitation of social welfare provisions. In the debate Roma and Sinti voices are rarely heard, this contributes to the dehumanisation of real Roma and Sinti which are presented as a "problem" which requires, according to the political side of the speaker, either the intervention of social workers or of the police. It is telling the fact that frequently Italian Roma and Sinti are dealt with in the electoral platform sections dedicated to immigrants.*[205]

---

203 Report of the Special Rapporteur on contemporary forms of racism, *supra* note 62, para. 64.

204 N. Sigona et al., *Political Participation and Media Representation of Roma and Sinti in Italy*, OsservAzione, July 26, 2006, [hereinafter Sigona et al.] at 41–42.

205 Id., at 42.

Finally, media coverage hardly reports the voices of the Roma, and so they rarely have the possibility of responding and giving their views through the media.[206]

The January 2008 European Conference on the Roma held in Rome under the auspices of the Department of Civil Liberties and Immigration of the Ministry of Interior, which had the aim of identifying possible solutions to the problems encountered by Roma, and which included the participation of several Roma and Sinti activists, should therefore be viewed optimistically.[207] Another positive step in this sense was taken with the creation of the "Federazione 'Rom e Sinti Insieme'" (hereafter Federazione), a democratic organisation led by a number of Italian and foreign Roma and Sinti, which has joined together 22 Roma and Sinti associations in 12 regions of Italy. Created on May 18, 2008, this organisation intends to define a political programme and an organisational strategy with the aim of ensuring active participation of Roma and Sinti, regardless of whether they are Italian or immigrants, and thus, in the long term, of improving the living conditions of the Roma and the respect of their rights.[208]

One of the main propositions of the Federazione is the recognition of the Roma as a minority through a modification of law 482/1999. A proposal in this sense was presented on July 3, 2007 (number 2858) and is currently pending with the Minister of Interior. This sheds light on the underlying prejudice that has lead to the non-recognition of the Roma amongst the recognised minorities which has led to the adoption of measures – such as the creation of nomad camps – that are not satisfactory in guaranteeing the full integration of the Roma and Sinti. According to the proposal, not recognising the Roma and the specificity of their culture implies a continued discrimination toward them. The first step should be the recognition of the Roma as a linguistic minority, which would allow for a revaluation of Roma and Sinti cultures and would favour their social integration locally and nationally.[209]

---

[206] Sigona et al., *supra* note 204, at 42.

[207] The CERD welcomed this Conference in its concluding observations on Italy. *See* CERD, Concluding observations on Italy, 2008, *supra* note 29, para. 4.

[208] The full description and programme of the Federazione "Rom e Sinti Insieme" can be viewed on the website of the organisation, http://comitatoromsinti.blogspot.com/, last visited Mar. 20, 2012. It should be pointed out that again no distinction is made between Italian and foreign Roma.

[209] Proposta di Legge n. 2858, July 3, 2007, Modifiche alla legge 15 dicembre 1999, n. 482, *per l'estensione delle disposizioni di tutela delle minoranze linguistiche storiche alle minoranze dei rom e dei sinti.* [hereinafter Proposta di Legge n. 2858].

The proposal wishes to incorporate international and European resolutions and recommendations on the topic, including the EChRML (which protects non-territorial languages) by adding to Article 1 of framework law 482/1999 an additional paragraph according to which:

> *the Republic promotes the development of the languages and cultures present in the various parts of the Country where the minority presence is such that it cannot be otherwise included within the field of application of the law.*[210]

The proposal also wishes to insert a paragraph 2(b) to Article 1, stating that:

> *The Republic promotes* [...] *the development of the languages and cultures protected as by paragraph 2, even when these are spread throughout the country and the minority presence is not such to fit in the sphere of application of the present law.*

In addition, Article 2(1) would add the words "Roma and Sinti" after the word "Croatian," so as to include Roma and Sinti among the recognised minority languages.[211]

What is needed to finally improve the situation is a drastic change which implies the abandonment of differential policies and the use of normal policies of cultural interchange and cultural recognition, thus allowing the participation of the Roma and Sinti in programmes involving them. This, together with the establishment of a constructive dialogue, should allow the majority society to better know the Roma and Sinti culture and thus lead to the elimination of discrimination against them. In this sense, the creation of the Federazione shows a positive trend as the Roma throughout Italy are finally raising their voices and acting together to start a dialogue with the government and the authorities and to affirm a culture of legality and the condemnation of abuses of power so as to promote a multicultural society.[212] The need to raise the Roma voices, include Roma as active subjects in political processes that have an effect on them, consult them on decisions that regard them and start a constructive dialogue with national and European institutions was underlined by Eva Rizzin, a young Sinti activist and founding member of the Federazione, in a number of interviews.[213]

---

210 Proposta di Legge n. 2858, *supra* note 209. *See also* http://comitatoromsinti.blogspot.com/, last visited Mar. 20, 2012.

211 Id.

212 Id.

213 *See*, for example, the interview for OsservAzione, available at http://www.osservazione.org/chefare_rizzin.htm, last visited Mar. 20, 2012, and the one in Vita,

Regrettably, little cooperation is forthcoming on the side of the authorities. In October 2010, the ACFC still highlighted the lack of a legal framework and a "comprehensive strategy for the integration and protection of Roma and Sinti in Italy" as a key area for action for the Italian authorities.[214] In its report on the situation of Roma and Sinti in Italy, published in May 2011, the Italian Senate's Human Rights Commission also pointed out that the current lack of a national plan on Roma and Sinti limits the use of European funds that are available for integration purposes.[215]

The High Commissioner for Human Rights of the Council of Europe has pointed out the need to create a task force at the national level, supporting and servicing a network of regional and local stakeholders that are active in social inclusion work for Roma and Sinti.[216] However, he added that:

> *for such a strategy to have a chance to produce long-term results, a genuine effort is needed in Italy to shift paradigm in dealing with issues relating to Roma and Sinti: the focus must be much more on social inclusion, non-discrimination and combating anti-Gypsyism and less on coercive measures such as forcible evictions and expulsions.*[217]

It is my contention that it is mainly by applying pressure at the legal and political level – which implies the adoption of a comprehensive national policy for the integration of Roma and Sinti – that real change can be achieved. Indeed, the views of society may take a long time to change, thus making the need of a deterrent against discriminatory behaviour urgent. The "Gypsy question" should no longer be seen only as a problem of public order but as a political and legal issue that has to be confronted with appropriate instruments. Italy does have a system in place that protects minorities which is quite advanced for those minorities that are recognised. However, the Italian legal system has failed the Roma, first because they are not recognised as a minority under the framework law, and second because the existing norms prohibiting discrimination are not properly applied.

---

a weekly magazine. *See* 'Minoranze. Parla Eva Rizzin della neonata Federazione Rom e Sinti Insieme. Rom, adesso per noi parliamo solo noi,' *Vita*, Aug. 29, 2008.

214 ACFC, Third Opinion on Italy, *supra* note 150, Executive Summary.

215 *Senato della Repubblica, Documentazione di Commissione n. 7, Commissione straordinaria per la tutela e la promozione dei diritti umani, Rapporto conclusivo dell'indagine sulla condizione di Rom, Sinti e Camminanti in Italia,* May 2011.

216 As seen in the preceding, a Contact Point for Roma has been established within UNAR in 2011.

217 Report by Thomas Hammarberg, *supra* note 157, paras. 42–34.

In the words of the former High Commissioner of National Minorities, van der Stoel, *"the existence of a minority is a question of fact and not of definition."*[218] In any event, the lack of an internationally accepted definition of minority should not delay the recognition of the Roma any further because various international bodies have clearly stated that the Roma are to be considered a minority.[219] Keeping this in mind, Italy should recognize the Roma and Sinti as a minority without delay because its current failure to do so discriminates between minorities.[220] Furthermore, the Roma and Sinti minority should be recognised because, due to the current state of racism in Italy against them, as proven by the latest developments, the failure of the government to provide such recognition is a factor tacitly encouraging anti-Romani racism. Besides guaranteeing the effective protection of the individual human rights of the Roma (i.e.: ensure the full application of existing norms against discrimination, or in other words, respect, protect and fulfil their human rights), the first measure that needs to be taken as a matter of urgency, thus, is the recognition of the Roma – at least, to begin with, of those who are Italian citizens – as a minority at the national level, an action which would guarantee policies of protection and promotion of their fundamental rights as a group, including their collective right to cultural identity. The next step would have to be the adoption of affirmative action policies and special measures aimed at the social inclusion of the Roma as a whole group – policies which can target both the Roma who are Italian citizens and those who are not (for example, the 2000/43 directive of the European Union does not differentiate in this sense). Thus, an approach encompassing the collective dimension – as discussed in chapter 4 – rather than only individual rights might be more appropriate in this case.

In the case of foreign Roma who do not fulfil the elements of citizenship, and until an appropriate solution is found (possibly through the adoption of an internationally accepted definition of minority with clear criteria which would be fulfilled by the Roma across Europe), the most urgent measures to adopt are the full implementation and application of international standards on the prohibition of discrimination (which Italy

---

218 Keynote address of the High Commissioner on National Minorities, Organization for Security and Cooperation in Europe Minorities' Seminar, Warsaw, 1994.

219 *See* chapter 2.

220 As was already mentioned, according to the ECtHR, *'the principle of equality of treatment is violated if the distinction has no objective and reasonable justification.' See Belgian Linguistics, supra* note 104, para. 10.

currently blatantly violates) so that they can also benefit from the measures in favour of other recognised Italian minorities. A model that could be adopted in this sense is the Belgian example. Indeed,

> *the Flemish parliament approved a decree for a policy in this field on 28 April 1998, describing ethnic-cultural minorities as the whole of allochthonous people, refugees, caravan dwellers and groups of foreigners in Belgium without a legal residence permit and those requesting relief or assistance due to their emergency situation.*[221]

It thus appears that in its definition of minority, Belgium also includes vulnerable migrants in need of supplementary inclusion measures, an approach not too distant from that recommended by the HRC in General Comment 23(50) according to which immigrants should not be denied the rights under Article 27 of the ICCPR either.[222] In addition, I observe that, considering the majority of foreign Roma living in Italy are in any case EU citizens and considering the approach of the ACFC which does not differentiate between citizens and non-citizens, they should eventually be granted the status of minority, in line with the principles expressed by the Council of Europe according to which the Roma are a real European minority and thus enjoying the protection granted by national norms to minorities.

5.6.1. *The Benefits of Collective Rights for the Roma of Italy*

As seen in chapter 4, collective rights are fundamental for the protection and preservation of the cultural identities of minorities and the human rights of their members, and cultural identity is considered to be the core of minority protection. The question that naturally arises then, is how the Roma and Sinti in Italy would benefit from a collective rights approach to their issues. This section briefly points out the practical benefits that an approach based on the implementation of collective rights would have on the Roma and Sinti minority of Italy.

It has been stated in chapter 4 that collective rights are needed to overcome the effects of past discrimination and can help to place minorities on equal footing with the majority society. Considering that the Roma and Sinti culture in Italy is highly despised and that Roma and Sinti are the

---

[221] *See* Compendium, Cultural Policies and Trends in Europe, *Belgium/ 4.2 Recent policy issues and debates, 4.2.1 Cultural minorities, groups and communities*, available at http://www.culturalpolicies.net/web/belgium.php?aid=421, last visited Mar. 20, 2012.

[222] General Comment 23(50), *supra* note 55.

subject of persecution and discrimination mostly due to their ethnicity and culture, it becomes clear that Roma and Sinti have less options and opportunities to live a dignified life than the rest of society. Collective rights imply the acknowledgement of the culture of the group and of the group itself and are even more important for minorities such as the Roma and Sinti who highly value their cultural membership to their group and whose life and relationships are often marked by their culture. Roma and Sinti identify themselves by reference to their membership to the Roma and Sinti group, and their well-being is often determined by the well-being of the whole group.

As seen in chapter 4, a strict individualist approach to minority issues might lead to the misrecognition of minorities and to the denial of their existence; it can lead members of minorities such as the Roma to seek to distance themselves from their culture so as to not be discriminated against, which, as we have already seen, has happened in Italy. Collective rights would allow group survival, in the sense that Roma and Sinti would not have to deny their identity for fear of being discriminated against and would not feel the need to abandon their group to have a better chance of being integrated into and accepted by the majority society. In this way, the culture and the life of the group could flourish, Roma and Sinti could feel more at ease in expressing their cultural identity and there would be a better chance for a constructive exchange and dialogue between the majority culture and that of Roma and Sinti, in which the majority society could have the possibility of learning about the history and the culture of the minority group. In this sense, learning about the "other" culture would be a first step toward a full understanding of a different, yet just as meaningful and interesting culture and way of life as well as toward the integration of the Roma and Sinti.

It has already been stated that a collective rights approach to Roma and Sinti issues in Italy would allow the recognition of their existence as a group, as well as of their culture – a fundamental aspect for their survival. This would eventually translate into the official recognition of the Roma and Sinti minority by the state and either into the adoption of a new law that officially recognises them and grants them special rights (and makes the application of the FCNM a more straightforward task) or in the application of the framework law 482/1999 to them as well. Roma and Sinti in Italy would thus be able to enjoy a minimum set of special rights[223]

[223] As seen in the course of this chapter, minorities which have a strong link to a territory or which have a kin state are usually in an advantaged position in making their claims.

that in Italy are normally afforded to officially recognised minority groups and that would allow for better protection of their culture and identity.

Collective rights allow for a certain form of autonomy, through which the Roma and Sinti in Italy could also determine their language rights (for example, to use their language in communications with public authorities) and could seek the financing of their own schools and media. A first step toward the empowerment of the Roma and Sinti minority would be the possibility of creating and running its schools (with a curriculum which includes the study of the Roma and Sinti history, culture, art and literature, as well as the study of Romanes and which, when possible, would allow mother tongue education in Romanes), its newspapers and tv channels, which would allow them to fully express their views and speak for themselves rather than being represented and portrayed by members of the majority society. It would give them the possibility of defending themselves against allegations of crimes coming from the majority society and of better organising themselves in terms of political and public awareness, as well as in terms of advocating their rights and their culture. It would also favour their participation in the life of the country, including political participation at the national and regional level, because they would gain more group consciousness and understand the importance of taking part in the life of the country not only as the objects of measures that target them, but also as the main actors in their destiny. In other words, Roma and Sinti would be able to have political representatives setting up political programmes and actions to favour the protection and promotion of the culture and identity of the group.

Finally, it should be underlined that collective rights would also allow better protection of Roma and Sinti from assimilationist policies by the state and would represent a better chance to put an end to the pattern and effect of discrimination against them. The general feeling among the majority of Italian society is that despite the fact that most of them are actually Italian citizens, Roma and Sinti are guests and foreigners who "should adapt to our norms and rules and live according to our way of life." As seen in the course of this chapter,[224] assimilationist and discriminatory policies have been widely applied to the Roma and Sinti in Italy. Through a series of emergency decrees, special restrictive measures have been put

Roma and Sinti, lacking any link with a specific territory, would not be able to make the same claims, yet they would have at least some minimum guarantees for the protection of their language, culture, history and by extention, identity.

[224] *See* section 5.4.2 *infra*.

in place that infringe on even the most basic rights of members of the Roma and Sinti communities and that are highly discriminatory as they single out the Roma and Sinti as a cause for social alarm. Roma are widely discriminated against in most fields of everyday life, from education to employment to access to health care and housing. The implementation of a collective right to cultural identity, allowing the Roma and Sinti to gain more political consciousness and to express their voices through their own representatives would favour the protection of the individual rights of the members of the Roma and Sinti minority. In fact, as previously stated,[225] collective rights also allow for a more effective protection of individual rights.

[225] *See* chapter 4, section 4.5.3.

CONCLUSION

This book has argued that the best approach to issues concerning the protection of extremely disadvantaged minorities such as the Roma is through the protection of their cultural identity by adopting a system that, besides applying the principles of equality and non-discrimination, encompasses the recognition of a collective right to cultural identity. To do this, it first provided a clarification of the concepts of culture and cultural identity because they are important for the identification of groups and are strictly linked to ethnicity. It thus showed that the Roma are a group and that, before anything else, they should be considered an ethnic group. However, doubts are raised about the status of the Roma as a minority. Indeed, an internationally accepted definition of minority is missing and although this has not been an obstacle to the application of existing instruments or to the protection of the cultural identity of minorities, the recognition of groups such as the Roma, whose status is not always clear, might not be a straightforward task. The effects have been disastrous in countries which have not followed the recommendations of international monitoring bodies on the recognition of minorities (including the Roma, which, according to various monitoring bodies, are to be considered a minority) and have unilaterally decided which groups should be recognised as minorities. When groups are not recognised as minorities, they cannot claim special rights for their protection, and their members can only resort to the application of individual human rights and of the principles of non-discrimination and equality to have their rights guaranteed. However, these individual rights are not sufficient in protecting the cultural identities of minorities (deemed the essence of minority protection). The book has thus maintained that the best way to protect minorities such as the Roma is through the recognition of collective rights, particularly a collective right to cultural identity. Finally, through the case study of Italy, it has been shown that where the law is vague, states have a high degree of freedom in the interpretation of international norms as well as in their implementation and are thus able to evade their international obligations: Italy is an example of a state that, although having ratified a large number of international human rights law instruments, does not automatically implement them at the domestic level, thus showing that the enforcement of international law is often not an easy task.

Evidence has thus demonstrated that when it comes to the protection of disadvantaged minorities such as the Roma, a deficiency in the law exists: the normative framework has loopholes that allow states to take unilateral decisions in the implementation of the law. Furthermore, a deficiency also exists in the application of the law even where this is clear, as almost nothing can be done to hold states accountable and to enforce international law at the domestic level.

The Roma as an Ethnic Group

Before addressing the main concerns of minority protection for the Roma in chapter I, it was necessary to clarify the meanings of culture and cultural identity and to establish whether the Roma, before being considered and recognised as a minority, are indeed a group. This book has demonstrated that despite the ample debate on whether they should be considered a group, the Roma are clearly an ethnic group. Despite their heterogeneity and their lack of a unified language, religion and culture, and notwithstanding the fact that they are spread across and beyond the continent without having made any territorial claims, elements can be found to ascertain that the Roma ought to be regarded as an ethnic group. Indeed, Roma have some common traits that should not be underestimated. They have common ancestry and geographic origins, which look back to a set of values and traditions that have been modified through contact with the majority society of the host countries; they all attach a high degree of importance to the group and to the family; and even their trans-nationality, the fact that they are spread across the continent, underlines their common way of life and traditions. Roma consider themselves as a unified, particular ethnic group and if anything, their common history of persecutions and discrimination can be used to prove that they should be considered a group.

Having established that the Roma are a group, it had to be considered whether they are an ethnic group. Due to the lack of a definition of "ethnic group" in international law, the definition provided by the House of Lords in *Mandla v. Dowell Lee*[1] has been followed because it is considered one of the most complete and accepted: when that definition is followed, it can be concluded that the Roma are an ethnic group.

[1] *Case of Mandla v. Dowell Lee*, [1983] 2AC 548.

The Roma as a Minority According to International Law

Having ascertained that the Roma are an ethnic group, chapter II determined whether they can be considered a minority: recognition as a minority is important to becoming the subject of special measures of protection and preservation of cultural identity. It has thus been explained that no internationally accepted definition of minority exists. However, despite that no instrument has actually adopted a definition that is internationally accepted or has provided, at most, a "description" or a working definition, through the interpretation that the monitoring bodies of the various instruments have provided, and through their jurisprudence, it has been possible to understand what groups should be recognised as minorities and it has been seen that the Roma should be considered a minority.

The lack of a clear and internationally, legally accepted definition of minority means that states have the final say when deciding which groups residing on their territory can be considered minorities, and this has caused the non-recognition of the Roma in Italy.

Collective Rights as a Better Guarantee of Minority Protection

Where groups are not recognised as minorities, they have no access to special measures and can only receive protection through individual human rights provisions and prohibition of discrimination and equality. Chapter III established that the application of the principles of equality and non-discrimination, despite being fundamental for minorities and the only applicable principles in which minorities are not officially recognised, are not enough to safeguard the real essence of minorities – that is, their cultural identities. The analysis of the case law of the Committee for the Elimination of Racial Discrimination (CERD), the Human Rights Committee (HRC) and the European Court of Human Rights (ECtHR) has shown that protection of cultural identity is not adequately achieved through the vindication of individual rights and the prohibition of discrimination.

Having ascertained that individual human rights and prohibition of discrimination do not provide sufficient safeguards for minority protection, it has been shown that special measures are needed to protect minorities' cultural identity, encompassing also the recognition of collective rights. Chapter IV, after exploring the debate between supporters and opponents of collective rights and revising the concept of cultural rights,

has thus shown how collective rights, in particular a collective right to cultural identity, are better suited to protect minorities.

Roma in Italy

Chapter V, focusing on Italy, has shown that the lack of an internationally accepted definition of minority binding on states has had disastrous effects for the Roma. It has proven how Italy, taking advantage of a deficiency in the law, has refused to recognise the Roma as a minority while recognising several other groups, thus continuing to discriminate against them. Despite recommendations and invitations from all international bodies to recognise the Roma among its minorities, Italy has thus far failed to do so and, as shown, it has denied them a series of special measures which are in place for other recognised minorities. Roma in Italy can therefore only resort to non-discrimination provisions to satisfy their rights. However, as shown in chapter III, non-discrimination provisions based on the protection of individual rights are not sufficient to protect minorities' identities when fully applied, and even less so in the case of Italy, where they are poorly implemented and where the Roma have little access to the legal system. Furthermore, the Italian authorities do not seem keen on at least ensuring protection of fundamental rights to the Roma. As seen in chapter V, when Roma are fiercely discriminated against on all grounds and become the target of racist attacks by the majority society, the authorities do not simply fail to act to protect them, but rather capitalise on the fears of the majority society to adopt a whole new system of norms and policies which is even more discriminatory and which denies the Roma their most basic rights.

What Next?

Roma in Europe, and even more so in Italy, are suffering on a number of grounds. Their everyday life is a battle for survival through extreme poverty and severe discrimination. Italy has ratified all the most important international human rights law instruments, including those on the protection of minorities, and has put in place an advanced system that provides excellent protection and promotion of the cultural identities of the recognised minorities. Roma living in Italy experience a situation which is dramatically different from that of other minority groups. In addition to not being recognised as a minority, there are no special measures for them and they cannot enjoy their collective right to cultural identity; furthermore, they cannot even enjoy their most basic rights.

In November 2008, a conference on minority languages was held in Macomer, Sardinia and representatives of all the recognised minority groups of Italy were invited.[2] They all expressed similar concerns on the protection of their identity, including the need for their languages to receive further attention in schools, in which they are already taught for several hours each week. It is a real paradox that recognised minorities talk of special measures for the protection of their identity to the point of demanding more hours for the teaching of their language, while the Roma, far from being recognised, have to face everyday discrimination in all fields of their life, must demand attention for their conditions, and are only at the initial stages of fighting for their fundamental human rights.

Unable to take advantage of the system of minority protection in Italy, and being the target of discrimination which they can hardly challenge, Roma who wish to be integrated in the Italy of today have to renounce their identity. Only too often do Roma activists and groups report episodes of Roma who have had to hide their ethnicity and identity to access homes, education or employment. For example, Roberto only confessed his ethnicity to his employer when, having been suggested to be part of a program favouring the employment of young Roma, he told Roberto that he would never employ "gypsies."[3] The 2009 season of the popular reality show "Big Brother," aired on Italian national television, had the "novelty" of having among its participants Mr Ferdi Berisa, a young Roma from Montenegro. Roma activists enthusiastically thought that this would be the chance to let the Roma be known to the public at large, but when the show started it became immediately obvious that Ferdi had renounced and rejected his cultural identity.

Unless something is done as a matter of urgency to end discrimination against the Roma and to protect and promote their cultural identity, there exists the risk that Roma culture will disappear under the pressure for acceptance by the majority society.

---

[2] For more information on the conference, see http://www.regione.sardegna.it/j/v/25?s=100354&v=2&c=220&t=1, last visited Mar. 20, 2012.

[3] http://www.flickr.com/photos/hidden_vice/3350572969/in/dateposted/, last visited Mar. 20, 2012.

APPENDIX I

FRAMEWORK CONVENTION FOR THE PROTECTION OF NATIONAL MINORITIES

(ETS No. 157)

Explanatory Report

Background

1. The Council of Europe has examined the situation of national minorities on a number of occasions over a period of more than forty years. In its very first year of existence (1949), the Parliamentary Assembly recognised, in a report of its Committee on Legal and Administrative Questions, the importance of "the problem of wider protection of the rights of national minorities". In 1961, the Assembly recommended the inclusion of an article in a second additional protocol to guarantee to national minorities certain rights not covered by the European Convention on Human Rights (ECHR). The latter simply refers to "association with a national minority" in the non-discrimination clause provided for in Article 14. Recommendation 285 (1961) proposed the following wording for the draft article on the protection of national minorities:

> "Persons belonging to a national minority shall not be denied the right, in community with the other members of their group, and as far as compatible with public order, to enjoy their own culture, to use their own language, to establish their schools and receive teaching in the language of their choice or to profess and practise their own religion."

2. The committee of experts, which had been instructed to consider whether it was possible and advisable to draw up such a protocol, adjourned its activities until a final decision had been reached on the Belgian linguistics cases concerning the language used in education (European Court of Human Rights. Judgment of 27 July 1968, Series A No. 6). In 1973 it concluded that, from a legal point of view, there was no special need to make the rights of minorities the subject of a further protocol to the ECHR. However, the experts considered that there was

no major legal obstacle to the adoption of such a protocol if it were considered advisable for other reasons.

3. More recently, the Parliamentary Assembly recommended a number of political and legal measures to the Committee of Ministers, in particular the drawing up of a protocol or a convention on the rights of national minorities. Recommendation 1134 (1990) contains a list of principles which the Assembly considered necessary for the protection of national minorities. In October 1991, the Steering Committee for Human Rights (CDDH) was given the task of considering, from both a legal and a political point of view, the conditions in which the Council of Europe could undertake an activity for the protection of national minorities, taking into account the work done by the Conference on Security and Co-operation in Europe (CSCE) and the United Nations, and the reflections within the Council of Europe.
4. In May 1992, the Committee of Ministers instructed the CDDH to examine the possibility of formulating specific legal standards relating to the protection of national minorities. To this end, the CDDH established a committee of experts (DH-MIN) which, under new terms of reference issued in March 1993, was required to propose specific legal standards in this area, bearing in mind the principle of complementarity of work between the Council of Europe and the CSCE. The CDDH and the DH-MIN took various texts into account, in particular the proposal for a European Convention for the Protection of National Minorities drawn up by the European Commission for Democracy through Law (the so-called Venice Commission), the Austrian proposal for an additional protocol to the ECHR, the draft additional protocol to the ECHR included in Assembly Recommendation 1201 (1993) and other proposals. This examination culminated in the report of the CDDH to the Committee of Ministers of 8 September 1993, which included various legal standards which might be adopted in this area and the legal instruments in which they could be laid down. In this connection, the CDDH noted that there was no consensus on the interpretation of the term "national minorities".
5. The decisive step was taken when the Heads of State and Government of the Council of Europe's member States met in Vienna at the summit of 8 and 9 October 1993. There, it was agreed that the national minorities which the upheavals of history have established in Europe had to be protected and respected as a contribution to peace and stability.

In particular, the Heads of State and Government decided to enter into legal commitments regarding the protection of national minorities. Appendix II of the Vienna Declaration instructed the Committee of Ministers:

– to draft with minimum delay a framework convention specifying the principles which contracting States commit themselves to respect, in order to assure the protection of national minorities. This instrument would also be open for signature by non-member States;
– to begin work on drafting a protocol complementing the European Convention on Human Rights in the cultural field by provisions guaranteeing individual rights, in particular for persons belonging to national minorities.

6. On 4 November 1993, the Committee of Ministers established an ad hoc Committee for the Protection of National Minorities (CAHMIN). Its terms of reference reflected the decisions taken in Vienna. The committee, made up of experts from the Council of Europe's member States, started work in late January 1994, with the participation of representatives of the CDDH, the Council for Cultural Co-operation (CDCC), the Steering Committee on the Mass Media (CDMM) and the European Commission for Democracy through Law. The High Commissioner on National Minorities of the CSCE and the Commission of the European Communities also took part, as observers.
7. On 15 April 1994, CAHMIN submitted an interim report to the Committee of Ministers, which was then communicated to the Parliamentary Assembly (Doc. 7109). At its 94th session in May 1994, the Committee of Ministers expressed satisfaction with the progress achieved under the terms of reference flowing from the Vienna Declaration.
8. A certain number of provisions of the framework Convention requiring political arbitration as well as those concerning the monitoring of the implementation were drafted by the Committee of Ministers (517bis meeting of Ministers' Deputies, 7 October 1994).
9. At its meeting from 10 to 14 October 1994, CAHMIN decided to submit the draft framework Convention to the Committee of Ministers, which adopted the text at the 95th Ministerial Session on 10 November 1994. The framework Convention was opened for signature by the Council of Europe's member States on 1 February 1995.

General Considerations

Objectives of the Framework Convention

10. The framework Convention is the first legally binding multilateral instrument devoted to the protection of national minorities in general. Its aim is to specify the legal principles which States undertake to respect in order to ensure the protection of national minorities. The Council of Europe has thereby given effect to the Vienna Declaration's call (Appendix II) for the political commitments adopted by the Conference on Security and Co-operation in Europe (CSCE) to be transformed, to the greatest possible extent, into legal obligations.

Approaches and Fundamental Concepts

11. In view of the range of different situations and problems to be resolved, a choice was made for a framework Convention which contains mostly programme-type provisions setting out objectives which the Parties undertake to pursue. These provisions, which will not be directly applicable, leave the States concerned a measure of discretion in the implementation of the objectives which they have undertaken to achieve, thus enabling them to take particular circumstances into account.
12. It should also be pointed out that the framework Convention contains no definition of the notion of "national minority". It was decided to adopt a pragmatic approach, based on the recognition that at this stage, it is impossible to arrive at a definition capable of mustering general support of all Council of Europe member States.
13. The implementation of the principles set out in this framework Convention shall be done through national legislation and appropriate governmental policies. It does not imply the recognition of collective rights. The emphasis is placed on the protection of persons belonging to national minorities, who may exercise their rights individually and in community with others (see Article 3, paragraph 2). In this respect, the framework Convention follows the approach of texts adopted by other international organisations.

Structure of the Framework Convention

14. Apart from its Preamble, the framework Convention contains an operative part which is divided into five sections.

15. Section I contains provisions which, in a general fashion, stipulate certain fundamental principles which may serve to elucidate the other substantive provisions of the framework Convention.
16. Section II contains a catalogue of specific principles.
17. Section III contains various provisions concerning the interpretation and application of the framework Convention.
18. Section IV contains provisions on the monitoring of the implementation of the framework Convention.
19. Section V contains the final clauses which are based on the model final clauses for conventions and agreements concluded within the Council of Europe.

Commentary on the Provisions of the Framework Convention

Preamble

20. The Preamble sets out the reasons for drawing up this framework Convention and explains certain basic concerns of its drafters. The opening words already indicate that this instrument may be signed and ratified by States not members of the Council of Europe (see Articles 27 and 29).
21. The Preamble refers to the statutory aim of the Council of Europe and to one of the methods by which this aim is to be pursued: the maintenance and further realisation of human rights and fundamental freedoms.
22. Reference is also made to the Vienna Declaration of Heads of State and Government of the member States of the Council of Europe, a document which laid the foundation for the present framework Convention (see also paragraph 5 above). In fact, the text of the Preamble is largely inspired by that declaration, in particular its Appendix II. The same is true of the choice of undertakings included in Sections I and II of the framework Convention.
23. The Preamble mentions, in a non-exhaustive way, three further sources of inspiration for the content of the framework Convention: the Convention for the Protection of Human Rights and Fundamental Freedoms (ECHR) and instruments which contain commitments regarding the protection of national minorities of the United Nations and the CSCE.
24. The Preamble reflects the concern of the Council of Europe and its member States about the risk to the existence of national minorities

and is inspired by Article 1, paragraph 1, of the United Nations Declaration on the Rights of Persons belonging to National or Ethnic, Religious and Linguistic Minorities (Resolution 47/135 adopted by the General Assembly on 18 December 1992).

25. Given that the framework Convention is also open to States which are not members of the Council of Europe, and to ensure a more comprehensive approach, it was decided to include certain principles from which flow rights and freedoms which are already guaranteed in the ECHR or in the protocols thereto (see also in connection with this, Article 23 of the framework Convention).

26. The reference to United Nations conventions and declarations recalls the work done at the universal level, for example in the International Covenant on Civil and Political Rights (Article 27) and in the Declaration on the Rights of Persons belonging to National or Ethnic, Religious and Linguistic Minorities. However this reference does not extend to any definition of a national minority which may be contained in these texts.

27. The reference to the relevant CSCE commitments reflects the desire expressed in Appendix II of the Vienna Declaration that the Council of Europe should apply itself to transforming, to the greatest possible extent, these political commitments into legal obligations. The Copenhagen Document in particular provided guidance for drafting the framework Convention.

28. The penultimate paragraph in the Preamble sets out the main aim of the framework Convention: to ensure the effective protection of national minorities and of the rights of persons belonging to those minorities. It also stresses that this effective protection should be ensured within the rule of law, respecting the territorial integrity and national sovereignty of States.

29. The purpose of the last recital is to indicate that the provisions of this framework Convention are not directly applicable. It is not concerned with the law and practice of the Parties in regard to the reception of international treaties in the internal legal order.

Section I

Article 1

30. The main purpose of Article 1 is to specify that the protection of national minorities, which forms an integral part of the protection of human rights, does not fall within the reserved domain of States.

The statement that this protection "forms an integral part of the international protection of human rights" does not confer any competence to interpret the present framework Convention on the organs established by the ECHR.

31. The article refers to the protection of national minorities as such and of the rights and freedoms of persons belonging to such minorities. This distinction and the difference in wording make it clear that no collective rights of national minorities are envisaged (see also the commentary to Article 3). The Parties do however recognise that protection of a national minority can be achieved through protection of the rights of individuals belonging to such a minority.

Article 2

32. This article provides a set of principles governing the application of the framework Convention. It is, *inter alia*, inspired by the United Nations Declaration on Principles of International Law concerning Friendly Relations and Co-operation among States in accordance with the Charter of the United Nations (General Assembly Resolution 2625 (XXV) of 24 October 1970). The principles mentioned in this provision are of a general nature but do have particular relevance to the field covered by the framework Convention.

Article 3

33. This article contains two distinct but related principles laid down in two different paragraphs

Paragraph 1

34. Paragraph 1 firstly guarantees to every person belonging to a national minority the freedom to choose to be treated or not to be treated as such. This provision leaves it to every such person to decide whether or not he or she wishes to come under the protection flowing from the principles of the framework Convention.
35. This paragraph does not imply a right for an individual to choose arbitrarily to belong to any national minority. The individual's subjective choice is inseparably linked to objective criteria relevant to the person's identity.
36. Paragraph 1 further provides that no disadvantage shall arise from the free choice it guarantees, or from the exercise of the rights which are connected to that choice. This part of the provision aims to secure

that the enjoyment of the freedom to choose shall also not be impaired indirectly.

Paragraph 2

37. Paragraph 2 provides that the rights and freedoms flowing from the principles of the framework Convention may be exercised individually or in community with others. It thus recognises the possibility of joint exercise of those rights and freedoms, which is distinct from the notion of collective rights. The term "others" shall be understood in the widest possible sense and shall include persons belonging to the same national minority, to another national minority, or to the majority.

Section II

Article 4

38. The purpose of this article is to ensure the applicability of the principles of equality and non-discrimination for persons belonging to national minorities. The provisions of this article are to be understood in the context of this framework Convention.

Paragraphs 1 and 2

39. Paragraph 1 takes the classic approach to these principles. Paragraph 2 stresses that the promotion of full and effective equality between persons belonging to a national minority and those belonging to the majority may require the Parties to adopt special measures that take into account the specific conditions of the persons concerned. Such measures need to be "adequate", that is in conformity with the proportionality principle, in order to avoid violation of the rights of others as well as discrimination against others. This principle requires, among other things, that such measures do not extend, in time or in scope, beyond what is necessary in order to achieve the aim of full and effective equality.
40. No separate provision dealing specifically with the principle of equal opportunities has been included in the framework Convention. Such an inclusion was considered unnecessary as the principle is already implied in paragraph 2 of this article. Given the principle of non-discrimination set out in paragraph 1 the same was considered true for freedom of movement.

Paragraph 3

41. The purpose of paragraph 3 is to make clear that the measures referred to in paragraph 2 are not to be regarded as contravening the principles of equality and non-discrimination. Its aim is to ensure to persons belonging to national minorities effective equality along with persons belonging to the majority.

Article 5

42. This article essentially aims at ensuring that persons belonging to national minorities can maintain and develop their culture and preserve their identity.

Paragraph 1

43. Paragraph 1 contains an obligation to promote the necessary conditions in this respect. It lists four essential elements of the identity of a national minority. This provision does not imply that all ethnic, cultural, linguistic or religious differences necessarily lead to the creation of national minorities (see in this regard the report of the CSCE meeting of experts, held in Geneva in 1991, section II, paragraph 4).
44. The reference to "traditions" is not an endorsement or acceptance of practices which are contrary to national law or international standards. Traditional practices remain subject to limitations arising from the requirements of public order.

Paragraph 2

45. The purpose of paragraph 2 is to protect persons belonging to national minorities from assimilation against their will. It does not prohibit voluntary assimilation.
46. Paragraph 2 does not preclude the Parties from taking measures in pursuance of their general integration policy. It thus acknowledges the importance of social cohesion and reflects the desire expressed in the preamble that cultural diversity be a source and a factor, not of division, but of enrichment to each society.

Article 6

47. This article is an expression of the concerns stated in Appendix III to the Vienna Declaration (Declaration and Plan of Action on combating racism, xenophobia, anti-Semitism and intolerance).

Paragraph 1

48. Paragraph 1 stresses a spirit of tolerance and intercultural dialogue and points out the importance of the Parties' promoting mutual respect, understanding and co-operation among all who live on their territory. The fields of education, culture and the media are specifically mentioned because they are considered particularly relevant to the achievement of these aims.
49. In order to strengthen social cohesion, the aim of this paragraph is, *inter alia,* to promote tolerance and intercultural dialogue, by eliminating barriers between persons belonging to ethnic, cultural, linguistic and religious groups through the encouragement of intercultural organisations and movements which seek to promote mutual respect and understanding and to integrate these persons into society whilst preserving their identity.

Paragraph 2

50. This provision is inspired by paragraph 40.2 of the Copenhagen Document of the CSCE. This obligation aims at the protection of all persons who may be subject to threats or acts of discrimination, hostility or violence, irrespective of the source of such threats or acts.

Article 7

51. The purpose of this article is to guarantee respect for the right of every person belonging to a national minority to the fundamental freedoms mentioned therein. These freedoms are of course of a universal nature, that is they apply to all persons, whether belonging to a national minority or not (see, for instance, the corresponding provisions in Articles 9, 10 and 11 of the ECHR), but they are particularly relevant for the protection of national minorities. For the reasons stated above in the commentary on the preamble, it was decided to include certain undertakings which already appear in the ECHR.
52. This provision may imply for the Parties certain positive obligations to protect the freedoms mentioned against violations which do not emanate from the State. Under the ECHR, the possibility of such positive obligations has been recognised by the European Court of Human Rights.
53. Some of the freedoms laid down in Article 7 are elaborated upon in Articles 8 and 9.

Article 8

54. This article lays down more detailed rules for the protection of freedom of religion than Article 7. It combines several elements from paragraphs 32.2, 32.3 and 32.6 of the CSCE Copenhagen Document into a single provision. This freedom of course applies to all persons and persons belonging to a national minority should, in accordance with Article 4, enjoy it as well. Given the importance of this freedom in the present context, it was felt particularly appropriate to give it special attention.

Article 9

55. This article contains more detailed rules for the protection of the freedom of expression than Article 7.

Paragraph 1

56. The first sentence of this paragraph is modelled on the second sentence of Article 10, paragraph 1, of the ECHR. Although the sentence refers specifically to the freedom to receive and impart information and ideas in the minority language, it also implies the freedom to receive and impart information and ideas in the majority or other languages.
57. The second sentence of this paragraph contains an undertaking to ensure that there is no discrimination in access to the media. The words "in the framework of their legal systems" were inserted in order to respect constitutional provisions which may limit the extent to which a Party can regulate access to the media.

Paragraph 2

58. This paragraph is modelled on the third sentence of Article 10, paragraph 1, of the ECHR.
59. The licensing of sound radio and television broadcasting, and of cinema enterprises, should be non-discriminatory and be based on objective criteria. The inclusion of these requirements, which are not expressly mentioned in the third sentence of Article 10, paragraph 1, of the ECHR, was considered important for an instrument designed to protect persons belonging to a national minority.
60. The words "sound radio", which also appear in paragraph 3 of this article, do not appear in the corresponding sentence in Article 10 of the

ECHR. They are used in order to reflect modern terminology and do not imply any material difference in meaning from Article 10 of the ECHR.

Paragraph 3

61. The first sentence of this paragraph, dealing with the creation and use of printed media, contains an essentially negative undertaking whereas the more flexibly worded second sentence emphasises a positive obligation in the field of sound radio and television broadcasting (for example the allocation of frequencies). This distinction reflects the relative scarcity of available frequencies and the need for regulation in the latter field. No express reference has been made to the right of persons belonging to a national minority to seek funds for the establishment of media, as this right was considered self-evident.

Paragraph 4

62. This paragraph emphasises the need for special measures with the dual aim of facilitating access to the media for persons belonging to national minorities and promoting tolerance and cultural pluralism. The expression "adequate measures" was used for the reasons given in the commentary on Article 4, paragraph 2 (see paragraph 39), which uses the same words. The paragraph complements the undertaking laid down in the last sentence of Article 9, paragraph 1. The measures envisaged by this paragraph could, for example, consist of funding for minority broadcasting or for programme productions dealing with minority issues and/or offering a dialogue between groups, or of encouraging, subject to editorial independence, editors and broadcasters to allow national minorities access to their media.

Article 10

Paragraph 1

63. The recognition of the right of every person belonging to a national minority to use his or her minority language freely and without interference is particularly important. The use of the minority language represents one of the principal means by which such persons can assert and preserve their identity. It also enables them to exercise their freedom of expression. "In public" means, for instance, in a

public place, outside, or in the presence of other persons but is not concerned in any circumstances with relations with public authorities, the subject of paragraph 2 of this article.

Paragraph 2

64. This provision does not cover all relations between individuals belonging to national minorities and public authorities. It only extends to administrative authorities. Nevertheless, the latter must be broadly interpreted to include, for example, ombudsmen. In recognition of the possible financial, administrative, in particular in the military field, and technical difficulties associated with the use of minority languages in relations between persons belonging to national minorities and the administrative authorities, this provision has been worded very flexibly, leaving Parties a wide measure of discretion.
65. Once the two conditions in paragraph 2 are met, Parties shall endeavour to ensure the use of a minority language in relations with the administrative authorities as far as possible. The existence of a "real need" is to be assessed by the State on the basis of objective criteria. Although contracting States should make every effort to apply this principle, the wording "as far as possible" indicates that various factors, in particular the financial resources of the Party concerned, may be taken into consideration.
66. The Parties' obligations regarding the use of minority languages do not in any way affect the status of the official language or languages of the country concerned. Moreover, the framework Convention deliberately refrains from defining "areas inhabited by persons belonging to national minorities traditionally or in substantial numbers". It was considered preferable to adopt a flexible form of wording which will allow each Party's particular circumstances to be taken into account. The term "inhabited ... traditionally" does not refer to historical minorities, but only to those still living in the same geographical area (see also Article 11, paragraph 3, and Article 14, paragraph 2).

Paragraph 3

67. This paragraph is based on certain provisions contained in Articles 5 and 6 of the European Convention on Human Rights. It does not go beyond the safeguards contained in those articles.

Article 11

Paragraph 1

68. In view of the practical implications of this obligation, the provision is worded in such a way as to enable Parties to apply it in the light of their own particular circumstances. For example, Parties may use the alphabet of their official language to write the name(s) of a person belonging to a national minority in its phonetic form. Persons who have been forced to give up their original name(s), or whose name(s) has (have) been changed by force, should be entitled to revert to it (them), subject of course to exceptions in the case of abuse of rights and changes of name(s) for fraudulent purposes. It is understood that the legal systems of the Parties will, in this respect, meet international principles concerning the protection of national minorities.

Paragraph 2

69. The obligation in this paragraph concerns an individual's right to display "in his or her minority language signs, inscriptions and other information of a private nature visible to the public". This does not, of course, exclude persons belonging to national minorities from being required to use, in addition, the official language and/or other minority languages. The expression "of a private nature" refers to all that is not official.

Paragraph 3

70. This article aims to promote the possibility of having local names, street names and other topographical indications intended for the public also in the minority language. In implementing this principle the States are entitled to take due account of the specific circumstances and the framework of their legal systems, including, where appropriate, agreements with other States. In the field covered by this provision, it is understood that the Parties are under no obligation to conclude agreements with other States. Conversely, the possibility of concluding such agreements is not ruled out. It is also understood that the legally binding nature of existing agreements remains unaffected. This provision does not imply any official recognition of local names in the minority languages.

Article 12

71. This article seeks to promote knowledge of the culture, history, language and religion of both national minorities and the majority population in an intercultural perspective (see Article 6, paragraph 1). The aim is to create a climate of tolerance and dialogue, as referred to in the preamble to the framework convention and in Appendix II of the Vienna Declaration of the Heads of State and Government. The list in the second paragraph is not exhaustive whilst the words "access to textbooks" are understood as including the publication of textbooks and their purchase in other countries. The obligation to promote equal opportunities for access to education at all levels for persons belonging to national minorities reflects a concern expressed in the Vienna Declaration.

Article 13

Paragraph 1

72. The Parties' obligation to recognise the right of persons belonging to national minorities to set up and manage their own private educational and training establishments is subject to the requirements of their educational system, particularly the regulations relating to compulsory schooling. The establishments covered by this paragraph may be subject to the same forms of supervision as other establishments, particularly with regard to teaching standards. Once the required standards are met, it is important that any qualifications awarded are officially recognised. The relevant national legislation must be based on objective criteria and conform to the principle of non-discrimination.

Paragraph 2

73. The exercise of the right referred to in paragraph 1 does not entail any financial obligation for the Party concerned, but neither does it exclude the possibility of such a contribution.

Article 14

Paragraph 1

74. The obligation to recognise the right of every person belonging to a national minority to learn his or her minority language concerns one

of the principal means by which such individuals can assert and preserve their identity. There can be no exceptions to this. Without prejudice to the principles mentioned in paragraph 2, this paragraph does not imply positive action, notably of a financial nature, on the part of the State.

Paragraph 2

75. This provision concerns teaching of and instruction in a minority language. In recognition of the possible financial, administrative and technical difficulties associated with instruction of or in minority languages, this provision has been worded very flexibly, leaving Parties a wide measure of discretion. The obligation to endeavour to ensure instruction of or in minority languages is subject to several conditions; in particular, there must be "sufficient demand" from persons belonging to the relevant national minorities. The wording "as far as possible" indicates that such instruction is dependent on the available resources of the Party concerned.
76. The text deliberately refrains from defining "sufficient demand", a flexible form of wording which allows Parties to take account of their countries' own particular circumstances. Parties have a choice of means and arrangements in ensuring such instruction, taking their particular educational system into account.
77. The alternatives referred to in this paragraph – "opportunities for being taught the minority language or for receiving instruction in this language" – are not mutually exclusive. Even though Article 14, paragraph 2, imposes no obligation upon States to do both, its wording does not prevent the States Parties from implementing the teaching of the minority language as well as the instruction in the minority language. Bilingual instruction may be one of the means of achieving the objective of this provision. The obligation arising from this paragraph could be extended to pre-school education.

Paragraph 3

78. The opportunities for being taught the minority language or for receiving instruction in this language are without prejudice to the learning of the official language or the teaching in this language. Indeed, knowledge of the official language is a factor of social cohesion and integration.

79. It is for States where there is more than one official language to settle the particular questions which the implementation of this provision shall entail.

Article 15

80. This article requires Parties to create the conditions necessary for the effective participation of persons belonging to national minorities in cultural, social and economic life and in public affairs, in particular those affecting them. It aims above all to encourage real equality between persons belonging to national minorities and those forming part of the majority. In order to create the necessary conditions for such participation by persons belonging to national minorities, Parties could promote – in the framework of their constitutional systems – inter alia the following measures:

- consultation with these persons, by means of appropriate procedures and, in particular, through their representative institutions, when Parties are contemplating legislation or administrative measures likely to affect them directly;
- involving these persons in the preparation, implementation and assessment of national and regional development plans and programmes likely to affect them directly;
- undertaking studies, in conjunction with these persons, to assess the possible impact on them of projected development activities;
- effective participation of persons belonging to national minorities in the decision-making processes and elected bodies both at national and local levels;
- decentralised or local forms of government.

Article 16

81. The purpose of this article is to protect against measures which change the proportion of the population in areas inhabited by persons belonging to national minorities and are aimed at restricting the rights and freedoms which flow from the present framework Convention. Examples of such measures might be expropriation, evictions and expulsions or redrawing administrative borders with a view to restricting the enjoyment of such rights and freedoms ("gerrymandering").
82. The article prohibits only measures which are aimed at restricting the rights and freedoms flowing from the framework Convention. It was

considered impossible to extend the prohibition to measures having the effect of restricting such rights and freedoms, since such measures may sometimes be entirely justified and legitimate. One example might be resettlement of inhabitants of a village in order to build a dam.

Article 17

83. This article contains two undertakings important to the maintenance and development of the culture of persons belonging to a national minority and to the preservation of their identity (see also Article 5, paragraph 1). The first paragraph deals with the right to establish and maintain free and peaceful contacts across frontiers, whereas the second paragraph protects the right to participate in the activities of non-governmental organisations (see also in this connection, the provisions on freedom of assembly and of association in Article 7).
84. The provisions of this article are largely based on paragraphs 32.4 and 32.6 of the Copenhagen Document of the CSCE. It was considered unnecessary to include an explicit provision on the right to establish and maintain contacts within the territory of a State, since this was felt to be adequately covered by other provisions of the framework Convention, notably Article 7 as regards freedom of assembly and of association.

Article 18

85. This article encourages the Parties to conclude, in addition to the existing international instruments, and where the specific circumstances justify it, bilateral and multilateral agreements for the protection of national minorities. It also stimulates transfrontier co-operation. As is emphasised in the Vienna Declaration and its Appendix II, such agreements and co-operation are important for the promotion of tolerance, prosperity, stability and peace.

Paragraph 1

86. Bilateral and multilateral agreements as envisaged by this paragraph might, for instance, be concluded in the fields of culture, education and information.

Paragraph 2

87. This paragraph points out the importance of transfrontier co-operation. Exchange of information and experience between States is

an important tool for the promotion of mutual understanding and confidence. In particular, transfrontier co-operation has the advantage that it allows for arrangements specifically tailored to the wishes and needs of the persons concerned.

Article 19

88. This article provides for the possibility of limitations, restrictions or derogations. When the undertakings included in this framework Convention have an equivalent in other international legal instruments, in particular the ECHR, only the limitations, restrictions or derogations provided for in those instruments are allowed. When the undertakings set forth in this framework Convention have no equivalent in other international legal instruments, the only limitations, restrictions or derogations allowed are those which, included in other legal instruments (such as the ECHR) in respect of different undertakings, are relevant.

Section III

Article 20

89. Persons belonging to national minorities are required to respect the national constitution and other national legislation. However, this reference to national legislation clearly does not entitle Parties to ignore the provisions of the framework Convention. Persons belonging to national minorities must also respect the rights of others. In this regard, reference may be made to situations where persons belonging to national minorities are in a minority nationally but form a majority within one area of the State.

Article 21

90. This provision stresses the importance of the fundamental principles of international law and specifies that the protection of persons belonging to national minorities must be in accordance with these principles.

Article 22

91. This provision, which is based on Article 60 of the ECHR, sets out a well-known principle. The aim is to ensure that persons belonging to

national minorities benefit from whichever of the relevant national or international human rights legislation is most favourable to them.

Article 23

92. This provision deals with the relationship between the framework Convention and the Convention for the Protection of Human Rights and Fundamental Freedoms, reference to which is included in the Preamble. Under no circumstances can the framework Convention modify the rights and freedoms safeguarded in the Convention for the Protection of Human Rights and Fundamental Freedoms. On the contrary, rights and freedoms enshrined in the framework Convention which are the subject of a corresponding provision in the Convention for the Protection of Human Rights and Fundamental Freedoms must be interpreted in accordance with the latter.

Section IV

Articles 24–26

93. To provide for overseeing the application of the framework Convention, the Committee of Ministers is entrusted with the task of monitoring the implementation by the Contracting Parties. The Committee of Ministers shall determine the modalities for the participation in the implementation mechanism by the Parties which are not members of the Council of Europe.
94. Each Party shall transmit to the Secretary General on a periodical basis and whenever the Committee of Ministers so requests information of relevance to the implementation of this framework Convention. The Secretary General shall transmit this information to the Committee of Ministers. However, the first report, the aim of which is to provide full information on legislative and other measures which the Party has taken to give effect to the undertakings set out in the framework Convention, must be submitted within one year of the entry into force of the framework Convention in respect of the Party concerned. The purpose of the subsequent reports shall be to complement the information included in the first report.
95. In order to ensure the efficiency of the monitoring of the implementation of the framework Convention, it provides for the setting up of an advisory committee. The task of this advisory committee is to assist

the Committee of Ministers when it evaluates the adequacy of the measures taken by a Party to give effect to the principles set out in the framework Convention.

96. It is up to the Committee of Ministers to determine, within one year of the entry into force of the framework Convention, the composition and the procedures of the advisory committee, the members of which shall have recognised expertise in the field of the protection of national minorities.

97. The monitoring of the implementation of this framework Convention shall, in so far as possible, be transparent. In this regard it would be advisable to envisage the publication of the reports and other texts resulting from such monitoring.

Section V

98. The final provisions contained in articles 27 to 32 are based on the model final clauses for conventions and agreements concluded within the Council of Europe. No article on reservations was included; reservations are allowed in as far as they are permitted by international law. Apart from Articles 27 and 29 the articles in this section require no particular comment.

Articles 27 and 29

99. The framework Convention is open for signature by the Council of Europe's member States and, at the invitation of the Committee of Ministers, by other States. It is understood that "other States" are those States which participate in the Conference on Security and Co-operation in Europe. These provisions take account of the Vienna Declaration, according to which the framework Convention should also be open for signature by non-member States (see Appendix II to the Vienna Declaration of the Council of Europe Summit).

APPENDIX II

EUROPEAN CHARTER FOR REGIONAL OR MINORITY LANGUAGES

(ETS No. 148)

Explanatory Report

Introduction

1. Many European countries have on their territory regionally based autochthonous groups speaking a language other than that of the majority of the population. This is a consequence of historical processes whereby the formation of states has not taken place on purely language-related lines and small communities have been engulfed by larger ones.
2. The demographic situation of such regional or minority languages varies greatly, from a few thousand speakers to several million, and so does the law and practice of the individual states with respect to them. However, what many have in common is a greater or lesser degree of precariousness. Moreover, whatever may have been the case in the past, nowadays the threats facing these regional or minority languages are often due at least as much to the inevitably standardising influence of modern civilisation and especially of the mass media as to an unfriendly environment or a government policy of assimilation.
3. For many years various bodies within the Council of Europe have been expressing concern over the situation of regional or minority languages. It is true that the Convention for the Protection of Human Rights and Fundamental Freedoms in its Article 14 lays down the principle of non-discrimination, in particular outlawing, at least with respect to the enjoyment of the rights and freedoms guaranteed by the Convention, any discrimination based on such grounds as language or association with a national minority. Important though this is, however, it creates only a right for individuals not to be subjected to discrimination, but not a system of positive protection for minority languages and the communities using them, as was pointed out by the Consultative Assembly as long ago as 1957 in its Resolution 136. In 1961,

in Recommendation 285, the Parliamentary Assembly called for a protection measure to supplement the European Convention to be devised in order to safeguard the rights of minorities to enjoy their own culture, to use their own language, to establish their own schools and so on.

4. Lastly, in 1981 the Parliamentary Assembly of the Council of Europe adopted Recommendation 928 on the educational and cultural problems of minority languages and dialects in Europe, and in the same year the European Parliament passed a resolution on the same questions. Both documents concluded that it was necessary to draw up a charter of regional or minority languages and cultures.
5. Acting on these recommendations and resolutions, the Standing Conference of Local and Regional Authorities of Europe (CLRAE) decided to undertake the preparation of a European charter for regional or minority languages, by reason of the part which local and regional authorities must be expected to play in relation to languages and cultures at local and regional level.
6. The preliminary work before the actual drafting of the charter involved a survey of the actual situation of regional and minority languages in Europe and, in 1984, a public hearing attended by some 250 people representing over 40 languages. The initial drafting was carried out with the assistance of a group of experts. In view of the strong and continuing interest of the Parliamentary Assembly of the Council of Europe and the European Parliament in this topic, the former participated in the drafting and contacts were maintained with competent members of the latter.
7. Finally, in its Resolution 192 (1988), the Standing Conference proposed the text of a charter which was designed to have the status of a convention.
8. Following this initiative, which was supported by the Parliamentary Assembly in its Opinion No. 142 (1988), the Committee of Ministers established an ad hoc committee of experts on regional or minority languages in Europe (CAHLR), with responsibility for drafting a charter bearing the Standing Conference's text in mind. This intergovernmental committee began work at the end of 1989. In view of their important role as promoters of the project, both the CLRAE and the Parliamentary Assembly were represented at its meetings. Before submitting the final text of the draft charter to the Committee of Ministers in 1992, the CAHLR consulted and took into account the opinions of a number of specialised committees within the Council of Europe (culture, education, human rights, legal co-operation, crime problems,

local and regional authorities, media), as well as the European Commission for Democracy through Law.

9. The charter was adopted as a convention by the Committee of Ministers at the 478th meeting of the Ministers' Deputies on 25 June 1992 and opened for signature on 5 November 1992 in Strasbourg.

General Considerations

Objectives of the Charter

10. As is made clear in the preamble, the charter's overriding purpose is cultural. It is designed to protect and promote regional or minority languages as a threatened aspect of Europe's cultural heritage. For this reason it not only contains a non-discrimination clause concerning the use of these languages but also provides for measures offering active support for them: the aim is to ensure, as far as reasonably possible, the use of regional or minority languages in education and the media and to permit their use in judicial and administrative settings, economic and social life and cultural activities. Only in this way can such languages be compensated, where necessary, for unfavourable conditions in the past and preserved and developed as a living facet of Europe's cultural identity.

11. The charter sets out to protect and promote regional or minority languages, not linguistic minorities. For this reason emphasis is placed on the cultural dimension and the use of a regional or minority language in all the aspects of the life of its speakers. The charter does not establish any individual or collective rights for the speakers of regional or minority languages. Nevertheless, the obligations of the parties with regard to the status of these languages and the domestic legislation which will have to be introduced in compliance with the charter will have an obvious effect on the situation of the communities concerned and their individual members.

12. The CLRAE conceived and presented its draft charter before the dramatic changes in central and eastern Europe and in the light of the needs of the countries which at that time were already members of the Council of Europe. Nevertheless, the relevance of the charter and its approach to the situation of the countries of central and eastern Europe has since been confirmed by the considerable interest expressed by the representatives of a number of these countries in the establishment of European standards on this topic.

13. While the draft charter is not concerned with the problem of nationalities who aspire after independence or alterations to frontiers, it may be expected to help, in a measured and realistic fashion, to assuage the problem of minorities whose language is their distinguishing feature, by enabling them to feel at ease in the state in which history has placed them. Far from reinforcing disintegrating tendencies, the enhancement of the possibility to use regional or minority languages in the various spheres of life can only encourage the groups who speak them to put behind them the resentments of the past which prevented them from accepting their place in the country in which they live and in Europe as a whole.
14. In this context it should be stressed that the charter does not conceive the relationship between official languages and regional or minority languages in terms of competition or antagonism. Rather, it deliberately adopts an intercultural and multilingual approach in which each category of language has its proper place. This approach corresponds fully to the values traditionally upheld by the Council of Europe and its efforts to promote closer relations between peoples, increased European co-operation and a better understanding between different population groups within the state on an intercultural basis.
15. The charter does not deal with the situation of new, often non-European languages which may have appeared in the signatory states as a result of recent migration flows often arising from economic motives. In the case of populations speaking such languages, specific problems of integration arise. The CAHLR took the view that these problems deserved to be addressed separately, if appropriate in a specific legal instrument.
16. Finally, it may be noted that some member states of the Council of Europe already implement policies which go further than some of the requirements of the charter. It is in no way intended that the provisions of the charter should detract from their right to do so.

Basic Concepts and Approach

Concept of Language

17. The concept of language as used in the charter focuses primarily on the cultural function of language. That is why it is not defined subjectively in such a way as to consecrate an individual right, that is the right to speak "one's own language", it being left to each individual to define that language. Nor is reliance placed on a politico-social or

ethnic definition by describing a language as the vehicle of a particular social or ethnic group. Consequently, the charter is able to refrain from defining the concept of linguistic minorities, since its aim is not to stipulate the rights of ethnic and/or cultural minority groups, but to protect and promote regional or minority languages as such.

Terminology used

18. In preference to other expressions such as "less widespread languages", the CAHLR opted for the term "regional or minority languages". The adjective "regional" denotes languages spoken in a limited part of the territory of a state, within which, moreover, they may be spoken by the majority of the citizens. The term "minority" refers to situations in which either the language is spoken by persons who are not concentrated on a specific part of the territory of a state or it is spoken by a group of persons, which, though concentrated on part of the territory of the state, is numerically smaller than the population in this region which speaks the majority language of the state. Both adjectives therefore refer to factual criteria and not to legal notions and in any case relate to the situation in a given state (for instance, a minority language in one state may be a majority language in another state).

Absence of Distinction between different "Categories" of Regional or Minority Languages

19. The authors of the charter were confronted by the problem of the major differences which exist in the situations of regional or minority languages in Europe. Some languages cover a relatively large territorial area, are spoken by a substantial population and enjoy a certain capability of development and cultural stability; others are spoken only by a very small proportion of the population, in a restricted territory, or in a very marked minority context and already with greatly impaired potential for survival and development.
20. Nevertheless, it was decided not to attempt to define different categories of languages according to their objective situation. Such an approach would not do justice to the diversity of language situations in Europe. In practice, each regional or minority language constitutes a special case and it is pointless to try and force them into distinct groups. The solution adopted was to preserve the single notion of regional or minority language, while enabling states to adapt their undertakings to the situation of each regional or minority language.

Absence of a List of Regional or Minority Languages in Europe

21. The charter does not specify which European languages correspond to the concept of regional or minority languages as defined in its first article. In fact the preliminary survey of the linguistic situation in Europe carried out by the Standing Conference of Local and Regional Authorities of Europe prompted the authors of the charter to refrain from appending a list of regional or minority languages. However expert its compilers, such a list would certainly be widely disputed on linguistic and other grounds. Moreover, its value would be limited, since at any rate with respect to the specific measures in Part III of the charter it is left largely up to the parties to determine which provisions shall apply to which language. The charter puts forward appropriate solutions for the different situations of individual regional or minority languages but does not prejudge what is the specific situation in concrete cases.

The Structure of the Charter

22. On the one hand, the charter establishes a common core of principles, set out in Part II, which apply to all regional or minority languages. On the other hand, Part III of the charter contains a series of specific provisions concerning the place of regional or minority languages in the various sectors of the life of the community: the individual states are free, within certain limits, to determine which of these provisions will apply to each of the languages spoken within their frontiers. In addition, a considerable number of provisions comprise several options of varying degrees of stringency, one of which must be applied "according to the situation of each language".
23. This flexibility takes account of the major differences in the de facto situations of regional or minority languages (number of speakers, degree of fragmentation, etc). It also has regard to the costs entailed by many of the provisions and the varying administrative and financial capacity of the European states. In this respect it is important that the parties are allowed to add to their commitments at a later stage, as their legal situation develops or their financial circumstances allow.
24. Finally, Part IV of the charter contains implementing provisions, including in particular the establishment of a European expert committee to monitor the application of the charter.

Commentary on the Provisions of the Charter

Preamble

25. The preamble sets out the reasons for having the charter drawn up and explains its basic philosophical approach.
26. The aim of the Council of Europe is to achieve a greater unity between its members in order to promote their common heritage and ideals. Linguistic diversity is one of the most precious elements of the European cultural heritage. The cultural identity of Europe cannot be constructed on the basis of linguistic standardisation. On the contrary, the protection and strengthening of its traditional regional and minority languages represents a contribution to the building of Europe, which, according to the ideals of the members of the Council of Europe, can be founded only on pluralist principles.
27. The preamble refers to the United Nations International Covenant on Civil and Political Rights and to the European Convention on Human Rights. In addition, it cites the commitments of a political nature adopted within the framework of the Conference on Security and Co-operation in Europe. Having regard to the present weakness of some of the historical regional or minority languages of Europe, however, the mere prohibition of discrimination against their users is not a sufficient safeguard. Special support which reflects the interests and wishes of the users of these languages is essential to their preservation and development.
28. The approach of the charter respects the principles of national sovereignty and territorial integrity. Each state is required to take into account a cultural and social reality and there is no question of challenging any political or institutional order. On the contrary, it is because the member states accept territorial and state structures as they are, that they believe it is necessary, within each state, but in a concerted manner, to take measures to promote languages of a regional or minority nature.
29. The affirmation of the principles of interculturalism and multilingualism serves to remove any misapprehension as to the aims of the charter, which by no means seeks to foster any kind of partitioning off of linguistic groups. On the contrary, it is recognised that in every state it is necessary to know the official language (or one of the official languages); consequently, none of the charter's provisions should be interpreted as intending to raising obstacles to the knowledge of official languages.

Part I – General provisions

Article 1 – Definitions

Definition of "regional or minority languages" (*Article 1, paragraph a*)

30. The definition employed in the charter emphasises three aspects:

Languages traditionally used by nationals of the State:

31. The purpose of the charter is not to resolve the problems arising out of recent immigration phenomena, resulting in the existence of groups speaking a foreign language in the country of immigration or sometimes in the country of origin in case of return. In particular, the charter is not concerned with the phenomenon of non-European groups who have immigrated recently into Europe and acquired the nationality of a European state. The expressions "historical regional or minority languages of Europe" (see second paragraph of the preamble) and languages "traditionally used" in the state (Article 1, paragraph a) show clearly that the charter covers only historical languages, that is to say languages which have been spoken over a long period in the state in question.

Different Languages:

32. These languages must clearly differ from the other language or languages spoken by the remainder of the population of the state. The charter does not concern local variants or different dialects of one and the same language. However, it does not pronounce on the often disputed question of the point at which different forms of expression constitute separate languages. This question depends not only on strictly linguistic considerations, but also on psycho-sociological and political phenomena which may produce a different answer in each case. Accordingly, it will be left to the authorities concerned within each state, in accordance with its own democratic processes, to determine at what point a form of expression constitutes a separate language.

Territorial Base:

33. The languages covered by the charter are primarily territorial languages, that is to say languages which are traditionally used in a

particular geographical area. That is why the charter seeks to define the "territory in which the regional or minority language is used". It is not only the territory within which that language is dominant or spoken by the majority, since many languages have become minority languages even in the areas where they have their traditional territorial base. The reason why the charter is mainly concerned with languages which have a territorial base is that most of the measures which it advocates necessitate the definition of a geographical field of application other than the state as a whole. Obviously there are situations in which more than one regional or minority language is spoken on a given territory; the charter also covers these situations.

Definition of the Territory of a Regional or Minority Language (Article 1, paragraph b)

34. The territory referred to is that where a regional or minority language is spoken to a significant extent, even if only by a minority, and which corresponds to its historical base. Since the terms used in the charter in this respect are inevitably fairly flexible, it is up to each state to define more precisely, in the spirit of the charter, the notion of regional or minority languages' territory, taking into account the provisions of Article 7, paragraph 1.b, regarding protection of the territory of regional or minority languages.
35. A key expression in this provision is "number of people justifying the adoption of the various protective and promotional measures". The authors of the charter avoided establishing a fixed percentage of speakers of a regional or minority language at or above which the measures laid down in the charter should apply. They preferred to leave it up to the state to assess, within the spirit of the charter, according to the nature of each of the measures provided for, the appropriate number of speakers of the language required for the adoption of the measure in question.

Definition of "Non-Territorial Languages" (Article 1, paragraph c)

36. "Non-territorial languages" are excluded from the category of regional or minority languages because they lack a territorial base. In other respects, however, they correspond to the definition contained in Article 1, paragraph a, being languages traditionally used on the territory of the state by citizens of the state. Examples of non-territorial languages are Yiddish and Romany.

37. In the absence of a territorial base, only a limited part of the charter can be applied to these languages. In particular, most of the provisions of Part III aim to protect or promote regional or minority languages in relation to the territory in which they are used. Part II can more easily be applied to non-territorial languages, but only *mutatis mutandis* and on the terms set out in Article 7, paragraph 5.

Article 2 – Undertakings

38. Article 2 distinguishes between the two main parts of the charter, namely Part II and Part III.

Implementation of Part II (Article 2, paragraph 1).

39. Part II is general in scope and applies in its entirety to all regional or minority languages spoken on the territory of a State Party. It will be noted, however, that the use of the expression "according to the situation of each language" shows that this part is drafted so as to cater for the very great variety of language situations that may be encountered in the various European countries and within each country. In particular, in the first paragraph the States Parties are required to undertake to match their policy, legislation and practice to a number of principles and objectives. These are fairly generally defined and allow the states concerned a broad measure of discretion as regards interpretation and application (see explanations below concerning Part II).
40. Although the States Parties are not free to grant or to refuse a regional or minority language the status which it is guaranteed under Part II of the charter, they are responsible, as authorities for the application of the charter, for deciding whether the form of expression used in a particular area of their territory or by a particular group of their nationals constitutes a regional or minority language within the meaning of the charter.

Implementation of Part III (Article 2, paragraph 2)

41. The purpose of Part III is to translate the general principles asserted in Part II into precise rules. It is binding on those contracting states which, in addition to the provisions of Part II, undertake to apply the provisions of Part III which they have chosen. In order to enable the charter to be adapted to the variety of linguistic situations encountered in the various European states, the authors of the charter have provided for a twofold modulation: firstly, the states are free to name

the languages to which they agree to Part III of the charter being applied and, secondly, for each of the languages for which they accept that the charter shall apply, they can determine the provisions of Part III to which they subscribe.

42. It is possible for a contracting state, without offending the letter of the charter, to recognise that a particular regional or minority language exists on its territory but consider it preferable, for reasons which lie within its discretion, not to extend to that language the benefit of the provisions of Part III of the charter. Clearly, however, the reasons which prompt a state to exclude a recognised regional or minority language completely from the benefit of Part III must be reasons compatible with the spirit, objectives and principles of the charter.

43. Once a State has agreed to apply Part III to a regional or minority language spoken on its territory, it will still have to determine which paragraphs of Part III are to be applied to that particular regional or minority language. Under paragraph 2 of Article 2, the parties undertake to apply at least 35 paragraphs or sub-paragraphs chosen from among the provisions of Part III. The role of the state in the choice between these different paragraphs will consist in matching the charter as closely as possible to the particular context of each regional or minority language.

44. For this purpose the conditions stipulated by Article 2, paragraph 2 are kept to a minimum designed to provide for a reasonable distribution of the parties' undertakings among the different articles of the charter and thus ensure that they do not ignore any of the major fields of protection of regional or minority languages (education, judicial authorities, administrative authorities and public services, media, cultural activities and facilities, economic and social life).

45. The expression "paragraphs or sub-paragraphs" refers to distinct provisions of the charter which stand on their own. Thus, if a state chooses paragraph 3 of Article 9, this paragraph will count as one unit for the purposes of Article 2, paragraph 2; the same applies if a state accepts sub-paragraph g of Article 8, paragraph 1. Where a given paragraph or sub-paragraph contains several options, the choice of one option will constitute a sub-paragraph for the purposes of Article 2, paragraph 2. For example, in Article 8, if a state chooses option a.iii in paragraph 1, this text will count as a "sub-paragraph". The position is different when the options are not necessarily alternatives but may be accepted cumulatively. Thus in Article 9, if a state chooses options a.iii and a. iv in paragraph 1, these texts will count as two sub-paragraphs within the meaning of Article 2.

46. The aim of these options is to introduce a further element of flexibility into the charter so as to take account of the wide disparities in the de facto situation of regional or minority languages. It is clear that certain provisions which are perfectly well adapted to a regional language practised by a large number of speakers are not suited to a minority language used only by a small group of persons. The role of the states will be, not to choose arbitrarily between these alternatives, but to seek for each regional or minority language the wording which best fits the characteristics and state of development of that language. The purpose of these alternative wordings is clearly expressed in the very text of the relevant articles or paragraphs of Part III, which provide that they are applicable "according to the situation of each language". Broadly speaking, and in the absence of other relevant factors, this would imply, for instance, that the larger the number of speakers of a regional or minority language and the more homogeneous the regional population, the "stronger" the option which should be adopted; a weaker alternative should be adopted only when the stronger option cannot be applied owing to the situation of the language in question.
47. It will therefore be for the states to choose in Part III provisions forming a coherent framework adapted to the specific situation of each language. They may also, if they prefer, adopt a general framework applying to all the languages or to a group of languages.

Article 3 – Practical Arrangements

48. Article 3 describes the procedure for the implementation of the principles just outlined in Article 2: each Contracting State specifies in its instrument of ratification, acceptance, approval or accession, firstly, those regional or minority languages to which Part III applies and, secondly, the paragraphs of Part III chosen for application to each language, it being understood that the paragraphs chosen need not be the same for each language.
49. The charter, in its Article 2, does not compel acceptance of both Parts II and III, since a state could confine itself to ratifying the convention without selecting any language for the purposes of the application of Part III. In such a case, only Part II would apply. In general, the spirit of the charter would require that states make use of the possibilities offered by Part III, which constitutes the essence of the protection afforded by the charter.

50. It is also clear that, at any time, a party may accept new obligations, for example by extending to an additional regional or minority language the benefit of the provisions of Part III of the charter or by subscribing, in respect of a language or all the minority or regional languages spoken on its territory, to paragraphs of the charter not previously accepted.
51. The wording of Article 3 takes account of the position in certain member states whereby a national language which has the status of an official language of the state, either on the whole or on part of its territory, may in other respects be in a comparable situation to regional or minority languages as defined in Article 1, paragraph a, because it is used by a group numerically smaller than the population using the other official language(s). If a state wishes such a less widely used official language to benefit from the measures of protection and promotion provided for by the charter, it is therefore enabled to determine that the charter shall apply to it. Such an extension of the application of the charter to an official language then holds good for all articles of the charter, including Article 4, paragraph 2.

Article 4 – Existing Regimes of Protection

52. This article relates to the combination of the charter with domestic legislation or international agreements laying down a legal status for linguistic minorities.
53. Where certain languages or the minorities who practise them already enjoy a status defined in domestic law or under international agreements, the purpose of the charter is clearly not to reduce the rights and guarantees recognised by those provisions. However, the protection afforded by the charter is additional to the rights and guarantees already granted by other instruments. For the application of all these undertakings, where competing provisions exist on the same subject the most favourable provisions should be applied to the minorities or languages concerned. Thus the existence of more restrictive provisions in domestic law or under other international undertakings must not be an obstacle to the application of the charter.
54. Paragraph 1 of this article is concerned with the specific case of the rights guaranteed by the European Convention on Human Rights. It seeks to exclude the possibility that any of the provisions of the charter might be so interpreted as to detract from the protection accorded thereby to the human rights of individuals.

Article 5 – Existing Obligations

55. As is already indicated in the preamble, the protection and promotion of regional or minority languages which is the objective of the charter must take place within the framework of national sovereignty and territorial integrity. This article makes explicit in this respect that the existing obligations of the parties remain unchanged. In particular the fact that, by ratifying the charter, a state has entered into undertakings with respect to a regional or minority language may not be used by another state having a special interest in that language or by the users of the language as a pretext for taking any action prejudicial to the sovereignty and territorial integrity of that state.

Article 6 – Information

56. The motive for the undertaking to provide information which is established by this article lies in the fact that the charter can never become fully effective if the competent authorities and interested organisations and individuals are not aware of the obligations which derive from it.

Part II – Objectives and Principles

Article 7

List of Objectives and Principles included in the Charter (Article 7, paragraph 1)

57. These provisions concern essentially objectives and principles and not precise implementing rules. These objectives and principles are considered to constitute the necessary framework for the preservation of regional or minority languages. They fall under six main headings.

Recognition of Regional or Minority Languages (Article 7, paragraph 1.a)

58. This is a question of recognition of the existence of these languages and of the legitimacy of their use. Such recognition must not be confused with recognition of a language as an official language. Admitting the existence of a language is a pre-condition for taking its specific features and needs into consideration and for action on its behalf.

Respect for the Geographical Area of each Regional or Minority Language (Article 7, paragraph 1.b)

59. Although the charter considers it desirable to ensure a consistency between the territory of a regional or minority language and an appropriate territorial administrative entity, it is clear that this objective cannot be achieved in all cases, since settlement patterns may be too complex and the determination of territorial administrative entities may legitimately depend on other considerations than the use of a language. Accordingly, the charter does not require that the territory of a regional or minority language should in all cases coincide with an administrative unit.
60. On the other hand, it does condemn practices which devise territorial divisions so as to render the use or survival of a language more difficult or to fragment a language community among a number of administrative or territorial units. If administrative units cannot be adapted to the existence of a regional or minority language, they must at least remain neutral and not have a negative effect on the language. In particular, local or regional authorities must be in a position to discharge their responsibilities in relation to these languages.

Need for Positive Action for the benefit of Regional or Minority Languages (Article 7, paragraph 1.c and d)

61. It is clear today that, by reason of the weakness of numerous regional or minority languages, the mere prohibition of discrimination is not sufficient to ensure their survival. They need positive support. This is the idea expressed in paragraph 1.c. In this paragraph it is left up to the states to determine the manner in which they intend acting to promote regional or minority languages in order to preserve them, but the charter emphasises that such action must be resolute.
62. Furthermore, as stated in paragraph 1.d, this effort of promotion must include action in favour of the possibility to use regional or minority languages freely, both orally and in writing, not only in private life and in individual relations, but also in community life, that is to say within the framework of institutions, social activities and economic life. The place which a regional or minority language may occupy in public contexts will obviously depend on its own particular features and will vary from one language to another. The charter does not lay down precise objectives in this respect but is content to call for an effort of promotion.

Guarantee of the Teaching and Study of Regional or Minority Languages (Article 7, paragraph 1.f and h)

63. A crucial factor in the maintenance and preservation of regional or minority languages is the place they are given in the education system. The charter is content in Part II to affirm the principle, leaving it to the states to define implementing measures. However, it requires that regional or minority languages be present "at all appropriate stages" of the education system. The arrangements for the teaching of the regional or minority language will obviously vary according to the level of education concerned. In particular, in some cases, provision will need to be made for teaching "in" the regional or minority language and in others only for teaching "of" the language. Only the teaching of the regional or minority language at levels for which the language would not be appropriate, in view of its own particular characteristics, could be left out of account.
64. While paragraph 1.f is concerned to establish or safeguard teaching in or of the language as an instrument of transmission of the language, paragraph 1.h provides for the promotion of studies and research on regional or minority languages in a university or equivalent setting; for such work is essential to the development of such languages in terms of vocabulary, grammar and syntax. The promotion of such studies is part of the general effort to promote regional or minority languages in order to encourage their intrinsic progress.

    Facilities afforded to non-speakers of regional or minority languages to acquire a knowledge of them (Article 7, paragraph 1.g)
65. The speakers of regional or minority languages know that, for their own personal fulfilment, they need to know the official language. However, in accordance with the emphasis placed in the preamble on the value of interculturalism and multilingualism, it is desirable that this spirit of receptiveness to several languages should not be confined to the speakers of regional or minority languages. In order to facilitate communication and understanding between language groups, the parties are called upon, in territories where a regional or minority language exists, to provide facilities for persons who are not native speakers of that language to learn it if they so desire.
66. It is well known that in some states the objective of the appropriate authorities is that the regional language should be the language normally and generally spoken in the region, and measures are taken to ensure that the language is known even by people for whom it is not

their native language. Such a policy is not contrary to the charter, but does not constitute the purpose of paragraph 1.g. This paragraph seeks only to ensure greater mutual permeability between language groups.

Relations between groups speaking a Regional or Minority Language (Article 7, paragraph 1.e and i)

67. It is necessary that groups speaking the same regional or minority language have the possibility of engaging in cultural exchanges and in general of developing their relations, in order to contribute together to the preservation and enrichment of their language. To this end, the charter seeks to prevent fragmented patterns of settlement, administrative divisions within a state or the fact that such groups are settled in different states from constituting an obstacle to relations between them.
68. Admittedly, such awareness of a shared identity between speakers of a regional or minority language must not be reflected negatively in exclusiveness or marginalisation in relation to other social groups. The objective of promoting cultural relations with speakers of different regional or minority languages therefore serves the goal both of cultural enrichment and of enhanced understanding between all groups in the state.
69. Paragraph 1.i adds a further dimension: the idea that such relations must also be able to develop across national frontiers if groups speaking the same or similar regional or minority languages are spread over several states. By definition, regional or minority languages are spoken in the state concerned by a relatively small number of speakers: for the purpose of mutual enrichment in the cultural sphere, the latter may need to be able to rely on the cultural resources available, across frontiers, to other groups speaking the same or a similar language. This is particularly important where a regional language in one state corresponds to a major cultural language, or even the national language, of another state and where transfrontier co-operation can enable the regional community to benefit from cultural activity in that more widespread language. It is important that states should recognise the legitimacy of such relations and not consider them suspect in terms of the loyalty which every state expects of its nationals or regard them as a threat to their territorial integrity. A language group will feel all the more integrated in the state of which it is a part if it is

recognised as such and if cultural contacts with its neighbouring communities are not hindered.

70. However, the states are left free to work out the most suitable arrangements for bringing such transnational exchanges about, especially bearing in mind the domestic and international constraints which some of them may face. More specific commitments are set out in Article 14 in Part III.

Elimination of Discrimination (Article 7, paragraph 2)

71. The prohibition of discrimination in respect of the use of regional or minority languages constitutes a minimum guarantee for the speakers of such languages. For this reason, the parties undertake to eliminate measures discouraging the use or jeopardising the maintenance or development of a regional or minority language.

72. However, the purpose of this paragraph is not to establish complete equality of rights between languages. As is indicated by its wording, and in particular by the insertion of the term "unjustified", it is in fact quite compatible with the spirit of the charter that in the pursuit of policies which relate to regional or minority languages certain distinctions could be made between languages. In particular, the measures laid down by each state in favour of the use of a national or official language do not constitute discrimination against regional languages on the sole grounds that these same measures are not taken for their benefit. However, such measures must not constitute an obstacle to the maintenance or development of the regional or minority languages.

73. At the same time, precisely because disparities exist between the situation of official languages and that of regional or minority languages and because those who practise the latter are often at a disadvantage, the charter accepts that positive measures may be necessary with the aim of preserving and promoting such languages. Provided that the measures have such an aim, and that they seek to do no more than promote equality between languages, they are not to be regarded as discriminatory.

Promotion of Mutual Respect and Understanding between Linguistic groups (Article 7, paragraph 3)

74. Respect for regional or minority languages and the development of a spirit of tolerance towards them are part of a general concern to

develop understanding for a situation of language plurality within a state. The development of this spirit of tolerance and receptiveness through the educational system and the media is an important factor in the practical preservation of regional or minority languages. The encouragement of the mass media to pursue such objectives is not considered to constitute illegitimate state influence; indeed respect for human rights, tolerance of minorities and avoidance of incitement to hatred are the kinds of objective which most European states do not hesitate to impose as obligations upon the media. In the same spirit, for speakers of regional or minority languages, this principle constitutes an important factor causing them to be receptive to majority languages and cultures.

Establishment of Bodies to Respresent the Interests of Regional or Minority Languages (Article 7, paragraph 4)

75. The CAHLR thought it important that in each state mechanisms should exist whereby the public authorities take account of the needs and wishes expressed by the speakers of regional or minority languages themselves. Consequently, it is recommended that for each regional or minority language there should be a promoting body responsible for representing the interests of the language at national level, carrying out practical measures to promote it, and monitoring the implementation of the charter in relation to that particular language. The expression "if necessary" indicates *inter alia* that, where such institutions already exist in one form or another, it is not intended to encourage states to establish new ones which would duplicate them.

Application of the Charter's Principles to Non-Territorial Languages (Article 7, paragraph 5)

76. Although the charter is primarily concerned with languages which are historically identified with a particular geographical area of the state, the CAHLR did not wish to ignore those languages traditionally spoken within the state but which have no precise territorial base.
77. However, it is recognised that, owing to the territorial field of application of a number of principles and objectives laid down in Part II and the practical difficulty of taking measures to implement them without defining their geographical scope, these provisions cannot without certain adjustments be applied to non-territorial languages.

Paragraph 5 accordingly specifies that they are to be applied only so far as possible to these languages.

78. Some of the provisions contained in paragraphs 1 to 4 can be applied without difficulty also to non-territorial languages; this is the case regarding the recognition of these languages, the measures to develop a spirit of respect, understanding and tolerance towards them, the prohibition of discrimination and the action to afford them positive support, the possibility for the groups speaking those languages to develop links with each other within the state and abroad, and the promotion of language research and study. On the other hand, it will not be possible to apply to non-territorial languages the provisions concerning administrative divisions and the facilities provided for non-speakers of these languages to acquire some knowledge of them, since such measures are capable of being taken only in a specified territory. Lastly, the objectives of making provision for the teaching and study of these non-territorial languages and the promotion of their use in public life can probably, for practical reasons, be implemented only with certain adjustments.

Part III – Measures to Promote the Use of Regional or Minority Languages in Public life in accordance with the undertakings entered into under Article 2, paragraph 2

Article 8 – Education

79. The provisions of paragraph 1 of this article relate only to the territory in which each regional or minority language is used. They are also to be applied "according to the situation of each of these languages". As indicated with reference to Article 2, paragraph 2 above, this stipulation is especially relevant to the choice of which option to accept for which language in sub-paragraphs a to f.

80. The phrase "and without prejudice to the teaching of the official language(s) of the state" is intended to avert any possibility of interpreting the provisions of Article 8, paragraph 1 – and in particular the first option in each of sub-paragraphs a to f – as excluding the teaching of the language(s) spoken by the majority. Such a tendency to form linguistic ghettos would be contrary to the principles of interculturalism and multilingualism underlined in the preamble and inimical to the interests of the population groups concerned. In the special circumstances of those countries where the charter applies to less widely

used official languages, this phrase should be interpreted as meaning that the provisions of paragraph 1 are without prejudice to the teaching of other official languages.

81. Article 8 deals with several levels of education: pre-school, primary, secondary, technical and vocational, university and adult education. For every one of these levels, different options are presented according to the situation of each regional or minority language.

82. Some of the sub-paragraphs employ the expression "in a number considered sufficient". This recognises that the public authorities cannot be required to take the measures concerned where the situation of the linguistic group makes it difficult to attain the minimum number of pupils required to form a class. On the other hand, given the particular circumstances of regional or minority languages, it is suggested that the normal quota required to constitute a class may be applied flexibly and a lower number of pupils may be "considered sufficient".

83. The wording of option iv in sub-paragraphs c and d takes account of the fact that national situations vary with regard to both the age of majority and the age at which such education may be completed. Depending on these circumstances, the wishes to be taken into account may be either those of the pupils themselves or those of their families.

84. It is recognised that not all education systems distinguish between secondary education and vocational education, the latter being merely regarded as a particular type of secondary education. Nevertheless, as made in sub-paragraphs c and d, this distinction takes account of the differences in systems of vocational training. In particular, in the case of countries where vocational training is largely carried out by means of apprenticeship and measures in favour of regional or minority languages are therefore difficult to apply, it enables the parties at least to accept the more stringent requirements in the field of general secondary education.

85. The provisions concerning university and adult education are comparable to those for other levels of education in as much as they offer an alternative between teaching in the regional or minority language and teaching of it as a subject of education. Morever, as in the case of pre-school education, a further solution is offered for those cases in which the public authorities have no direct competence for the type of education concerned. In certain states, the number of speakers of a regional or minority language might be judged insufficient for the provision of university education in or of that language. In this

connection, the example has been cited of states which, by virtue either of a specific agreement or of a general agreement on the recognition of diplomas, recognise the university degree obtained by a speaker of a regional or minority language at a university of another state in which the same language is used.

86. Paragraph 1.g is motivated by a concern not to isolate the teaching of regional or minority languages from their cultural context. These languages are often related to a separate history and specific traditions. This history and regional or minority culture constitutes a component of Europe's heritage. It is accordingly desirable that non-speakers of the languages concerned should have access to it too.

87. Where a state undertakes to guarantee that a regional or minority language is taught, it must see that the necessary means are available in terms of finance, staff and teaching aids. This necessary consequence does not need to be specified in the charter. However, where staff are concerned, the question also arises of their competence and therefore of their training. This is a fundamental aspect, which is why specific provision is made for it in paragraph 1.h.

88. Considering the fundamental importance of teaching and, more specifically, of the school system, for the preservation of regional or minority languages, the CAHLR considered it necessary to provide for a specific body or bodies to monitor what was being done in this field. The characteristics of such a supervisory institution are not specified in paragraph 1.i. It could accordingly be an education authority body or an independent institution. This function could also be conferred on the body provided for in Article 7, paragraph 4, of the charter. In any case, the charter requires the findings of the monitoring to be made public.

89. The charter normally confines the protection of regional or minority languages to the geographical area where they are traditionally spoken. But paragraph 2 of Article 8 constitutes an exception to this rule. It is motivated by the realisation that in modern circumstances of mobility the principle of territoriality may no longer be sufficient in practice for the effective protection of a regional or minority language. In particular, a substantial number of speakers of such languages have migrated to the major cities. However, in view of the difficulties involved in the extension of educational provision for regional or minority languages outside their traditional territorial base, Article 8, paragraph 2, is drafted flexibly in terms of the undertakings involved and in any case applies only where such measures are justified by the number of users of the language concerned.

Article 9 – Judicial authorities

90. Paragraph 1 of this article applies to those judicial districts in which the number of residents using the regional or minority languages justifies the measures concerned. This stipulation corresponds in part to the general rule in most of the provisions of the charter, which is concerned to protect regional or minority languages within the territory in which they are traditionally used. For higher courts located outside the territory in which the regional or minority language is used, it is then a matter for the state concerned to take account of the special nature of the judicial system and its hierarchy of instances.
91. The wording of the introductory sentence of Article 9, paragraph 1, also reflects the concern of the CAHLR to protect fundamental principles of the judicial system, such as equality of the parties and avoidance of undue delays in the process of law, against possible misuse of the facilities for recourse to regional or minority languages. This legitimate concern does not, however, justify any general restriction of a party's undertakings under this paragraph; rather, abuse of the possibilities offered will have to be determined by the judge in individual cases.
92. A distinction is made between criminal, civil and administrative proceedings and the options provided for are adapted to the particular nature of each. As is indicated by the words "and/or", some of these options may be adopted cumulatively.
93. The provisions of Article 9, paragraph 1, relate to proceedings before courts of law. Depending on the particular arrangements for the administration of justice obtaining in each state, the term "courts" should, where appropriate, be understood as covering other bodies exercising a judicial function. This is especially relevant in the case of sub-paragraph c.
94. The first option of sub-paragraphs a, b and c of Article 9, paragraph 1, employs the expression "conduct the proceedings in the regional or minority languages". This expression implies, at any rate, that the relevant regional or minority language is used in the courtroom and in those proceedings in which the party speaking this language takes part. However, it is up to each state, in the light of the particular characteristics of its judicial system, to determine the precise scope of the expression "conduct the proceedings".
95. It should be noted that paragraph 1.a.ii, whereby the parties undertake to guarantee the accused the right to use his/her regional or minority language, goes beyond the right of the accused, as laid down

in Article 6, paragraph 3.e, of the European Convention on Human Rights, to have the free assistance of an interpreter if he cannot understand or speak the language used in court. Like sub-paragraphs b.ii and c.ii, it is based on the consideration that even if speakers of a regional or minority language are able to speak the official language, when it comes to justifying themselves before a court of law, they may feel the need to express themselves in the language which is emotionally closest to them or in which they have greater fluency. It would therefore run counter to the purpose of the charter for its application to be limited to situations of practical necessity. On the other hand, given that this provision goes beyond the strictly human rights aspect by in effect giving a free choice to the accused and requires facilities to be provided in accordance with his or her decision, it was considered reasonable to allow states some discretion as to whether to accept it or not and to limit its application to certain judicial districts.

96. The purpose of paragraph 1.d is to provide that the translation or interpretation which may be rendered necessary by the application of Article 9, paragraphs 1.b and c, shall be free of charge. In the case of those states which do not choose this sub-paragraph, it is up to them to resolve this question either according to the existing legal provisions or by adopting new, specific provisions which would take account of the need to promote regional or minority languages. Consequently, the costs could be borne wholly or partly by the person who makes the request for a given act, or shared among the parties, etc.

97. Paragraph 2 concerns the validity of legal documents drawn up in a regional or minority language. Its scope is in fact limited in as much as it does not indicate all the conditions for the validity of a legal document but confines itself to stipulating that the fact that a document is drafted in a regional or minority language cannot by itself alone be a ground for denying its validity. Moreover, it does not preclude a state from providing for additional formalities in such a case, for example the need for a particular formula of certification to be added in the official language. Paragraph 2.b implies that the contents of the document invoked by the party using the regional or minority language are made known, directly or indirectly (advertisement, state information service, etc.), to the other party or to interested third parties who do not speak the regional or minority language, in a form they can understand.

98. The application of Article 9, paragraph 2, is without prejudice to the application of treaties and conventions on mutual assistance in legal matters, in each of which the question of the languages to be used is explicitly dealt with.
99. Paragraph 3 concerns the translation of legislative texts into regional or minority languages. The phrase "unless they are otherwise provided" refers to cases where the text already exists in a regional or minority language because it has already been translated into a similar or identical language which is the official language of another state.

Article 10 – Administrative Authorities and Public Services

100. The purpose of this article is to allow the speakers of regional or minority languages to exercise their rights as citizens and fulfil their civic duties in conditions that respect their mode of expression.
101. The provisions are mainly designed to improve communication between the public authorities and those who use regional or minority languages. It is true that social and cultural situations have evolved in such a way that the very great majority of the people speaking these languages are bilingual and able to use an official language in order to communicate with the public authorities. However, allowing the use of regional or minority languages in relations with those authorities is fundamental to the status of these languages and their development and also from a subjective standpoint. Clearly, if a language were to be completely barred from relations with the authorities, it would in fact be negated as such, for language is a means of public communication and cannot be reduced to the sphere of private relations alone. Furthermore, if a language is not given access to the political, legal or administrative sphere, it will gradually lose all its terminological potential in that field and become a "handicapped" language, incapable of expressing every aspect of community life.
102. Article 10 distinguishes, in the types of action taken by the public authorities, three categories:

- action by administrative authorities of the state: that is to say the traditional acts of the public authorities, especially in the form of the exercise of public prerogatives or powers under ordinary law (paragraph 1);

- action by local and regional authorities, that is general sub-national territorial authorities with powers of self-government (paragraph 2);
- action by bodies providing public services, whether under public or private law, where they remain under public control: postal services, hospitals, electricity, transport, and so on (paragraph 3).

103. In each field, with suitable adaptations to the specific nature of the authorities or bodies concerned, account is taken of the diversity of linguistic situations. In some cases the characteristics of the regional or minority language allow it to be recognised as a "quasi-official" language, thus making it, on its territory, a working language, or the normal means of communication, of the public authorities. (Recourse to the official or most widely-spoken language remains the norm in contacts with persons who do not speak the regional or minority language.) Alternatively, the language may at least be used in relations which such authorities may have with persons who address them in that language. Where, however, the objective situation of a regional or minority language makes such solutions impracticable, minimum undertakings are provided to safeguard the position of the speakers of the language concerned: oral or written applications or documents may legitimately be submitted in the regional or minority language, but without entailing any obligation to reply in that language.

104. The undertakings of the parties in paragraphs 1 and 3 are qualified by the phrase "as far as this is reasonably possible". This proviso is not intended to be a substitute for the exercise of the faculty, accorded to the parties by Articles 2, paragraph 2 and 3, paragraph 1, of omitting some of the provisions of Part III of the charter from their undertakings in respect of each particular language. However, it does seek to take account of the fact that some of the measures provided for have significant implications in terms of finance, staffing or training. An acceptance of a particular provision with respect to a given language necessarily entails a commitment to provide the resources and make the administrative arrangements required to render it effective. Nevertheless, it is recognised that there may be some circumstances in which total and unqualified application of the provision in question is not, or not yet, realistic. The phrase "as far as this is reasonably possible" allows the parties, in the implementation of the relevant provisions, to determine in individual cases whether such circumstances obtain.

105. The terms of paragraph 2, and in particular the undertaking of the parties to "allow and/or encourage", are drafted so as to take account of the principle of local and regional autonomy. They do not signify that less importance is attached to the application of the provisions set out therein, which concern the public authorities closest to the citizen. More generally, the CAHLR was aware that the application of some of the charter's provisions falls within the competence of local or regional authorities and may entail substantial costs for those concerned. The parties should ensure that the implementation of the charter respects the principle of local autonomy as defined in the European Charter of Local Self-Government, and in particular its Article 9, paragraph 1, which stipulates that: "Local authorities shall be entitled, within national economic policy, to adequate financial resources of their own, of which they may dispose freely within the framework of their powers."

106. Paragraph 2.a provides for the use of regional or minority languages "within the framework" of the regional or local authority. This formulation is intended to indicate that a regional or minority language may be used as a working language by the authority concerned; however, it does not imply that the regional or minority language may be used when communicating with central government.

Article 11 – Media

107. The time and space which regional or minority languages can secure in the media is vital for their safeguard. Today no language can keep its influence unless it has access to the new forms of mass communications. The development of these throughout the world and the progress of technology are leading to the weakening of the cultural influence of less widely-spoken languages. For the major media, especially television, the size of the audience is generally the decisive factor. But regional and minority languages represent a small cultural market. Despite the new opportunities offered them by the advances in broadcasting technology, it remains true that to have access to the media they need public support. However, the media constitute a field where public intervention is limited and action by means of regulations is not very effective. The public authorities act in this field essentially by encouragement and the provision of aid. With a view to ensuring that such encouragement and aid is provided in support of regional or minority languages, the charter asks states to give undertakings on various levels.

108. The measures provided for in this article are for the benefit of the users of regional or minority languages within the respective geographical areas of those languages. However, the wording of paragraph 1 in this respect, which differs from the formulation in other articles, takes account of the special nature in particular of the audiovisual media. Thus even if the measures are taken with reference to a particular territory, their effects may extend well beyond it; on the other hand, the measures need not be taken within the territory in question, provided that they benefit those who live there.

109. It is recognised that the public authorities in the different states have varying degrees of control over the media. For this reason it is specified in paragraphs 1 and 3 that the extent of their commitment is determined by the extent of their competence, powers or legitimate role in this field. It is underlined, moreover, that in every country the legitimate role of the state in creating the legal framework and conditions within which the purpose of this article can be achieved is circumscribed by the principle of the autonomy of the media.

110. Paragraph 1 of Article 11 makes a distinction between the undertakings which are proposed for the benefit of regional or minority languages in the field of radio and television, according to whether or not the latter carry out a public service mission. Such a mission, which may be performed by a public or private broadcasting body, involves the provision of a broad range of programmes including the consideration of minority tastes and interests. In this context the state can make provision (for instance, in legislation or in the broadcaster's specifications) for the broadcasting of programmes in regional or minority languages. Sub-paragraph a deals with this situation. On the other hand, where broadcasting is conceived as a purely private-sector function, the state can do no more than "encourage and/or facilitate" (sub-paragraphs b and c). Only the latter situation applies to the written press (sub-paragraph e). Where relevant, the undertaking given by the parties includes the allocation of the necessary frequencies to those broadcasting in regional or minority languages.

111. However minimal the role of the state may be in relation to the media, it normally at least retains the power to guarantee freedom of communication or take measures involving the elimination of obstacles to such freedom. For this reason, paragraph 2 does not contain the same proviso as paragraph 1 concerning the extent of the competence of public authorities. The undertaking to guarantee freedom of reception relates not only to obstacles deliberately placed in the way

of the reception of programmes broadcast from neighbouring countries but also to passive obstacles resulting from the failure of the competent authorities to take any action to make such reception possible.

112. In view of the fact that broadcasts from a neighbouring state may not be subject to the same legitimate conditions as those produced on the relevant party's own territory, the third sentence of this paragraph introduces a safeguard which is worded in the same terms as Article 10, paragraph 2, of the European Convention on Human Rights concerning freedom of expression. It should be pointed out, however, with respect to television, that for those states which are parties to the European Convention on Transfrontier Television, the circumstances and conditions under which the freedoms guaranteed by Article 11, paragraph 2, of the charter can be restricted will be determined by that convention, in particular by the principle of non-restriction of the retransmission on their territories of programme services which comply with the terms of the Convention on Transfrontier Television. Moreover, the provisions of this paragraph do not affect the need for copyright to be respected.

113. Article 11, paragraph 3, provides for the representation of the interests of the users of regional or minority languages in the bodies responsible for ensuring media pluralism. Such structures exist in most European countries. The words "or taken into account" were inserted in response to the possible difficulties involved in determining who were the representatives of the users of these languages. However, the CAHLR considered that it was sufficient that the linguistic groups be represented on similar terms to other categories of the population. This could be arranged, for example, through the bodies representing regional or minority languages which are provided for in Article 7, paragraph 4, of the charter.

Article 12 – Cultural Activities and Facilities

114. In this field, as in the case of Article 11, states are asked to commit themselves to the extent to which the public authorities have competence, powers or a legitimate role, enabling them to take effective action. However, since the public authorities have an undoubted influence on the conditions in which cultural facilities are used, the charter requires them to see that regional or minority languages have an appropriate place in the functioning of such facilities.

115. In paragraph 1.a states are asked in general to encourage initiatives typical of the modes of cultural expression specific to regional or minority languages. The means for this support are those usually drawn on for cultural promotion purposes. The expression "the different means of access to works..." covers – depending on the type of cultural activity concerned – publication, production, presentation, diffusion, transmission, and so on.

116. By reason of their limited number of speakers among the population, regional and minority languages do not have the same cultural productivity as the more widely-spoken languages. In order to promote their use and also allow their speakers access to a vast cultural heritage, it is therefore necessary to have recourse to the techniques of translation, dubbing, post-synchronisation and subtitling (paragraph 1.c). The avoidance of cultural barriers implies, however, a two-way process. It is therefore essential to the viability and status of regional or minority languages that important works produced in them should become known to a wider public. That is the purpose of paragraph 1.b.

117. With regard to the functioning of cultural institutions, that is to say of bodies whose function it is to undertake or support cultural activities in a variety of forms, states are asked to see that such institutions accord sufficient importance in their programmes to the knowledge and use of regional or minority languages and to their attendant cultures (Article 12, paragraph 1.d to f). The charter cannot of course specify how regional or minority languages are to be incorporated in the activities of these institutions. It speaks simply of making "appropriate allowance" for them. The role of states in this sphere is generally one of guidance and supervision; they are not asked to further this objective themselves, but merely to "ensure" that it is pursued.

118. The charter also provides for the creation for each regional or minority language of a body responsible for collecting, keeping a copy of and disseminating works in that language (Article 12, paragraph 1.g). Having regard to the weak situation in which many regional or minority languages find themselves, it is necessary to organise this type of work systematically, the manner of its organisation being left to states to decide. For the purposes of the implementation of this paragraph g, it may be necessary for certain states to adapt their legislation on legal deposit and archives so that the body envisaged can take part in the conservation of works in regional or minority languages.

119. The application of Article 12, paragraph 1, relates to the territory in which regional or minority languages are used, even though it is

recognised that in practice many of its provisions have implications extending beyond that territory. However, having regard to the nature of cultural promotion and to needs arising outside of the areas in which the languages are traditionally used (in particular as a result of internal migration), Article 12, paragraph 2, introduces provisions corresponding to those of Article 8, paragraph 2.

120. All countries seek to promote their national culture abroad. In order to give a complete and faithful picture of that culture, such promotion should not neglect regional or minority languages and cultures. This undertaking, which is provided for in Article 12, paragraph 3, constitutes one way of applying the principle of the recognition of regional or minority languages embodied in Article 7, paragraph 1.a, of Part II of the charter.

Article 13 – Economic and Social Life

121. In the economic and social systems which characterise the Council of Europe countries, intervention by the public authorities in economic and social life is mainly confined to the promulgation of laws and regulations. In these circumstances, the possibilities of action on the part of the authorities to see that regional or minority languages receive due consideration in these sectors are limited. Nevertheless, the charter provides for a certain number of measures in this field. It seeks, on the one hand, to eliminate measures to ban or discourage the use of such languages in economic and social life and proposes, on the other hand, a number of positive measures.

122. The provisions of Article 13, paragraph 1, give concrete application to the principle of non-discrimination. This is why they are intended to apply throughout the territory of contracting states and not only in the parts of that territory where regional or minority languages are used.

123. Article 13, paragraph 2, of the charter lists various concrete measures in support of regional or minority languages in this sector. For practical reasons, they are confined to the geographical areas in which these languages are used. With regard to the proviso "as far as this is reasonably possible", reference should be made to the explanations under Article 10 above (see paragraph 104). Finally, the undertakings of the parties extend only as far as the public authorities have competence, a proviso which, however, is relevant only to subparagraph c.

Article 14 – Transfrontier Exchanges

124. This article expands and develops the idea set out in Article 7, paragraph 1.i, and reference is therefore made to the explanations given above (see paragraphs 69–70).

125. In many fields, transfrontier co-operation develops between the neighbouring regions of different states. It is noted that in certain cases such a situation could still be seen as a problem in terms of territorial integrity. With European states now moving closer together, however, it now presents an opportunity for the states concerned to employ a "cultural factor" to enhance their mutual understanding. The Council of Europe has drawn up an outline convention on transfrontier co-operation at local and regional level. While it is desirable that such co-operation should develop in a general manner, paragraph b underlines that this is particularly the case where one and the same regional language is spoken on either side of the border.

126. The co-operation envisaged may extend to such matters as school twinnings, teacher exchanges, the mutual recognition of diplomas and qualifications, the joint organisation of cultural activities, the further circulation of cultural assets (books, films, exhibitions, etc) and the transfrontier activities of cultural agencies (theatre companies, lecturers, etc). In some circumstances, it may also be a satisfactory (and less expensive) means of implementing undertakings entered into under other articles of the charter: for example, with respect to the provision of higher education facilities as laid down in Article 8, paragraph 1.e, a bilateral agreement could make arrangements for the students concerned to attend appropriate institutions in a neighbouring state.

Part IV – Application of the Charter

Articles 15–17

127. To enable its application to be monitored by the Council of Europe, its member states and the general public, the charter has opted for a system of periodical reports by the parties on the action taken in pursuance of its provisions. The reports are triennial; however the first report, which is intended to describe the situation of the regional or minority languages at the time when the charter enters into force for the state concerned, is to be presented within one year of that date.

128. In order to ensure the efficiency of this system for monitoring the implementation of the charter, the latter provides for the setting up of a committee of experts to examine the reports submitted by the various parties. It will also be possible for the committee of experts to be approached by bodies or associations wishing to supply further information or describe specific situations relating to the application of the charter, especially Part III thereof (Article 16, paragraph 2). Only bodies legally established in one of the parties will have access to this committee of experts for matters concerning that party. The purpose of this rule is to prevent groups whose headquarters is outside the party concerned by the application of the charter from using the monitoring system set up under it to generate discord among the parties.

129. It should be emphasised that this is not a quasi-judicial complaints procedure. The committee of experts is merely instructed to monitor the implementation of the charter and receive information to that end. The bodies referred to in Article 16 may not ask it to act as a more or less judicial appeal body.

130. The committee of experts may verify any information submitted with the states concerned and must call on them for further explanations or information for the purposes of carrying out its investigations. The results will be communicated to the Committee of Ministers, together with the comments of the states concerned, on the occasion of the presentation of the experts' reports. Although it might appear that, in the interests of openness, these reports should be published automatically, it was felt that, since they might contain proposals for recommendations which the Committee of Ministers might make to one or more states, it should be left up to the Committee of Ministers to judge case by case to what extent the reports should be published.

131. The number of members of the committee of experts will be the same as the number of parties to the charter. They must be persons of recognised competence in the field of regional or minority languages. At the same time, by placing emphasis on the intrinsically personal trait of the "highest integrity", the charter makes clear that the experts appointed to the committee, in carrying out their task, should be free to act independently and not be subject to instructions from the governments concerned.

132. This machinery for the monitoring of the application of the charter by a committee of experts will make it possible to assemble a body of

objective information concerning the situation of regional or minority languages, while respecting to the full the specific responsibilities of states.

Part V – Final Provisions

133. The final clauses contained in Articles 18 to 23 are based on the model final clauses for conventions and agreements concluded within the Council of Europe.
134. It was decided not to include among these final provisions a territorial clause enabling states to exclude part of their territories from the scope of the charter. This is because it is already an intrinsic characteristic of the present charter that it is concerned especially with particular territories, namely those on which regional or minority languages are used; moreover, contracting states already have the right, under Article 3, paragraph 1, to specify those regional or minority languages to which their detailed undertakings will apply.
135. Under Article 21, the parties have the right to make reservations only in respect of paragraphs 2 to 5 of Article 7 of the charter. The CAHLR considered that contracting states should not have the possibility to make reservations with regard to Article 7, paragraph 1, since this paragraph contains objectives and principles. As far as Part III is concerned, it took the view that, in a text which already allowed the parties so much choice as to the undertakings they entered into, reservations would be inappropriate.
136. In view of the importance of the subject-matter of the charter for many states which are not, or not yet, members of the Council of Europe, it was decided that the charter should be an open convention, to which non-member states may be invited to accede (Article 20).

APPENDIX III

UNITED NATIONS HUMAN RIGHTS COMMITTEE GENERAL COMMENT NO. 18: NON-DISCRIMINATION

1. Non-discrimination, together with equality before the law and equal protection of the law without any discrimination, constitute a basic and general principle relating to the protection of human rights. Thus, article 2, paragraph 1, of the International Covenant on Civil and Political Rights obligates each State party to respect and ensure to all persons within its territory and subject to its jurisdiction the rights recognized in the Covenant without distinction of any kind, such as race, colour, sex, language, religion, political or other opinion, national or social origin, property, birth or other status. Article 26 not only entitles all persons to equality before the law as well as equal protection of the law but also prohibits any discrimination under the law and guarantees to all persons equal and effective protection against discrimination on any ground such as race, colour, sex, language, religion, political or other opinion, national or social origin, property, birth or other status.
2. Indeed, the principle of non-discrimination is so basic that article 3 obligates each State party to ensure the equal right of men and women to the enjoyment of the rights set forth in the Covenant. While article 4, paragraph 1, allows States parties to take measures derogating from certain obligations under the Covenant in time of public emergency, the same article requires, *inter alia,* that those measures should not involve discrimination solely on the ground of race, colour, sex, language, religion or social origin. Furthermore, article 20, paragraph 2, obligates States parties to prohibit, by law, any advocacy of national, racial or religious hatred which constitutes incitement to discrimination.
3. Because of their basic and general character, the principle of non-discrimination as well as that of equality before the law and equal protection of the law are sometimes expressly referred to in articles relating to particular categories of human rights. Article 14, paragraph 1, provides that all persons shall be equal before the courts and tribunals, and paragraph 3 of the same article provides that, in the determination of any criminal charge against him, everyone shall be entitled, in full

equality, to the minimum guarantees enumerated in subparagraphs (a) to (g) of paragraph 3. Similarly, article 25 provides for the equal participation in public life of all citizens, without any of the distinctions mentioned in article 2.

4. It is for the States parties to determine appropriate measures to implement the relevant provisions. However, the Committee is to be informed about the nature of such measures and their conformity with the principles of non-discrimination and equality before the law and equal protection of the law.

5. The Committee wishes to draw the attention of States parties to the fact that the Covenant sometimes expressly requires them to take measures to guarantee the equality of rights of the persons concerned. For example, article 23, paragraph 4, stipulates that States parties shall take appropriate steps to ensure equality of rights as well as responsibilities of spouses as to marriage, during marriage and at its dissolution. Such steps may take the form of legislative, administrative or other measures, but it is a positive duty of States parties to make certain that spouses have equal rights as required by the Covenant. In relation to children, article 24 provides that all children, without any discrimination as to race, colour, sex, language, religion, national or social origin, property or birth, have the right to such measures of protection as are required by their status as minors, on the part of their family, society and the State.

6. The Committee notes that the Covenant neither defines the term "discrimination" nor indicates what constitutes discrimination. However, article 1 of the International Convention on the Elimination of All Forms of Racial Discrimination provides that the term "racial discrimination" shall mean any distinction, exclusion, restriction or preference based on race, colour, descent, or national or ethnic origin which has the purpose or effect of nullifying or impairing the recognition, enjoyment or exercise, on an equal footing, of human rights and fundamental freedoms in the political, economic, social, cultural or any other field of public life. Similarly, article 1 of the Convention on the Elimination of All Forms of Discrimination against Women provides that "discrimination against women" shall mean any distinction, exclusion or restriction made on the basis of sex which has the effect or purpose of impairing or nullifying the recognition, enjoyment or exercise by women, irrespective of their marital status, on a basis of equality of men and women, of human rights and fundamental freedoms in the political, economic, social, cultural, civil or any other field.

7. While these conventions deal only with cases of discrimination on specific grounds, the Committee believes that the term "discrimination" as used in the Covenant should be understood to imply any distinction, exclusion, restriction or preference which is based on any ground such as race, colour, sex, language, religion, political or other opinion, national or social origin, property, birth or other status, and which has the purpose or effect of nullifying or impairing the recognition, enjoyment or exercise by all persons, on an equal footing, of all rights and freedoms.
8. The enjoyment of rights and freedoms on an equal footing, however, does not mean identical treatment in every instance. In this connection, the provisions of the Covenant are explicit. For example, article 6, paragraph 5, prohibits the death sentence from being imposed on persons below 18 years of age. The same paragraph prohibits that sentence from being carried out on pregnant women. Similarly, article 10, paragraph 3, requires the segregation of juvenile offenders from adults. Furthermore, article 25 guarantees certain political rights, differentiating on grounds of citizenship.
9. Reports of many States parties contain information regarding legislative as well as administrative measures and court decisions which relate to protection against discrimination in law, but they very often lack information which would reveal discrimination in fact. When reporting on articles 2 (1), 3 and 26 of the Covenant, States parties usually cite provisions of their constitution or equal opportunity laws with respect to equality of persons. While such information is of course useful, the Committee wishes to know if there remain any problems of discrimination in fact, which may be practised either by public authorities, by the community, or by private persons or bodies. The Committee wishes to be informed about legal provisions and administrative measures directed at diminishing or eliminating such discrimination.
10. The Committee also wishes to point out that the principle of equality sometimes requires States parties to take affirmative action in order to diminish or eliminate conditions which cause or help to perpetuate discrimination prohibited by the Covenant. For example, in a State where the general conditions of a certain part of the population prevent or impair their enjoyment of human rights, the State should take specific action to correct those conditions. Such action may involve granting for a time to the part of the population concerned certain preferential treatment in specific matters as compared with the rest of

the population. However, as long as such action is needed to correct discrimination in fact, it is a case of legitimate differentiation under the Covenant.

11. Both article 2, paragraph 1, and article 26 enumerate grounds of discrimination such as race, colour, sex, language, religion, political or other opinion, national or social origin, property, birth or other status. The Committee has observed that in a number of constitutions and laws not all the grounds on which discrimination is prohibited, as cited in article 2, paragraph 1, are enumerated. The Committee would therefore like to receive information from States parties as to the significance of such omissions.
12. While article 2 limits the scope of the rights to be protected against discrimination to those provided for in the Covenant, article 26 does not specify such limitations. That is to say, article 26 provides that all persons are equal before the law and are entitled to equal protection of the law without discrimination, and that the law shall guarantee to all persons equal and effective protection against discrimination on any of the enumerated grounds. In the view of the Committee, article 26 does not merely duplicate the guarantee already provided for in article 2 but provides in itself an autonomous right. It prohibits discrimination in law or in fact in any field regulated and protected by public authorities. Article 26 is therefore concerned with the obligations imposed on States parties in regard to their legislation and the application thereof. Thus, when legislation is adopted by a State party, it must comply with the requirement of article 26 that its content should not be discriminatory. In other words, the application of the principle of non-discrimination contained in article 26 is not limited to those rights which are provided for in the Covenant.
13. Finally, the Committee observes that not every differentiation of treatment will constitute discrimination, if the criteria for such differentiation are reasonable and objective and if the aim is to achieve a purpose which is legitimate under the Covenant.

APPENDIX IV

UNITED NATIONS HUMAN RIGHTS COMMITTEE GENERAL COMMENT NO. 23: THE RIGHTS OF MINORITIES (ART. 27)

1. Article 27 of the Covenant provides that, in those States in which ethnic, religious or linguistic minorities exist, persons belonging to these minorities shall not be denied the right, in community with the other members of their group, to enjoy their own culture, to profess and practise their own religion, or to use their own language. The Committee observes that this article establishes and recognizes a right which is conferred on individuals belonging to minority groups and which is distinct from, and additional to, all the other rights which, as individuals in common with everyone else, they are already entitled to enjoy under the Covenant.
2. In some communications submitted to the Committee under the Optional Protocol, the right protected under article 27 has been confused with the right of peoples to self-determination proclaimed in article 1 of the Covenant. Further, in reports submitted by States parties under article 40 of the Covenant, the obligations placed upon States parties under article 27 have sometimes been confused with their duty under article 2.1 to ensure the enjoyment of the rights guaranteed under the Covenant without discrimination and also with equality before the law and equal protection of the law under article 26.

3.1. The Covenant draws a distinction between the right to self-determination and the rights protected under article 27. The former is expressed to be a right belonging to peoples and is dealt with in a separate part (Part I) of the Covenant. Self-determination is not a right cognizable under the Optional Protocol. Article 27, on the other hand, relates to rights conferred on individuals as such and is included, like the articles relating to other personal rights conferred on individuals, in Part III of the Covenant and is cognizable under the Optional Protocol.[1]

[1] *See* Official Records of the General Assembly, Thirty-ninth Session, Supplement No. 40 (A/39/40), annex VI, General Comment No. 12 (21) (article 1), also issued in document

3.2. The enjoyment of the rights to which article 27 relates does not prejudice the sovereignty and territorial integrity of a State party. At the same time, one or other aspect of the rights of individuals protected under that article – for example, to enjoy a particular culture – may consist in a way of life which is closely associated with territory and use of its resources.[2] This may particularly be true of members of indigenous communities constituting a minority.

4. The Covenant also distinguishes the rights protected under article 27 from the guarantees under articles 2.1 and 26. The entitlement, under article 2.1, to enjoy the rights under the Covenant without discrimination applies to all individuals within the territory or under the jurisdiction of the State whether or not those persons belong to a minority. In addition, there is a distinct right provided under article 26 for equality before the law, equal protection of the law, and non-discrimination in respect of rights granted and obligations imposed by the States. It governs the exercise of all rights, whether protected under the Covenant or not, which the State party confers by law on individuals within its territory or under its jurisdiction, irrespective of whether they belong to the minorities specified in article 27 or not.[3] Some States parties who claim that they do not discriminate on grounds of ethnicity, language or religion, wrongly contend, on that basis alone, that they have no minorities.

5.1. The terms used in article 27 indicate that the persons designed to be protected are those who belong to a group and who share in common a culture, a religion and/or a language. Those terms also indicate that the individuals designed to be protected need not be citizens of the State party. In this regard, the obligations deriving from article 2.1 are also relevant, since a State party is required under that article to ensure that the rights protected under the Covenant are available to all individuals within its territory and subject to its jurisdiction, except rights which are expressly made to apply to citizens, for example,

CCPR/C/21/Rev.1; *id.*, Forty-fifth Session, Supplement No. 40, (A/45/40), Vol. II, annex IX, sect. A, Communication No. 167/1984 (Bernard Ominayak, Chief of the Lubicon Lake Band v. Canada), views adopted on 26 March 1990.

[2] *See id.*, Forty-third Session, Supplement No. 40 (A/43/40), annex VII, sect. G, Communication No. 197/1985 (Kitok v. Sweden), views adopted on 27 July 1988.

[3] *See id.*, Forty-second Session, Supplement No. 40 (A/42/40), annex VIII, sect. D, Communication No. 182/1984 (F.H. Zwaan-de Vries v. the Netherlands), views adopted on 9 April 1987; *id.*, sect. C, Communication No. 180/1984 (L.G. Danning v. the Netherlands), views adopted on 9 April 1987.

political rights under article 25. A State party may not, therefore, restrict the rights under article 27 to its citizens alone.

5.2. Article 27 confers rights on persons belonging to minorities which "exist" in a State party. Given the nature and scope of the rights envisaged under that article, it is not relevant to determine the degree of permanence that the term "exist" connotes. Those rights simply are that individuals belonging to those minorities should not be denied the right, in community with members of their group, to enjoy their own culture, to practise their religion and speak their language. Just as they need not be nationals or citizens, they need not be permanent residents. Thus, migrant workers or even visitors in a State party constituting such minorities are entitled not to be denied the exercise of those rights. As any other individual in the territory of the State party, they would, also for this purpose, have the general rights, for example, to freedom of association, of assembly, and of expression. The existence of an ethnic, religious or linguistic minority in a given State party does not depend upon a decision by that State party but requires to be established by objective criteria.

5.3. The right of individuals belonging to a linguistic minority to use their language among themselves, in private or in public, is distinct from other language rights protected under the Covenant. In particular, it should be distinguished from the general right to freedom of expression protected under article 19. The latter right is available to all persons, irrespective of whether they belong to minorities or not. Further, the right protected under article 27 should be distinguished from the particular right which article 14.3 (f) of the Covenant confers on accused persons to interpretation where they cannot understand or speak the language used in the courts. Article 14.3 (f) does not, in any other circumstances, confer on accused persons the right to use or speak the language of their choice in court proceedings.[4]

6.1. Although article 27 is expressed in negative terms, that article, nevertheless, does recognize the existence of a "right" and requires that it shall not be denied. Consequently, a State party is under an obligation to ensure that the existence and the exercise of this right are protected against their denial or violation. Positive measures of protection are,

---

[4] *See id.*, Forty-fifth Session, Supplement No. 40, (A/45/40), Vol. II, annex X, sect. A, Communication No. 220/1987 (T.K. v. France), decision of 8 November 1989; *id.*, sect. B, Communication No. 222/1987 (M.K. v. France), decision of 8 November 1989.

therefore, required not only against the acts of the State party itself, whether through its legislative, judicial or administrative authorities, but also against the acts of other persons within the State party.

6.2. Although the rights protected under article 27 are individual rights, they depend in turn on the ability of the minority group to maintain its culture, language or religion. Accordingly, positive measures by States may also be necessary to protect the identity of a minority and the rights of its members to enjoy and develop their culture and language and to practise their religion, in community with the other members of the group. In this connection, it has to be observed that such positive measures must respect the provisions of articles 2.1 and 26 of the Covenant both as regards the treatment between different minorities and the treatment between the persons belonging to them and the remaining part of the population. However, as long as those measures are aimed at correcting conditions which prevent or impair the enjoyment of the rights guaranteed under article 27, they may constitute a legitimate differentiation under the Covenant, provided that they are based on reasonable and objective criteria.

7. With regard to the exercise of the cultural rights protected under article 27, the Committee observes that culture manifests itself in many forms, including a particular way of life associated with the use of land resources, especially in the case of indigenous peoples. That right may include such traditional activities as fishing or hunting and the right to live in reserves protected by law.[5] The enjoyment of those rights may require positive legal measures of protection and measures to ensure the effective participation of members of minority communities in decisions which affect them.

8. The Committee observes that none of the rights protected under article 27 of the Covenant may be legitimately exercised in a manner or to an extent inconsistent with the other provisions of the Covenant.

9. The Committee concludes that article 27 relates to rights whose protection imposes specific obligations on States parties. The protection of these rights is directed towards ensuring the survival and continued development of the cultural, religious and social identity of the minorities concerned, thus enriching the fabric of society as a whole.

---

[5] *See supra* notes 1 and 2, Communication No. 167/1984 (Bernard Ominayak, Chief of the Lubicon Lake Band v. Canada), views adopted on 26 March 1990, and Communication No. 197/1985 (Kitok v. Sweden), views adopted on 27 July 1988.

Accordingly, the Committee observes that these rights must be protected as such and should not be confused with other personal rights conferred on one and all under the Covenant. States parties, therefore, have an obligation to ensure that the exercise of these rights is fully protected and they should indicate in their reports the measures they have adopted to this end.

APPENDIX V

GENERAL COMMENT NO. 20

NON-DISCRIMINATION IN ECONOMIC, SOCIAL AND CULTURAL RIGHTS (ART. 2, PARA. 2, OF THE INTERNATIONAL COVENANT ON ECONOMIC, SOCIAL AND CULTURAL RIGHTS)

I. Introduction and Basic Premises

1. Discrimination undermines the fulfilment of economic, social and cultural rights for a significant proportion of the world's population. Economic growth has not, in itself, led to sustainable development, and individuals and groups of individuals continue to face socio-economic inequality, often because of entrenched historical and contemporary forms of discrimination.
2. Non-discrimination and equality are fundamental components of international human rights law and essential to the exercise and enjoyment of economic, social and cultural rights. Article 2, paragraph 2, of the International Covenant on Economic, Social and Cultural Rights (the Covenant) obliges each State party "to guarantee that the rights enunciated in the present Covenant will be exercised without discrimination of any kind as to race, colour, sex, language, religion, political or other opinion, national or social origin, property, birth or other status".
3. The principles of non-discrimination and equality are recognized throughout the Covenant. The preamble stresses the "equal and inalienable rights of all" and the Covenant expressly recognizes the rights of "everyone" to the various Covenant rights such as, inter alia, the right to work, just and favourable conditions of work, trade union freedoms, social security, an adequate standard of living, health and education and participation in cultural life.
4. The Covenant also explicitly mentions the principles of non-discrimination and equality with respect to some individual rights. Article 3 requires States to undertake to ensure the equal right of men and women to enjoy the Covenant rights and article 7 includes the "right to equal remuneration for work of equal value" and "equal opportunity

for everyone to be promoted" in employment. Article 10 stipulates that, inter alia, mothers should be accorded special protection during a reasonable period before and after childbirth and that special measures of protection and assistance should be taken for children and young persons without discrimination. Article 13 recognizes that "primary education shall be compulsory and available free to all" and provides that "higher education shall be made equally accessible to all".

5. The preamble, Articles 1, paragraph 3, and 55, of the Charter of the United Nations and article 2, paragraph 1, of the Universal Declaration of Human Rights prohibit discrimination in the enjoyment of economic, social and cultural rights. International treaties on racial discrimination, discrimination against women and the rights of refugees, stateless persons, children, migrant workers and members of their families, and persons with disabilities include the exercise of economic, social and cultural rights,[1] while other treaties require the elimination of discrimination in specific fields, such as employment and education.[2] In addition to the common provision on equality and non-discrimination in both the Covenant and the International Covenant on Civil and Political Rights, article 26 of the International Covenant on Civil and Political Rights contains an independent guarantee of equal and effective protection before and of the law.[3]
6. In previous general comments, the Committee on Economic, Social and Cultural Rights has considered the application of the principle of non-discrimination to specific Covenant rights relating to housing, food, education, health, water, authors' rights, work and social security.[4] Moreover, general comment No. 16 focuses on State parties' obligations under article 3 of the Covenant to ensure equal rights of

---

[1] *See* the International Convention on the Elimination of All Forms of Racial Discrimination (ICERD); the Convention on the Elimination of All Forms of Discrimination against Women (CEDAW); the Convention relating to the Status of Refugees; the Convention relating to the Status of Stateless Persons; the Convention on the Rights of the Child; the International Convention on the Protection of the Rights of All Migrant Workers and Members of Their Families; and the Convention on the Rights of Persons with Disabilities.

[2] ILO Convention No. 111 concerning Discrimination in Respect of Employment and Occupation (1958); and the UNESCO Convention against Discrimination in Education.

[3] *See* general comment No. 18 (1989) of the Human Rights Committee on non-discrimination.

[4] The Committee on Economic, Social and Cultural Rights (CESCR), general comment No. 4 (1991): The right to adequate housing; general comment No. 7 (1997): The right to adequate housing: forced evictions (art. 11, para. 1); general comment No. 12 (1999): The right to adequate food; general comment No. 13 (1999): The right to education (art. 13); general comment No. 14 (2000): The right to the highest attainable standard of health

men and women to the enjoyment of all Covenant rights, while general comments Nos. 5 and 6 respectively concern the rights of persons with disabilities and older persons.[5] The present general comment aims to clarify the Committee's understanding of the provisions of article 2, paragraph 2, of the Covenant, including the scope of State obligations (Part II), the prohibited grounds of discrimination (Part III), and national implementation (Part IV).

II. Scope of State Obligations

7. Non-discrimination is an immediate and cross-cutting obligation in the Covenant. Article 2, paragraph 2, requires States parties to guarantee non-discrimination in the exercise of each of the economic, social and cultural rights enshrined in the Covenant and can only be applied in conjunction with these rights. It is to be noted that discrimination constitutes any distinction, exclusion, restriction or preference or other differential treatment that is directly or indirectly based on the prohibited grounds of discrimination and which has the intention or effect of nullifying or impairing the recognition, enjoyment or exercise, on an equal footing, of Covenant rights.[6] Discrimination also includes incitement to discriminate and harassment.
8. In order for States parties to "guarantee" that the Covenant rights will be exercised without discrimination of any kind, discrimination must be eliminated both formally and substantively:[7]

   (a) **Formal discrimination**: Eliminating formal discrimination requires ensuring that a State's constitution, laws and policy documents do not discriminate on prohibited grounds; for example, laws

(art. 12); general comment No. 15 (2002): The right to water (arts. 11 and 12); general comment No. 17 (2005): The right of everyone to benefit from the protection of the moral and material interests resulting from any scientific, literary or artistic production of which he is the author (art. 15, para. 1 (c); general comment No. 18 (2005): The right to work (art. 6); and general comment No. 19 (2008): The right to social security.

[5] CESCR, general comment No. 5 (1994): Persons with disabilities; and general comment No. 6 (1995): The economic, social and cultural rights of older persons.

[6] For a similar definition *see* art. 1, ICERD; art. 1, CEDAW; and art. 2 of the Convention on the Rights of Persons with Disabilities (CRPD). The Human Rights Committee comes to a similar interpretation in its general comment No. 18, paragraphs 6 and 7. The Committee has adopted a similar position in previous general comments.

[7] CESCR, general comment No. 16 (2005): The equal right of men and women to the enjoyment of all economic, social and cultural rights (art. 3).

should not deny equal social security benefits to women on the basis of their marital status;

(b) **Substantive discrimination**: Merely addressing formal discrimination will not ensure substantive equality as envisaged and defined by article 2, paragraph 2.[8] The effective enjoyment of Covenant rights is often influenced by whether a person is a member of a group characterized by the prohibited grounds of discrimination. Eliminating discrimination in practice requires paying sufficient attention to groups of individuals which suffer historical or persistent prejudice instead of merely comparing the formal treatment of individuals in similar situations. States parties must therefore immediately adopt the necessary measures to prevent, diminish and eliminate the conditions and attitudes which cause or perpetuate substantive or de facto discrimination. For example, ensuring that all individuals have equal access to adequate housing, water and sanitation will help to overcome discrimination against women and girl children and persons living in informal settlements and rural areas.

9. In order to eliminate substantive discrimination, States parties may be, and in some cases are, under an obligation to adopt special measures to attenuate or suppress conditions that perpetuate discrimination. Such measures are legitimate to the extent that they represent reasonable, objective and proportional means to redress de facto discrimination and are discontinued when substantive equality has been sustainably achieved. Such positive measures may exceptionally, however, need to be of a permanent nature, such as interpretation services for linguistic minorities and reasonable accommodation of persons with sensory impairments in accessing health-care facilities.

10. Both direct and indirect forms of differential treatment can amount to discrimination under article 2, paragraph 2, of the Covenant:

(a) **Direct discrimination** occurs when an individual is treated less favourably than another person in a similar situation for a reason related to a prohibited ground; e.g. where employment in educational or cultural institutions or membership of a trade union is based on the political opinions of applicants or employees. Direct discrimination also includes detrimental acts or omissions on the

---

[8] *See* also CESCR general comment No. 16.

basis of prohibited grounds where there is no comparable similar situation (e.g. the case of a woman who is pregnant);

(b) **Indirect discrimination** refers to laws, policies or practices which appear neutral at face value, but have a disproportionate impact on the exercise of Covenant rights as distinguished by prohibited grounds of discrimination. For instance, requiring a birth registration certificate for school enrolment may discriminate against ethnic minorities or non-nationals who do not possess, or have been denied, such certificates.

Private Sphere

11. Discrimination is frequently encountered in families, workplaces, and other sectors of society. For example, actors in the private housing sector (e.g. private landlords, credit providers and public housing providers) may directly or indirectly deny access to housing or mortgages on the basis of ethnicity, marital status, disability or sexual orientation while some families may refuse to send girl children to school. States parties must therefore adopt measures, which should include legislation, to ensure that individuals and entities in the private sphere do not discriminate on prohibited grounds.

Systemic Discrimination

12. The Committee has regularly found that discrimination against some groups is pervasive and persistent and deeply entrenched in social behaviour and organization, often involving unchallenged or indirect discrimination. Such systemic discrimination can be understood as legal rules, policies, practices or predominant cultural attitudes in either the public or private sector which create relative disadvantages for some groups, and privileges for other groups.

Permissible Scope of Differential Treatment

13. Differential treatment based on prohibited grounds will be viewed as discriminatory unless the justification for differentiation is reasonable and objective. This will include an assessment as to whether the aim and effects of the measures or omissions are legitimate, compatible with the nature of the Covenant rights and solely for the purpose of promoting the general welfare in a democratic society. In addition, there must be a clear and reasonable relationship of proportionality between the aim sought to be realized and the measures or omissions

and their effects. A failure to remove differential treatment on the basis of a lack of available resources is not an objective and reasonable justification unless every effort has been made to use all resources that are at the State party's disposition in an effort to address and eliminate the discrimination, as a matter of priority.

14. Under international law, a failure to act in good faith to comply with the obligation in article 2, paragraph 2, to guarantee that the rights enunciated in the Covenant will be exercised without discrimination amounts to a violation. Covenant rights can be violated through the direct action or omission by States parties, including through their institutions or agencies at the national and local levels. States parties should also ensure that they refrain from discriminatory practices in international cooperation and assistance and take steps to ensure that all actors under their jurisdiction do likewise.

III. Prohibited Grounds of Discrimination

15. Article 2, paragraph 2, lists the prohibited grounds of discrimination as "race, colour, sex, language, religion, political or other opinion, national or social origin, property, birth or other status". The inclusion of "other status" indicates that this list is not exhaustive and other grounds may be incorporated in this category. The express grounds and a number of implied grounds under "other status" are discussed below. The examples of differential treatment presented in this section are merely illustrative and they are not intended to represent the full scope of possible discriminatory treatment under the relevant prohibited ground, nor a conclusive finding that such differential treatment will amount to discrimination in every situation.

Membership of a Group

16. In determining whether a person is distinguished by one or more of the prohibited grounds, identification shall, if no justification exists to the contrary, be based upon self-identification by the individual concerned. Membership also includes association with a group characterized by one of the prohibited grounds (e.g. the parent of a child with a disability) or perception by others that an individual is part of such a group (e.g. a person has a similar skin colour or is a supporter of the rights of a particular group or a past member of a group).

Multiple Discrimination[9]

17. Some individuals or groups of individuals face discrimination on more than one of the prohibited grounds, for example women belonging to an ethnic or religious minority. Such cumulative discrimination has a unique and specific impact on individuals and merits particular consideration and remedying.

A. *Express Grounds*

18. The Committee has consistently raised concern over formal and substantive discrimination across a wide range of Covenant rights against indigenous peoples and ethnic minorities among others.

"Race and colour"

19. Discrimination on the basis of "race and colour", which includes an individual's ethnic origin, is prohibited by the Covenant as well as by other treaties including the International Convention on the Elimination of Racial Discrimination. The use of the term "race" in the Covenant or the present general comment does not imply the acceptance of theories which attempt to determine the existence of separate human races.[10]

Sex

20. The Covenant guarantees the equal right of men and women to the enjoyment of economic, social and cultural rights.[11] Since the adoption of the Covenant, the notion of the prohibited ground "sex" has evolved considerably to cover not only physiological characteristics but also the social construction of gender stereotypes, prejudices and expected roles, which have created obstacles to the equal fulfilment of economic, social and cultural rights. Thus, the refusal to hire a woman,

---

[9] *See* para. 27 of the present general comment on intersectional discrimination.

[10] *See* the outcome document of the Durban Review Conference, para. 6: "*Reaffirms* that all peoples and individuals constitute one human family, rich in diversity, and that all human beings are born free and equal in dignity and rights; and strongly rejects any doctrine of racial superiority along with theories which attempt to determine the existence of so-called distinct human races."

[11] *See* art. 3 of the Covenant, and CESCR general comment No. 16.

on the ground that she might become pregnant, or the allocation of low-level or part-time jobs to women based on the stereotypical assumption that, for example, they are unwilling to commit as much time to their work as men, constitutes discrimination. Refusal to grant paternity leave may also amount to discrimination against men.

Language

21. Discrimination on the basis of language or regional accent is often closely linked to unequal treatment on the basis of national or ethnic origin. Language barriers can hinder the enjoyment of many Covenant rights, including the right to participate in cultural life as guaranteed by article 15 of the Covenant. Therefore, information about public services and goods, for example, should also be available, as far as possible, in languages spoken by minorities, and States parties should ensure that any language requirements relating to employment and education are based on reasonable and objective criteria.

Religion

22. This prohibited ground of discrimination covers the profession of religion or belief of one's choice (including the non-profession of any religion or belief), that may be publicly or privately manifested in worship, observance, practice and teaching.[12] For instance, discrimination arises when persons belonging to a religious minority are denied equal access to universities, employment, or health services on the basis of their religion.

Political or other Opinion

23. Political and other opinions are often grounds for discriminatory treatment and include both the holding and not-holding of opinions, as well as expression of views or membership within opinion-based associations, trade unions or political parties. Access to food assistance schemes, for example, must not be made conditional on an expression of allegiance to a particular political party.

---

[12] *See* also the General Assembly's Declaration on the Elimination of All Forms of Intolerance and of Discrimination Based on Religion or Belief, proclaimed by the General Assembly in its resolution 36/55 of 25 November 1981.

National or Social Origin

24. "National origin" refers to a person's State, nation, or place of origin. Due to such personal circumstances, individuals and groups of individuals may face systemic discrimination in both the public and private sphere in the exercise of their Covenant rights. "Social origin" refers to a person's inherited social status, which is discussed more fully below in the context of "property" status, descent-based discrimination under "birth" and "economic and social status".[13]

Property

25. Property status, as a prohibited ground of discrimination, is a broad concept and includes real property (e.g. land ownership or tenure) and personal property (e.g. intellectual property, goods and chattels, and income), or the lack of it. The Committee has previously commented that Covenant rights, such as access to water services and protection from forced eviction, should not be made conditional on a person's land tenure status, such as living in an informal settlement.[14]

Birth

26. Discrimination based on birth is prohibited and article 10, paragraph 3, of the Covenant specifically states, for example, that special measures should be taken on behalf of children and young persons "without any discrimination for reasons of parentage". Distinctions must therefore not be made against those who are born out of wedlock, born of stateless parents or are adopted or constitute the families of such persons. The prohibited ground of birth also includes descent, especially on the basis of caste and analogous systems of inherited status.[15] States parties should take steps, for instance, to prevent, prohibit and eliminate discriminatory practices directed against members of descent-based communities and act against the dissemination of ideas of superiority and inferiority on the basis of descent.

---

[13] *See* paras. 25, 26 and 35, of the present general comment.

[14] *See* CESCR general comments Nos. 15 and 4 respectively.

[15] For a comprehensive overview of State obligations in this regard, *see* general comment No. 29 (2002) of the Committee on the Elimination of All Forms of Racial Discrimination on art. 1, para. 1, regarding descent.

B. Other Status[16]

27. The nature of discrimination varies according to context and evolves over time. A flexible approach to the ground of "other status" is thus needed in order to capture other forms of differential treatment that cannot be reasonably and objectively justified and are of a comparable nature to the expressly recognized grounds in article 2, paragraph 2. These additional grounds are commonly recognized when they reflect the experience of social groups that are vulnerable and have suffered and continue to suffer marginalization. The Committee's general comments and concluding observations have recognized various other grounds and these are described in more detail below. However, this list is not intended to be exhaustive. Other possible prohibited grounds could include the denial of a person's legal capacity because he or she is in prison, or is involuntarily interned in a psychiatric institution, or the intersection of two prohibited grounds of discrimination, e.g. where access to a social service is denied on the basis of sex and disability.

Disability

28. In its general comment No. 5, the Committee defined discrimination against persons with disabilities[17] as "any distinction, exclusion, restriction or preference, or denial of reasonable accommodation based on disability which has the effect of nullifying or impairing the recognition, enjoyment or exercise of economic, social or cultural rights".[18] The denial of reasonable accommodation should be included in national legislation as a prohibited form of discrimination on the basis of disability.[19] States parties should address discrimination, such as prohibitions on the right to education, and denial of reasonable accommodation in public places such as public health facilities and

---

[16] *See* para. 15 of the present general comment.

[17] For a definition, *see* CRPD, art. 1: "Persons with disabilities include those who have long-term physical, mental, intellectual or sensory impairments which in interaction with various barriers may hinder their full and effective participation in society on an equal basis with others."

[18] *See* CESCR general comment No. 5, para. 15.

[19] *See* CRPD, art. 2: "'Reasonable accommodation' means necessary and appropriate modification and adjustments not imposing a disproportionate or undue burden, where needed in a particular case, to ensure to persons with disabilities the enjoyment or exercise on an equal basis with others of all human rights and fundamental freedoms."

the workplace,[20] as well as in private places, e.g. as long as spaces are designed and built in ways that make them inaccessible to wheelchairs, such users will be effectively denied their right to work.

Age

29. Age is a prohibited ground of discrimination in several contexts. The Committee has highlighted the need to address discrimination against unemployed older persons in finding work, or accessing professional training or retraining, and against older persons living in poverty with unequal access to universal old-age pensions due to their place of residence.[21] In relation to young persons, unequal access by adolescents to sexual and reproductive health information and services amounts to discrimination.

Nationality

30. The ground of nationality should not bar access to Covenant rights,[22] e.g. all children within a State, including those with an undocumented status, have a right to receive education and access to adequate food and affordable health care. The Covenant rights apply to everyone including non-nationals, such as refugees, asylum-seekers, stateless persons, migrant workers and victims of international trafficking, regardless of legal status and documentation.[23]

Marital and Family Status

31. Marital and family status may differ between individuals because, inter alia, they are married or unmarried, married under a particular legal regime, in a de facto relationship or one not recognized by law, divorced or widowed, live in an extended family or kinship group or have differing kinds of responsibility for children and dependants or a particular number of children. Differential treatment in access to

[20] *See* CESCR general comment No. 5, para. 22.

[21] *See*, further, CESCR general comment No. 6.

[22] This paragraph is without prejudice to the application of art. 2, para. 3, of the Covenant, which states: "Developing countries, with due regard to human rights and their national economy, may determine to what extent they would guarantee the economic rights recognized in the present Covenant to non-nationals."

[23] *See* also general comment No. 30 (2004) of the Committee on the Elimination of All Forms of Racial Discrimination on non-citizens.

social security benefits on the basis of whether an individual is married must be justified on reasonable and objective criteria. In certain cases, discrimination can also occur when an individual is unable to exercise a right protected by the Covenant because of his or her family status or can only do so with spousal consent or a relative's concurrence or guarantee.

Sexual Orientation and Gender Identity

32. "Other status" as recognized in article 2, paragraph 2, includes sexual orientation.[24] States parties should ensure that a person's sexual orientation is not a barrier to realizing Covenant rights, for example, in accessing survivor's pension rights. In addition, gender identity is recognized as among the prohibited grounds of discrimination; for example, persons who are transgender, transsexual or intersex often face serious human rights violations, such as harassment in schools or in the workplace.[25]

Health Status

33. Health status refers to a person's physical or mental health.[26] States parties should ensure that a person's actual or perceived health status is not a barrier to realizing the rights under the Covenant. The protection of public health is often cited by States as a basis for restricting human rights in the context of a person's health status. However, many such restrictions are discriminatory, for example, when HIV status is used as the basis for differential treatment with regard to access to education, employment, health care, travel, social security, housing and asylum.[27] States parties should also adopt measures to address widespread stigmatization of persons on the basis of their health status, such as mental illness, diseases such as leprosy and women who have suffered obstetric fistula, which often undermines the ability of

---

[24] *See* CESCR general comments Nos. 14 and 15.

[25] For definitions, *see* the Yogyakarta Principles on the Application of International Human Rights Law in relation to Sexual Orientation and Gender Identity.

[26] *See* CESCR general comment No. 14, paras. 12(b), 18, 28 and 29.

[27] *See* the guidelines published by the Office of the High Commissioner for Human Rights and the Joint United Nations Programme on HIV/AIDS (UNAIDS) (2006), "International Guidelines on HIV/AIDS and Human Rights, 2006 Consolidated Version". Available online at: http://data.unaids.org/Publications/IRC-pub07/JC1252-Intern Guidelines_en.pdf.

individuals to enjoy fully their Covenant rights. Denial of access to health insurance on the basis of health status will amount to discrimination if no reasonable or objective criteria can justify such differentiation.

Place of Residence

34. The exercise of Covenant rights should not be conditional on, or determined by, a person's current or former place of residence; e.g. whether an individual lives or is registered in an urban or a rural area, in a formal or an informal settlement, is internally displaced or leads a nomadic lifestyle. Disparities between localities and regions should be eliminated in practice by ensuring, for example, that there is even distribution in the availability and quality of primary, secondary and palliative health-care facilities.

Economic and Social Situation

35. Individuals and groups of individuals must not be arbitrarily treated on account of belonging to a certain economic or social group or strata within society. A person's social and economic situation when living in poverty or being homeless may result in pervasive discrimination, stigmatization and negative stereotyping which can lead to the refusal of, or unequal access to, the same quality of education and health care as others, as well as the denial of or unequal access to public places.

IV. National Implementation

36. In addition to refraining from discriminatory actions, States parties should take concrete, deliberate and targeted measures to ensure that discrimination in the exercise of Covenant rights is eliminated. Individuals and groups of individuals, who may be distinguished by one or more of the prohibited grounds, should be ensured the right to participate in decision-making processes over the selection of such measures. States parties should regularly assess whether the measures chosen are effective in practice.

Legislation

37. Adoption of legislation to address discrimination is indispensable in complying with article 2, paragraph 2. States parties are therefore

encouraged to adopt specific legislation that prohibits discrimination in the field of economic, social and cultural rights. Such laws should aim at eliminating formal and substantive discrimination, attribute obligations to public and private actors and cover the prohibited grounds discussed above. Other laws should be regularly reviewed and, where necessary, amended in order to ensure that they do not discriminate or lead to discrimination, whether formally or substantively, in relation to the exercise and enjoyment of Covenant rights.

Policies, Plans and Strategies

38. States parties should ensure that strategies, policies, and plans of action are in place and implemented in order to address both formal and substantive discrimination by public and private actors in the area of Covenant rights. Such policies, plans and strategies should address all groups distinguished by the prohibited grounds and States parties are encouraged, among other possible steps, to adopt temporary special measures in order to accelerate the achievement of equality. Economic policies, such as budgetary allocations and measures to stimulate economic growth, should pay attention to the need to guarantee the effective enjoyment of the Covenant rights without discrimination. Public and private institutions should be required to develop plans of action to address non-discrimination and the State should conduct human rights education and training programmes for public officials and make such training available to judges and candidates for judicial appointments. Teaching on the principles of equality and non-discrimination should be integrated in formal and non-formal inclusive and multicultural education, with a view to dismantling notions of superiority or inferiority based on prohibited grounds and to promote dialogue and tolerance between different groups in society. States parties should also adopt appropriate preventive measures to avoid the emergence of new marginalized groups.

Elimination of Systemic Discrimination

39. States parties must adopt an active approach to eliminating systemic discrimination and segregation in practice. Tackling such discrimination will usually require a comprehensive approach with a range of laws, policies and programmes, including temporary special measures. States parties should consider using incentives to encourage public and private actors to change their attitudes and behaviour in

relation to individuals and groups of individuals facing systemic discrimination, or penalize them in case of non-compliance. Public leadership and programmes to raise awareness about systemic discrimination and the adoption of strict measures against incitement to discrimination are often necessary. Eliminating systemic discrimination will frequently require devoting greater resources to traditionally neglected groups. Given the persistent hostility towards some groups, particular attention will need to be given to ensuring that laws and policies are implemented by officials and others in practice.

Remedies and Accountability

40. National legislation, strategies, policies and plans should provide for mechanisms and institutions that effectively address the individual and structural nature of the harm caused by discrimination in the field of economic, social and cultural rights. Institutions dealing with allegations of discrimination customarily include courts and tribunals, administrative authorities, national human rights institutions and/or ombudspersons, which should be accessible to everyone without discrimination. These institutions should adjudicate or investigate complaints promptly, impartially, and independently and address alleged violations relating to article 2, paragraph 2, including actions or omissions by private actors. Where the facts and events at issue lie wholly, or in part, within the exclusive knowledge of the authorities or other respondent, the burden of proof should be regarded as resting on the authorities, or the other respondent, respectively. These institutions should also be empowered to provide effective remedies, such as compensation, reparation, restitution, rehabilitation, guarantees of non-repetition and public apologies, and State parties should ensure that these measures are effectively implemented. Domestic legal guarantees of equality and non-discrimination should be interpreted by these institutions in ways which facilitate and promote the full protection of economic, social and cultural rights.[28]

Monitoring, Indicators and Benchmarks

41. States parties are obliged to monitor effectively the implementation of measures to comply with article 2, paragraph 2, of the Covenant.

---

[28] *See* CESCR general comments Nos. 3 and 9. *See* also the practice of the Committee in its concluding observations on reports of States parties to the Covenant.

Monitoring should assess both the steps taken and the results achieved in the elimination of discrimination. National strategies, policies and plans should use appropriate indicators and benchmarks, disaggregated on the basis of the prohibited grounds of discrimination.[29]

---

[29] *See* CESCR general comments Nos. 13, 14, 15, 17 and 19, and its new reporting guidelines (E/C.12/2008/2).

BIBLIOGRAPHY

Articles

Acton, T. and Gheorghe, N., 'Dealing with Multiculturality: Minority, Ethnic, National and Human Rights,' in *Office for Democratic Institutions and Human Rights Bulletin* Spring (1995) Vol. 3, 2.

Alfredsson, G., 'A Frame an Incomplete Painting: Comparison of the Framework Convention for the Protection of National Minorities with International Standards and Monitoring Procedures,' (2000) *International Journal of Minority and Group Rights* Vol. 7, n. 4, pp. 291–304.

——, 'Emerging or newly restored democracies – Strengthening of democratic institutions and development,' paper presented at *Workshop I: Human rights, fundamental freedoms and the rights of minorities, essential components of democracy, Conference on Parliamentary Democracy* (Strasbourg: Council of Europe, 1991).

——, 'Minority Rights and A New World Order' in Gomien, D. (ed.), *Broadening the Frontiers of Human Rights – Essays in Honour of Asbjørn Eide* (Oslo: Scandinavian University Press, 1993), pp. 55–78.

——, 'Minority Rights: A Summary of Existing Practice' in Phillips, A. and Rosas, A. (eds), *The UN Minority Rights Declaration* (Turku/Åbo: Åbo Akademi University, Institute for Human Rights, 1993), pp. 73–79.

——, 'Minority Rights: A Summary of Existing Practice' in Phillips, A. and Rosas, A. (eds), *Universal Minority Rights* (London: Minority Rights Group International 1995), pp. 77–86.

——, "Minority Rights and Democracy," discussion paper on Human Rights, fundamental freedoms and the Rights of Minorities, submitted to the Third Strasbourg Conference on Parliamentary Democracy, Strasbourg, 1991 [SXB.CONF (III) 8], reproduced in Compendium of Documents from this Conference, Parliamentary Assembly of the Council of Europe, Strasbourg, 1992, pp. 85–101.

Alfredsson, G. and de Zayas, A., 'Minority Rights: Protection by the United Nations' *Human Rights Law Journal* Vol. 14, No. 1–2 (1993), pp. 1–9.

Andrews, J., 'Gypsies and the Law' 22 *European Law Review* 365 (1997).

Andrysek, O., 'Report on the Definition of Minorities,' SIM Special No. 8 (Utrecht: Netherland Institute of Human Rights, 1989).

Arlati, A., 'La lunga marcia del popolo senza patria' 606 *Gli Zingari* 7 (1997).

——, 'Le persecuzioni contro gli zingari: una pagina tragica e poco conosciuta,' 606 *Gli Zingari* 27 (1997).

——, 'Gli Zingari in Italia' 602 *Gli Zingari* 36 (1997).

——, 'Gli Zingari e il Fascismo' 606 *Gli Zingari* 34 (1997).

Baka, A., 'The Convention and the Protection of Minorities Under International Law,' in Macdonald, R. St. J. et al. (eds), *The European System for the Protection of Human Rights* (Dordrecht : M. Nijhoff, 1993), pp. 875–888.

Barnett, H., 'The Rights of Gypsies – Landmark or Signpost?' *New Law Journal* 1628 (8 November 1996).

Barsh, R.L., 'The United Nations and Protection of Minorities' *Nordic Journal of International Law*, Vol. 58, No. 2 (1989), pp. 188–197.

Bartole, S., 'Minoranze Nazionali', *Novissimo Digesto Italiano* Appendix V (1982).

Bauman, S., 'Modernity and Ambivalence,' 7 (2–3) (1990) *Theory, Culture and Society* 143.

——, 'Soil, Blood and Identity,' 40 (4) (1992) *The Sociological Review* 675.

Bayefsky, A.F., 'The principle of Equality or Non-discrimination in International Law', 11 (1990) *Human Rights Quarterly* 1.

Berting, J., 'Social Change, Human Rights and the Welfare State in Europe', in Berting, J., Baehr, P.R., Burgers, J.H., Flinterman, C, de Klerk, B, Kroes, R., van Minnen, C.A. and VanderWal, K. (eds.), *Human Rights in a Pluralist World* (London: Meckler, 1990), pp. 189–208.

Blumkin, S.B., 'Protection of Minorities: For Individuals or for Groups?' in Chandra, S. (ed.), *International Protection of Minorities* (Delhi: Mittal, 1986), pp. 1–46.

Boutros-Ghali, B., 'The Right to Culture and the Universal Declaration of Human Rights,' in *Cultural Rights as Human Rights* (Paris: UNESCO, 1970), pp. 73–75.

Bowring, B., 'Multicultural Citizenship: A More Viable Framework for Minority Rights?' in Fottrell, D. and Bowring, B. (eds.), *Minority and Groups Rights in the New Millenium* (Netherlands: Kluwer Law International, 1999), pp. 1–23.

Brearley, M., 'The Persecution of Gypsies in Europe,' *American Behavioral Scientist*, Vol. 45, No. 4 (2001), 588–599.

Brown, C., 'Universal Human Rights: A Critique' *The International Journal of Human Rights* Vol. 1 No. 2 (Summer 1997), pp. 41–65.

Cahn, C., Lawmaking in Traditional Romani Communities and International Human Rights Law and Norms: Case Study of the Real and Potential Role of the Romani Kris, forthcoming in the European Yearbook of Minority Issues, 2010.

Campbell, S., 'Gypsies: the Criminalisation of a Way of Life?' *Criminal Law Review* 28 (January 1995).

Capotorti, F. 'Protection of Minorities under Multinational Agreements on Human Rights,' *Italian Yearbook of International Law* (1976) 3.

Castangia, I., 'L'Europa delle persone e le minoranze zingare' year XLVI, *Jus, Rivista di Scienze Giuridiche* 191 (January-April 1999).

Clough Marinaro, I., 'Integration or marginalization? The failures of social policy for the Roma in Rome,' 8 (2) *Modern Italy* 203.

Cohen, Y., 'From National State to International Community,' in *Cultural Rights as Human Rights* (Paris: UNESCO, 1970), pp. 76–87.

Cohen-Jonathan, G., 'Article 10,' in Pettiti, L.E. et. al. (eds.), *La Convention Européenne des Droits de l'Homme. Commentaire Article par Article* (Paris: Economica, 1995), pp. 365–408.

Dell'Agnese, E and Vitale, T., 'Rom and Sinti, una galassia di minoranze senza territorio,' in Amitti, G., and Rosina, A., (eds.), *Tra identità ed integrazione: passato e presente delle minoranze nell'Europa mediterranea* (Milan: Franco Angeli, 2007), pp. 123–145.

Deschênes, J., 'Qu'est-ce qu'un minorité? Conclusion générale sur les droits des minorités' *Les Cahiers de Droit*, Vol. 27, No. 1 (1986), pp. 255–291.

De Nova, R., 'The International Protection of National Minorities and Human Rights' *Howard LJ* 11 (1965) 275.

De Witte, B., 'Politics versus law in the EU's approach to ethnic minorities,' in Zielonka, J. (ed.) *Europe Unbound. Enlarging and Reshaping the Boundaries of the European Union* (London: Routledge, 2002), pp. 137–160.

——, 'The constitutional resources for an EU Minority Protection Policy' in Toggenburg, G. (ed.) *Minority protection and the enlarged European Union: the way forward* (Budapest: OSI/LGI, 2004), pp. 109–124.

Dinstein, Y., 'Collective Human Rights of Peoples and Minorities' *International and Comparative Law Quarterly* Vol. 25, No. 1 (1976), pp. 102–120.

Dinstein, Y., 'Cultural Rights' *Israel Yearbook on Human Rights* 58 (1970).

Donnelly, J., 'Human Rights, Individual Rights and Collective Rights,' in Berting, J. et al. (eds.), *Human Rights in a Pluralist World. Individuals and Collectivities* (London: Westport 1990), pp. 39–62.

Eddison, E., *The Protection of Minorities at the Conference on Security and Co-operation in Europe,* Published by the Human Rights Centre of the University of Essex, No. 5 (1993).

Eide, A., 'Cultural Rights and Individual Rights' in Eide, A. et al. (eds.), *Economic, Social and Cultural Rights* (Netherlands: Kluwer Law International, 2001), pp. 289–301.

——, 'Minority Protection and World Order: Towards a Framework for Law and Policy,' in *Universal Minority Rights,* Phillips, A. and Rosas, A. (eds.) (London: Minority Rights Group International 1995) pp. 87–112.

——, 'Minority Situations: In Search of Peaceful and Constructive Solutions' 66 (1991) *Notre Dame Law Review* 1311.

Ermacora, F., 'The Protection of Minorities before the United Nations,' *Recueil des cours de l'Académie de droit internationale,* Tome 182, Vol. IV (1984), pp. 247–370.

Fenet, A., 'Europe et les Minorités' in Fenet, A. et al (eds.), *Le Droit et les Minorités. Analyses et Textes* (Bruxelles: Bruylant, 1995), pp. 83–195.

Fiss, O.M., 'Groups and the Equal Protection Clause' (1976) 5 *Philosophy and Public Affairs* 107.

Fredman, S., 'Combating Racism with Human Rights: The Right to Equality,' in Fredman, S. (ed.), *Discrimination and Human Rights: The Case of Racism* (Oxford: Oxford University Press, 2001), pp. 9–44.

Freeman, M., 'Are there collective human rights?' *Political Studies* Vol. 43 Special Issue (1995), 25–40.

——, 'Is a Political Science of Human Rights Possible?' *Netherlands Quarterly of Human Rights* Vol. 19/2 (2001) 123.

——, 'Liberalism, Socialism and Human Rights' *Essex Papers in Politics and Government* Number 86 April 1992.

Galenkamp, M., 'Collective Rights: Much Ado About Nothing' *Netherlands Quarterly of Human Rights* Vol. 9, No. 3 (1991) 291.

——, 'Collective Rights,' *SIM* (*Netherlands Institute of Human Rights*) *special,* No. 16, 1995, pp. 53–106.

Gerards, J., 'Equality as a Legal Argument', available at http://ivr-enc.info/index.php?title=Equality_as_Legal_Argument.

Geroe, M. and Gump, T., 'Hungary and a New Paradigm for the Protection of Ethnic Minorities in Central and Eastern Europe,' 32 *Columbia Journal of Transnational Law* (1994–1995), pp. 673–705.

Gilbert, G., 'The Burgeoning minority rights jurisprudence of the European Court of Human Rights' 24 *Human Rights Quarterly* 736 (2002).

——, 'The Council of Europe and minority rights' 18 Vol. 1 (1996) *Human Rights Quarterly* 160.

——, 'The Cultural and Political Autonomy of Minorities,' *L'Observateur Des Nations Unies* 2007 – 2, Vol. 23, pp. 225–250.

——, 'The Legal Protection Accorded to Minority Groups in Europe' *Netherlands Yearbook of International Law* Vol. 23 (1992) 67.

Gheorghe, N. and Mirga, A., 'The Roma in the Twenty-First Century: A Policy Paper,' available at http://www.eurozine.com/article/2001-03-12-mirga-gheorgh-en.html.

Glazer, N., 'Individual Rights against Group Rights' in Kymlicka, W. (ed.), *The Rights of Minorities Cultures* (Oxford: Oxford University Press, 1995), 123–138.

Goodwin, M., '*D.H. and Others v. Czech Republic*: a major set-back for the development of non-discrimination norms in Europe,' *German Law Journal* Vol. 7 No. 4 (2006), 421.

Graham, K., 'The Moral Significance of Collective Entities,' 44 *Inquiry* 21.

Green, L., 'Two Views of Collective Rights,' Vol. 4 No. 2 (1991) *Canadian Journal of Law and Jurisprudence* 315.

Haarsher, G., 'European Culture, Individual Rights, Collective Rights,' in Berting, J., Baehr, P.R., Burgers, J.H., Flinterman, C, de Klerk, B, Kroes, R., van Minnen, C.A. and VanderWal, K. (eds.), *Human Rights in a Pluralist World* (London: Meckler, 1990), pp. 149–153.

Habermas, J., 'Citizenship and National Identity: Some Reflections on the Future of Europe' *Praxis International* 12, 1 April 1992, Vol. 12, No. 1, pp. 1–19.

Habermas, J 'Struggles for Recognition in the Democratic Constitutional State,' in Gutman, A. (ed.), *Multiculturalism – Examining the Politics of Recognition* (Princeton: Princeton University Press, 1994), pp. 107–148.

Hancock, I., 'American Roma: the hidden Gypsy world,' *Interface 28,* November 1997, pp. 19–22.

——, 'Genocide of the Roma in the Holocaust,' in *Patrin Web Journal*, available at http://www.reocities.com/~patrin/genocide.htm.

Hannikainen, L., 'Legal Nature of Minority Rights as Part of Human Rights, Limitations, Derogations, Reservations, and Interpretative Statements,' in Weller, M. (ed.), *Universal Minority Rights* (Oxford University Press: Oxford, 2007), pp. 27–48.

Hannum, H., 'Contemporary Developments in the International Protection of the Rights of Minorities' *Notre Dame Law Review,* Vol. 66 (1991), 1431–1448.

——, 'The Limits of Sovereignty and Majority Rule: Minorities, Indigenous Peoples ad the Right to Autonomy,' in Lutz, E. et al (eds.), *New Directions in Human Rights,* (Philadelphia: University of Pennsylvania Press, 1989).

Hartney, M., 'Some Confusions Concerning Collective Rights,' Vol. 4 No. 2 (1991) *Canadian Journal of Law and Jurisprudence* 293.

Heintze, H., 'Article 1,' in Weller, M. (ed.) *The Rights of Minorities in Europe* (Oxford: Oxford University Press, 2005), pp. 77–96.

Henrard, K., 'Non-discrimination and Full and Effective Equality,' in Weller, M. (ed.), *Universal Minority Rights* (Oxford University Press: Oxford, 2007), pp. 75–147.

——, 'The Interrelationship between Individual Human Rights, Minority Rights and the Right to Self-Determination and Its Importance for the Adequate Protection of Linguistic Minorities, *The Global Review of Ethnopolitics* Vol. 1, No. 1, September 2001, pp. 41–61.

——, 'Education and Multiculturalism: the Contribution of Minority Rights?' 7 *International Journal on Minority and Group Rights* 393 (2000).

Hoffman, R., 'The Framework Convention for the Protection of National Minorities: An Introduction,' in Weller, M. (ed.), *The Rights of Minorities in Europe* (Oxford: Oxford University Press, 2005), pp. 1–24.

Holmes, H., 'Anti-Discrimination Rights without Equality', 68 (n. 2, March 2005) *The Modern Law Review* 175.

Howard, R., 'Dignity, Community and Human Rights,' in An-Na'im, A.A. (ed.) *Human Rights in Cross-Cultural Perspectives* (Philadelphia: University of Pennsylvania Press, 1992), pp. 81–102.

Hughes, J. and Sasse, G., 'Monitoring the Monitors: EU Enlargement Conditionality and Minority Protection in the CEECs,' *Journal on Ethnopolitics and Minority Issues in Europe*, Issue 1/2003.

Javonic, M.A., 'Recognizing Minority Identities Through Collective Rights,' 27 Vol. 2 (2005) *Human Rights Quarterly* 625.

Johnston, D., 'Native Rights as Collective Rights: A Question of Group Self-Preservation' in Kymlicka, W. (ed.), *The Rights of Minorities Cultures* (Oxford: Oxford University Press, 1995), 179–201.

Jones, P., 'Human Rights, Group Rights, and Peoples' Rights, 21 (1999) *Human Rights Quarterly* 80.

——, 'Group Rights and Group Oppression,' Volume 7, Number 4 (1999) *The Journal of Political Philosophy*, 353.

Juliver, P. 'Are Collective Rights Anti-Human? Theories on Self-Determination and Practice in Soviet Successor States' 11 *Netherlands Quarterly of Human Rights* n.3 (1993), pp. 267–282.

Karpati, M., 'Una storia di diritti negati tra rigetto e tentativi di assimilazione' Atti del convegno Conosciamo i Rom e i Sinti Milano, Opera Nomadi di Milano, 1998 *Romano Drom* 9 (1998).

Kawczynski, R., 'Nationality: Roma Citizenship: Europe,' in *Roma Rights*, available at http://www.errc.org/cikk.php?cikk=1760.

Kis, J., 'Beyond the Nation State,' 63 *SOC. RES.* 191 (1995).

Kovats, M., 'Hungary: politics difference and equality' in Guy, W. (ed.), *Between past and future: the Roma of Central and Eastern Europe* (Hatfield: University of Hertfordshire Press, 2001).

——, 'The emergence of a European Roma Policy,' in Guy, W. (ed.), *Between Past and Future. The Roma of Central and Eastern Europe* (Hatfield: University of Hertfordshire Press, 2001), pp. 93–116.

Kubosova, L., *EU gives blessing for Italy's Roma fingerprint scheme*, EU Observer, 5 September 2008, available at http://euobserver.com/9/26691/?rk=1.

Kukathas, C., 'Are There Any Cultural Rights?' in Kymlicka, W. (ed.), *The Rights of Minorities Cultures* (Oxford: Oxford University Press, 1995), pp. 228–256.

Kymlicka, W., 'Individual and Community Rights,' in Baker, J. (ed.), *Group Rights* (Toronto: University of Toronto Press, 1994), pp. 17–33.

——, *Minority Rights and the New International Politics of Diversity*, a paper presented at the Colloquium in Legal & Social Philosophy, The Global Diffusion of Minority and Indigenous Rights, 28 February 2007, University College London.

Lauterpacht, H. *International Law, Collected Papers*, Vol. 1 (1970).

Legesse, A. 'Human Rights in African Political Culture' in Thompson, K.W. (ed.), *The Moral Imperatives of Human Rights: A World Survey* (Washington: University Press of America 1980).

Leiris, M., *Race and Culture* (UNESCO, 1958).

L'Heureux Dubé, C., 'Making a Difference: The Pursuit of Equality and a Compassionate Justice,' 13 *South African Journal on Human Rights* 335 (1997).

Liégeois, J.P., 'Il discorso dell'ordine. Pubblici poteri e minoranze culturali', *Lacio Drom*, Vol. 5 (1980), pp. 9–29.

Liew Ten, C., 'Liberalism and Multiculturalism' in Clark, G.L. et al (eds.), *Multiculturalism, Difference and Postmodernism* (Melbourne: Cheshire, 1993), pp. 54–67.

Machnyikova, Z., 'Article 7,' in Weller, M. (ed.) *The Rights of Minorities in Europe* (Oxford: Oxford University Press, 2005), pp. 193–224.

——, 'Article 8,' in Weller, M. (ed.) *The Rights of Minorities in Europe* (Oxford: Oxford University Press, 2005), pp. 225–261.

——, 'Religious Rights,' in Weller, M. (ed.) *Universal Minority Rights* (Oxford University Press: Oxford, 2007), pp. 179–202.

Mahalic, D., and Mahalic, J.G., 'The Limitation Provisions of the International Convention on the Elimination of All Forms of Racial Discrimination,' Vol. 9, No. 1 (Feb., 1987) *Human Rights Quarterly* 74.

Malik, M., 'Communal Goods as Human Rights,' in Gearty, C., and Tomkins, A., Human Rights Quarterly (eds.), *Understanding Human Rights* (London: Mansell, 1996), pp. 138–169.

Malinverni, G., 'The draft Convention for the Protection of Minorities / Proposal of the European Commission for Democracy through Law' *Human Rights Law Journal* Vol. 12, No. 6–7 (1991), pp. 265–273.

Malloy, T.H., 'Title and Preamble,' in Weller, M. (ed.), *The Rights of Minorities in Europe* (Oxford: Oxford University Press, 2005), pp. 49–73.

Margalit, A. and Halbertal, M., 'Liberalism and the Right to Culture' *Social Research, Vo. 61 n. 3, Fall 1994*, pp. 491–510.

Marie, J.B., 'Le Droits Culturels : Interface entre les Droits de l'Individu et les droits des Communautés' in Meyer-Bisch, P. (ed.), *Le Droits Cultures, une catégorie sous-développée de droits de l'homme, Actes du VIIIe Colloque interdisciplinaire sur le droits de l'homme* (Switzerland: Editions Universitaires Fribourg Suisse, 1993), pp. 197–213.

Marko, J., 'Constitutional Recognition of Ethnic Difference–Towards an Emerging European Minimum Standard?,' in Verstichel, A. et al. (eds.), *The Framework Convention for the Protection of National Minorities: A Useful Pan-European Instrument?* (Antwerpen: Intersentia, 2008), pp. 19–32 .

Marquand, C., 'Human Rights protection and Minorities,' *PL* 359 (1994) at 365.

Marushiakova, E. and Popov, V., 'Historical and Ethnographic Background: Gypsies, Roma and Sinti,' in Guy, W. (ed.), *Between past and future, the Roma of Central and Eastern Europe,* (Great Britain: University of Hertfordshire Press, 2001), pp. 33–53.

McDonald, M., 'Should Communities Have Rights?' in An-Na'im, A.A. (ed.) *Human Rights in Cross-Cultural Perspectives* (Philadelphia: University of Pennsylvania Press, 1992), pp. 133–161.

McDonald, L., 'Can Collective and Individual Rights Coexist,' 22 (1998) *University of Melbourne Law Review* 310.

McKean, W.A., 'The Meaning of Discrimination in International and Municipal Law' (1970) *BYIL* Vol., 44, pp. 177–192.

McGoldrick, D., 'Multiculturalism and its Discontent,' *Human Rights Law Review* 5:1 (2005), pp. 27–56.

Meron, T. 'The Meaning and Reach of the International Convention on the Elimination of All Forms of Racial Discrimination," Vol. 79 (n. 2) (April 1985) *The American Journal of International Law* 283.

Meyer-Bisch, P., 'Le Droits Culturels Forment-ils une Catégorie Spécifique de Droits de l'Homme? Quelques difficultés logiques' in Meyer-Bisch, P. (ed.), *Le Droits Cultures, une catégorie sous-développée de droits de l'homme, Actes du VIIIe Colloque interdisciplinaire sur le droits de l'homme* (Switzerland: Editions Universitaires Fribourg Suisse, 1993), pp. 17–43.

Narveson, J., 'Collective Rights?,' Vol. 4 No. 2 (1991) *Canadian Journal of Law and Jurisprudence* 329.

Newton, L., 'Reverse Discrimination as Unjustified' (1973) *Ethics* 83 No. 4, pp. 308–312.

Nowak, M., 'The Evolution of Minority Rights in International Law, Comments' in Brölmann, C., Lefeber, R., and Zieck, M. (eds.) *Peoples and Minorities in International Law* (Dordrecht: Nijhoff, 1993), pp. 104–117.

O'Connell, R., 'Substantive Equality in the European Court of Human Rights?', 107 *Mich. L. Rev. First Impressions* 129 (2009).

Osella, C., 'Nomadi incalzati dal consumismo' 5 December 1999, *Zingari Oggi* 12 (1999).

O'Keefe, R., 'The "Right to Take Part in Cultural Life" under article 15 of the ICESCR' *ICLQ* 1998 (904).

Okely, J., 'Cultural ingenuity and travelling autonomy: not copying, just choosing,' in Acton, T. and Mundy, G. (eds.), Romani culture and Gypsy identity (Great Britain: University of Hertfordshire Press, 1997), pp. 188–203.

——, 'Ethnic identity and place of origin: the Traveller Gypsy in England,' in Vermeulen, H. and Boissevain, J. (eds.), *Ethnic Challenge: The Politics of Ethnicity in Europe* (Göttingen, 1984), pp. 50–65.

——, 'Gypsy Identity,' in Adams, B., Okely, J., Morgan D. and Smith, D. (eds.), *Gypsies and Government Policy in England: A Study of the Travellers' Way of Life in Relation to the Policies and Practices of Central and Local Government* (London: Heinemann Educational 1975), pp. 27–54.

O'Nions, H., 'The Right to Respect for Roma and Family Life: the First in a Series of "Gypsy Cases" to challenge UK Legislation,' (1996) 5 *Web JCLI.*

Packer, J., 'On the Definition of Minorities' in Packer, J. and Myntti, K. (eds.), *The Protection of Ethnic and Linguistic minorities in Europe* (Ebo/Turku: Ebo Akademi University, 1993), pp. 23–65.

——, 'Problems in Defining Minorities' in Fottrell, D and Bowring, B. (eds.), *Minority and Groups Rights in the New Millennium* (Netherlands: Kluwer Law International, 1999), pp. 223–274.

Packer, J. and Holt, S., 'Article 9,' in Weller, M. (ed.) *The Rights of Minorities in Europe* (Oxford: Oxford University Press, 2005), pp. 263–300.

Palermo, F., 'A Never-Ending Story? The Italian Draft Bill on the Protection of Linguistic Minorities' in Trifunovska, S. (ed.), *Minority Rights in Europe: European Minorities and Languages* (The Hague: TMC Asser Press, 2000), pp. 55–66.

——, 'La Corte "applica" il Titolo V alle minoranze linguistiche e chiude alle Regioni,' in Vol. 3 (2009) *Giurisprudenza Costituzionale* 1780.

——, 'La tutela giuridica delle minoranze linguistiche in Italia,' in Lengas, *Revue de Sociolinguistique*, 44, 1998, pp. 99–114.

Palermo, R., 'Le minoranze linguistiche in Italia dopo la legge generale di tutela,' *Quo vadis Romania? – Zeitschrift für eine aktuelle Romanistik*, Vol. (23), 2004, pp. 35–46.

Parekh, B., *What is multiculturalism*, paper conveyed at a seminar, available at www.india-seminar.com/1999/484/484%20parekh.htm.

Partsch, K.J., 'Fundamental Principle of Human Rights: self-determination, equality and non-discrimination' in The International Dimensions of Human Rights, Vasak, K. (ed.) (Westport, Connecticut: Greenwood Press, 1982), pp. 61–86.

Pejic, J., 'Minority Rights in International Law' 19 (No. 3) *Human Rights Quarterly* 666 (1997).

Pestieau, J., 'Minority Rights: Caught between Individual Rights and Collective Rights,' Vol. 4 No. 2 (1991) *Canadian Journal of Law and Jurisprudence* 361.

Pike, J., 'Dunromain' 145 *Solicitor's Journal* 45, 2001.

Pizzorusso, A., 'Commento all'art. 6', in G. Branca (ed.), *Commentario alla Costituzione*, Bologna-Roma (1975).

Pogány, I., 'Minority Rights and the Roma of Central and Eastern Europe,' (2006) *Human Rights Law Review* 6:1.

Pospíšil, I., *The Protection of National Minorities and the Concept of Minority in the EU Law*, a paper presented at the ECPR 3rd Pan-European Conference, Bilgi University, Istanbul, 21–23 September 2006.

Prott, H.L.V., 'Cultural Rights as Peoples Rights' in Crawford, J. (ed.), *The Rights of Peoples*, (Oxford: Clarendon, 1988), pp. 93–107.

Ramaga, P.V., 'The Basis of Minority Identity,' 14 (No. 3) *Human Rights Quarterly* 409 (1992).

——, 'The Group Concept in Minority Protection' 15 (No. 3) *Human Rights Quarterly* 575 (1993).

——, 'Relativity of the Minority Concept,' 14 (No. 1) *Human Rights Quarterly* 104 (1992).

Rodley, N., 'Conceptual Problems in the Protection of Minorities: International Legal Developments' 17 (Vol. 1) *Human Rights Quarterly* 48 (1995).

Rosas, A., 'The Protection of Minorities in Europe: A General Overview' in Packer, J. and Myntti, K. (eds.), *The Protection of Ethnic and Linguistic minorities in Europe* (Ebo/Turku: Ebo Akademi University, 1993), pp. 9–14.

Roth, S.J., 'Toward a Minority Convention: It's Need and Content,' *Israel Yearbook on Human Rights*, Vol. 20 (1990), pp. 93–126.

Sanders, D., 'Collective Rights' 13 *Human Rights Quarterly* 3 (1991), pp. 368–386.

Shaw, M.N., 'The Definition of Minority in International Law' *Israel Yearbook on Human Rights* Vol. 20 (1990), pp. 13–43.

Silverman, C., Persecution and Politicization: Roma (Gypsies) of Eastern Europe, Vol. 19 No. 2 (Summer 1995) *Nationalism in Eastern Europe*.

Sigona, F., 'Locating 'The Gypsy Problem'. The Roma in Italy: Stereotyping, Labelling and 'Nomad Camps',' *Journal of Ethnic and Migration studies*, Vol. 31, No. 4, July 2005, pp. 741–756.

——, 'The Governance of Romani People in Italy: discourse, policy and practice,' 16: 5 (2011) *Journal of Modern Italian Studies*, pp. 590–606.

Simon, T., 'Minorities in International Law', X (1997) *Canadian Journal of Law and Jurisprudence* 2.

Simoni, A., 'I decreti "emergenza nomadi": il nuovo volto di un vecchio problema,' X volume 3–4 (2008) *Diritto immigrazione e cittadinanza* 44.

——, 'I giuristi e il problema di una gente vagabonda. Considerazioni intorno a un libro di inizio Novecento nato da un incontro con i rom meridionali' 3 *Italia Romanì* 265 (2001).

——, 'Il giurista e gli Zingari: lezioni dalla Common Law' 30 (No. 4) *Politica del Diritto* 629 (1999).
——, 'I matrimoni degli Zingari. Considerazioni a partire dal recente dibattito sulla Gypsy Law' 2 *Daimon* 115 (2002).
——, 'La discriminazione razziale alla vigilia dell'attuazione della direttiva 43/2000: considerazioni a partire da alcune recenti pronunce giurisprudenziali,' *Diritto, Immigrazione, cittadinanza,* 2002, Vol. 4, p. 81.
——, 'La mendicità, gli Zingari e la cultura giuridica italiana: uno schizzo di tappe e problemi' Anno XIV 3 *Polis* 371 (2000).
——, *Report on Measures to Combat Discrimination Directives 2000/43/EC and 2000/78/EC, Country Report Italy,* December 2004.
——, 'Sicurezza, legalità e lo spettro degli "zingari,"' *Reset* 107, May-June 2008.
——, 'Stato di diritto e rom. Breve rassegna storica e comparata su di un problema mai risolto', in D'Isola, I., Sullam, M., Baldoni, G., Baldini, G. and Frassanito, G. (eds), *Alla periferia del mondo. Il popolo dei rom escluso dalla storia* (Fondazione Roberto Franceschi: Milano, 2003), pp. 54–75.
Shepherd, G., 'Foreword,' in Campbell, P.J. and Mahoney-Norris, K. (eds.), *Democratisation and the Protection of Human Rights* (Praeger: Westport, 1998).
Sohn, L.B. 'The Rights of Minorities,' in Henkin, L. (ed.), *The International Bill of Rights* (New York: Columbia University Press, 1981), pp. 270–289.
Solimano, N. and Mori, T., *A Roma Ghetto in Florence,* The UNESCO Courier (June 2000).
Stavenhagen, R., 'Cultural Rights and Universal Human Rights' in Eide, A. (ed.), *Economic, Social and Cultural Rights: A Textbook* (Dordrecht: Martinus Nijhoff, 1995), pp. 63–77.
——, 'Cultural Rights: A Social Science Perspective,' in Eide, A., Krause, C. and Rosas, A. (eds.), *Economic, Social and Cultural Rights – A textbook* (Martinus Nijhoff Publishers: Dordrecht, 2001), pp. 85–110.
——, 'Human Rights and Peoples' Rights: The Question of Minorities' *NJHR* 16 (1987).
——, 'The Right to Cultural Identity' in Berting, J., Baehr, P.R., Burgers, J.H., Flinterman, C, de Klerk, B, Kroes, R., van Minnen, C.A. and VanderWal, K. (eds.), *Human Rights in a Pluralist World* (London: Meckler, 1990), pp. 255–258.
Stewart, M., 'The puzzle of Roma persistence: group identity without a nation,' in Acton, T. and Mundy, G. (eds.), *Romani culture and Gypsy Identity*, (Great Britain: University of Hertfordshire Press, 1997), pp. 82–96.
Symonides, J., 'Cultural Rights,' in Symonides, J. (ed.), *Human Rights: Concept and Standards* (Paris: UNESCO, 2000), pp. 267–278.
Tabory, M., 'Minority Rights in the CSCE Context' in Dinstein, Y. and Tabory, M. (eds.) *The Protection of Minorities and Human Rights* (Dordrecht: Kluwer, 1993), pp. 187–211.
Tanner, H., 'The Roma Persecution,' in *Patrin Web Journal*, available at http://www.reocities.com/~patrin/porraimos.htm.
Tavani, C., 'Keeping the Criminality Myth Alive: Stigmatisation of Roma through the Italian Media,' *The Roma Rights Quarterly* n. 1, 2005.
Thelen, P., 'Roma Policy: The Long Walk Towards Political Participation,' in *Roma in Europe. From Social Exclusion to Active Participation,* Thelen, P., (ed.) (Skopie: Friedrich Ebert Stiftung, 2005), pp. 7–74.
Thio, L.A., 'Developing a "Peace and Security" Approach towards Minorities' Problems,' 52 (Vol. 1) (2003) *International and Comparative Law Quarterly.*
Thompson, R.H., 'Ethnic Minorities and the Case for Collective Rights' *American Anthropologist,* New Series, Vol. 99, No. 4 (December 1997), pp 786–798.
Tomuschat, C., 'Evolving Procedural Rules: The United Nations Human Rights Committee's First two Years of Dealing with Individual Communications,' in *Human Rights Law Journal* Vol. 1, No. 1 (1980), pp. 249–257.
Topidi, K., 'European Union Standards and Mechanisms for the Protection of Minorities and the Prevention of Discrimination,' in *Mechanisms for the implementation of minority rights* (Strasbourg: Council of Europe Publishing, 2004), pp. 183–202.

Thornberry, P., 'Article 12,' in Weller, M. (ed.) *The Rights of Minorities in Europe* (Oxford: Oxford University Press, 2005), pp. 365–393.

——, 'Article 13,' in Weller, M. (ed.) *The Rights of Minorities in Europe* (Oxford: Oxford University Press, 2005), pp. 393–406.

——, 'The UN Declaration on the Rights of Persons Belonging to National or Ethnic, Religious and Linguistic Minorities: Background, Analysis, Observations and an Update' in Phillips, A. and Rosas, A. (eds), *Universal Minority Rights* (Ebo/Turku: Ebo Akademi University, 1995), pp. 13–76.

VanderWal, K., 'Collective Human Rights: a Western View' in Berting, J., Baehr, P.R., Burgers, J.H., Flinterman, C, de Klerk, B, Kroes, R., van Minnen, C.A. and VanderWal, K. (eds.) *Human Rights in a Pluralist World* (London: Meckler, 1990), pp. 83–98.

Van Dyke, V., 'Collective Entities and Moral Rights: Problems in Liberal-Democratic Thought,' 44 *The Journal of Politics* (1982) 21.

——, 'The Cultural Rights of Peoples,' *Universal Human Rights,* Vol. 2 No. 2, April-June 1980, pp.1–21.

Van Roermund, B.C., 'Justice, Rights and Human Dignity: Some Aspects of Coherence in the Legal Concept of a Person,' *Windsor Yearbook of Access to Justice,* Vol. 7 (1987), pp. 46–65.

Vasak, K., 'Pour une troisième génération des droits de l'homme,' in Swinarski, C. (ed.), *Essays on International Humanitarian Law and Red Cross Principles in Honour of Jean Picket* (The Hague: Martinus Nijhoff, 1984), pp. 837–850.

Vassallo Paleologo, F., 'Il diritto speciale, Associazione Studi Giuridici sull'Immigrazione' Palermo, March 2001, available at www.terrelibere.it/rom.htm.

Vitale T., "Un popolo senza requisiti. La condizione dei rom e dei sinti nell'Italia di oggi", in Scarpelli, F. and Rossi, E. (eds.) *Il Porrajmos dimenticato. Le persecuzioni dei rom e dei sinti in Europa* (Milan: Edizioni Opera Nomadi, 2004), pp. 90–101.

Waldron, J., 'Minority Cultures and the Cosmopolitan Alternative' *University of Michigan Journal of Law Reform, Vol. 35 n. 3/4, 1991,* pp. 751–781.

Webber, J., 'Jews and Judaism in contemporary Europe: religious or ethnic group,' *Ethnic and Racial Studies,* Vol. 20, No. 2, April 1997, pp. 257–279.

Weiwei, L., Equality and Non-Discrimination Under International Human Rights Law, *Research Notes 2003/2004, Norwegian Centre for Human Rights.*

Weller, M., 'Article 15,' in Weller, M. (ed.) *The Rights of Minorities in Europe* (Oxford: Oxford University Press, 2005), pp. 429–461.

——, 'Effective Participation of Minorities in Public Life,' in Weller, M. (ed.), *Universal Minority Rights,* (Oxford: Oxford University Press, 2007), pp. 477–516.

——, 'Preface,' in Weller, M. (ed.), *Universal Minority Rights* (Oxford University Press: Oxford, 2007).

Wilhem, M., 'L'Entendue des Droits a L'Identité a la Lumiére des Droits Autochtones' in Meyer-Bisch, P (ed.), *Le Droits Cultures, une catégorie sous-développée de droits de l'homme, Actes du VIIIe Colloque interdisciplinaire sur le droits de l'homme* (Switzerland: Editions Universitaires Fribourg Suisse, 1993), pp. 212–244.

Williams, C.H., 'The Cultural Rights of Minorities: Recognition and Implementation' in J. Plichtova (ed.), *Minorities in Politics: Cultural and Language Rights* (Bratislava: Czechoslovak Committee of the European Cultural Foundation, 1992), pp. 106–121.

Wright, J., 'Minority Groups, Autonomy and Self-determination' *Oxford Journal of Legal Studies* 1999 19 (605).

——, 'The OSCE and the Protection of Minority Right' 18 (Vol. 1) *Human Rights Quarterly* 190 (1996).

——, 'The Protection of Minority Rights in Europe: from Conference to Implementation' 2 (No.1) *The International Journal of Human Rights* 1 (Spring 1998).

Zorzella, N., 'Gli "zingari" stranieri e i meandri del diritto italiano" in Simoni, A., (ed.) *Stato di Diritto e Identità Rom,* (Turin: L'Harmattan Italia, 2005), pp. 140–166.

Zvobgo, E.J.M. 'A Third World View' in Kommers, D.P. and Loescher, G.D. (eds.), *Human Rights and American Foreign Policy* (Notre Dame: University of Notre Dame Press, 1979).

Books

Alla periferia del mondo: il popolo dei rom e sinti escluso dalla storia, D'Isola, I., Sullam, M., Baldoni, G., Baldini, G. and Frassanito, G. (eds), Fondazione Roberto Franceschi Onlus (ed.) (Milan: Fondazione Roberto Franceschi Onlus, 2003).

Anatomy of the Auschwitz Death Camp, Gutman, Y. and Berenbaum, M. (eds.) (USA: Indiana University Press, 1994).

Bancroft, A., *Roma and Gypsy Travellers in Europe: modernity, race, space and exclusion* (Aldershot: Ashgate, 2005).

Barany, Z., *The East European Gypsies* (USA: Cambridge University Press, 2002).

Benoit-Rohmer, F., *The Minority Question in Europe: Towards a Coherent System of Protection for National Minorities* (Strasbourg: Council of Europe, 1996).

Between past and future, the Roma of Central and Eastern Europe, Guy, W. (ed.) (Hatfield: University of Hertfordshire Press, 2001).

Bin, R., and Pitruzzella, G., *Diritto Costituzionale* (G. Giappicchelli Editore: Torino, 2001).

Bobbio, N., *The Age of Rights* (Cambridge: Polity Press, 1996).

Boero, M.L. and Sulas, F.S., *Zingari a scuola* (Italy: Irrsae, 1996).

Bossuyt, M.J., *Guide to the "Travaux Préparatoires" of the International Covenant on Civil and Political Rights* (Dordrecht: Martinus Nijhoff, 1987).

Broadening the Frontiers of Human Rights – Essays in Honour of Asbjørn Eide, Gomien, D. (ed.) (Scandinavian University Press: Oslo, 1993).

Calabrò, A., *Il vento non soffia più* (Italy: Marsilio, 1992).

Children of Minorities, Gypsies, Costarelli, S. (ed.) (Florence, Italy: UNICEF, International Child Development Centre, 1993).

Clebert, J.P., *The Gypsies* (Harmondsworth, 1967).

Crowe, D.M., *A History of the Gypsies of Eastern Europe and Russia* (St. Martin's Press: New York, 1994).

Cultural Rights and Wrongs, A Collection of Essays in Commemoration of the 50th Anniversary of the Universal Declaration of Human Rights, Niec, H. (ed.) (Paris: UNESCO Publishing, 2001).

Cultural Rights as Human Rights (UNESCO: Paris, 1970).

Danbakli, M., *Roma, Gypsies: Text Issued by International Institution* (Paris, Centre de Reserches Tsiganes-Hatfield: University of Hertfordshire Press, 2001).

Democratisation and the Protection of Human Rights, Campbell, P.J. and Mahoney-Norris, K. (eds.) (Praeger: Westport, 1998).

De Visscher, C., *The Stabilization of Europe* (Chicago: University of Chicago Press, 1924).

Discrimination and Human Rights, Fredman, S. (ed.) (Oxford: Oxford University Press, 2001).

Donders, Y.M., *Towards a Right to Cultural Identity?* (Antwerp: Intersentia, 2002).

Donnelly, J., *International Human Rights* (Boulder: Westview Press, 1998).

——, *Universal Human Rights in Theory and Practice* (Ithaca: Cornell University Press, 2003).

Economic, Social and Cultural Rights: A Textbook, Eide, A. (ed.) (Dordrecht: Martinus Nijhoff, 1995).

Economic, Social and Cultural Rights – A textbook, Eide, A., Krause, C. and Rosas, A. (eds.), (Martinus Nijhoff Publishers: Dordrecht, 2001).

Eide, A., *New Approaches to Minority Protection* (London: Minority Rights Group, 1993).

Essays on International Humanitarian Law and Red Cross Principles in Honour of Jean Picket, C. Swinarski (ed.) (The Hague: Martinus Nijhoff, 1984).

Ethnic Challenge: The Politics of Ethnicity in Europe, Vermeulen, H. and Boissevain, J. (eds.), (Göttingen, 1984).

Europe Unbound. Enlarging and Reshaping the Boundaries of the European Union, Zielonka, J. (ed.) (London: Routledge, 2002).

Finkielkraut, A., *La défaite de la pensée* (Paris, 1987).

Fonseca, I., *Bury Me Standing. The Gypsies and their Journey* (New York: Vintage Departures, 1996).
Fraser, A., *The Gypsies* (United Kingdom: Blackwell, 1995).
Freeman, M., *Human Right: An Interdisciplinary Approach* (Cambridge: Polity Press, 2002).
Galenkamp, M. *Individualism versus Collectivism – The concept of collective rights* (Gouda Quint: Deventer, 1998).
Galston, W., *Liberal Pluralism* (United Kingdom: Cambridge University Press, 2002).
Ghandhi, P.R., *International Human Rights Documents* (Oxford, Oxford University Press, 2002).
Gomien, D., Harris, D.J. and Zwaak, L., *Law and Practice of the European Convention on Human Rights and the European Social Charter* (Strasbourg: Council of Europe, 1996).
Gottfried, T., *Martyrs to Madness* (Connecticut, Twenty-First Century Books, 2000).
Governments, Ethnic Groups and Political Representation. Comparative Studies on Governments and non-dominant Ethnic Groups in Europe 1850–1940, Alderman, G. (ed.) (Dartmouth: New York University Press, 1993).
Group Rights, Baker, J. (ed.) (Toronto: University of Toronto Press, 1994).
Gypsies, an Interdisciplinary Reader, Tong, D. (ed.) (New York : Garland Publishing Inc., 1998).
Gypsies and Government Policy in England: A Study of the Travellers' Way of Life in Relation to the Policies and Practices of Central and Local Government, Adams, B., Okely, J., Morgan, D., and Smith, D. (eds.), (London: Heinemann Educational 1975).
Habermas, J., *The Inclusion of the Other* (USA: MIT Press 1999).
Hancock, I., *The Pariah Syndrome* (USA, Karoma Publishers, 1987).
Hannum, H., *Autonomy, Sovereignty and Self-Determination: The Accommodation of Conflicting Rights* (Philadelphia: University of Pennsylvania Press, 1990).
Harris, D.J., O'Boyle, M. and Warbrick, C., *Law of the European Convention on Human Rights* (London: Buttersworth, 1995).
Henrard, K., *Devising and Adequate System of Minority Protection* (The Netherlands: Kluwer Law International, 2000).
Human Rights and American Foreign Policy, Kommers, D.P. and Loescher, G.D. (eds.) (Notre Dame: University of Notre Dame Press, 1979).
Human Rights in Cross-Cultural Perspectives, An-Na'im, A.A. (ed.) (Philadelphia: University of Pennsylvania Press, 1992).
Human Rights in a Pluralist World, Berting, J. et al. (eds.) (London: Westport, 1990).
Human Rights: Concept and Standards, Symonides, J. (ed.) (Paris: UNESCO, 2000).
Il Porrajmos dimenticato. Le persecuzioni dei rom e dei sinti in Europa, Scarpelli, F. and Rossi, E. (eds.) (Milan: Edizioni Opera Nomadi, 2004).
International Protection of Minorities, Chandra, S. (ed.) (Delhi: Mittal, 1986).
I rom e l'azione pubblica, Bezzecchi, G., Pagani, M. and Vitale, T. (eds.) (Italy: Teti Editore, 2008).
Kenrick, D. and Puxon, G., *Gypsies under the Swastika* (United Kingdom: University of Hertfordshire Press, 1995).
Kymlicka, W., *Liberalism, Community and Culture* (Oxford: Clarendon, 1989).
——, *Multicultural Citizenship: a Liberal Theory of Minority Rights* (Oxford: Oxford University Press, 1995).
La Convention Européenne des Droits de l'Homme. Commentaire Article par Article, Pettiti, L.E. et. al. (eds.) (Paris: Economica, 1995).
Lador-Lederer, J.J., *International Group Protection: Aims and Methods in Human Rights* (Leiden: A.W. Sijthoff, 1968).
Le Droit et les Minorités. Analyses et Textes, Fenet, A. et al (eds.) (Bruxelles: Bruylant, 1995).
Lerner, N., *Group Rights and Discrimination in International Law* (Dordrecht: Martinus-Nijhoff, 1991).
——, *Group Rights and Discrimination in International Law* (Dordrecht: Martinus-Nijhoff, 2003).

Liégeois, J.P., *Gypsies and Travellers: Socio-cultural Data, Socio-political Data* (Strasbourg, 1987).
——, *Gypsies. An Illustrated History*, translated by Tony Berre (London: Al Saqui Books, 1986).
——, *Rom, Sinti, Kalé... zingari e viaggianti in Europa* (Rome: Lacio Drom, 1995).
——, *Roma in Europe* (Strasbourg: Council of Europe Publishing, 2007).
L'urbanistica del disprezzo. Campi Rom e società italiana, Brunello, P. (ed) (Rome: Manifestolibri, 1996).
Le Droits Cultures, une catégorie sous-développée de droits de l'homme, Actes du VIIIe Colloque interdisciplinaire sur le droits de l'homme, Meyer-Bisch, P. (ed.) (Switzerland: Editions Universitaires Fribourg Suisse, 1993).
Lewy, G., *The Nazi Persecution of the Gypsies* (New York, Oxford University Press, 2000).
Mayall, D. *Gypsy Identities 1500–2000* (London: Routledge, 2004).
Mc Kean, W., *Equality and Discrimination under International Law* (Oxford: Clarendon Press, 1985).
Mechanisms for the Implementation of Minority Rights (Strasbourg: Council of Europe Publishing, 2005).
Meijknecht, A., *Minority protection: standards and reality: implementation of Council of Europe standards in Slovakia, Romania and Bulgaria* (The Hague: T.M.C. Asser Press, 2004).
Meron, T., *Human Rights Law Making in the United Nations: A Critique of Instruments and Process* (Oxford: Clarendon, 1986).
Minority and Group Rights in the New Millennium, Fottrell, D. and Bowring, B. (eds) (The Netherlands: Kluwer Law International, 1999).
Minorities in Politics: Cultural and Language Rights, Plichtova, J. (ed.) (Bratislava: Czechoslovak Committee of the European Cultural Foundation, 1992).
Minority protection and the enlarged European Union: the way forward, Toggenburg, G. (ed.) (Budapest: OSI/LGI, 2004).
Minority Rights in Europe: European Minorities and Languages, Trifunovska, S. (ed.) (The Hague: TMC Asser Press, 2000).
Müller-Hill, B., *Murderous Science,* USA, Cold Spring Harbor Laboratory Press, 1998.
Multiculturalism, Difference and Postmodernism, Clark, G.L. et al (eds.) (Melbourne: Cheshire, 1993).
Multiculturalism – Examining the Politics of Recognition, Gutmann, A. (ed.) (Princeton: Princeton University Press, 1994).
Musgrave, T.D., *Self-determination and National Minorities* (Oxford: Oxford University Press, 1997).
New Directions in Human Rights, Lutz, E. et al (eds.) (Philadelphia: University of Pennsylvania Press, 1989).
Nowak, M., *UN Convention on Civil and Political Rights: CCPR Commentary* (Strasbourg: N. P. Engel, Kehl, 1993).
O'Nions, H., *Minority Rights Protection in International Law. The Roma of Europe* (United Kingdom: Ashgate, 2007).
Palley, C., *Constitutional Law and Minorities* (London: Minority Rights Group, 1978).
Parekh, B., *Rethinking Multiculturalism – Cultural Diversity and Political Theory,* (Basingstoke: Macmillan Press, 2000).
Pentassuglia, G., *Minorities in International Law* (Strasbourg: Council of Europe Publishing, 2002).
Peoples and Minorities in International Law, Brölmann, C., Lefeber, R., and Zieck M. (eds.) (Dordrecht: Nijhoff, 1993).
Piasere, L., *I rom d'Europa. Una storia moderna* (Roma-Bari: Laterza, 2004).
——, *Popoli delle Discariche. Saggi di antropologia zingari* (Rome: CISU, 1991).
——, *Un Mondo di Mondi* (Italy: L'Ancora, 1999).
Postma, K., *Changing prejudice in Hungary: a Study on the Collapse of State Socialism and its Impacts on Prejudice against Gypsies and Jews* (Amsterdam: Thesis Publishers, 1996).

Revelli, M., *Fuori Luogo. Cronaca da un campo rom* (Italy: Bollati Boringhieri, 1999).
Roma in Europe. From Social Exclusion to Active Participation, Thelen, P. (ed.) (Skopie: Friedrich Ebert Stiftung, 2005).
Romani culture and Gypsy Identity, Acton, T. and Mundy, G. (eds.) (Great Britain: University of Hertfordshire Press, 1997).
Rom e Sinti in Italia: Tra Stereotipi e Diritti Negati, Cherchi, R. and Loy, G. (eds.) (Rome: Ediesse, 2009).
Roossens, E., *Creating Ethnicity: The Process of Ethnogenesis* (Newbury: Sage, 1989).
Sigler, J.A., *Minority Rights: A Comparative Analysis* (London: Greenwood Press, 1983).
Solimano, N. and Mori, T. *A Roma Ghetto in Florence,* The UNESCO Courier (June 2000).
Sorrentino, F., *Le Fonti del Diritto Italiano* (Cedam: Italy, 2009).
Spiliopoulou Åkermark, A., *Justification of Minority Protection in International Law* (The Hague: Kluwer Law International, 1997).
Spinelli, A.S., *Baro Romano Drom* (Rome: Meltemi editore, 2003).
Scholarship and the Gypsy Struggle, T. Acton (ed.) (Great Britain, University of Hertfordshire Press, 2002).
Sibley, D., *Outsiders in Urban Societies* (New York: St. Martin's Press, 1981).
Stamatopoulou, E., *Cultural Rights in International Law, Article 27 of the Universal Declaration of Human Rights and Beyond* (Leiden: Martinus Nijhoff Publishers, 2007).
Stato di Diritto e Identità Rom, A. Simoni (ed.) (Turin: L'Harmattan Italia, 2005).
Stavenhagen, R., *The Ethnic Question: Conflicts Development and Human Rights* (Tokyo: UN University Press, 1990).
Stewart, M., *The time of the Gypsies* (USA: Westview Press, 1997).
The European System for the Protection of Human Rights, Macdonald, R.St.J. et al. (eds) (Dordrecht: M. Nijhoff, 1993).
The Gypsies of Eastern Europe, Crowe, D. and Kolsti, J. (eds.) (USA: M. E. Sharpe, Inc., 1991).
The Human Rights Reader, Ishay, M. (ed.) (New York: Routledge, 1997).
The International Bill of Rights, Henkin, K. (ed) (New York: Columbia University Press, 1981).
The International Dimensions Of Human Rights, Vasak, K. (ed.) (Westport, Connecticut: Greenwood Press, 1982).
The Moral Imperatives of Human Rights: A World Survey, Thompson, K.W. (ed.) (Washington: University Press of America 1980).
The Protection of Ethnic and Linguistic minorities in Europe, J. Packer and K. Myntti (eds.) (Ebo/Turku: Ebo Akademi University, 1993).
The Protection of Minorities and Human Rights, Dinstein, Y. and Tabory, M. (eds.) (Dordrecht: Kluwer, 1993).
The Rights of Minorities Cultures, Kymlicka, W. (ed.) (Oxford: Oxford University Press, 1995).
The Rights of Minorities in Europe, Weller, M. (ed) (Oxford: Oxford University Press, 2005).
The Rights of Peoples, Crawford, J. (ed.) (Oxford: Clarendon, 1988).
The UN Minority Rights Declaration, Phillips, A. and Rosas, A. (eds) (Turku/Åbo: Åbo Akademi University, Institute for Human Rights, 1993).
Thornberry, P., *International Law and the Rights of Minorities* (Oxford: Oxford University Press, 1991).
Thornberry, P. and Martín Estébanez, M.A., *Minority Rights in Europe,* (Germany: Council of Europe Publishing, 2004).
Thurner, E., *National Socialism and Gypsies in Austria* (USA: The University of Alabama Press, 1998).
Torbisco Casals, N., *Group Rights as Human Rights: A Liberal Approach to Multiculturalism* (Springer: Doordrecht, 2006).
Tra identità ed integrazione: passato e presente delle minoranze nell'Europa mediterranea, Amitti, G., and Rosina, A., (eds.) (Milan: Franco Angeli, 2007).
Understanding Human Rights, Gearty, C., and Tomkins, A., (eds.) (London: Mansell, 1996).
Universal Minority Rights, Phillips, A. and Rosas, A. (eds.) (London: Minority Rights Group International 1995).
Universal Minority Rights, Weller, M. (ed.) (Oxford University Press: Oxford, 2007).

Van der Stoel, M. *Peace and Stability through Human and Minority Rights* (Baden-Baden: Nomos Verlagsgesellschaft, 1999).
Van Dyke, V., *Human Rights, Ethnicity, and Discrimination* (USA: Greenwood Press, 1985).
Viaggio, G., *Storia degli Zingari in Italia* (Italy: CSZ-ANICIA, 1997).
Welhengama, G., *Minorities' Claims: From Autonomy to Secession* (Hampshire: Ashgate Publishing Limited, 2000.
Zanghì, C., *Le minoranze* (Rome: Rizzoli, 1995).
Zatta, P., *Scuola di stato e nomadi* (Italy: Francisci, 1986).
Zingari Ieri e Oggi, Tarpati, M., (ed.) (Rome: Edizioni Lacio Drom, 1993).

Documents

Council of Europe

Advisory Committee on the Framework Convention

Council of Europe, Advisory Committee on the Framework Convention for the Protection National Minorities, *Comments of the Government of Italy on the second opinion of the Advisory Committee on the Implementation of the Framework Convention for the Protection of National Minorities in Italy*, GVT/COM/INF/OP/II(2005)003, October 4, 2005.
Council of Europe, Advisory Committee on the Framework Convention for the Protection National Minorities, *Commentary on the Effective Participation of Persons Belonging to National Minorities in Cultural, Social and Economic Life and in Public Affairs*, ACFC/31DOC(2008)001, February 27, 2008.
Council of Europe, Advisory Committee on the Framework Convention on National Minorities, *Commentary on Education under the Framework Convention for the Protection of National Minorities*, ACFC/25DOC(2006)002, March 2, 2006.
Council of Europe, Advisory Committee on the Framework Convention for the Protection of National Minorities, *Opinion on Albania*, ACFC/INF/OP/I(2003)004, September 12, 2002.
Council of Europe, Advisory Committee on the Framework Convention for the Protection of National Minorities, *Opinion on Armenia*, ACFC/INF/OP/I(2003)001, May 16, 2002.
Council of Europe, Advisory Committee on the Framework Convention for the Protection of National Minorities, *Opinion on Estonia*, ACFC/INF/OP/I(2002)005, September 14, 2001.
Council of Europe, Advisory Committee on the Framework Convention for the Protection of National Minorities, *Opinion on Finland*, ACFC/INF/OP/I(2001)002, September 22, 2000.
Council of Europe, Advisory Committee on the Framework Convention for the Protection of National Minorities, *Opinion on Germany*, ACFC/INF/OP/I(2002)008, March 1, 2002.
Council of Europe, Advisory Committee on the Framework Convention for the Protection of National Minorities, *Opinion on Hungary*, ACFC/INF/OP/I(2001)004, 22 September 2000.
Council of Europe, Advisory Committee on the Framework Convention for the Protection of National Minorities, *Opinion on Italy*, ACFC/INF/OP/I(2002)007, September 14, 2001.
Council of Europe, Advisory Committee on the Framework Convention for the Protection National Minorities, *Opinion on Sweden*, ACFC/INF/OP/I(2003)006, August 25, 2002.
Council of Europe, Advisory Committee on the Framework Convention for the Protection of National Minorities, *Report submitted by Italy pursuant to article 25, paragraph 1 of the Framework Convention for the Protection of National Minorities*, May 3, 1999, ACFC/SR(1999)007.

Council of Europe, Advisory Committee on the Framework Convention for the Protection of National Minorities, *Second report submitted by Italy pursuant to article 25, paragraph 1 of the Framework Convention for the Protection of National Minorities*, May 14, 2004, ACFC/SR/II(2004)006.

Council of Europe, Advisory Committee on the Framework Convention for the Protection of National Minorities, *Second Opinion on the Czech Republic*, February 25, 2005, ACFC/INF/OP/II(2005)002.

Council of Europe, Advisory Committee on the Framework Convention for the Protection of National Minorities, *Second Opinion on Italy*, February 24, 2005, ACFC/INF/OP/II(2005)003.

Council of Europe, Advisory Committee on the Framework Convention for the Protection of National Minorities, *Second Report Submitted by Switzerland Pursuant to Article 25, Paragraph 1 of the Framework Convention for the Protection of "National Minorities*, January 31, 2007, ACFC/SR/II(2007)002.

Council of Europe, Advisory Committee on the Framework Convention for the Protection of National Minorities, *Third Opinion on Italy*, October 15, 2010, ACFC/OP/III(2010)008, 30 May 2011.

Reports

Alfredsson, *G., Report on "Equality and non-discrimination: minority rights",* 7th International Colloquy on the European Convention on Human Rights, Council of Europe, Strasbourg 1990, H/Coll(90)6.

Bindig, R., *Report of the Committee on Legal Affairs and Human Rights,* Council of Europe, Committee on Legal Affairs and Human Rights, Document number 8920, January 29, 2001.

Council of Europe Commissioner for Human Rights, *Memorandum by Thomas Hammarberg Commissioner for Human Rights of the Council of Europe Following his visit to Italy on 19–20 June 2008,* Strasbourg, July28, 2008 CommDH(2008)18.

Council of Europe, Committee on Legal Affairs and Human Rights, *Report on the Legal Situation of the Roma in Europe,* April 19, 2002.

Council of Europe, European Charter for Regional or Minority Languages – Explanatory Report, DELA(92)2.

Council of Europe, European Commission Against Racism and Intolerance, *Second Report on Italy,* June 22, 2001, CRI (2002) 4.

Council of Europe, Preparatory Work of the Ad Hoc Committee for the Portection of National Minorities (CAHMIN), *Explanatory Report to the Framework Convention for the Protection of National Minorities*, CAHMIN H(1995)010.

Council of Europe, Office of the Commissioner for Human Rights, *Report by Mr Alvaro Gil-Robles, Commissioner for Human Rights, On his visit to Italy, 10–17 June 2005, for the attention of the Committee of Ministers and the Parliamentary Assembly,* CommDH(2005)9, Strasbourg December 14, 2005.

Council of Europe, Parliamentary Assembly, Committee on Legal Affairs and Human Rights, Rapporteur Mr J. Berényi, *The situation of Roma in Europe and relevant activities of the Council of Europe, Introductory memorandum,* AS/Jur (2008) 29 rev, September 3, 2008, Declassified by the Committee on 9 September 2008.

European Commission for Democracy through Law, *Proposal for a European Convention for the Protection of Minorities, Explanatory Report,* Council of Europe, CDL(91)8, 1991.

Hammarberg, T., *Report of the Commissioner for Human Rights of the Council of Europe Following his visit to Italy from 26 to 27 May 2011,* CommDH(2011)26, September 7, 2011.

Recommendations and Resolutions

Appendix to Resolution ResChS(2006)4 Information provided by the Permanent Representative of Italy during consideration by the Committee of Ministers of the report transmitted by the European Committee of Social Rights concerning Collective complaint No. 27/2004.

Council of Europe, Committee of Ministers, Appendix to Resolution DH (2000) 44, April 10, 2000, *Canea Catholic Church v. Greece.*

Council of Europe, Committee of Ministers, Appendix to Resolution DH (2000) 99, July 24, 2000, *Sidiropoulos v. Greece.*

Council of Europe, Committee of Ministers, Recommendation (2001)17 *on improving the economic and employment situation of Roma/Gypsies and Travellers in Europe,* November 27, 2001.

Council of Europe, Committee of Ministers, Recommendation (2008)5 *on policies for Roma and/or Travellers in Europe,* February 20, 2008.

Council of Europe, Committee of Ministers, Recommendation (2000)4 *on the education of Roma/Gypsy children in Europe,* February 3, 2000.

Council of Europe, Committee of Ministers, Resolution ResCMN(2002)10 *on the implementation of the Framework Convention for the Protection of National Minorities by Italy,* July 3, 2002.

Council of Europe, Committee of Ministers, Resolution ResCMN(2006)5 *on the implementation of the Framework Convention for the Protection of National Minorities by Italy,* June 14, 2006.

Council of Europe, Committee of Ministers, Resolution (75) 13 Containing Recommendations on the Social Situation of Nomads in Europe, adopted by the Committee of Ministers on May 22, 1975 at the 245th meeting of the Ministers' Deputies.

Council of Europe, Consultative Assembly, Recommendation 563 (1969) *on the situation of Gypsies and other travellers in Europe,* September 30, 1969.

Council of Europe, European Commission Against Racism and Intolerance, *General Policy Recommendation N. 7 on National Legislation to Combat Racism and Racial Discrimination,* December 13, 2002.

Council of Europe, Committee of Ministers, Resolution ResChS(2006)4, Collective complaint No. 27/2004, by the European Roma Rights Centre against Italy, *Adopted by the Committee of Ministers on 3 May 2006 at the 963rd meeting of the Ministers' Deputies.*

Council of Europe, European Commission Against Racism and Intolerance, *General Policy Recommendation N. 3: Combating Racism and Intolerance against Roma/Gypsies,* CRI (98) 29 rev, March 6, 1998.

Council of Europe, Parliamentary Assembly, Recommendation 1134 (1990) *on the rights of minorities,* October 1, 1990.

Council of Europe, Parliamentary Assembly, Recommendation 1201 (1993) *on an additional protocol on the rights of national minorities to the European Convention on Human Rights,* February 1, 1993.

Council of Europe, Parliamentary Assembly, Recommendation 1203 (1993) *On the Situation of Roma in Europe,* February 2, 1993.

Council of Europe, Parliamentary Assembly, Recommendation 1557 (2002) *The Legal Situation of Roma in Europe,* 25 April 25, 2002.

Council of Europe, *Recommendations of the Assembly – Replies by the Committee of Ministers*: Document 8306 (Communication).

Council of Europe, Standing Conference of Local and Regional Authorities of Europe, Resolution 125(1981) *on the role and responsibility of local and regional authorities in regard to the cultural and social problems of populations of nomadic origins,* October 29, 1981.

Council of Europe, Standing Conference of Local and Regional Authorities of Europe, Resolution 249(1993) *on Gypsies in Europe: the role and responsibility of local and regional authorities,* March 18, 1993.

Meetings/Various

Committee of experts on issues relating to the protection of national minorities (DH-MIN), *Results of the exchange of information on the question to which groups the Framework Convention will be applied*, Strasbourg, January 15, 1999, DH-MIN (98) 4, Addendum I.

Council of Europe Doc. CAHMIN (94)12, Preliminary Draft Framework Convention for the Protection of National Minorities, April 1994.

CoE Doc. CAHMIN (94)35, December 1994.

Council of Europe, Commission for Democracy through Law, *Proposal for a European Convention for the Protection of Minorities*, reproduced in *Human Rights Law Journal*, Vol. 12, 1991, No. 6–7, pp. 269–273.

Council of Europe, Committee of Ministers, *Secretariat of the Framework Convention for the Protection of National Minorities*, 799th meeting, June 13, 2002.

Council of Europe, European Commission for Democracy Through Law (Venice Commission), *Vademecum of Venice Commission, Opinions and Reports Concerning the Protection of Minorities*, CDL-MIN(2007)001, Strasbourg, March 6, 2007.

Council of Europe Roundtable, *Roma and Statistics*, MG-S-ROM (2000) 13.

Council of Europe, Secretariat of the Framework Convention for the Protection of National Minorities, Committee of Ministers, 799th meeting, June 13, 2002.

European Commission for Democracy through Law, *Proposal for a European Convention for the Protection of Minorities*, Council of Europe, CDL(91)7, 1991.

European Union

Directives

Council Directive 2000/43/EC *implementing the principle of equal treatment between persons irrespective of racial or ethnic origin*, Official Journal L 180, July 19, 2000 P, 0022–0026.

Council Directive 95/46/EC *on the protection of individuals with regard to the processing of personal data and on the free movement of such data*, October 24, 1995.

Council Directive 2004/83/EC, *on minimum standards for the qualification and status of third country nationals or stateless persons as refugees or as persons who otherwise need international protection and the content of the protection granted.*

Council Directive 2003/86/CE *on the Right to Family Reunification*, September 22, 2003.

Council Directive 2004/38/EC *on the right of citizens of the European Union and their family members to move and reside freely within the territory of the EU*, April 29, 2004.

European Union, *Race Equality Directive*, 2000/43/EC, June 29, 2000.

European Union Directive 2000/78/EC *establishing a general framework for equal treatment in employment and occupation, and to the framework decision on combating racism and xenophobia.*

Reports

Commission of the European Communities, *Commission report on the implementation of the Action Plan against racism*, COM (96) 495, October 1996.

European Commission Against Racism and Intolerance (ECRI), *Second Report on Italy*, June 22, 2001.

European Commission Against Racism and Intolerance (ECRI), *Third Report on Italy*, December 16, 2005.

European Monitoring Centre on Racism and Xenophobia, *Racism and Xenophobia in the EU Member States: trends, developments and good practice,* Annual Report 2003/2004, Part 2.

European Monitoring Centre on Racism and Xenophobia, *Racism and Xenophobia in the EU Member States: trends, developments and good practice in 2002,* Annual Report Part 2.

European Monitoring Centre on Racism and Xenophobia, *The Annual Report on the Situation regarding Racism and Xenophobia in the Member States of the EU,* 2006.

European Union Agency for Fundamental Rights, *Report on Racism and Xenophobia in the Member States of the EU.*

European Union Agency for Fundamental Rights, *Annual Report, 2008.*

European Union High Level Advisory Group of Experts, *'Ethnic Minorities on the Labour Market – An Urgent Call for Better Social Inclusion,'* report published by the Commission in 2007.

Simoni, A., *Report on Measures to Combat Discrimination Directives 2000/43/EC and 2000/78/EC, Country Report Italy,* December 2004.

Simoni, A., Boni, G., *A comparison of national anti-discrimination legislation on the grounds of racial or ethnic origins, religion or belief with the Council Directives, Italy,* Niessen, J. and Chopin, J. (eds), *Anti-discrimination Legislation in EU Member States, Minority Policy Group,* European Monitoring Centre on Racism and Xenophobia, Vienna, 2002.

Recommendations/Resolutions

European Commission, Composite Paper, Reports on Progress towards Accession by each of the candidate countries, October 13, 1999.

European Community, Council of the Ministers of Education, *Communication on Education in the European Community: Medium Term Perspectives, 1988–1992,* May 24, 1988.

European Community, Council of the Ministers of Education, Resolution 89/C 153/02 *on school provision for gypsy and traveller children,* May 22, 1989.

European Parliament Resolution *on the census of the Roma on the basis of ethnicity in Italy,* P6_TA-PROV(2008)0361, July 10, 2008.

European Parliament, Resolution *on the situation of Gypsies in the European Community,* A3-0124/94, April 21, 1994.

European Parliament Resolution *on the situation of the Roma in the European Union,* P6_TA(2005)0151, April 8, 2005.

European Parliament Resolution *on the situation of Roma women in the European Union* (2005/2164(INI)), P6_TA(2006)0244, June 1, 2006.

European Parliament Resolution on application of Directive 2004/38/EC *on the right of EU citizens and their family members to move and reside freely within the territory of the Member States,* B6-0462/2007 / P6-TA-PROV(2007)0534, November 15, 2007.

European Parliament Resolution *on a European strategy on the Roma,* P6_TA(2008)0035, January 31, 2008.

Resolution on linguistic and cultural minorities in the European Community *A3-0042/94.*

CSCE/OSCE

Conferences

Conference for Security and Co-operation in Europe, *Human Dimension Seminar on Case Studies on National Minorities. Issues: Positive Results,* Warsaw, May 24–28, 1993.

Conference for Security and Co-operation in Europe, *second Conference on the Human Dimension of the CSCE, Copenhagen 5 June – 29 July 1990, Document of the Copenhagen meeting of the Conference on the Human Dimension of the CSCE.*

Conference for Security and Co-operation in Europe, *third Conference on the Human Dimension of the CSCE, Moscow 10 September-15 October 1991, Document of the Moscow meeting of the Conference on the Human Dimension of the CSCE.*
Conference for Security and Co-operation in Europe, *1992 Summit, Helsinki 9–10 July 1992, CSCE Helsinki Document 1992, The Challenges of Change.*
Consolidated Summary of CSCE Human Dimension Seminar on Roma in the CSCE Region, Opening Speech by Mr. Peter Leuprecht, Deputy Secretary General of the Council of Europe, Warsaw, September 20, l994.
Organisation for Security and Co-operation in Europe, *Background Paper Summarising and Analysing Information Gathered During the Project through Participation of Romani STOs in the OSCE Election Observation Missions and Prague Workshop on Romani Political Participation, prepared for the OSCE Conference on Romani and Sinti Affairs,* 10–14 September 2001, Bucharest, compiled by Ilona Klimova, University of Cambridge, August 2001.
Organisation for Security and Co-operation in Europe, *High Commissioner on National Minorities, Summary: Seminar on Roma in the OSCE area, 14–15 June 2000, Bratislava,* The Hague, October 2000.
OSCE ODIHR, *Human Dimension Seminar, Case Studies on National Minorities Issues: Positive Results,* Warsaw, May 24–28, 1993, Key-Note Address of Mr. M. van der Stoel, CSCE High Commissioner on National Minorities.

Reports

Conference for Security and Cooperation in Europe, High Commissioner on National Minorities, *High Commissioner on National Minorities' Report on the Roma in the CSCE Region*, 1993.
Gheorghe, N. and Tanaka, J., *Rapporteurs' Report of the OSCE Review, Meeting, 1996 (Vienna)*, Public policies concerning Roma and Sinti in the OSCE region, OSCE Human Dimension Implementation Meeting, October 1998, Background Paper 4.
Office of the OSCE High Commissioner on National Minorities, *Note on the Possible Use of Terminology in the Process of Incorporating into Domestic Law International Standards for the Protection of Minorities*, 2003.
Organisation for Security and Co-operation in Europe, *High Commissioner on National Minorities, Report on the situation of Roma and Sinti in the OSCE area,* March 2000.
OSCE/ODIHR Contact Point for Roma and Sinti Issues, *Rating action on Roma rights: Keeping track of progress*, October-November 2008.
OSCE/ODIHR, *Implementation of the Action Plan on Improving the Situation of Roma and Sinti Within the OSCE Area,* Status Report 2008.
Report of the CSCE Meeting of Experts on National Minorities, 30 ILM 1692 (1991).

Recommendations, Resolutions and Commitments

Organisation for Security and Co-operation in Europe, *Charter for European Security,* Istanbul, November 1999.
Organisation for Security and Co-operation in Europe, *Istanbul Summit Declaration,* November 19, 1999.
Organisation for Security and Co-operation in Europe, *Office for Democratic Institutions and Human Rights, OSCE Commitments and Recommendations relating to Roma and Sinti,* Warsaw, 2003.
Organisation for Security and Co-operation in Europe, *Office for Democratic Institutions and Human Rights, Implementation of the Action Plan on Improving the Situation of Roma and Sinti Within the OSCE Area,* Status Report 2008.

Organisation for Security and Co-operation in Europe, *Parliamentary Assembly on Roma and Sinti, Resolution on Roma Education,* Berlin, July 2002.
OSCE 1998 Oslo Ministerial Decision, *Decision on the enhancement of the OSCE's operational capabilities regarding Roma and Sinti Issues*: MC(7).DEC/5.

United Nations

Reports/Studies

Capotorti, F., *Study on the Rights of Persons belonging to Ethnic, Religious and Linguistic Minorities,* UN Doc. E/CN.4/Sub.2/384/Rev. 1, 1979.
Chernichenko, S., *The Definition of Minorities – Second Working Paper for the UN Working Group on Minorities,* UN Doc. E/CN.4/Sub.2/AC.5/1997/WP.1, April 1997.
Deschênes, J., *Proposal Concerning a Definition of the Term "Minority",* UN Doc. E/CN.4/Sub.2/1985/31 of 14 May 1985.
Eide, A., *Protection of Minorities,* Progress report, UN Document E/CN.4/Sub.2/1990/46.
——, *Preliminary Report: Possible ways and means of facilitating the peaceful and constructive solution of problems involving minorities*, UN Document E/CN.4/Sub.2/1991/43.
——, *Protection of Minorities,* Second progress report, UN Document E/CN.4/Sub.2/1992/37.
——, *Protection of Minorities: Possible ways and means of facilitating the peaceful and constructive solution of problems involving minorities*, UN Doc. E/CN.4/Sub.2/1993/34.
——, *Final Text of the Commentary to the Declaration on the Rights of Persons Belonging to National or Ethnic, Religious, and Linguistic Minorities*, UNGA Res. A/47/135. 1992.
Minority Rights Group International, Possible United Nations Mechanisms for the Protection and Promotion of the Rights of Minorities, E/CN.4/Sub.2/AC.5/2003/WP.3 May 5, 2003.
Palley, C., *Protection of Minorities,* UN Document E/CN.4/Sub.2/1989/43.
Report of the Working Group on the right of persons belonging to national, religious and linguistic minorities, UN Doc. E/CN.4/1991/53, 1991, March 5, 1991.
'Rights of Persons Belonging to National or Ethnic, Religious and Linguistic Minorities,' report of a technical meeting of experts on minorities which took place at Geneva from 2 to 4 February 1993, UN Document E/CN.4/1993/85.
Shaheed, R., *Report of the independent expert in the field of cultural rights*, submitted pursuant to resolution 10/23 of the Human Rights Council, A/HRC/14/36, March 22, 2010.
Study of Discrimination in Education, UN Doc E/CN.4/Sub.2/181.
Türk, D., *Realisation of Economic, Social and Cultural Rights*, UN Doc. E/CN.4/Sub.2/1989/19.
Yeung Sik Yuen, Y.K.J., *Human rights problems and protections of Roma, United Nations Commission on Human Rights, Sub-Commission on the Promotion and Protection of Human Rights, 52nd Session,* E/CN.4/Sub.2/2000/28, June 23, 2000.

General Assembly and Human Rights Commission/Council

United Nations *Body of Principles for the Protection of All Persons under Any Form of Detention or Imprisonment,* A/RES/43/173 of December 9, 1988.
United Nations Commission on Human Rights, Resolution 1992/65 *on the protection of Roma (Gypsies) on Human Rights*, March 4, 1992.
United Nations Commission on Human Rights, *Rights of persons belonging to national, ethnic, religious and linguistic minorities,* E/CN.4/1992/L.72.
United Nations General Assembly, *Declaration on the Rights of persons belonging to national or ethnic, religious and linguistic minorities,* G.A. Res. 47/135, December 18, 1992.

United Nations General Assembly, *Vienna Declaration and Programme of Action*, A/CONF.157/23, July 12, 1993.
United Nations General Assembly, *World Conference against Racism, Racial Discrimination, Xenophobia and Related Intolerance, Study on the effect of racial discrimination on the children of minorities and those of migrant workers in the fields of education, training and employment, report by the Secretary General*, A/CONF.189/PC.1/11, April 10, 2000.
United Nations Human Rights Council, *Report of the Special Rapporteur on contemporary forms of racism, racial discrimination, xenophobia and related intolerance, Doudou Diène. Mission to Italy*, A/HRC/4/19/Add.4, February 27, 2007.
37 UN GAOR Supp. (No. 18), UN Doc. A/37/18 (1982).
38 U.N. GAOR Supp. (No. 18), U.N. Doc. A/38118 (1983).
United Nations Declaration on the Rights of Indigenous Peoples, adopted by the General Assembly with Resolution A/RES/61/295, September 13, 2007.
UN Doc. E/CN.4/52, Sec. V, December 6, 1947.
UN Doc. E/CN.4/358, January 30, 1950.
UN Doc E/CN.4/Sub.2/SR.66, October 17, 1951.
UN Doc E/CN.4/1991/53.
UN Doc. E/CN.4/Sub.2/AC.5/2000/CRP.1.
UN Doc. E/CN.4/Sub.2/AC.5/2001/CRP.4.

Human Rights Committee

United Nations Human Rights Committee, *Comments by the Government of Italy concluding observations of the Human Rights Committee*, CCPR/C/ITA/CO/5/Add.1, February 19, 2007.
United Nations Human Rights Committee, *Concluding Observations of the Human Rights Committee: Bosnia and Herzegovina*, CCPR/C/BIH/CO/1, November 22, 2006.
United Nations Human Rights Committee, *Concluding Observations of the Human Rights Committee: Bulgaria*, CCPR/C/79/Add.24, August 3, 1993.
United Nations Human Rights Committee, *Concluding Observations of the Human Rights Committee: Czech Republic*, CCPR/C/CZE/CO/2, August 9, 2007.
United Nations Human Rights Committee, *Concluding Observations of the Human Rights Committee: France*, CCPR/C/FRA/CO/4, July 31, 2008.
United Nations Human Rights Committee, *Concluding Observations of the Human Rights Committee: Hungary*, CCPR/CO/74/HUN, September 25, 2002.
United Nations Human Rights Committee, *Concluding Observations of the Human Rights Committee: Italy*, CCPR/C/79/Add.94, August 18, 1998.
United Nations Human Rights Committee, *Concluding Observations of the Human Rights Committee: Italy*, CCPR/C/ITA/CO/5, April 24, 2006.
United Nations Human Rights Committee, *Concluding Observations of the Human Rights Committee: Romania*, CCPR/C/79/Add.111, July 28, 1999.
United Nations Human Rights Committee, *Concluding Observations of the Human Rights Committee: Slovakia*, CCPR/CO/78/SVK, August 22, 2003.
United Nations Human Rights Committee, *Fourth periodic reports of States parties due in 1995 : Italy*, CCPR/C/103/Add.4, May 28, 1997.
United Nations Human Rights Committee, *General Comment 12, The Right to Self-Determination of Peoples*, March 13, 1984.
United Nations Human Rights Committee, *General Comment 18, Non-discrimination*, U.N. Doc. HRI/GEN/1/Rev.1 at 26 (1994).
United Nations Human Rights Committee, *General Comment 20, Article 7*, March 10, 1992.
United Nations Human Rights Committee, *General Comment 23(50), Article 27*, UN Doc. CCPR/C/21/Rev.1/Add.5, 1994.

United Nations Human Rights Committee, *Summary record of the 1679th meeting: Italy*, CCPR/C/SR.1679, July 28, 1998.

Committee on Economic Social and Cultural Rights

United Nations Committee on Economic, Social and Cultural Rights, *General Comment No. 13*, E/C.12/1999/10, 21st session, 1999.

United Nations Committee on Economic, Social and Cultural Rights, General Comment 17 *The right of everyone to benefit from the protection of the moral and material interests resulting from any scientific, literary or artistic production of which he or she is the author (article 15, paragraph 1 (c), of the Covenant)*, E/C.12/GC/17, January 12, 2006.

United Nations, Committee on Economic, Social and Cultural Rights, *General Comment No. 20, Non-Discrimination in Economic, Social and Cultural Right*, E/C.12/GC/20, June 10, 2009.

United Nations, Committee on Economic, Social and Cultural Rights, *General Comment 21, Right of Everyone to Take Part in Cultural Life*, E/C.12/GC/21, December 21, 2009.

Committee on the Elimination of Racial Discrimination

United Nations Committee on the Elimination of Racial Discrimination, *Concluding observations of the Committee on the Elimination of Racial Discrimination: Hungary*, CERD/C/304/Add.4, March 28, 1996.

United Nations Committee on the Elimination of Racial Discrimination, *Concluding observations of the Committee on the Elimination of Racial Discrimination: Italy*, CERD/C/304/Add.68, 7 April 1999.

United Nation Committee on the Elimination of Racial Discrimination, *Concluding observations of the Committee on the Elimination of Racial Discrimination: Italy*, CERD/C/304/Add.68, April 7, 1999.

United Nation Committee on the Elimination of Racial Discrimination, *Concluding observations of the Committee on the Elimination of Racial Discrimination: Italy*, A/56/18, August 8, 2001.

United Nations Committee on the Elimination of Racial Discrimination, *Concluding observations of the Committee on the Elimination of Racial Discrimination, Italy*, CERD/C/ITA/CO/15, May 16, 2008.

United Nations Committee on the Elimination of Racial Discrimination, *Fifteenth periodic reports of States parties due in 2005 Addendum Italy*, CERD/C/ITA/15, March 29, 2006.

United Nations Committee on the Elimination of Racial Discrimination, *General Recommendation 32, The meaning and scope of special measures in the International Convention on the Elimination of Racial Discrimination*, Seventy-fifth session, August 2009.

United Nation Committee on the Elimination of Racial Discrimination, *General Recommendation 27, Discrimination against Roma*, 57th Session, August 16, 2000, document A/55/18 annex V.

United Nations Committee on the Elimination of Racial Discrimination, *Implementation of the ICERD, article 7: Teaching, Education, Culture and Information as means of Eliminating Racial Discrimination'* (New York: United Nations, 1985).

United Nations Committee on the Elimination of Racial Discrimination, *Reports submitted by States parties under article 9 of the Convention, Sixteenth to eighteenth periodic reports of States parties due in 2009, Italy*, CERD/C/ITA/16–18, June 21, 2011.

United Nation Committee on the Elimination of Racial Discrimination, *Summary Record of the 1075th Meeting: Italy*, CERD/C/SR.1075, March 6, 1995.

United Nation Committee on the Elimination of Racial Discrimination, *Thirteenth periodic reports of States Parties due in 2001, Addendum, Italy,* CERD/C/406/ADD.1, October 17, 2000.
United Nations Committee on the Elimination of Racial Discrimination, 22nd Sess. (486th mtg.) U.N. Doc. CERDIC/SR.486 (1980).
United Nations Committee on the Elimination of Racial Discrimination, 26th Sess. (577th mtg.) U.N. Doc. CERDIC/SR.577 (1982).
United Nations Committee on the Elimination of Racial Discrimination, 30th Sess. (685th mtg.) U.N. Doc. CERD/C/SR.685 (1984).
United Nations Committee on the Elimination of Racial Discrimination, 30th Sess. (678th mtg.), U.N. Doc. CERDIC/SR.678 (1984).

Other Committees

United Nations Committee Against Torture, *Concluding Observations of the Committee against Torture : Italy.* A/54/44,paras.163–169, May 7, 1999.
United Nations Committee on the Rights of the Child, *Concluding observations of the Committee on the Rights of the Child: Italy,* CRC/C/15/Add. 41, November 27, 1995.

Secretariat

United Nations Secretariat, *Working Paper on Best Practices in the Area of Minority Protection,* UN Doc. E/CN.4/Sub.2/AC.5/1998/WP.2, May 27, 1998.
United Nations Secretary General, *Report: Rights of Persons Belonging to National or Ethnic, Religion and Linguistic Minorities,* UN Doc. E/CN.4/1998/90, December 29, 1997.
United Nations Secretary General, *Report: Rights of Persons Belonging to National or Ethnic, Religion and Linguistic Minorities,* UN Doc. E/CN.4/1997/82, January 8, 1997.
United Nations Secretary General, *Report: Rights of Persons Belonging to National or Ethnic, Religion and Linguistic Minorities,* UN Doc. E/CN.4/1996/88, January 26, 1996.
United Nations Secretary General, *Report: Possible Ways and Means of Facilitating the Peaceful and Constructive Solution of Problems involving Minorities,* UN Doc. E/CN.4/Sub.2/1995/33, June 14, 1995.
United Nations Secretary General, *Memorandum: Definition and Classification of Minorities,* UN Doc. CN.4/Sub.2/85, 1950.
World Conference to Combat Racism and Discrimination UN Doc. A/33/262 (1978).

UNESCO

United Nations Educational, Scientific and Cultural Organisation (UNESCO), *Cultural Rights as Human Rights,* Paris, 1970.
UNESCO Declaration on Race and Racial Prejudice.
UNESCO Declaration on Race and Racial Prejudice, Explanatory Report, Doc 20/C/18 annex.

Working Group on Minorities

United Nations Working Group on Minorities, *Report on its Fourth Session,* UN Doc. E/CN.4/Sub.2/1998/18, July 5, 1998.

United Nations Working Group on Minorities, *Report on its Third Session*, UN Doc. E/CN.4/Sub.2/1997/18, July 10, 1997.
United Nations Working Group on Minorities, *Report on its Second Session*, UN Doc. E/CN.4/Sub.2/1996/28, July 8, 1996.
United Nations Working Group on Minorities, *Report on its First Session*, UN Doc. E/CN.4/Sub.2/1996/2, November 30, 1995.

Interviews

Osservazione

Eva Rizzin, at http://www.osservazione.org/chefare_rizzin.htm.
Dijana Pavlovic, at http://www.osservazione.org/chefare_pavlovic.htm.
Nazzareno Guarneri, at http://www.osservazione.org/chefare_guarnieri.htm.
Interview with Yuri del Bar, at http://www.osservazione.org/chefare_yuri.htm.

Terra

Eva Rizzin, available at http://www.tg5.mediaset.it/video/2006/01/vedivideo_3198.shtml.

Legal Instruments

Council of Europe

1950 Convention for the Protection of Human Rights and Fundamental Freedoms.
1952 First Protocol to the 1950 Convention for the Protection of Human Rights and Fundamental Freedoms.
1963 Fourth Protocol to the 1950 Convention for the Protection of Human Rights and Fundamental Freedoms.
1992 European Charter for Regional or Minority Languages.
1995 Framework Convention for the Protection of National Minorities.
1997 Council of Europe, European Convention on Nationality, ETS 166.
2000 Twelfth Protocol to the 1950 Convention for the Protection of Human Rights and Fundamental Freedoms.

European Union

2000 Charter of Fundamental Rights of the European Union.
Treaty of Amsterdam.
Treaty of Lisbon.
Treaty on the European Union.

International

1948 Universal Declaration on Human Rights.
1948 Convention on the Prevention and Punishment of the Crime of Genocide.

1960 UNESCO Convention Against Discrimination in Education.
1966 UNESCO Declaration of the Principles of International Cultural Co-operation, UNESCO Doc 14C/8.I., 4 November 1966.
1966 International Covenant on Civil and Political Rights.
1966 International Covenant on Economic Social and Cultural Rights.
1966 International Convention on the Elimination of All Forms of Racial Discrimination.
1984 Convention against Torture and Other Cruel, Inhuman or Degrading Treatment or Punishment.
1989 United Nations Convention on the Rights of the Child.
1992 Declaration on the Rights of Persons Belonging to National or Ethnic, Religious and Linguistic Minorities.
2001 World Conference against Racism, Racial Discrimination, Xenophobia and Related Intolerance.

Italian

The following can be found in Di Majo, A., *Codice Civile, con la Costituzione, il Trattato C.E.E. e le principali norme complementari,* Milan, Dott. A Giuffrè Editore, 1997:

1. Codice Civile.
2. Costituzione della Repubblica Italiana.
3. Decreto del Presidente della Repubblica 12 Ottobre 1993, n. 572. Regolamento di esecuzione della legge 5 febbraio 1992, n. 91, recante nuove norme sulla cittadinanza.
4. Legge 5 Febbraio 1992, n. 91. Nuove norme sulla cittadinanza.

Codice di procedura penale.
Codice Penale.

Decreti del Presidente del Consiglio dei Ministri (D.P.C.M)

D.P.C.M. of May 12, 1999, *Misure di protezione temporanea, a fini umanitari, da assicurarsi nel territorio dello Stato a favore delle persone provenienti dalle zone di guerra dell'area balcanica.*
D.P.C.M n. 535/99 of December 9, 1999, *Regolamento concernente i compiti del Comitato per i minori stranieri, a norma dell'articolo 33, commi 2 e 2-bis, del decreto legislativo 25 luglio 1998, n. 286.*
D.P.C.M of May 21, 2008, *Dichiarazione dello stato di emergenza in relazione agli insediamenti di comunità nomadi nel territorio delle regioni Campania, Lazio e Lombardia.*
Linee guida del ministero dell'interno, July 17, 2008, *per l'attuazione delle ordinanze del Presidente del Consiglio dei Ministri del 30.5.2008, nn. 3676, 3677 e 3673, concernenti insediamenti di comunità nomadi nelle Regioni Campania, Lazio e Lombardia.*

Laws

Law 125 of April 10, 1991, *Azioni positive per la realizzazione della parità uomo-donna nel lavoro.*
Law 91/1992 of February 5, 1992, *New norms on citizenship.*
Law 225/92 of February 24, 1992, *Istituzione del Servizio Nazionale della Protezione Civile. Ecologia.*
Law 205/1993 of June 25, 1993, *Misure urgenti in materia di discriminazione razziale, etnica e religiosa* (*Legge Mancino*) (Urgent measures relating to racial, ethnic and religious discrimination).

Law 40/1998 of March 6, 1998, *Disciplina dell'immigrazione e norme sulla condizione dello straniero.*

Law 162 of May 21, 1998, *Modifiche alla legge 5 febbraio 1992, n. 104, concernenti misure di sostegno in favore di persone con handicap grave.*

Law 482/1999 of December 15, 1999, *Norms concerning the protection of linguistic and historical minorities.*

Law 85/2006 of February 24, 2006, *Modifiche al codice penale in materia di reati di opinione.*

Law 101 of June 6, 2008, *Conversione in legge, con modificazioni, del decreto-legge 8 aprile 2008, n. 59, recante disposizioni urgenti per l'attuazione di obblighi comunitari e l'esecuzione di sentenze della Corte di giustizia delle Comunità europee.*

Law 189/2002 of July 30, 2002 *Modifica alla normativa in materia di immigrazione e di asilo.*

Legislative Decrees

Legislative Decree 286/98 of July 25, 1998, *Testo unico delle disposizioni concernenti la disciplina dell'immigrazione e norme sulla tutela dello straniero* (*Consolidated Law on Immigration*).

Legislative Decree 215 of July 9, 2003 implementing Directive 2000/43/EC.

Legislative Decree 216 of July 9, 2003 implementing Directive 2000/78/CE.

Legislative Decree 3/2007 of January 8, 2007, *Attuazione della direttiva 2003/109/CE relativa allo status di cittadini di Paesi terzi soggiornanti di lungo periodo.*

Legislative Decree 5/2007 of January 8, 2007, *Attuazione della direttiva 2003/86/CE relativa al diritto di ricongiungimento familiare.*

Legislative Decree 30 of February 6, 2007, *Attuazione della direttiva 2004/38/CE relativa al diritto dei cittadini dell'Unione e dei loro familiari di circolare e di soggiornare liberamente nel territorio degli Stati membri.*

Legislative Decree 181/2007 of October 31, 2007, *Disposizioni urgenti in materia di allontanamento dal territorio nazionale per esigenze di pubblica sicurezza.*

Legislative Decree 249 of Janurary 2, 2008, *Misure urgenti in materia di espulsioni e di allontanamenti per terrorismo e per motivi imperativi di pubblica sicurezza.*

Legislative Decree 92 of May 23, 2008, *Misure urgenti in materia di sicurezza pubblica.*

Law Proposals, Circulars and Resolutions

Circolare Ministeriale n. 207 del 16 Luglio 1986 del Ministero dell'Istruzione, *Scolarizzazione degli alunni zingari e nomadi nella scuola materna, elementare e secondaria di primo grado.*

Circolare 151/85 del 5 Luglio 1985 *Oggetto Problema dei nomadi.*

Progetto di legge No. 169, *Norme in materia di tutela delle minoranze linguistiche.*

Proposta di Legge n. 2858, July 3, 2007, Modifiche alla legge 15 dicembre 1999, n. 482, *per l'estensione delle disposizioni di tutela delle minoranze linguistiche storiche alle minoranze dei rom e dei sinti.*

Risoluzione del Consiglio e dei Ministri dell'Istruzione riuniti in sede di Consiglio, del 22 Maggio 1989, *concernente la scolarizzazione dei figli degli zingari e dei girovaghi.*

Government/Parliament Reports

Commissione per le Politiche di Integrazione, Dipartimento per gli Affari Sociali, Presidenza del Consiglio dei Ministri, *Rom e Sinti: un'integrazione possibile. Italia ed Europa a confronto*, Naples, June 23–24, 2000.

Commissione per le politiche di integrazione degli immigrati, *Secondo Rapporto sull'Integrazione degli immigrati in Italia, Chapter 3.7, Rom e Sinti: un'integrazione possibile,* (Rome: Dipartimento per gli Affari Sociali, December 13, 2000).
Marta, C., 'Le Politiche per i Rom e Sinti in Italia,' in Commissione per le Politiche di Integrazione, Dipartimento per gli Affari Sociali, Presidenza del Consiglio dei Ministri, *Rom e Sinti: un'integrazione possibile. Italia ed Europa a confronto*, Naples, June 23–24, 2000, pp. 43–49.
Ministero dell'Interno, Ufficio centrale per i problemi delle zone di confine e delle minoranze etniche, *Primo rapporto sullo stato delle minoranze in Italia,* 1994.
Ministry of Public Education – National Observatory on Integration of foreign pupils, *La via italiana per la scuola interculturale e l'integrazione degli alunni*, (Rome: Ministry of Public Education, 2007).
Ministero per le Pari Opportunità, *Un Anno di Attività Contro la Discriminazione Razziale, Rapporto 2005, Relazione al Presidente del Consiglio dei Ministri sull'attività Svolta dall'Ufficio Nazionale Antidiscriminazioni Razziali,* Dicembre 2005.
Presidenza del Consiglio dei Ministri, Dipartimento per le Pari Opportunità, UNAR, Ufficio Nazionale Antidiscriminationi Razziali, *L'efficacia degli strumenti di tutela nel contrasto alle discriminazioni razziali,* Relazione 2007.
Scalia, G.M., *Le Comunità "sprovviste di territorio." I Rom, i Sinti e i Camminanti in Italia* (Italy: Ministero dell'Interno, Dipartimento per le Libertà Civili e l'Immigrazione, 2006).
Senato della Repubblica, Documentazione di Commissione n. 7, Commissione straordinaria per la tutela e la promozione dei diritti umani, *Rapporto conclusivo dell'indagine sulla condizione di Rom, Sinti e Camminanti in Italia,* May 2011.
Volpiani, P., *Rom e Sinti: Verso una Strategia di Inclusione Sociale*, UNAR (2011).

Newspapers and Magazines Articles

Amadori, G., 'Vita da Baby Ladro,' *Panorama,* July 10, 2008.
'Asili vietati ai figli dei clandestini. Ultimatum del governo alla Moratti', *La Repubblica,* January 9, 2008.
'Bimbi rumeni insultati a scuola', *L'Unità*, November 12, 2007.
'Bombe carta e sputi romeni nel mirino', *Il Manifesto*, November 6, 2007.
Bonerandi, E., 'Milano, cinesi in rivolta, guerra con vigili e polizia', *La Repubblica*, April 13, 2007.
'Cassazione, se i nomadi sono ladri è legittima la discriminazione,' *La Repubblica*, June 29, 2008.
'Cesena: Minacciata una donna perché rumena', *Corriere di Romagna*, November 7, 2007.
'Chiti: sbarchi clandestini in calo rispetto 2006', *ANSA*, May 16, 2007.
'Classi per stranieri: il no di Veltroni: "Dio ce ne scampi." Alemanno frena,' *Corriere della Sera*, October 15, 2008.
De Florio, A. 'Scontro sulle espulsioni, niente voto bipartisan', *Il Messaggero*, November 22, 2007.
Di Caro, P., 'Fini: impossibile integrarsi con chi ruba,' *Corriere della Sera*, November 4, 2007.
'Europe's Spectral Nation,' *The Economist,* May 12, 2001, pp. 29–31.
Ferrarella, L., 'Troppo emotive, basta leggi subito dopo i fatti di cronaca,' *Corriere della Sera*, November 21, 2007.
Hooper, J., 'Italy: Court inflames Roma discrimination row,' *The Guardian,* July 1, 2008.
Ignazi, P., 'In difesa degli Zingari,' *L'Espresso,* July 17, 2008.
'Immigrati, servono metodi da SS', *Il Corriere della Sera*, December 5, 2007.
Isman, G., 'Ci hanno aggredito con i bastoni, è una vendetta per Tor di Quinto,' *La Repubblica*, November 3, 2007.
'ISTAT: la popolazione in Italia oltre il traguardo dei 60 milioni,' *La Repubblica*, February 26, 2009.

Italy: Roma-Gypsy camp dismantled again in capital, available at http://www.adnkronos.com/AKI/English/Security/?id=3.0.2548154333.
Kubosova, L., *EU gives blessing for Italy's Roma fingerprint scheme*, EU Observer, September 5, 2008.
Liso, O., 'Rogo al campo rom, politici indagati', *La Repubblica*, March 1, 2007.
Luglio, M., 'Giù le baracche ma i rom non se ne vanno', *La Repubblica,* November 2, 2007.
Maisto, T., Radice, E., '"Marocchino!" Botte a scuola dai compagni', *La Repubblica*, November 6, 2007.
McDougall, D., 'Why do the Italians hate us?', *The Observer*, August 17, 2008.
'Minoranze. Parla Eva Rizzin della neonata Federazione Rom e Sinti Insieme. Rom, adesso per noi parliamo solo noi,' *Vita*, August 29, 2008.
'Niente borsa di studio agli extracomunitari', *Corriere della Sera,* December 2, 2007.
Poverini, C., 'Aiuto, sono di sinistra ma sto diventando razzista', *La Repubblica*, May 7, 2007.
'Prefettura, Mosca lascia il posto a Pecoraro,' *La Repubblica*, November 14, 2008.
'Razzisti imbrattano il centro di accoglienza', *Il Firenze*, November 3, 2007.
Rigetti, C., 'Il TAR Lombardia boccia le ordinanze sul modello Cittadella,' *Metropoli*, May 2008.
'Roma: nomade ubriaco travolge 13 persone alla fermata del bus', Corriere della Sera, November 5, 2008.
Romano, A., 'Valle dei Templi vietata ai bimbi di colore', *La Repubblica*, July 10, 2007.
'Rumeno ferito: "Mi hanno accoltellato tre italiani"', *L'Unità – Roma,* November 27, 2007.
Ruotolo, G., 'Criminalità. Il pericolo arriva da est', *La Stampa*, May 17, 2007.
Salvia, L., 'Maroni: giusto espellere i Rom. Saremo più duri di Sarkozy,' *Corriere della Sera*, August 21, 2010.
'Scuolabus separati per bimbi rom', *Corriere della Sera*, January 12, 2008.
'Un maiale-day contro la moschea', *Corriere della Sera,* September 14, 2007.
Viaggio, M., 'Demolita la "bidonville" di Ponte Mammolo,' *Il Giornale*, December 5, 2007.
Vuolo, P., 'In 40 all'assalto del campo rom armati di molotov, sassi e catene', *Il Messaggero*, September 21, 2007.
When Brussels Trumps Rome, The Berlusconi government is forced to soften its anti-immigration measures, *The Economist*, October 23, 2008.

NGOS' Reports

Amnesty International, *La Risposta Sbagliata* (2010).
Bencini, C. and Cerretelli, S. (COSPE), *Enar Shadow Report 2007, Racism in Italy.*
Bencini, C. and Cerretelli, S. (COSPE), *Enar Shadow Report 2006, Racism in Italy.*
Bencini, C. and Cerretelli, S. (COSPE), ENAR *Shadow Report 2002: Italy.*
Brearley, M., *The Roma/Gypsies of Europe: a persecuted people*, Institute for Jewish Policy Research Policy Paper, No. 3, December 1996.
Censis, *L'immagine degli immigrati e delle minoranze etniche nei media*, November 2002, Roma, available at http://www.edscuola.it/archivio/stranieri/immagine_immigrati.pdf.
Cahn, C., 'Towards Realising a Right to Positive Action for Roma in Europe: Connors v. UK,' 1 *Roma Rights Quarterly* 13 (2005).
Censis, *41° rapporto annuale sulla situazione sociale del paese,* (Rome: Censis, 2007).
Centre on Housing Rights and Evictions, Associazione Studi Giuridici sull'Immigrazione, European Roma Grassroots Organization, European Roma Rights Centre, OsservAzione, National Roma Centrum, Cultural Center "O Del Amenca", Policy Center for Roma and Minorities, Roma Center for Social Intervention and Studies, Roma Women Association in Romania, *Memorandum: Request for Expedited Engagement of Follow-Up Procedure and/or Urgent Action/Early Warning Procedure Concerning Italy ICERD Compliance.*

Centre on Housing Rights and Evictions, OsservAzione, Policy Center for Roma and Minorities, *Memorandum Concerning the Necessity to Apply Treaty Measures in the Matter of the Italy Emergency.*

Cerretelli, S., ENAR (European Network Against Racism) *Shadow Report 2003: Italy.*

Chahrokh, H., Klug. W. and Bilger, V., *Migrants, minorities and legislation: Documenting legal measures and remedies against discrimination in 15 Member States of the European Union. Report submitted by the International Centre for Migration Policy Development (ICMPD) on behalf of the European Monitoring Centre on Racism and Xenophobia (EUMC),* December 2004.

Compendium, Cultural Policies and Trends in Europe, *Belgium/ 4.2 Recent policy issues and debates, 4.2.1 Cultural minorities, groups and communities,* at http://www.cultural policies.net/web/belgium.php?aid=421.

Dimitras, P.E., *Recognition of Minorities in Europe: Protecting Rights and Dignity,* Minority Rights Group International, 2004.

European Roma Information Office, *The Situation of Roma in an Enlarged European Union*

European Roma Rights Center, *Il paese dei campi. La segregazione razziale dei Rom in Italia, serie Rapporti nazionali,* number 9, October 2000.

European Roma Rights Center, *Implementing Roma Rights in Europe: Written Submission by the European Roma Rights Center to the Parliamentary Assembly of the Council of Europe "Hearing on the Situation of Roma in Member States of the Council of Europe,"* March 4, 2002.

European Roma Rights Center, *Written Comments of the European Roma Rights Center Concerning the Republic of Hungary For Consideration by the United Nations Committee on the Elimination of Racial Discrimination at its 61st Session,* August 5–23, 2002.

European Roma Rights Center, *Written Comments of the European Roma Rights Center Concerning the Republic of Hungary For Consideration by the United Nations Human Rights Committee at its 74th Session,* March 18 – April 5, 2002.

European Roma Rights Center, *Written Comments of the European Roma Rights Center Concerning Italy For Consideration by the United Nations Committee on the Elimination of Racial Discrimination at its 54th session,* March 8–9, 1999.

Human Rights Watch/Helsinki, *Rights Denied, the Roma of Hungary,* USA, Human Rights Watch, 1996.

Human Rights Watch, *Every Day Intolerance: Racist and Xenophobic Violence in Italy* (2011).

Kádár, A., Farkas, L., Pardavi, M., *Implementing European Anti-discrimination Law. Legal analysis of national and European anti-discrimination legislation, A comparison of the EU Racial Equality Directive & Protocol n. 12 with anti-discrimination legislation in Hungary, Hungarian Helsinki Committee,* European Roma Rights Center, Interights, Migration Policy Group, September 2001.

La Questione Zingara in Italia, Centro di Studi Maria Luisa Sigillo, Enzo Civitareale, Nessun Luogo E' Lontano, at http://www.nessunluogoelontano.it/download/eventi/C03_03.pdf.

Legal Defence Bureau for National and Ethnic Minorities (NEKI), *White Booklet 2000, The annual report of the Legal Defence Bureau for National and Ethnic Minorities (NEKI),* Budapest, 2000.

Liégeois, J.P. and Gheorghe, N., *Roma/Gypsies, a European Minority,* United Kingdom, Minority Rights Group International Report, 1995.

Miceli, R., Sicurezza e Paura, *Working Paper n. 127,* IRES Piemonte, October 1999.

Open Society Institute, Center on Housing Rights and Evictions, the European Roma Rights Centre (ERRC), Romani Criss and the Roma Civic Alliance in Romania, *Security a la Italiana: Fingerprinting, Extreme Violence and Harassment of Roma in Italy,* July 2008.

Opera Nomadi, *L'educazione dei bambini zingari e nomadi,* Italy, Opera Nomadi, 1991.

OsservAzione, *Cittadinanze Imperfette: Rapporto sulla discriminazione razziale di Rom e Sinti in Italia* (Italy: Edizioni Spartaco, 2006).

OsservAzione, *Political Participation and Media Representation of Roma and Sinti in Italy,* July 26, 2006.

Osservazioni del Tavolo Rom sul Regolamento delle aree destinate ai nomadi nel territorio del Comune di Milano, available at http://coopofficina.splinder.com/post/19826090.

Save the Children, *Denied a Future? The Rights to Education of Roma, Gypsy and Traveller Children in Europe,* Vol. 2, United Kingdom, Save the Children, 2001.

Sigona, N., Monasta, L., Saudino, F. and Torre, A., *Political Participation and Media Representation of Roma and Sinti in Italy,* OsservAzione, July 26, 2006.

Pleşe, B., 'Strasbourg Court finally redresses racial discrimination,' 1 *Roma Rights Quarterly* 109 (2004).

RAXEN, *Annual Report 2007 ITALY,* July 2008.

Rivera, A., and Andrisani, P., National Focal Point Italy, *Analytical Study on Discrimination and Racist Violence in Italy: 2000–2002,* September 2002, COSPE – Cooperazione per lo Sviluppo dei Paesi Emergenti.

Rivera, A., RAXEN National Focal Point Italy, *National Analytical Study on Racist Violence and Crime.*

Roma in Italy: forced nomadism, 2 Snapshots from around Europe 1999, at http://errc.org/rr_nr2_1999/snap18.shtml.

Save the Children, *Denied a Future? The right to education of Roma/Gypsy and Traveller Children In Europe, International Legislation Handbook,* United Kingdom, Save the Children, 2001.

Szente, V.L., 'Field Report: Italy', 3 (1997) *Roma Rights* 51.

The Institute of Race Relations, *European Race Audit,* Bulletin n. 28, October 1998.

Thornberry, P., *Minorities and Human Righs Law,* Minority Rights Group Report No. 73 (Minority Rights Group: London, 1987).

Vassallo Paleologo, F., *Analytical Report on Legislation,* RAXEN National Focal Point Italy, Co-operation for the Development of Emerging Countries, Vienna, 2004.

Written Comments of the European Roma Rights Centre (ERRC), the Centre On Housing Rights and Evictions (COHRE), OsservAzione and Sucar Drom Concerning Italy for Consideration by the United Nations Committee on the Elimination of Racial Discrimination at its 72nd Session.

Web-sites

www.amnesty.org
www.asgi.it
www.coe.int
www.errc.org
www.eu.europa.int
www.geocites.com
www.hrw.org
www.irr.org.uk
www.justiceinitiative.org
www.neki.hu
www.osce.org
www.osservazione.org
www.romaniunion.org
www.savethechildren.org
www.un.org
www.unar.it
www.unhchr.org
www.youtube.com

TABLE OF CASES

European Court of Justice

Case Defrenne v. SABENA (1978) ECR 1365
Horst Bickel and Ulrich Franz, Case C-274/96 (1998), ECR I-4139
Case 4/73 *Nold v. Commission of the European Communities* (1974), ECR 491
Roman Angonese v. Cassa di Risparmio di Bolzano, Case C-281/98 (2000), ECR I-4139
Case 36/75 *Rutili v. Minister for the Interior* (1975) ECR 1219
Case of Strauder v. City of Ulm, Case 29/69 [1969] ECR 1219

European Commission on Human Rights and European Court of Human Rights

Belgian Linguistics Case, Commission Report of 24 June 1965, B.3 (1967)
Belgian Linguistics Case, Eur. Comm. Hum. Rts., Series A No. 6
Case of Al-Nashif et al. *v. Bulgaria*, Eur. Ct. Hum. Rts. (Fourth Section), Application number 50963/99, December 6, 1999 and January 25, 2001
Case of Anguelova v. Bulgaria, Eur. Ct. Hum. Rts., Application number 38361/97, June 13, 2002
Case of Airey v. Ireland, Eur. Ct. H. R., October 9, 1979, Series A n. 32
Case of Arslan and others v. Turkey, Eur. Ct. Hum. Rts., Application number 23462/94, July 8, 1999
Case of Aziz v. Cyprus, Eur. Ct. Hum. Rts, Application number 69949/01, June 22, 2004
Case of Beard v. the United Kingdom, Eur. Ct. Hum. Rts., Application number 24882/94, January 18, 2001
Case of Bekir-Ousta and others v. Greece, Eur. Ct. Hum. Rts., Application number 35151/05, October 11, 2007
Case of Buckley v. the United Kingdom, Eur. Ct. Hum. Rts., Application number 20348/92, September 25, 1996
Case of Buckley v. the United Kingdom, (1997) 23 EHRR 101
Case of Buckley v. United Kingdom, (1995) 19 EHRR CD20
Case of Buscarini and Others v. San Marino, Eur. Ct. Hum. Rts., Application number 24645/94, February 18, 1999
Case of Campbell and Cosans v. the United Kingdom, Eur. Ct. Hum. Rts., Application numbers 7511/76 and 00007743/76, February 25, 1982
Case of Canea Catholic Church v. Greece, Eur. Ct. Hum. Rts., December 16, 1997
Case of Cha'are Shalom ve Tsedek v. France, Eur. Ct. Hum. Rts., Application number 27417/95, June 27, 2000
Case of Chahal v. United Kingdom, (1996) 23 EHRR
Case of Chapman v. the United Kingdom, Eur. Ct. Hum. Rts., Application number 27238/95, January 18, 2001
Case of Church of Scientology & 128 of its members v. Sweden, Eur. Comm. H. R., Application number 8282/78, July 12, 1980, D. R. 21
Case of Čonka v. Belgium, Eur. Ct. Hum. Rts, Application number 51564/99, February 5, 2002
Case of Coster v. the United Kingdom, Eur. Ct. Hum. Rts., Application number 24876/94, January 8, 2001

Case of Cyprus v. Turkey, Eur. Comm. Hum. Rts., Application number 24781/94, June 4, 1999
Case of Cyprus v. Turkey, Eur. Ct. Hum. Rts., Application number 25781/94, May 10, 2001
Case of D. H. and Others v. the Czech Republic, Eur. Ct. Hum. Rts., Application number 57325/00, February 7, 2006
Case of D. H. and Others v. the Czech Republic (Grand Chamber) Eur. Ct. Hum. Rts., Application number 57325/00, November 13, 2007
Case of Denizci v. Cyprus, Eur. Ct. Hum. Rts., Application number 25316-25321/94 and 27207/95, 23 August 2001
Case of Dudgeon v. United Kingdom, Eur. Ct. Hum. Rts, October 22, 1982, Series A No. 45
Case of Erdogu v. Turkey, Eur. Ct. Hum. Rts., Application number 25723/94, June 15, 2000
Case of Folgerø and Others v. Norway, Eur. Ct. Hum. Rts., Application number 15472/02, June 29, 2007
Case of Fredin v. Sweden (1991) 13 EHRR 784
Case of Freedom and Democracy Party (ÖZDEP) v. Turkey, Eur. Ct. Hum. Rts., Application number 23885/94, December 8, 1999
Case of G and E v. Norway, European Commission of Human Rights, DR 9278 & 9415/81, 35 DR 30, 1983
Case of Gorzelik and others v.Poland (2004) 38 EHRR 4
Case of Hamidovic v. Italy, Eur. Ct. Hum. Rts., the application is pending before the Court (Application number 31956/05)
Case of Handyside v. the United Kingdom, Eur. Ct. Hum. Rts. (Series A No 24), Application number 5493/72, December 7, 1976
Case of Hasan and Chaush v. Bulgaria, Eur. Ct. Hum. Rts., Application number 30985/96, October 26, 2000
Case of Hasan and Eylem Zengin v. Turkey, Eur. Ct. Hum. Rts., Application number 1448/04, October 9, 2007
Case of Hoffman v. Austria, Eur. Comm. Hum. Rts., Report of January 16, 1992, Series A no 255-C
Case of Hoffman v. Austria, Eur. Ct. Hum. Rts., June 23, 1993, Series A no 255-C
Case of Ibrahim Aksoy v. Turkey, Eur. Ct. Hum. Rts., Application number 28635/95, October 10, 2000
Case of Incal v. Turkey, Eur. Ct. Hum. Rts., Application number 41/1997/825/1031 June 9, 1998
Case of Informationsverein Lentia and others v. Austria, Eur. Ct. Hum. Rts., Series A n. 276 24 November 1993
Case of Jane Smith v. the United Kingdom, Eur. Ct. Hum. Rts., Application number 25154/94, January 18, 2001
Case of Kokkinakis v. Greece, Eur. Ct. Hum. Rts., Application number14307/88, May 25, 1993
Case of Larkos v. Cyprus, Eur. Ct. Hum. Rts., Application number 29515/95, February 18, 1999
Case of Lee v. the United Kingdom, Eur. Ct. Hum. Rts., Application number 25289/94, January 18, 2001
Case of Lindsay and Others v. the United Kingdom, March 8, 1979, D. R. 15 (247)
Case of Maaouia v. France, 33 EHRR 42, October 5, 2000
Case of Manoussakis and others v. Greece, Application number 18748/91, Eur. Ct. Hum. Rts., September 26, 1996
Case of Mathieu-Mohin and Clerfayt v.Belgium, Eur. Ct. Hum. Rts, Application number 9267/81, March 2, 1987
Case of McGuinness v. the United Kingdom, Eur. Ct. Hum. Rts., Application number 39511/98, June 8, 1999, admissibility decision
Case of Metropolitan Church of Bessarabia and Others v. Moldova, Eur. Ct. Hum. Rts., Application number 45701/99, 13 December 2001
Case of Moureaux v. Belgium, Eur. Comm. Hum. Rts., Application number 9267/81, July 12, 1983, D. R. 33 (97)
Case of Muonio Saami Village v. Sweden, Eur. Ct. Hum. Rts. (First Section), Application number 28222/95, February 15, 2000

Case of Murphy v. Ireland, Eur. Ct. Hum. Rts., Application number 44179/98, December 3, 2003
Case of Nachova and others v. Bulgaria, Eur. Ct. Hum. Rts., Application number 43577/98 and 00043579/98, February 26, 2004
Case of Noack and Others v. Germany, Eur. Ct. Hum. Rts. (First Section), Application number 46346/99, May 25, 2000
Case of Orsus and Others v. Croatia, Eur. Ct. Hum. Rts., Application No. 15766/03, July 17, 2008
Case of Orsus and Others v. Croatia (Grand Chamber), Eur. Ct. Hum. Rts., Application number 15766/03, March 16, 2010
Case of Otto Preminger Institute v. Austria, Eur. Ct. Hum. Rts., Series A no 295-A, September 20, 1994
Case of Otto Preminger Institute v. Austria, Eur. Comm. H. R., Series A no 295-A, Report of January 14, 1993
Case of Özgür Gündem v. Turkey, Eur. Ct. Hum. Rts., Application number 23144/93, March 16, 2000
Case of Petrovic v. Austria, application No. 20458/92, Eur. Ct. Hum. Rts., March 23, 1998
Case of Podkolzina v. Latvia, Eur. Ct. Hum. Rts., Application number 46726/99, April 9, 2002
Case of Raif Oglu v. Greece, Eur. Ct. Hum. Rts. (Third Section), Application number 33738/96, March 16, 1999
Case of Raif Oglu v. Greece, Eur. Ct. Hum. Rts. (Third Section), Application number 33738/96, June 27, 2000
Case Relating to Certain Aspects of the Laws on the Use of Languages in Education in Belgium v. Belgium, 23/7/1968 (No. 6) 1 EHHR 252
Case of Sampanis and Others v. Greece, Eur. Ct. Hum. Rts., Application number 32526/05, June 5, 2008
Case of Sejdić and Finci vs Bosnia and Hercegovina, communicated in March 2008
Case of Sener v. Turkey, Eur. Ct. Hum. Rts., Application number 26680/95, July 18, 2000
Case of Serif v. Greece, Eur. Ct. Hum. Rts. Application number 38178/97, December 14, 1999
Case of Sidiropoulos and others v. Greece, Eur. Ct. Hum. Rts., Application number 26695/95, July 10, 1998
Case of Sidiropoulos and others v. Greece, Eur. Comm. Hum. Rts., Report of April 11, 1997
Case of Soering v. United Kingdom, (1989) 11 EHRR 439
Case of Stankov and United Macedonian Organisation ILINDEN v. Bulgaria, Eur. Ct. Hum. Rts., Application numbers 29221/95 and 29225/95, October 2, 2001
Case of Sulejmanovic & others and Sejdovic & Sulejmanovic v. Italy, Eur. Ct. Hum. Rts., Application numbers 57574/00 and 57575/00, November 8, 2002
Case of United Communist Party (TBKP) v. Turkey, Eur. Ct. Hum. Rts., Application number 19392/92, October 28, 1996
Case of United Communist Party (TBKP) v. Turkey, Eur. Ct. Hum. Rts., Application number 133/1996/752/951, January 30, 1998
Case of Thlimmenos v. Greece (2000) 31 EHRR 411
Case of Varey v. the United Kingdom, Eur. Ct. Hum. Rts. Application number 26662/95, December 21, 2000, case struck out of the list
Case of Velikova v. Bulgaria, Eur. Ct. Hum. Rts. Application number 41488/98, May 18, 2000
Case of Welfare Party (Refah Partisi) and others v. Turkey, Eur. Ct. Hum. Rts., Application numbers 41349/98, 41342/98, 41343/98 and 41344/98, July 31, 2001
Case of Wingrove v. the United Kingdom, Eur. Ct. Hum. Rts., November 25, 1996
Case of X. v. the United Kingdom, Eur. Ct. Hum. Rts, Application number 8160/78, March 12, 1981
Case of X, Y, Z v. FRG, Eur. Comm. Hum. Rts., Application number 6850/74, May 18, 1976

European Committee of Social Rights

Centre on Housing Rights and Evictions (COHRE) v. Italy, Complaint 58/2009, Decision on the merits, June 25, 2010

Human Rights Committee

Apirana Mahuika v. New Zealand, Communication number 547/1993 (October 27, 2000) UN Doc. CCPR/C/70/D/547/1993 (October 27, 2000)
Ballantyne, Davidson, McIntyre v. Canada, Communication numbers 359/1989 and 385/1989, (March 31, 1993) UN Doc. CCPR/C/47/D/359/1989 and 385/1989/Rev.1
C. L. D. v. France, Communication number 228/1987 (July 18, 1988), U.N. Doc. Supp. No. 40 (A/43/40) at 252 (1988)
Hopu and Bessert v. France, Communication number 549/1993 (July 29, 1997) CCPR/C/60/D/549/1993/Rev.1
Ilmari Länsman et al *v. Finland,* Communication number 511/1992 (November 8, 1994) A/50/40 (1995)
Kitok v. Sweden, Communication number 197/1985 (August 10, 1988), CCPR/C/33/D/197/185
Lovelace v. Canada, Communication number 24/1977 (July 31, 1980), CCPR/C/OP/1 at 37 (1984)
Ominayak, Chief of the Lubicon Lake Band v. Canada, Communication number 167/1984 (May 10, 1990), CCPR/C/38/D/167/1984
T. K. v. France, Communication number 220/1987 (November 8, 1989) CCPR/C/37/D/220/1987
Waldman v. Canada, Communication number 694/1996 (November 3, 1999) UN Doc A/55/40, CCPR/C/67/D/694/1996

Committee on the Elimination of Racial Discrimination

Koptova v. Slovak Republic, Communication number 13/1998 (November 1, 2000) CERD/C/57/D/13/1998
Lacko v. Slovak Republic, Communication number 11/1998 (August 8, 2001) CERD/C/59/D/11/1998

International Court of Justice

Reparation for Injuries Suffered in the Service of the United Nations, International Court of Justice, Advisory Opinion, April 11, 1949, *ICJ Reports* 1949
South West Africa Case, International Court of Justice, Advisory Opinion, *ICJ Reports* 1996
Western Sahara, International Court of Justice, Advisory Opinion, October 16, 1975, *ICJ Reports* 1975

Permanent Court of International Justice

Greco-Bulgarian Communities case (PCIJ, Series B/17, 1930)
Minority Schools in Albania, 1935 PCIJ (ser. A/B) No. 64
Rights of minorities in Upper Silesia (Minority Schools) (PCIJ Reports, Series A, n. 14, 4 1928)

Italy Cases

Consiglio di Stato, Sentenza n. 6050, November 16, 2011 *'Stato di emergenza dichiarato nel territorio delle Regioni Lombardia, Lazio e Campania in relazione agli insediamenti di comunità nomadi'*
Corte Costituzionale della Repubblica Italiana, Pronunciation No. 183/1973
Corte Costituzionale della Repubblica Italiana, Pronunciation No. 312/1983
Corte Costituzionale della Repubblica Italiana, Pronunciation No. 170/1984
Corte Costituzionale della Repubblica Italiana, Pronunciation No. 153/1987
Corte Costituzionale della Repubblica Italiana, Pronunciation No. 188/1990
Corte Costituzionale della Repubblica Italiana, Pronunciation No. 62/1992
Corte Costituzionale della Repubblica Italiana, Pronunciation No. 15/1996
Corte Costituzionale della Repubblica Italiana, Pronunciation No. 10/1993
Corte Costituzionale della Repubblica Italiana, Pronunciation No. 12, July 27, 2000, number 376
Corte Costituzionale della Repubblica Italiana, Pronunciation No. 5, July 17, 2001, number 252
Corte Costituzionale della Repubblica Italiana, Pronunciation No. 159, May 18, 2009
Tribunale Civile di Mantova, Ricorso ex artt. 43 e 44 TU d.lgs. 286/98 e art. 11 e ss. d.lgs. 215/2003
Tribunale Ordinario di Roma, ricorso rejected on August 13, 2008
TAR, Tribunale Amministrativo Regionale per il Lazio, Roma, ricorso 7785/2008, rejected on October 22, 2008
Tribunale di Milano, ricorso ex artt. 44 D.Lgs. N. 286/1998 e 2 D.Lgs. N. 215/2003

United Kingdom Cases

Case of Mandla v. Dowell Lee, [1983] 2AC 548
CRE v Dutton [1989] 1 All ER 304
Regina v. Immigration Officer at Prague Airport and another (Respondents) ex parte European Roma Rights Centre and others (Appellants), December 9, 2004, [2004] UKHL 55

United States Cases

Regents of the University of California v Bakke, 438, US 265 (1978)

INDEX